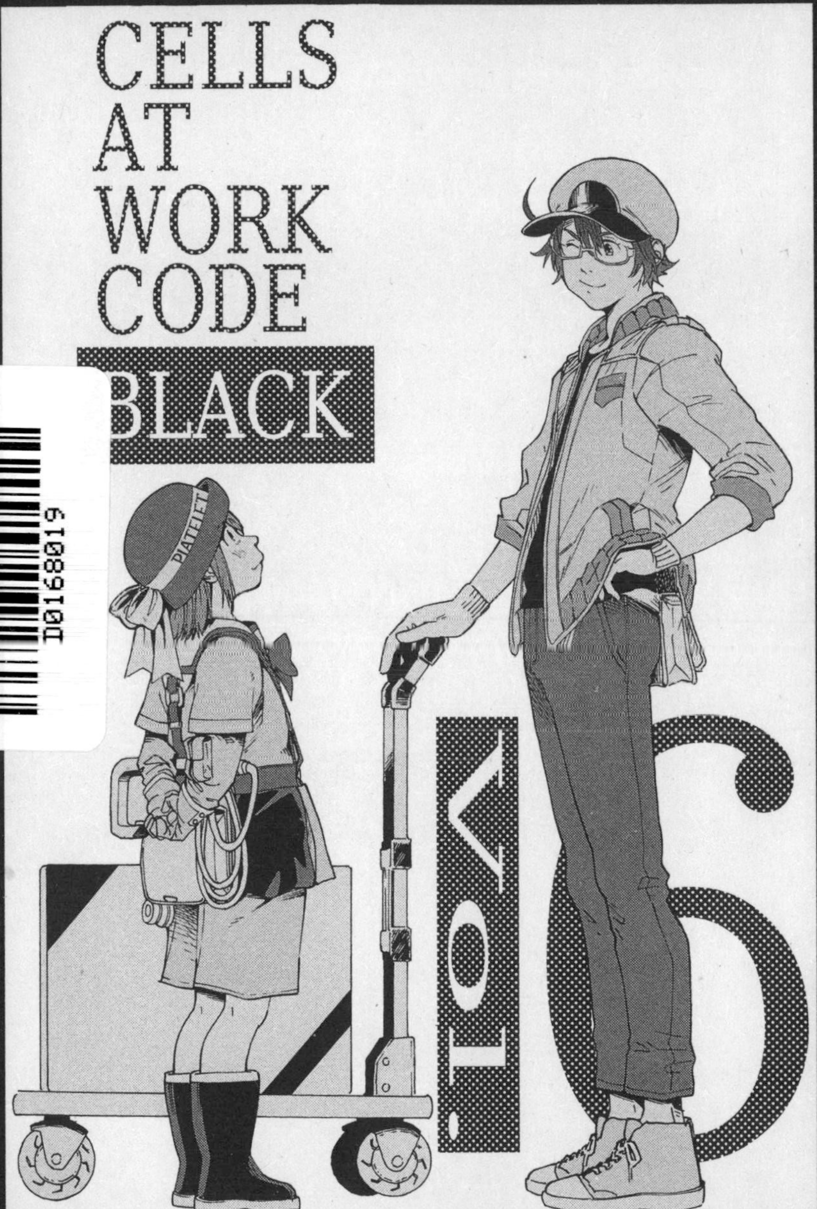
CELLS AT WORK CODE BLACK
PLATELET
Vol. 6

Table of Contents

Warning: This volume contains depictions of suicide.
If you are experiencing suicidal thoughts or feelings, you are not alone, and
there is help. Call the National Suicide Prevention Lifeline at 1-800-273-TALK (8255)
or go to suicidepreventionlifeline.org.

32. GASTRIC LAVAGE, TEARS, TEARS

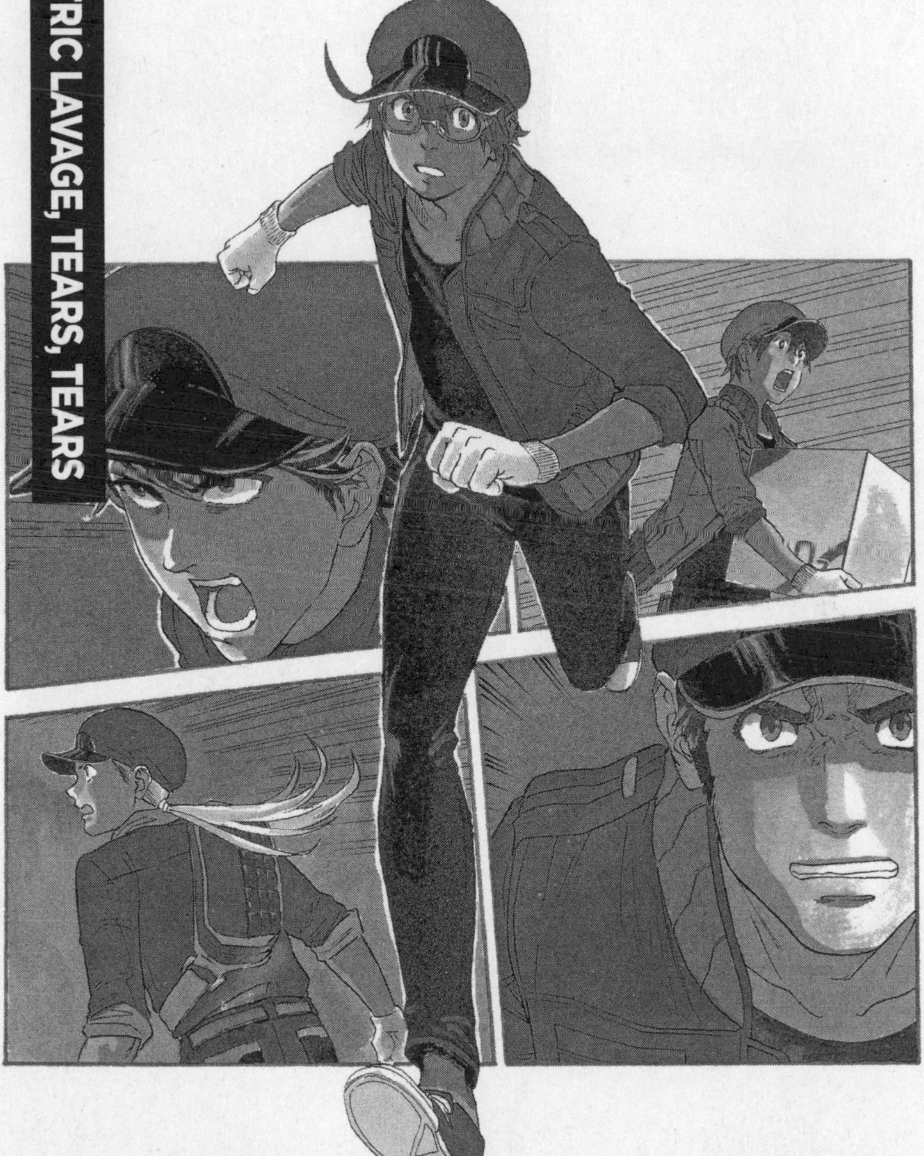

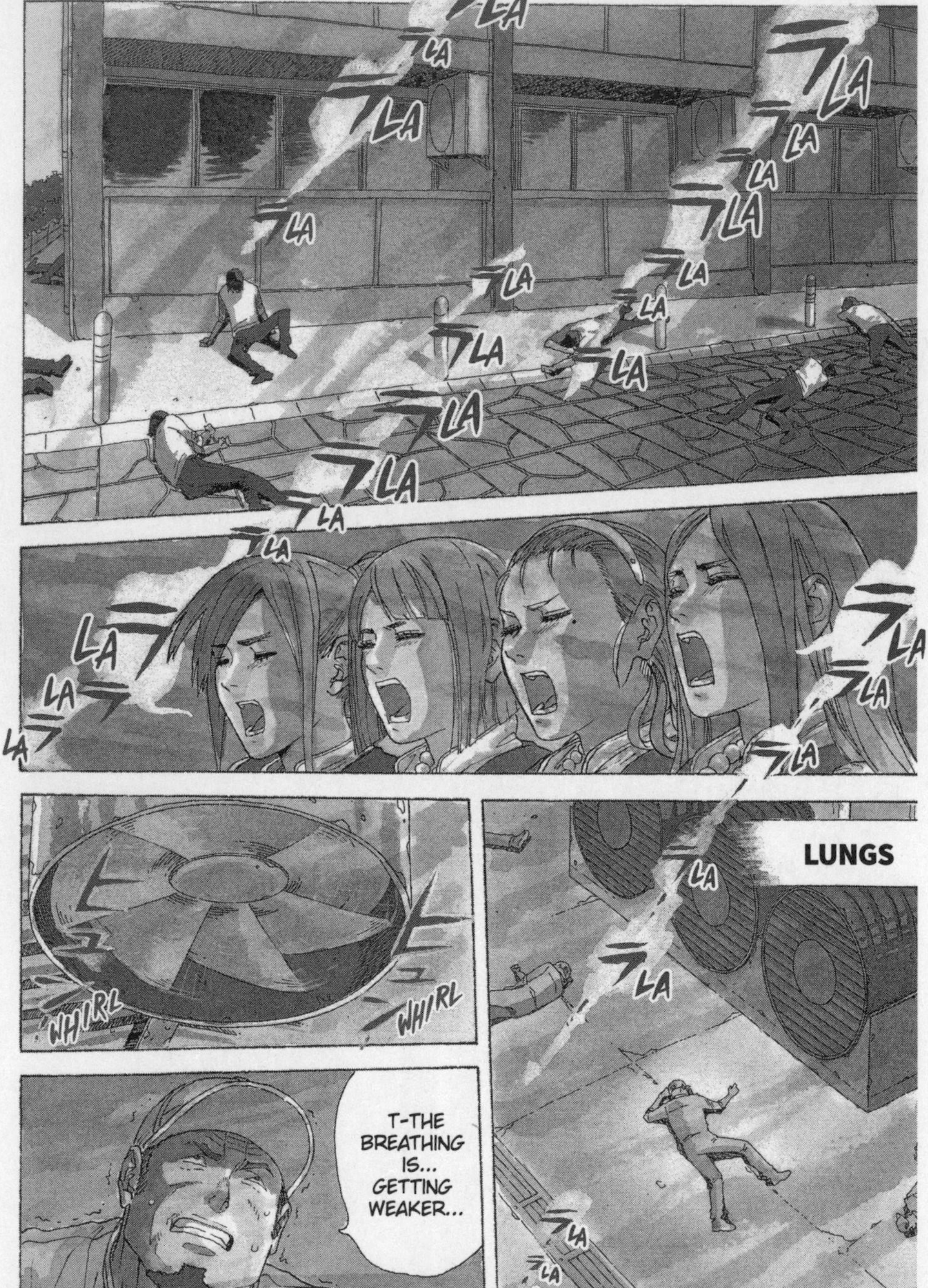

LA
LA
LA
LA
LA
LA
LA
LA
LA
LA
LA
LA
LA
LA
LA
LA
LA
LA
LA
LA
LA
LA
LA
LA
LA
LUNGS
LA
LA
LA
LA
WHIRL
WHIRL
T-THE BREATHING IS... GETTING WEAKER...

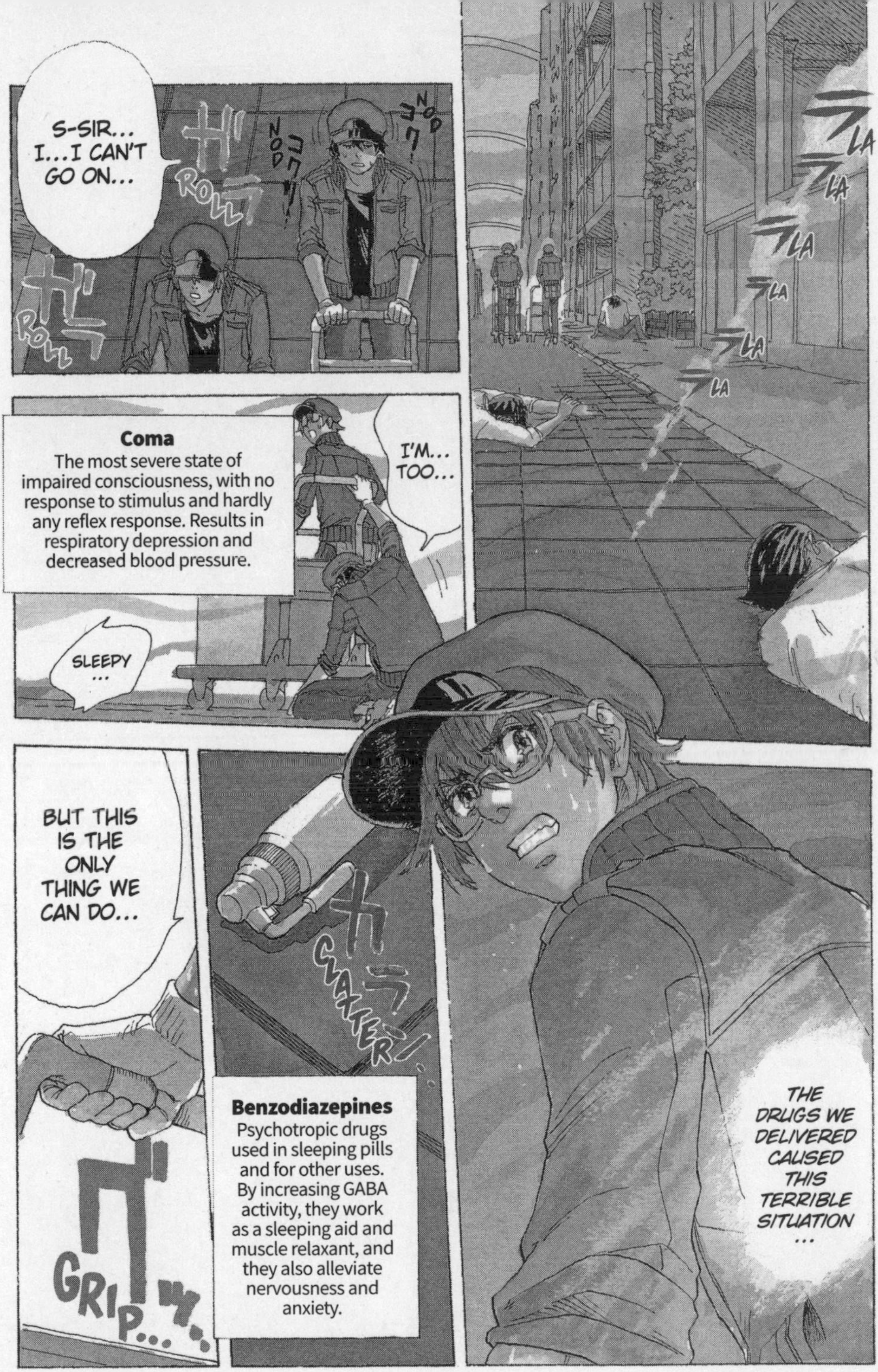
LA
LA
LA
LA
LA
LA
S-SIR... I...I CAN'T GO ON...
NOD NOD
ROLL
ROLL
I'M... TOO...
Coma
The most severe state of impaired consciousness, with no response to stimulus and hardly any reflex response. Results in respiratory depression and decreased blood pressure.
SLEEPY...
THE DRUGS WE DELIVERED CAUSED THIS TERRIBLE SITUATION...
CLATTER
Benzodiazepines
Psychotropic drugs used in sleeping pills and for other uses. By increasing GABA activity, they work as a sleeping aid and muscle relaxant, and they also alleviate nervousness and anxiety.
BUT THIS IS THE ONLY THING WE CAN DO...
GRIP...

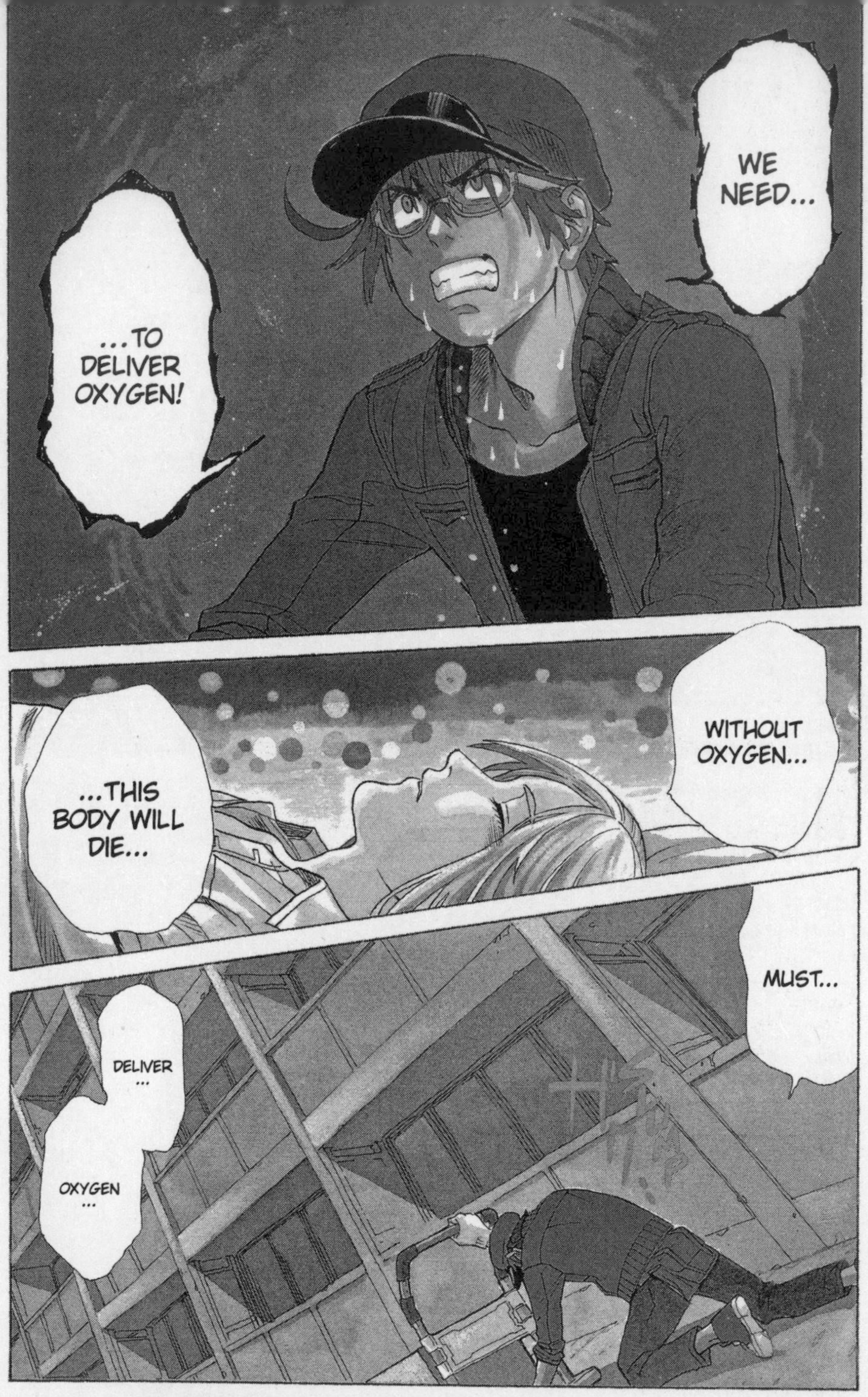
WE NEED...
...TO DELIVER OXYGEN!
WITHOUT OXYGEN...
...THIS BODY WILL DIE...
MUST...
DELIVER ...
OXYGEN ...

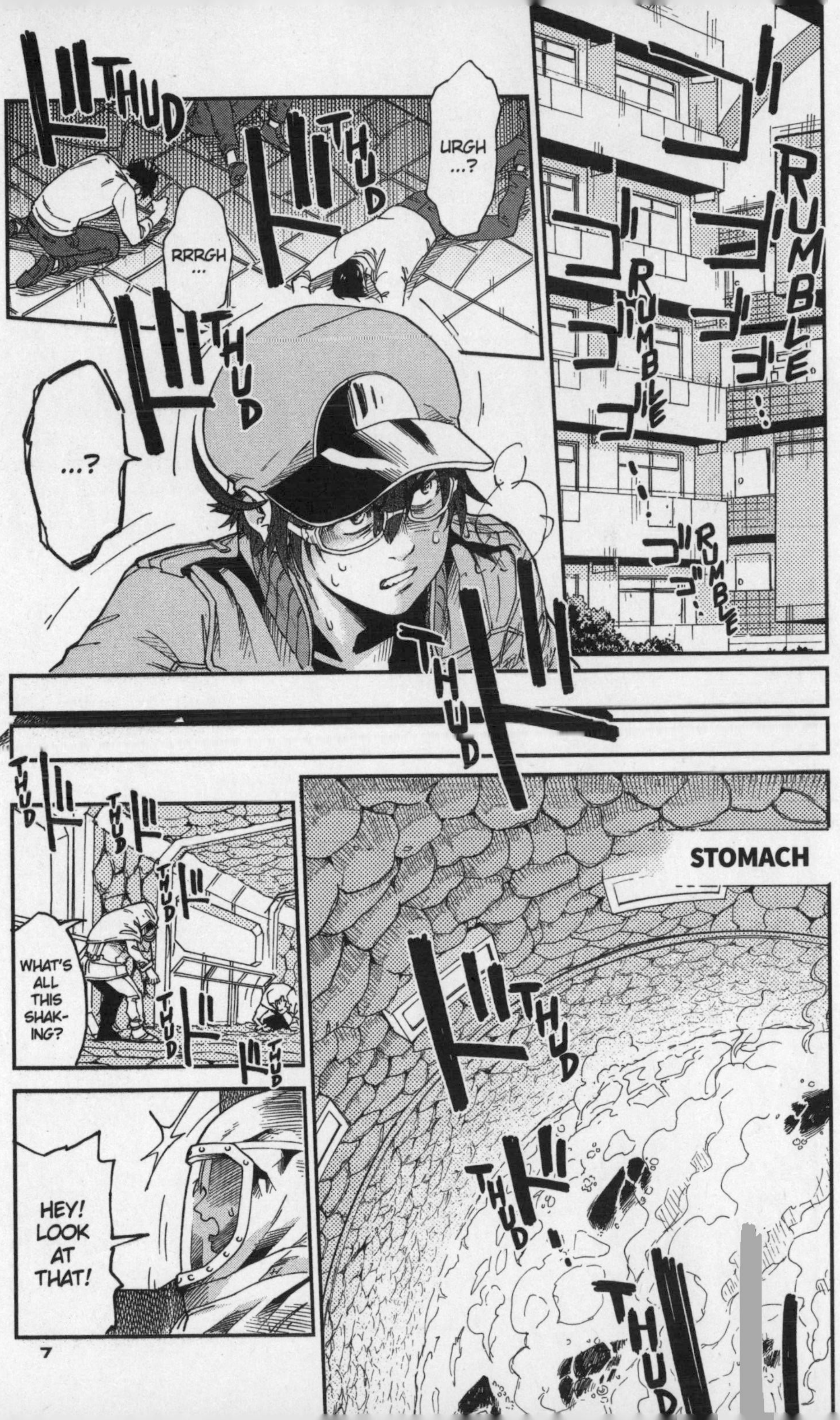
RUMBLE
RUMBLE
RUMBLE
THUD
THUD
URGH ...?
RRRGH ...
THUD
...?
THUD
STOMACH
THUD
THUD
THUD
THUD
THUD
THUD
THUD
THUD
WHAT'S ALL THIS SHAK-ING?
HEY! LOOK AT THAT!

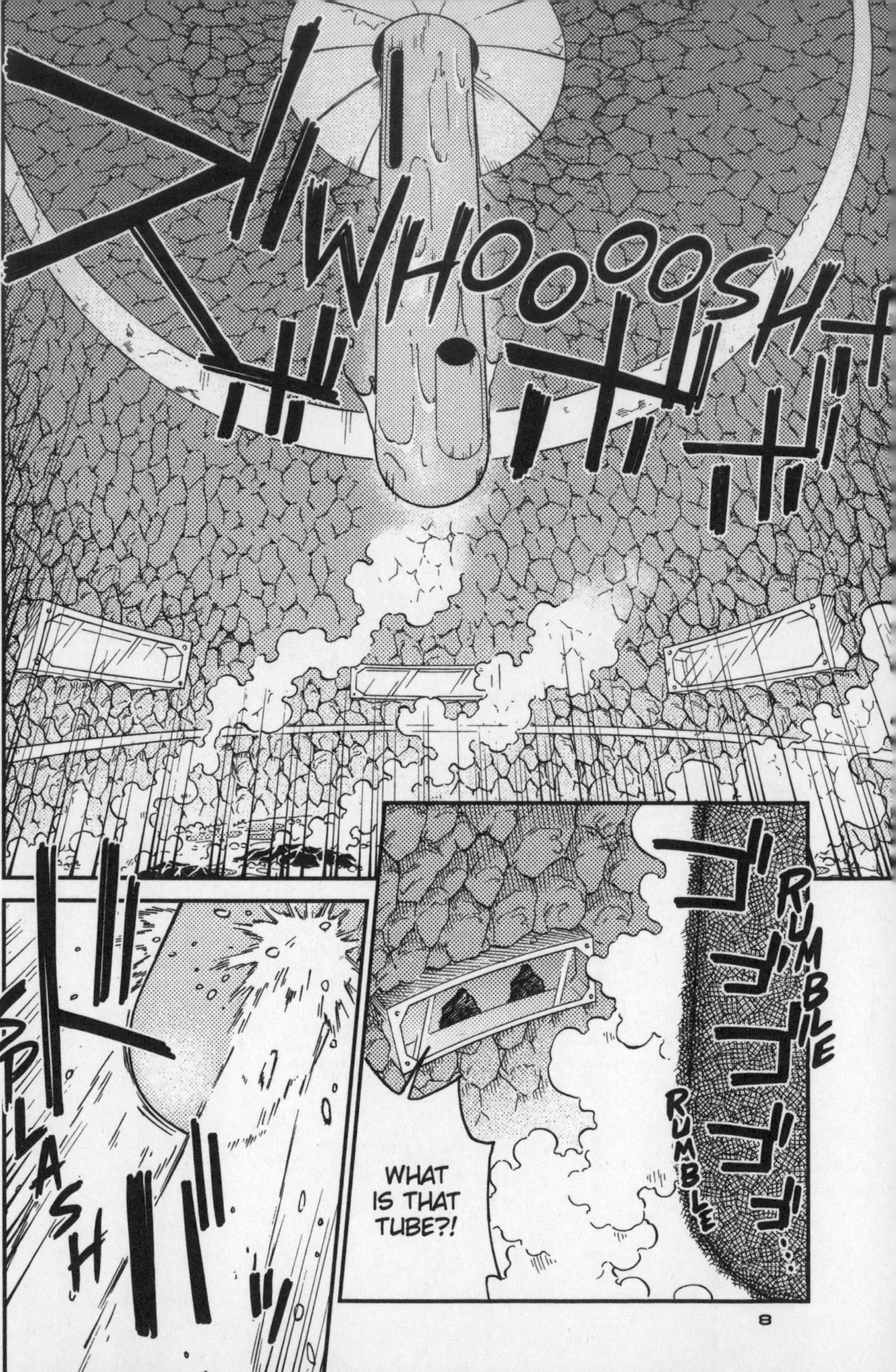
WHOOOSH
RUMBLE
RUMBLE
WHAT IS THAT TUBE?!
SPLASH

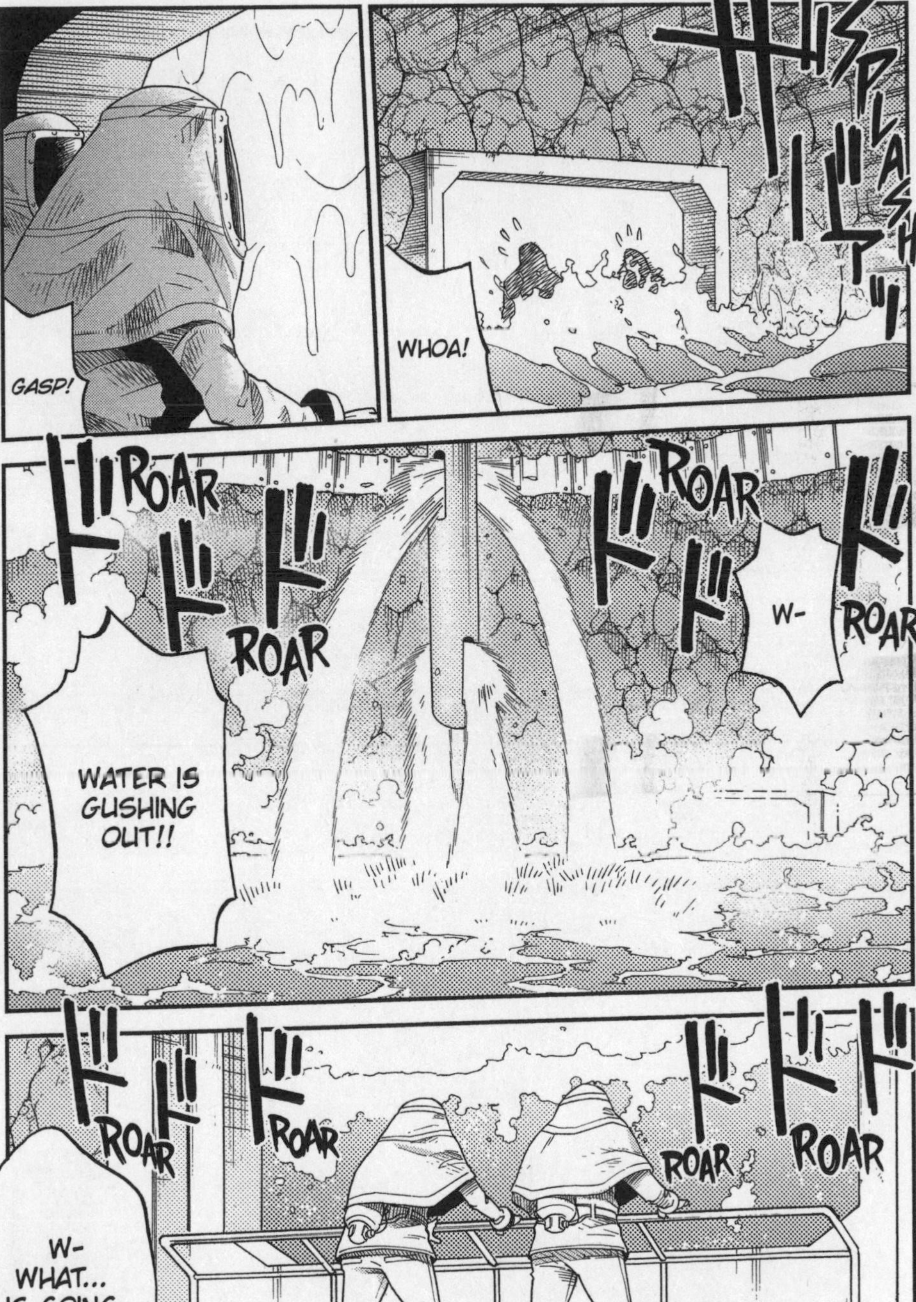
SPLASH
WHOA!
GASP!
ROAR
ROAR
W-
ROAR
ROAR
ROAR
WATER IS GUSHING OUT!!
ROAR
ROAR
ROAR
ROAR
W- WHAT... IS GOING ON?

WHAT'S HAPPENING?! GIVE ME AN UPDATE!

BEEEEP

BEEEEP

RRG!

WHAT THE...

WOBBLE

WOBBLE

W-WHAT...?!

A TUBE INSERTED FROM OUTSIDE IS RELEASING LARGE AMOUNTS OF WATER INTO THE STOMACH!

HEY! AT THIS RATE, IT'S GOING TO OVERFLOW!

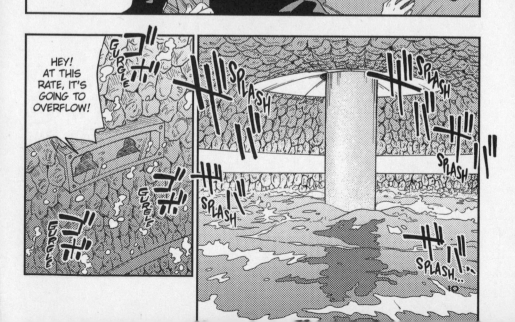

GURGLE

GURGLE

GURGLE

SPLASH

SPLASH

SPLASH

SPLASH

SPLASH...

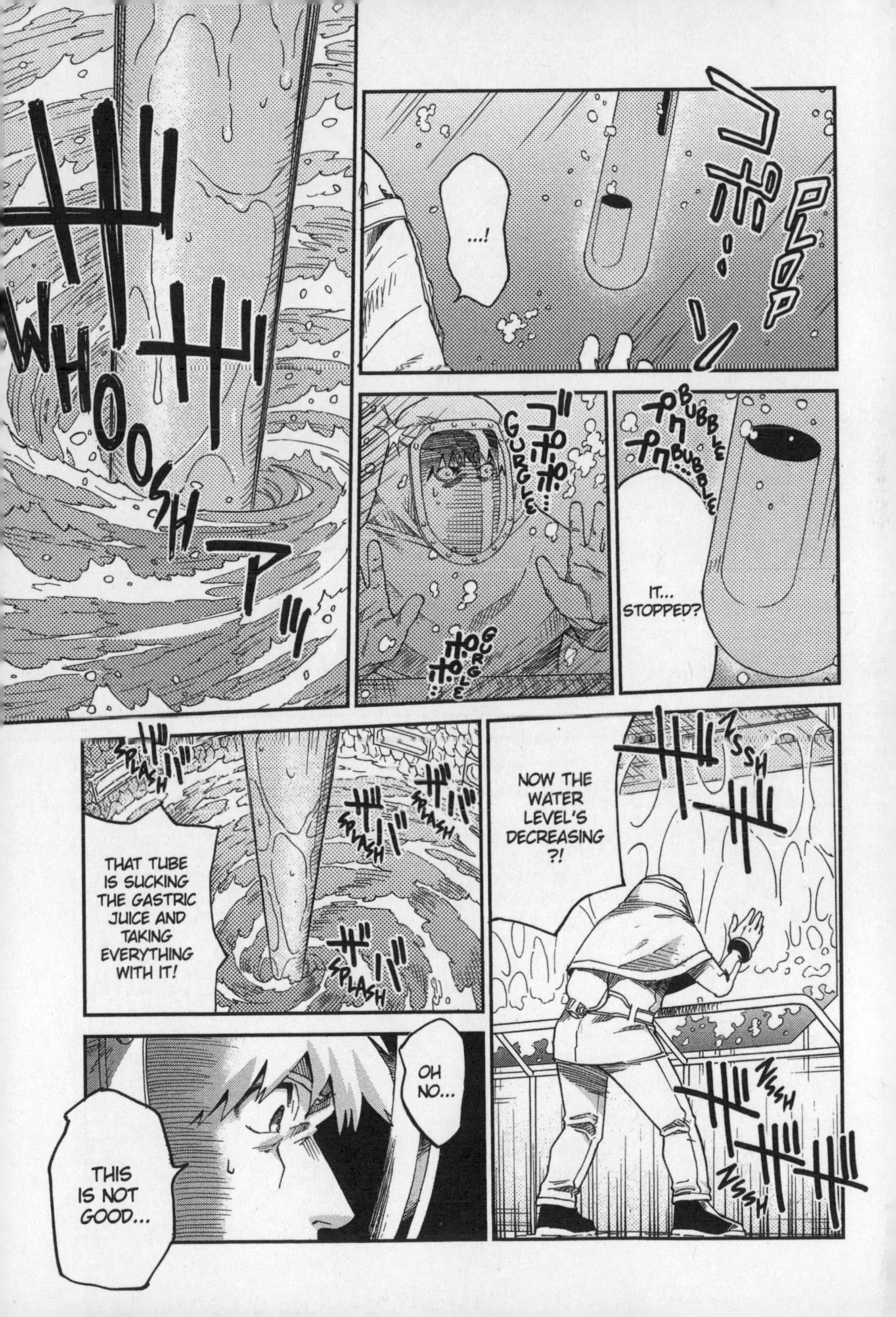

PLOOP
...!
BUBBLE BUBBLE
IT... STOPPED?
GURGLE...
GURGLE
WHOOSH
NSSH
NOW THE WATER LEVEL'S DECREASING ?!
NSSH
NSSH
SPLASH
SPLASH
SPLASH
THAT TUBE IS SUCKING THE GASTRIC JUICE AND TAKING EVERYTHING WITH IT!
SPLASH
OH NO...
THIS IS NOT GOOD...

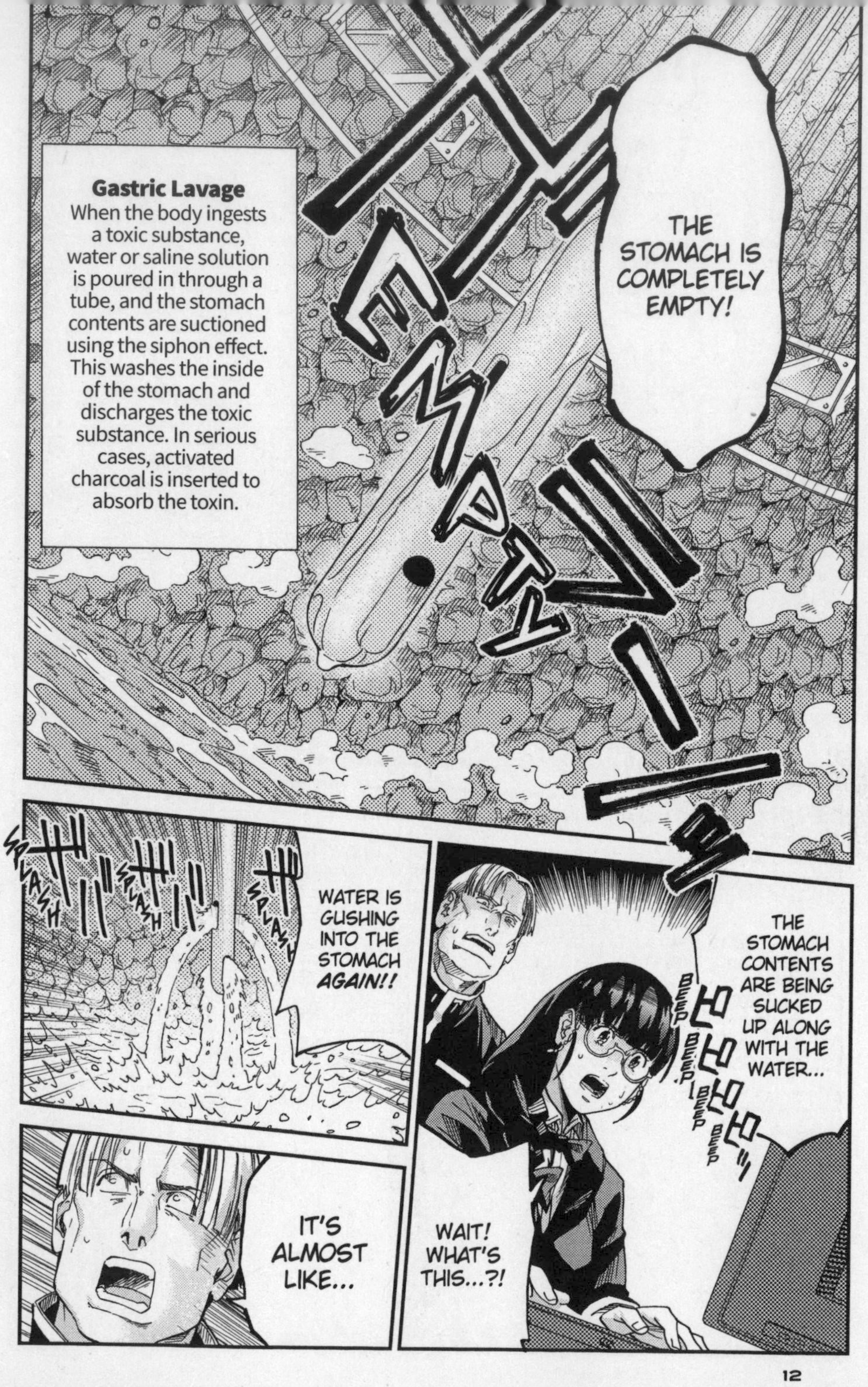
THE STOMACH IS COMPLETELY EMPTY!
EMPTY
Gastric Lavage
When the body ingests a toxic substance, water or saline solution is poured in through a tube, and the stomach contents are suctioned using the siphon effect. This washes the inside of the stomach and discharges the toxic substance. In serious cases, activated charcoal is inserted to absorb the toxin.
THE STOMACH CONTENTS ARE BEING SUCKED UP ALONG WITH THE WATER...
BEEP BEEP BEEP BEEP
WAIT! WHAT'S THIS...?!
WATER IS GUSHING INTO THE STOMACH AGAIN!!
SPLASH SPLASH SPLASH
IT'S ALMOST LIKE...

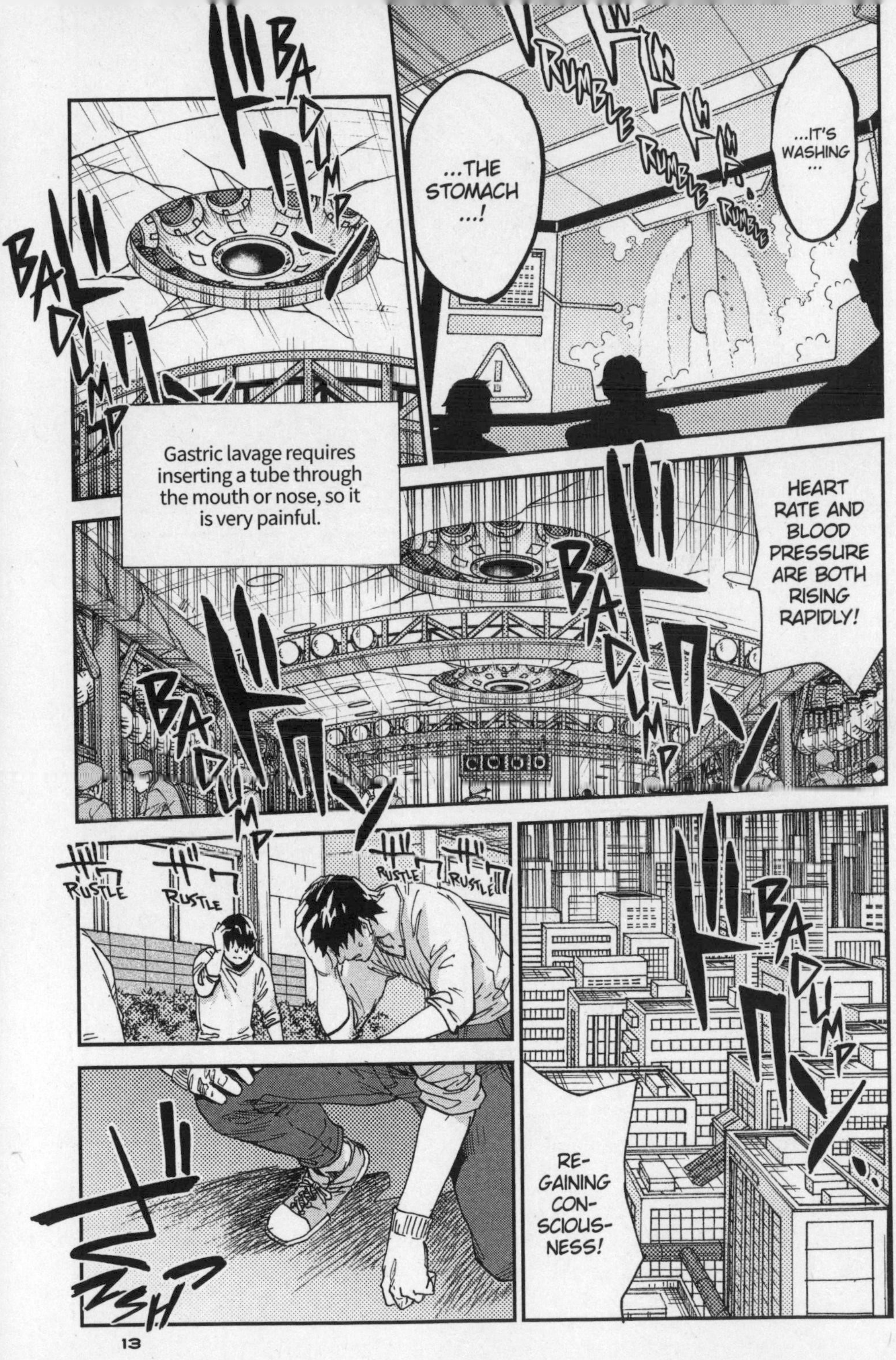
...IT'S WASHING ...
RUMBLE RUMBLE RUMBLE
...THE STOMACH ...!
BADUMP
BADUMP
Gastric lavage requires inserting a tube through the mouth or nose, so it is very painful.
HEART RATE AND BLOOD PRESSURE ARE BOTH RISING RAPIDLY!
BADUMP
BADUMP
BADUMP
RE-GAINING CON-SCIOUS-NESS!
RUSTLE RUSTLE
RUSTLE RUSTLE
SHH

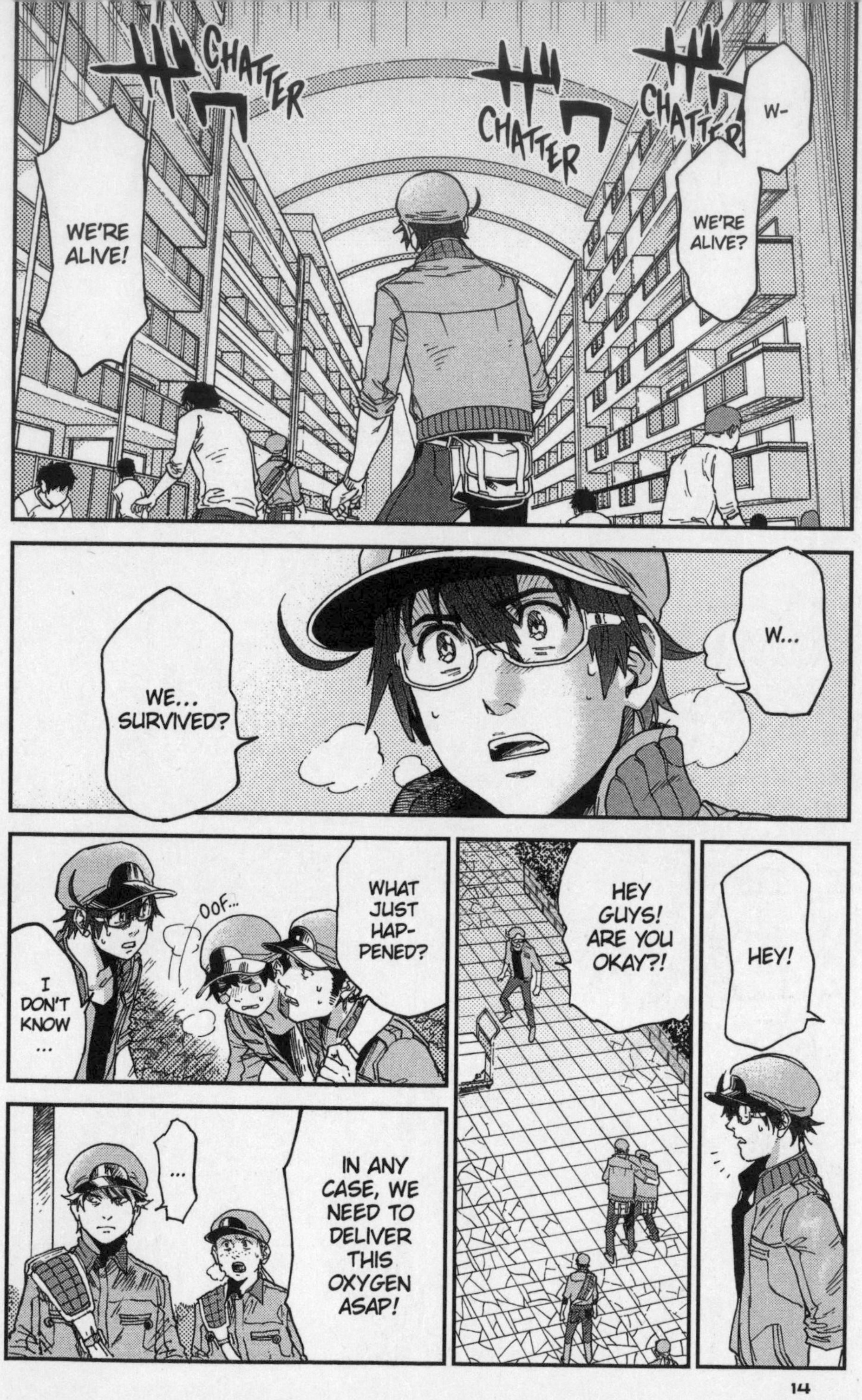
CHATTER
W-
WE'RE ALIVE?
CHATTER
CHATTER
WE'RE ALIVE!
W...
WE... SURVIVED?
HEY!
HEY GUYS! ARE YOU OKAY?!
WHAT JUST HAP-PENED?
OOF...
I DON'T KNOW ...
IN ANY CASE, WE NEED TO DELIVER THIS OXYGEN ASAP!
...

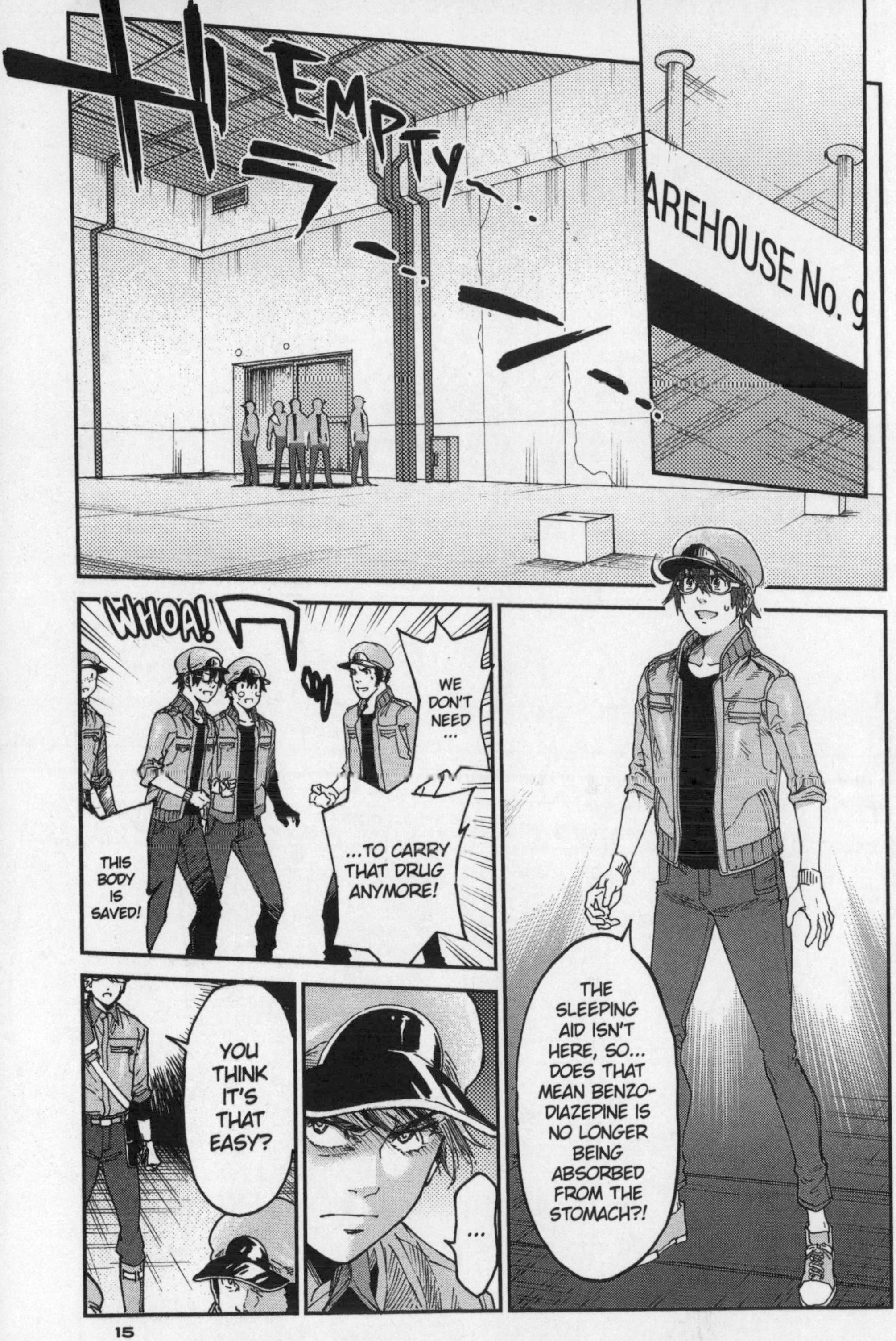
EMPTY...
AREHOUSE No. 9
THE SLEEPING AID ISN'T HERE, SO... DOES THAT MEAN BENZO-DIAZEPINE IS NO LONGER BEING ABSORBED FROM THE STOMACH?!
WE DON'T NEED...
...TO CARRY THAT DRUG ANYMORE!
WHOA!
THIS BODY IS SAVED!
...
YOU THINK IT'S THAT EASY?

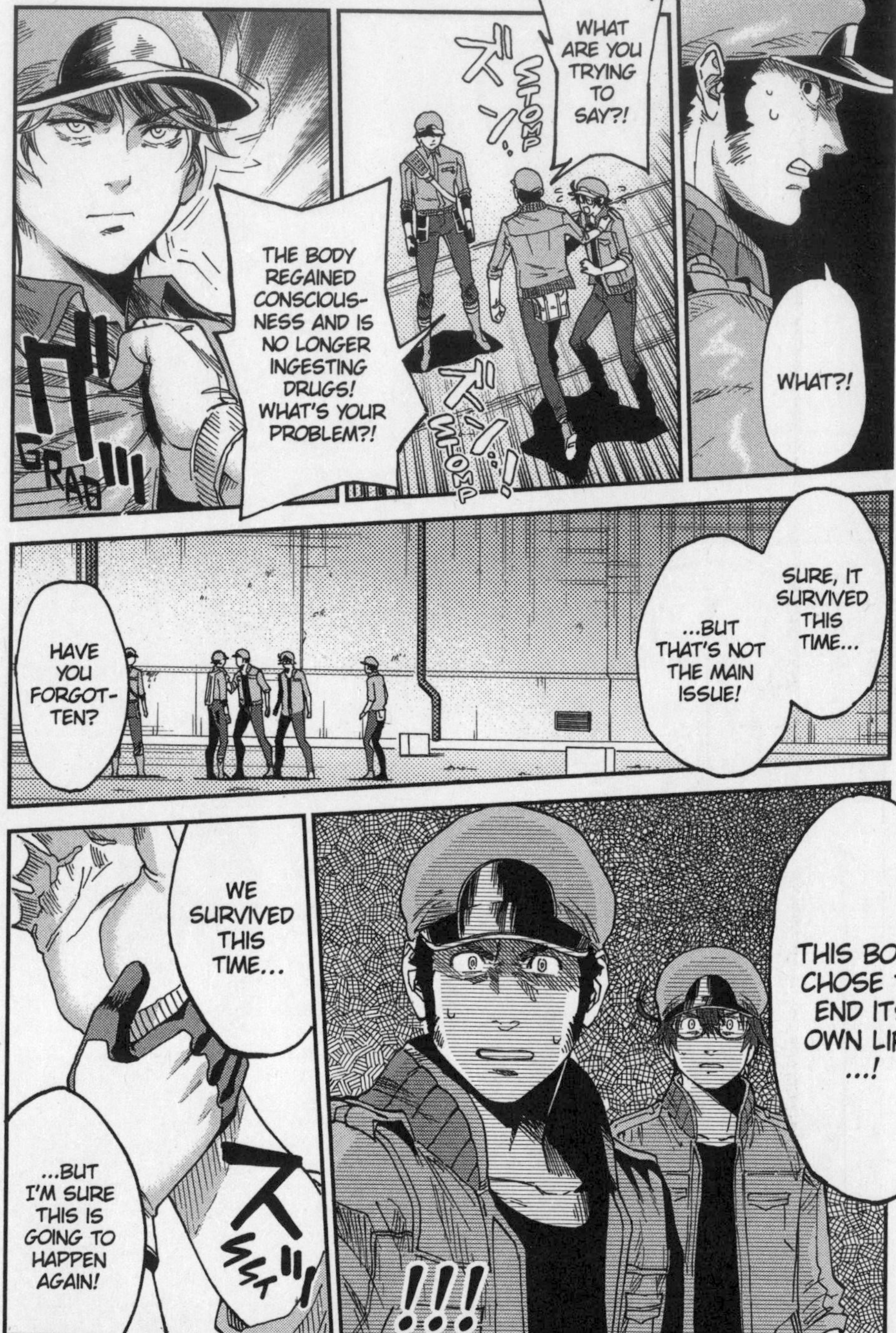
WHAT?!
WHAT ARE YOU TRYING TO SAY?!
STOMP
THE BODY REGAINED CONSCIOUSNESS AND IS NO LONGER INGESTING DRUGS! WHAT'S YOUR PROBLEM?!
STOMP
GRAB
SURE, IT SURVIVED THIS TIME...
...BUT THAT'S NOT THE MAIN ISSUE!
HAVE YOU FORGOTTEN?
THIS BODY CHOSE TO END ITS OWN LIFE ...!
!!!
WE SURVIVED THIS TIME...
...BUT I'M SURE THIS IS GOING TO HAPPEN AGAIN!
YANK

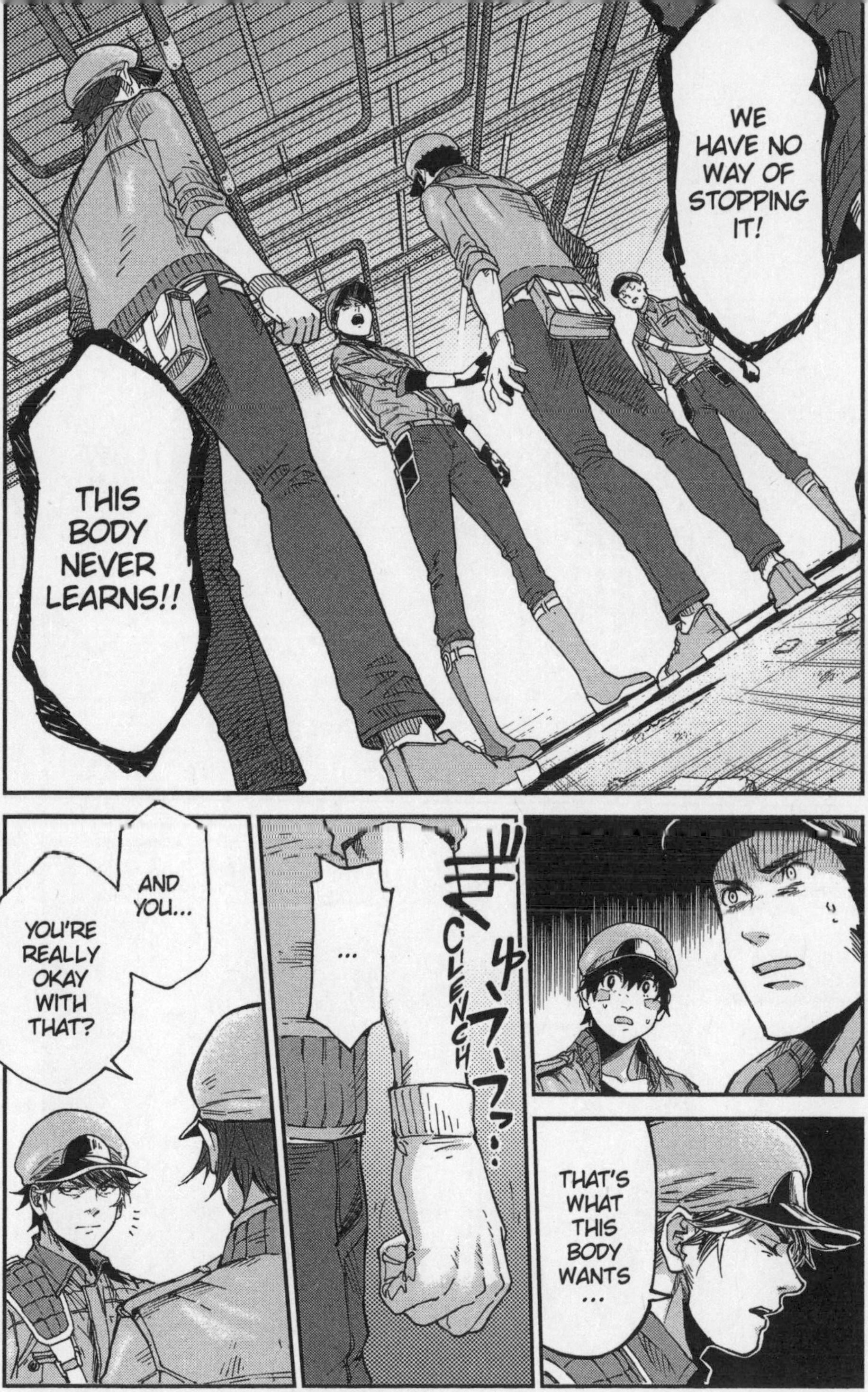
WE HAVE NO WAY OF STOPPING IT!
THIS BODY NEVER LEARNS!!
THAT'S WHAT THIS BODY WANTS...
...
CLENCH
AND YOU...
YOU'RE REALLY OKAY WITH THAT?

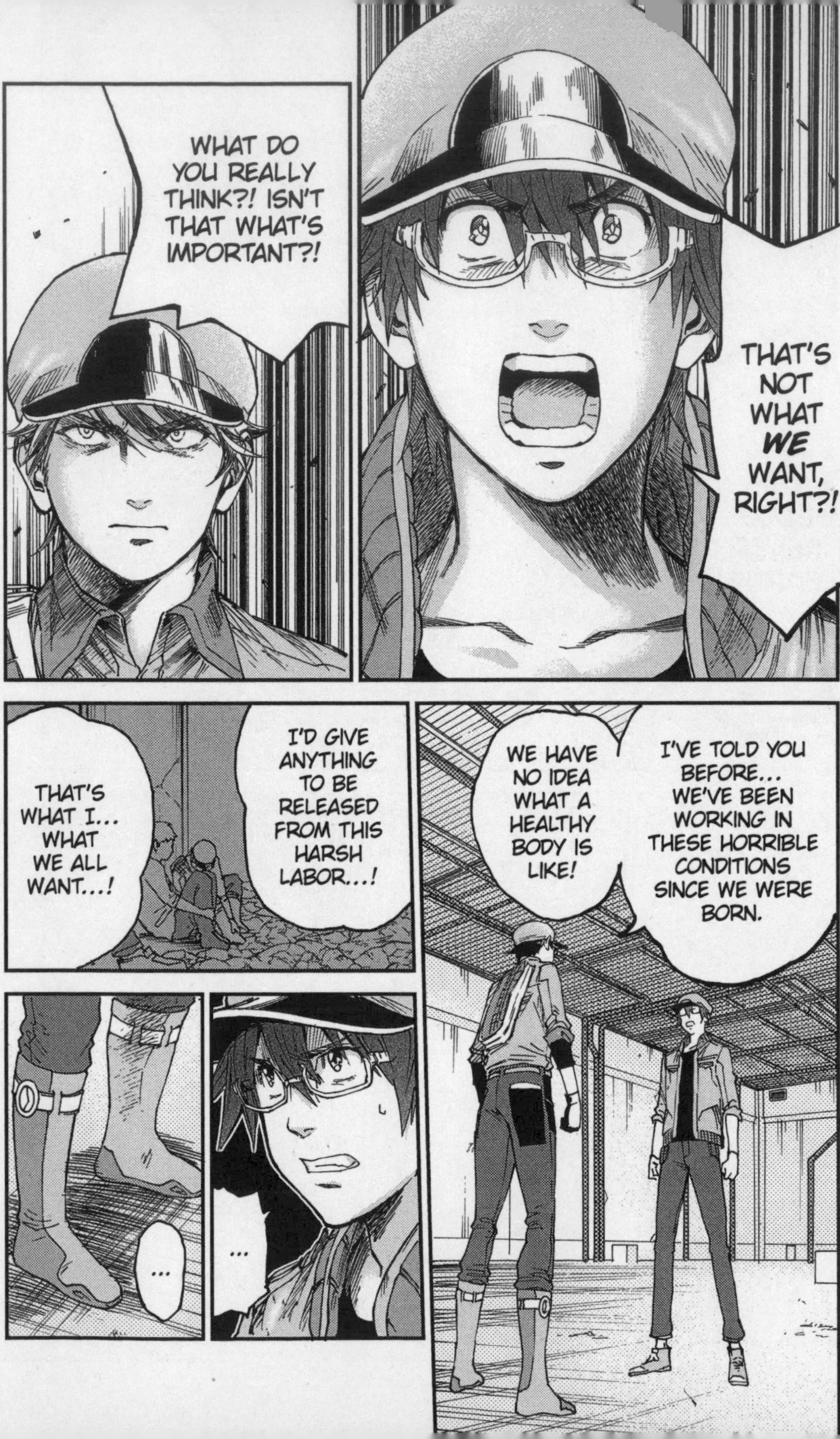
THAT'S NOT WHAT WE WANT, RIGHT?!
WHAT DO YOU REALLY THINK?! ISN'T THAT WHAT'S IMPORTANT?!
I'VE TOLD YOU BEFORE... WE'VE BEEN WORKING IN THESE HORRIBLE CONDITIONS SINCE WE WERE BORN.
WE HAVE NO IDEA WHAT A HEALTHY BODY IS LIKE!
I'D GIVE ANYTHING TO BE RELEASED FROM THIS HARSH LABOR...!
THAT'S WHAT I... WHAT WE ALL WANT...!
...
...

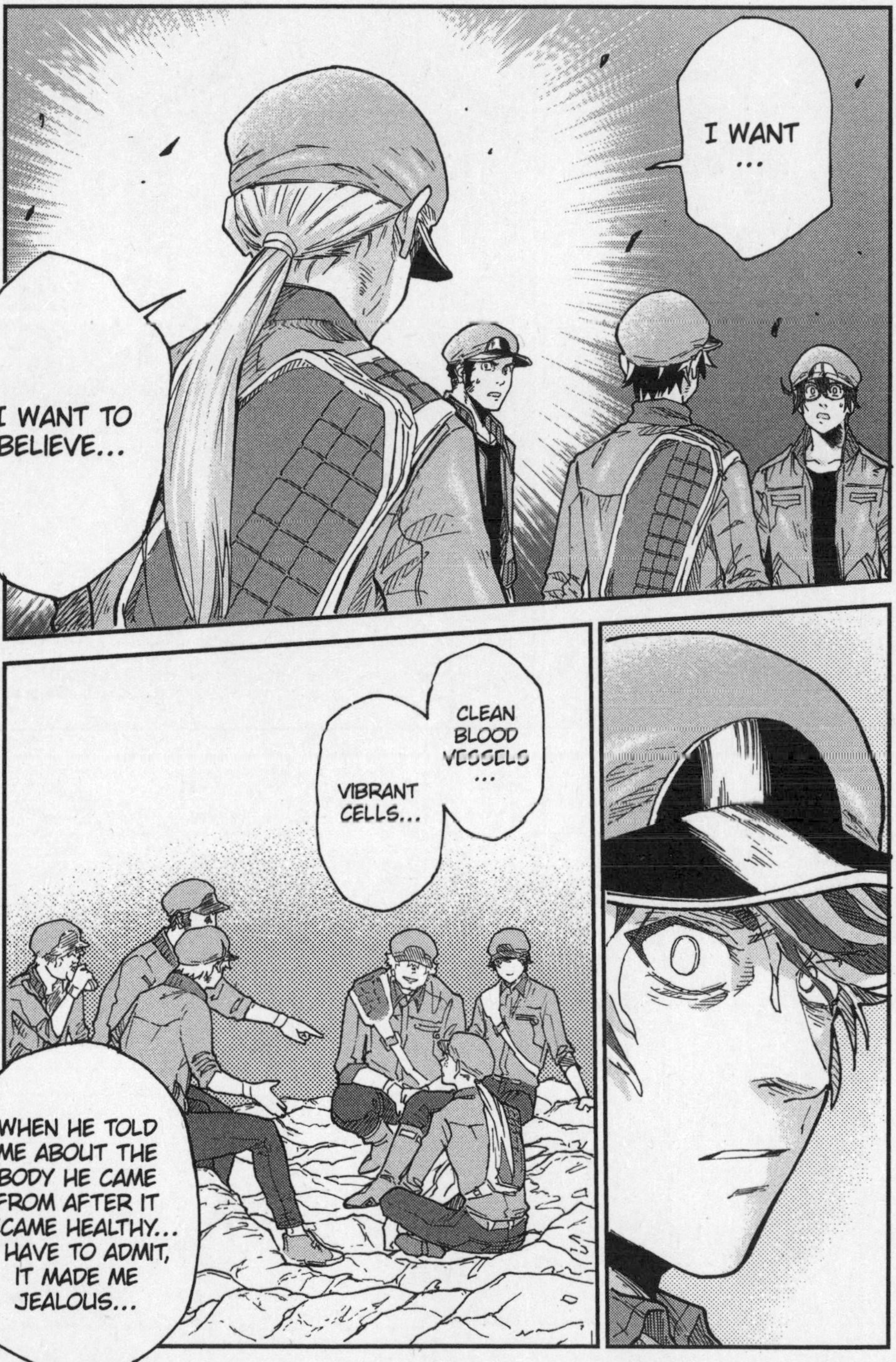
I WANT ...
I WANT TO BELIEVE...
CLEAN BLOOD VESSELS ...
VIBRANT CELLS...
WHEN HE TOLD ME ABOUT THE BODY HE CAME FROM AFTER IT BECAME HEALTHY... I HAVE TO ADMIT, IT MADE ME JEALOUS...

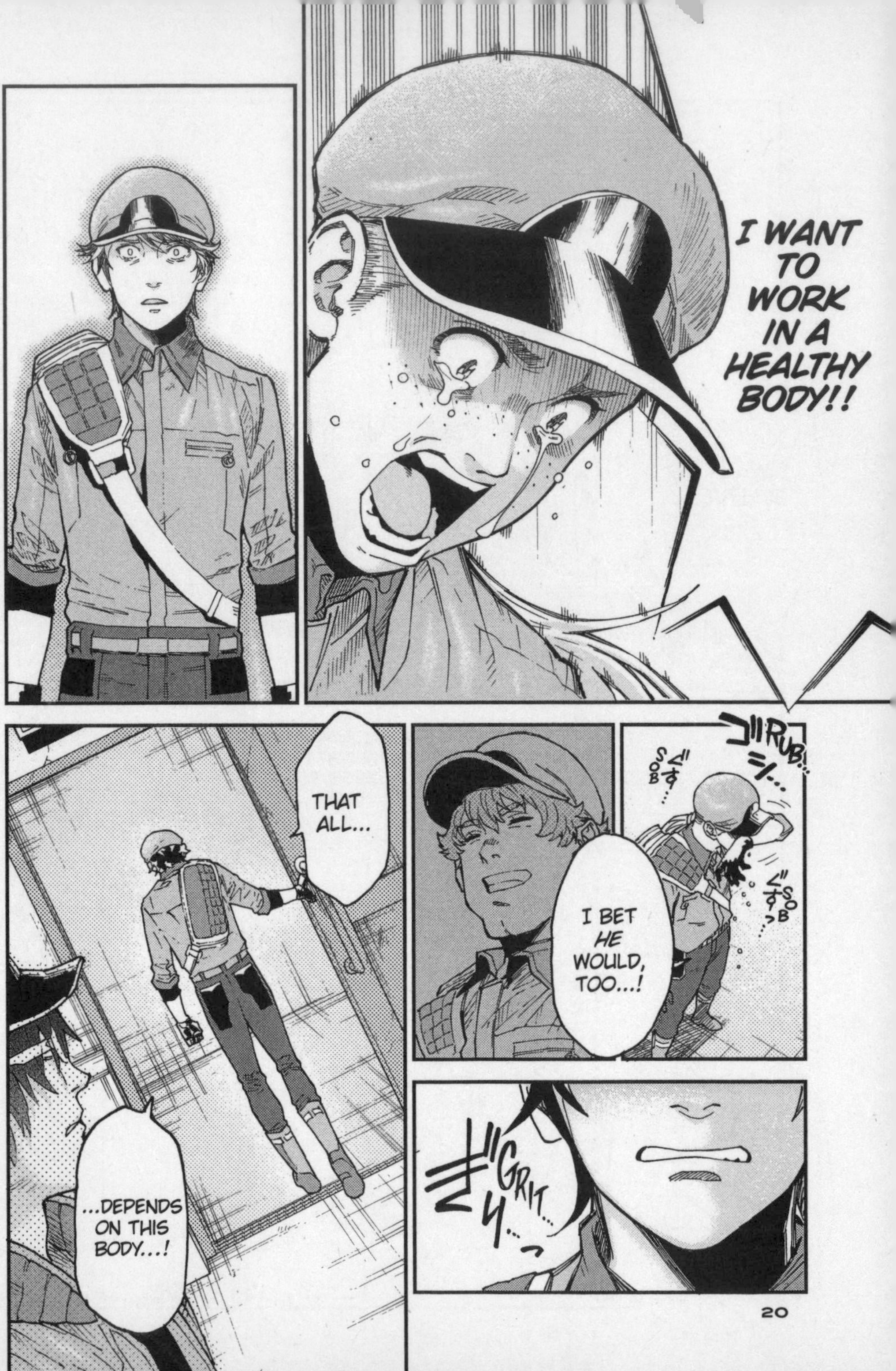
I WANT TO WORK IN A HEALTHY BODY!!
RUB...
SOB...
SOB...
I BET HE WOULD, TOO...!
GRIT...
THAT ALL...
...DEPENDS ON THIS BODY...!

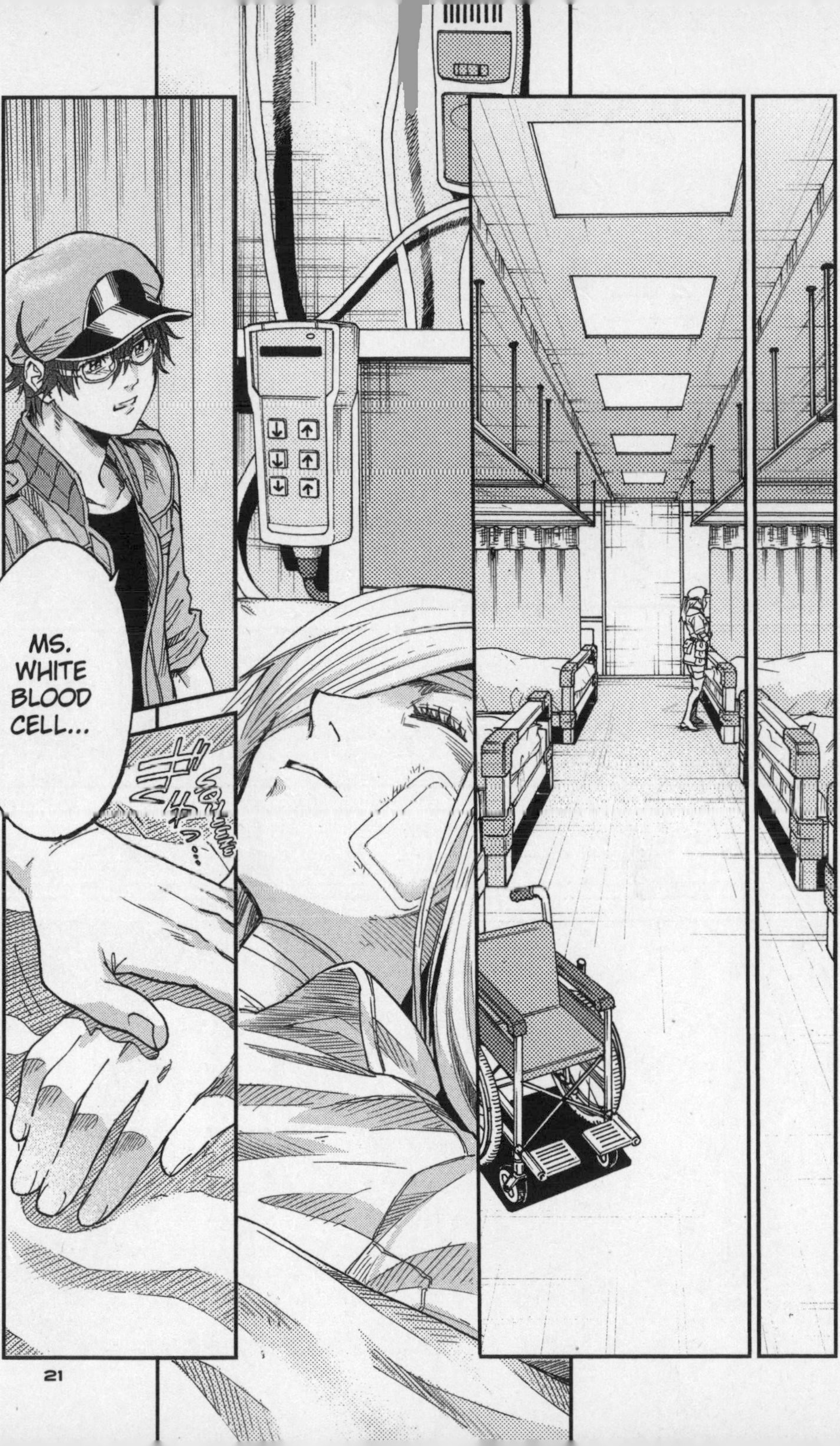
MS. WHITE BLOOD CELL...

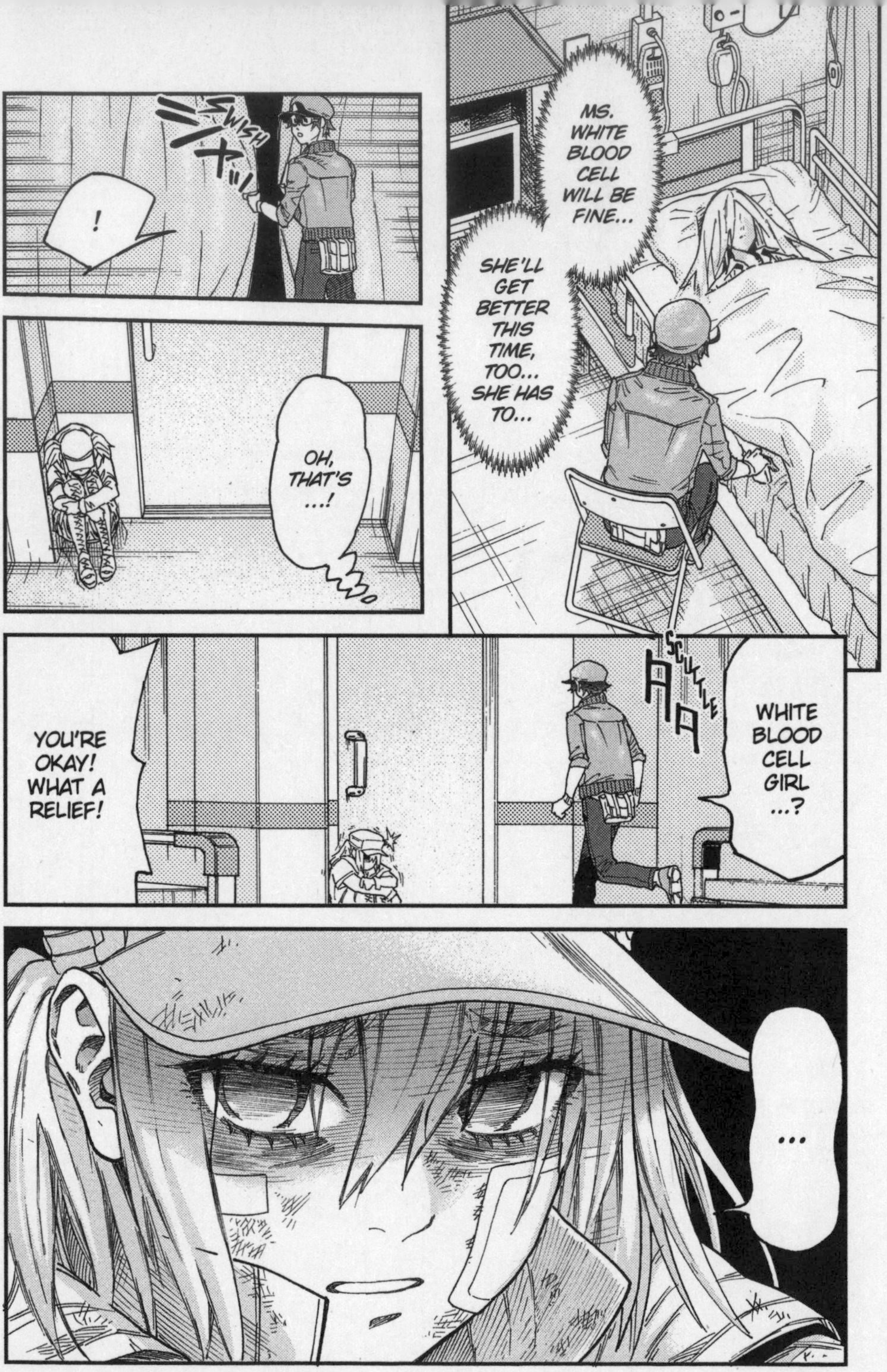
MS. WHITE BLOOD CELL WILL BE FINE...
SHE'LL GET BETTER THIS TIME, TOO... SHE HAS TO...
SWISH
!
OH, THAT'S ...!
SCUTTLE
WHITE BLOOD CELL GIRL ...?
YOU'RE OKAY! WHAT A RELIEF!
...

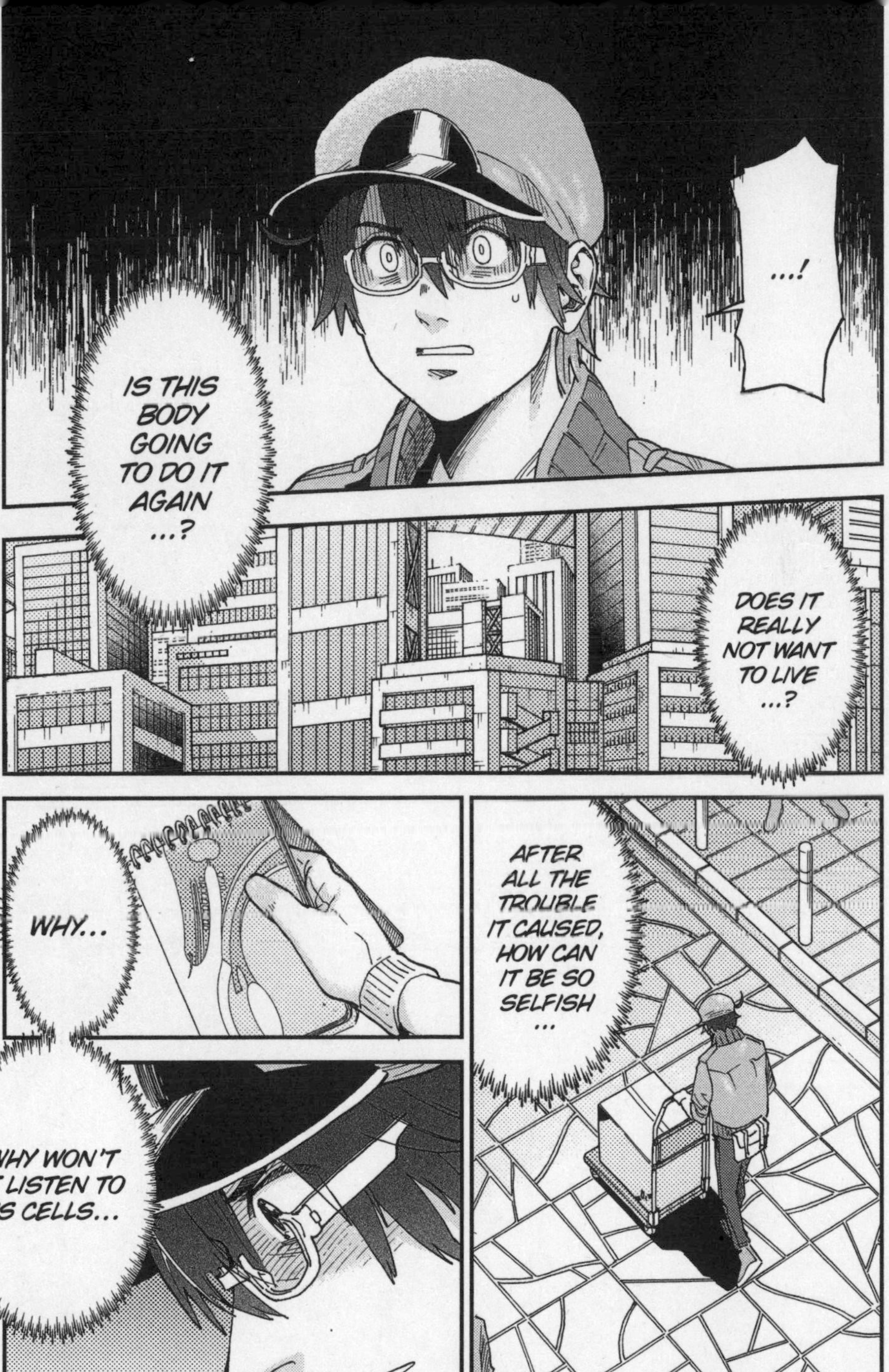
...!
IS THIS BODY GOING TO DO IT AGAIN ...?
DOES IT REALLY NOT WANT TO LIVE ...?
AFTER ALL THE TROUBLE IT CAUSED, HOW CAN IT BE SO SELFISH ...
WHY...
WHY WON'T IT LISTEN TO US CELLS...

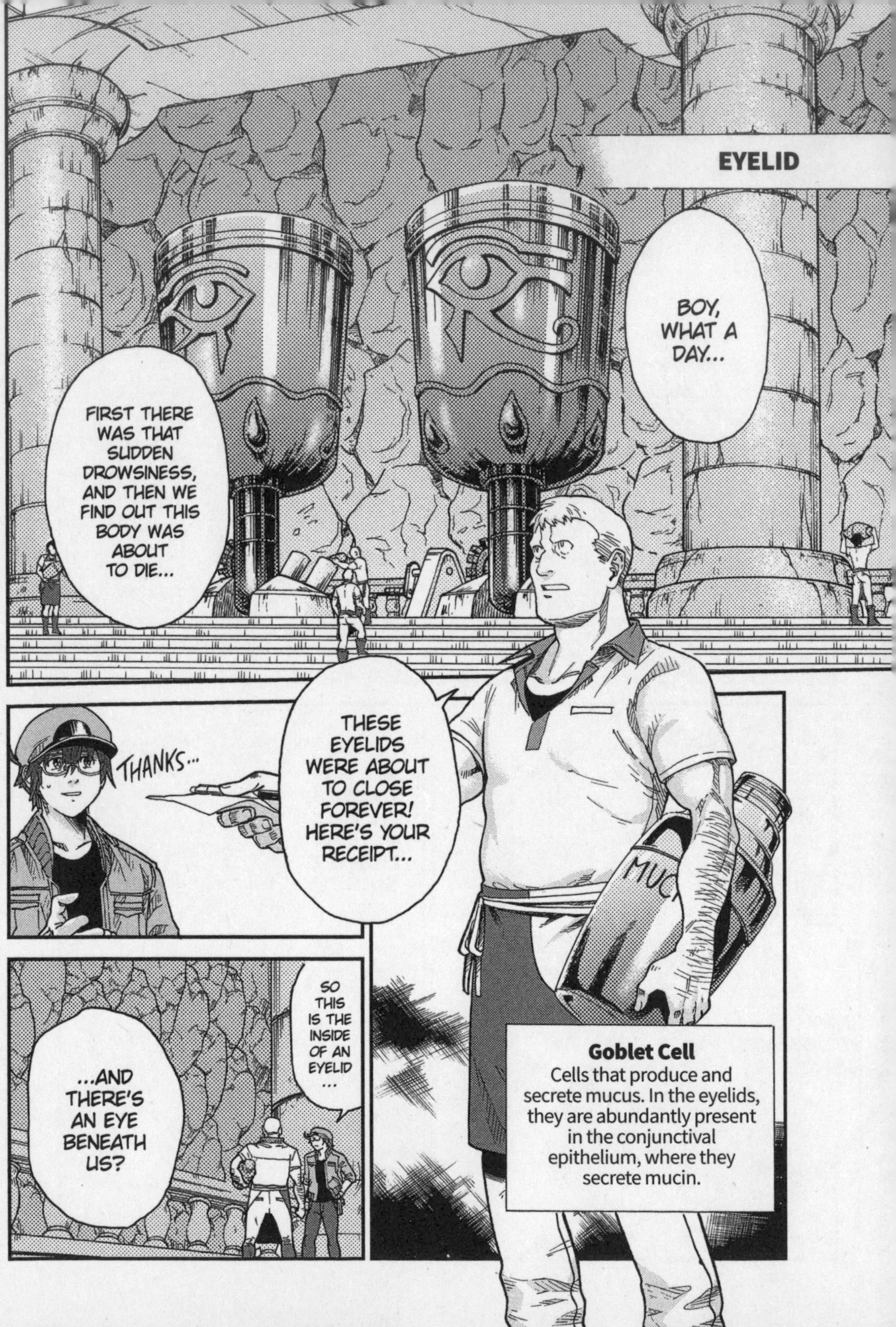
EYELID
BOY, WHAT A DAY...
FIRST THERE WAS THAT SUDDEN DROWSINESS, AND THEN WE FIND OUT THIS BODY WAS ABOUT TO DIE...
THESE EYELIDS WERE ABOUT TO CLOSE FOREVER! HERE'S YOUR RECEIPT...
MUC
Goblet Cell
Cells that produce and secrete mucus. In the eyelids, they are abundantly present in the conjunctival epithelium, where they secrete mucin.
THANKS...
SO THIS IS THE INSIDE OF AN EYELID...
...AND THERE'S AN EYE BENEATH US?

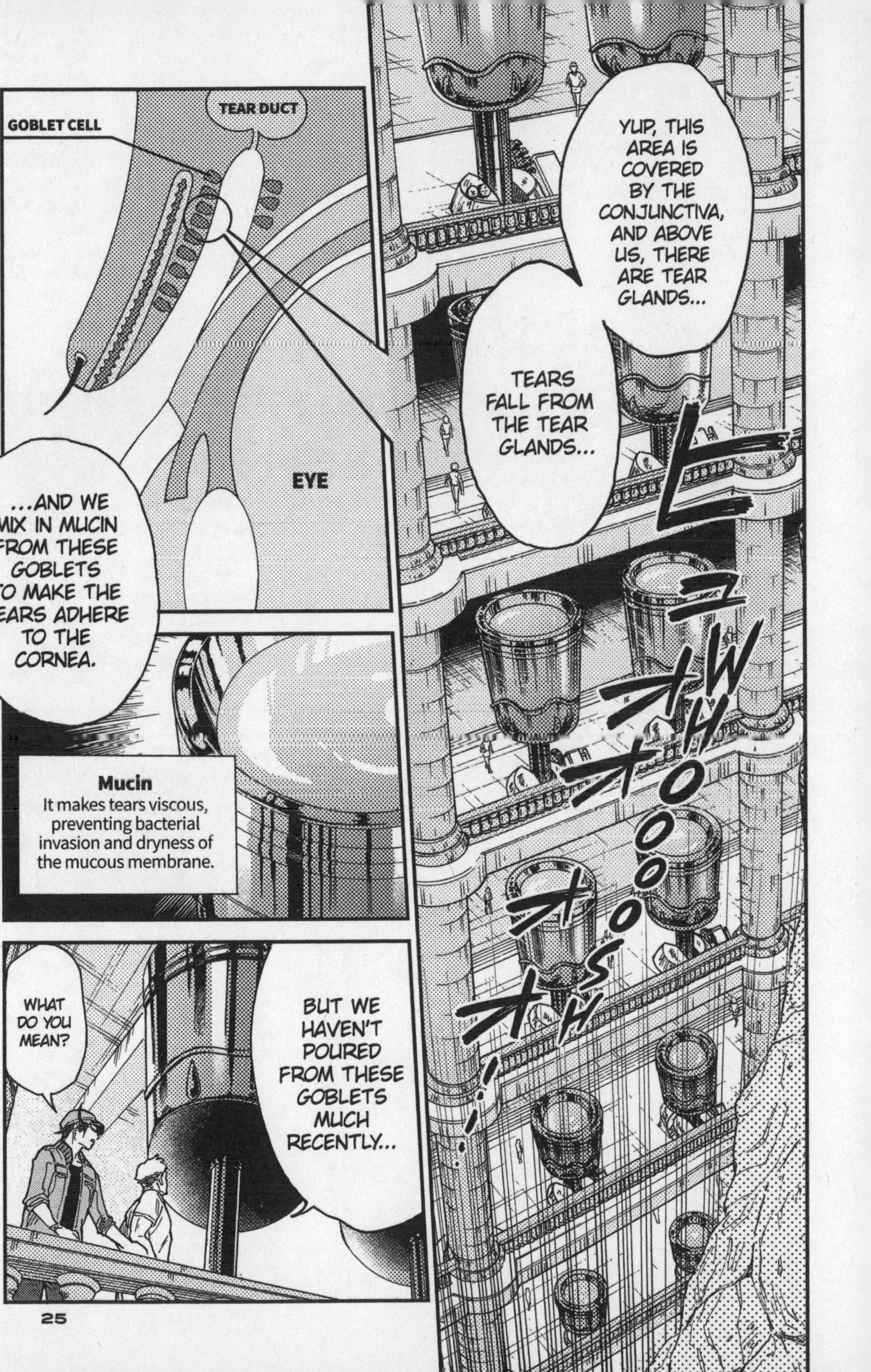
YUP, THIS AREA IS COVERED BY THE CONJUNCTIVA, AND ABOVE US, THERE ARE TEAR GLANDS...
TEARS FALL FROM THE TEAR GLANDS...
WHOOOOOSH!!
TEAR DUCT
GOBLET CELL
EYE
...AND WE MIX IN MUCIN FROM THESE GOBLETS TO MAKE THE TEARS ADHERE TO THE CORNEA.
Mucin
It makes tears viscous, preventing bacterial invasion and dryness of the mucous membrane.
BUT WE HAVEN'T POURED FROM THESE GOBLETS MUCH RECENTLY...
WHAT DO YOU MEAN?

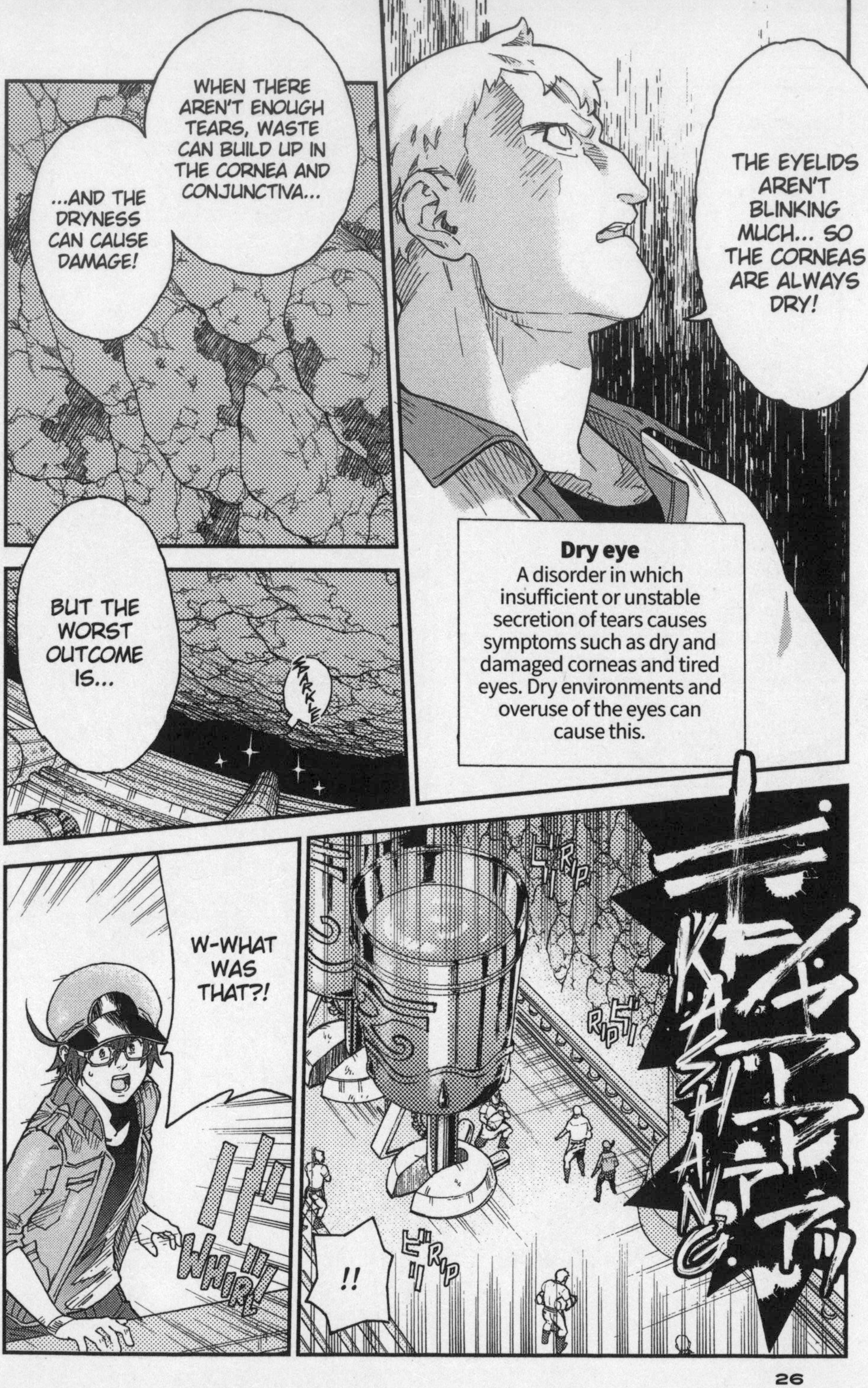
THE EYELIDS AREN'T BLINKING MUCH... SO THE CORNEAS ARE ALWAYS DRY!
Dry eye
A disorder in which insufficient or unstable secretion of tears causes symptoms such as dry and damaged corneas and tired eyes. Dry environments and overuse of the eyes can cause this.
WHEN THERE AREN'T ENOUGH TEARS, WASTE CAN BUILD UP IN THE CORNEA AND CONJUNCTIVA...
...AND THE DRYNESS CAN CAUSE DAMAGE!
BUT THE WORST OUTCOME IS...
SPARKLE
KASHANG
RIP
RIP
RIP
!!
W-WHAT WAS THAT?!
WHIRL

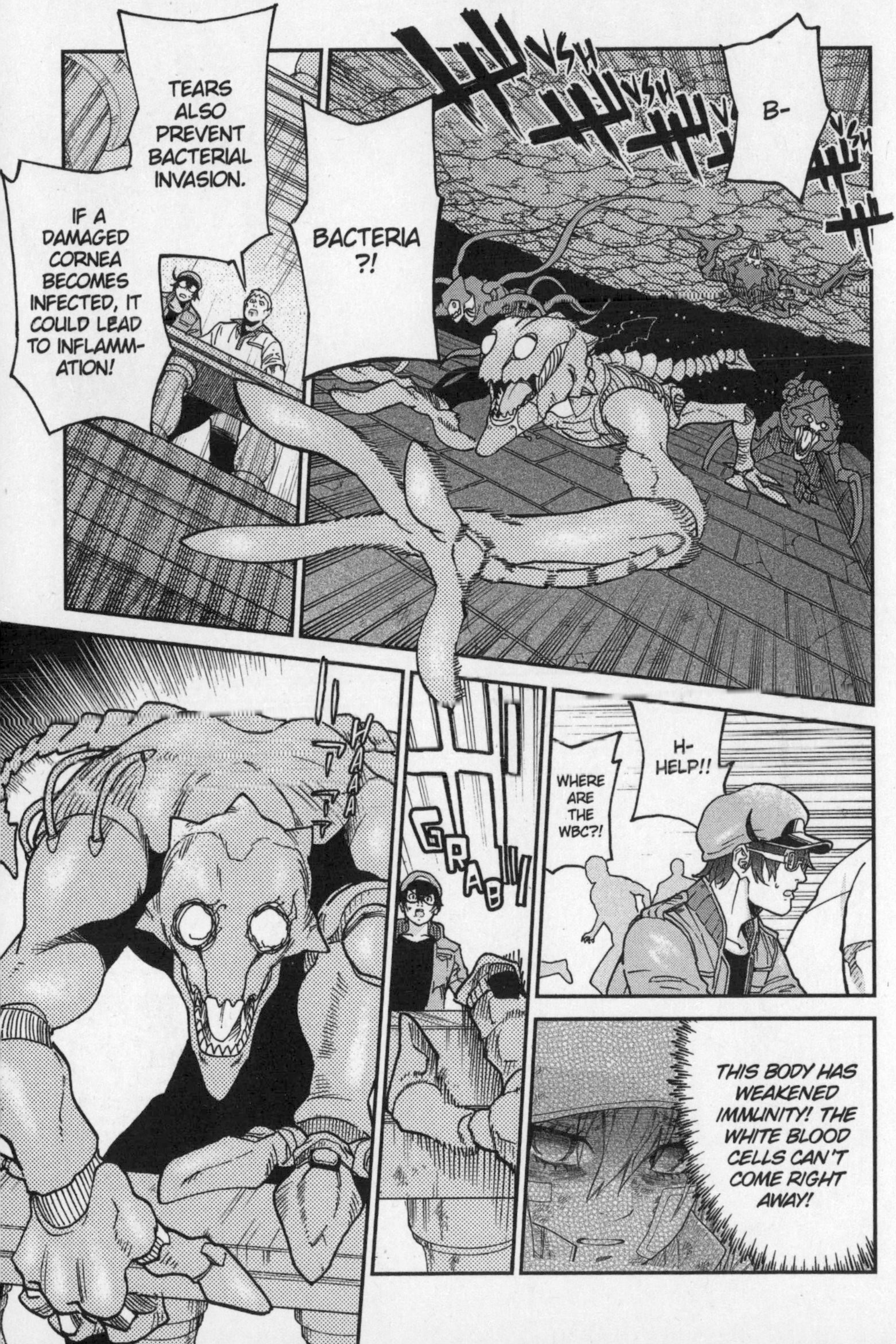
B-
VSH
VSH
VSH
TEARS ALSO PREVENT BACTERIAL INVASION.
BACTERIA?!
IF A DAMAGED CORNEA BECOMES INFECTED, IT COULD LEAD TO INFLAMMATION!
H- HELP!!
WHERE ARE THE WBC?!
THIS BODY HAS WEAKENED IMMUNITY! THE WHITE BLOOD CELLS CAN'T COME RIGHT AWAY!
GRAB
HAAAA

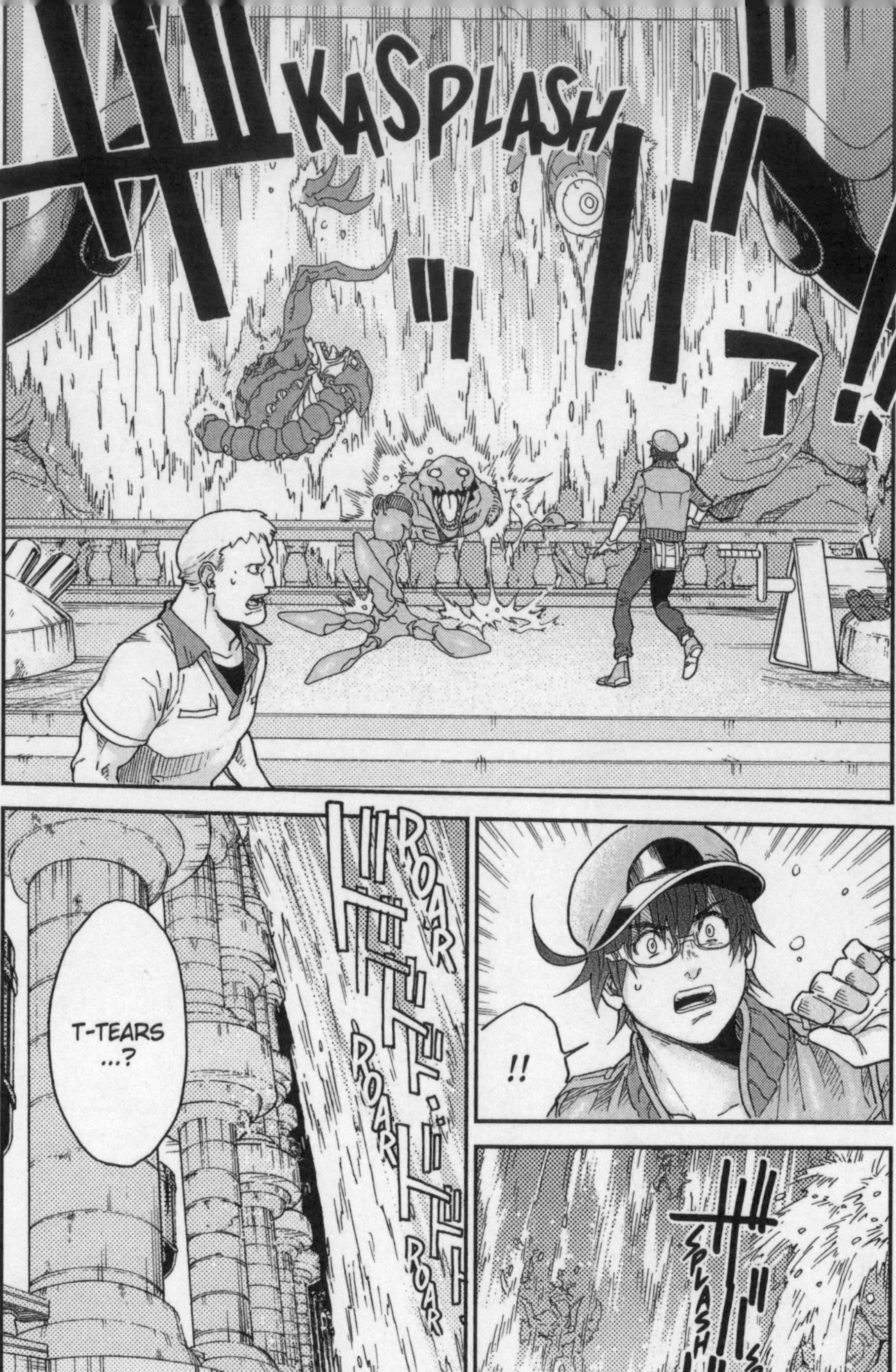
KASPLASH
!!
SPLASH...
SPLASH...
ROAR
ROAR
ROAR
ROAR
T-TEARS ...?

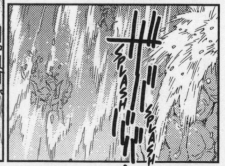

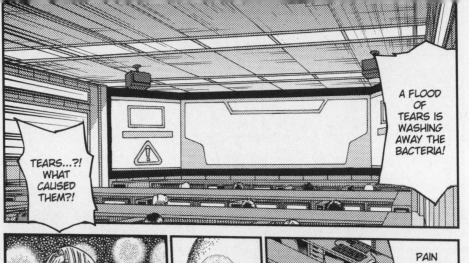

A FLOOD OF TEARS IS WASHING AWAY THE BACTERIA!

TEARS...?! WHAT CAUSED THEM?!

PAIN SOME-WHERE IN THE BODY ...?!

N-NO...

IS SOMETHING WRONG WITH THE TEAR GLANDS ?!

NO...!

THEN WHAT WAS THE CAUSE?!

WHAT'S THIS SINGING ...?

THE PARA-SYMPATHETIC NERVES ARE FULLY ACTIVATED!

THESE ARE...

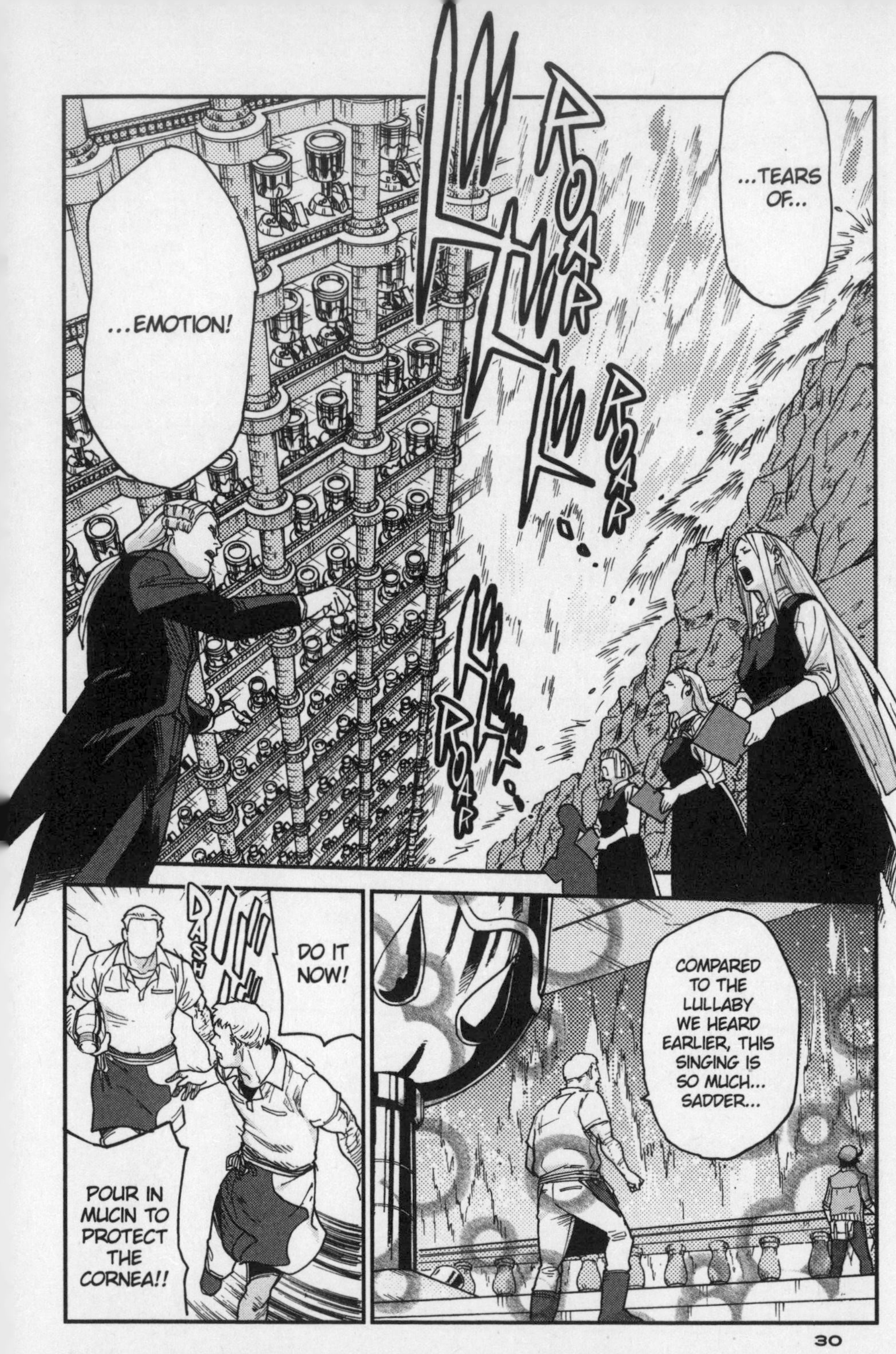
...TEARS OF...
ROAR
ROAR
...EMOTION!
ROAR
COMPARED TO THE LULLABY WE HEARD EARLIER, THIS SINGING IS SO MUCH... SADDER...
DO IT NOW!
DASH
POUR IN MUCIN TO PROTECT THE CORNEA!!

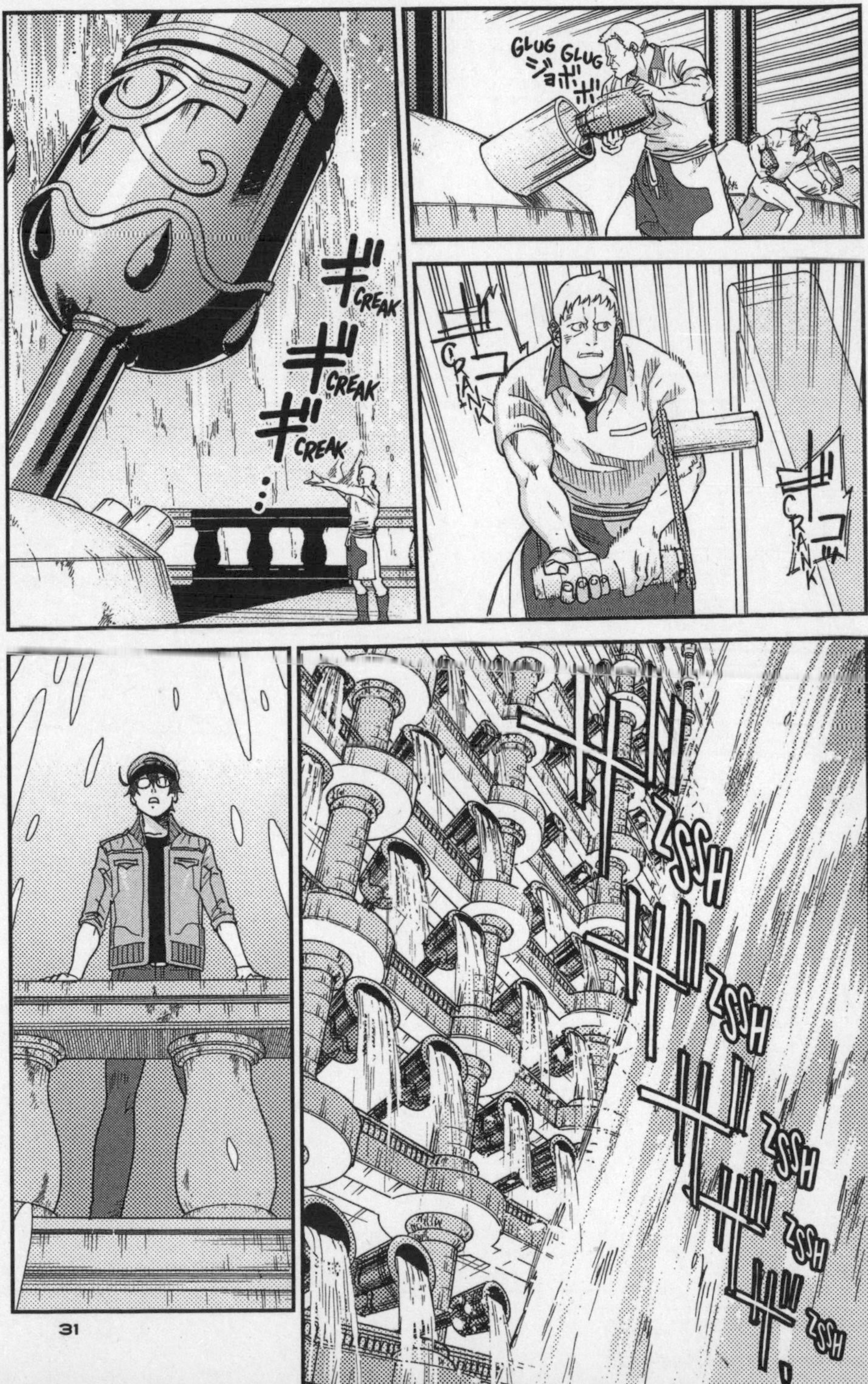
GLUG GLUG
ジョボボ
CRANK
CRANK
CREAK
CREAK
CREAK
...
ZSSH
ZSSH
ZSSH
ZSSH
ZSSH

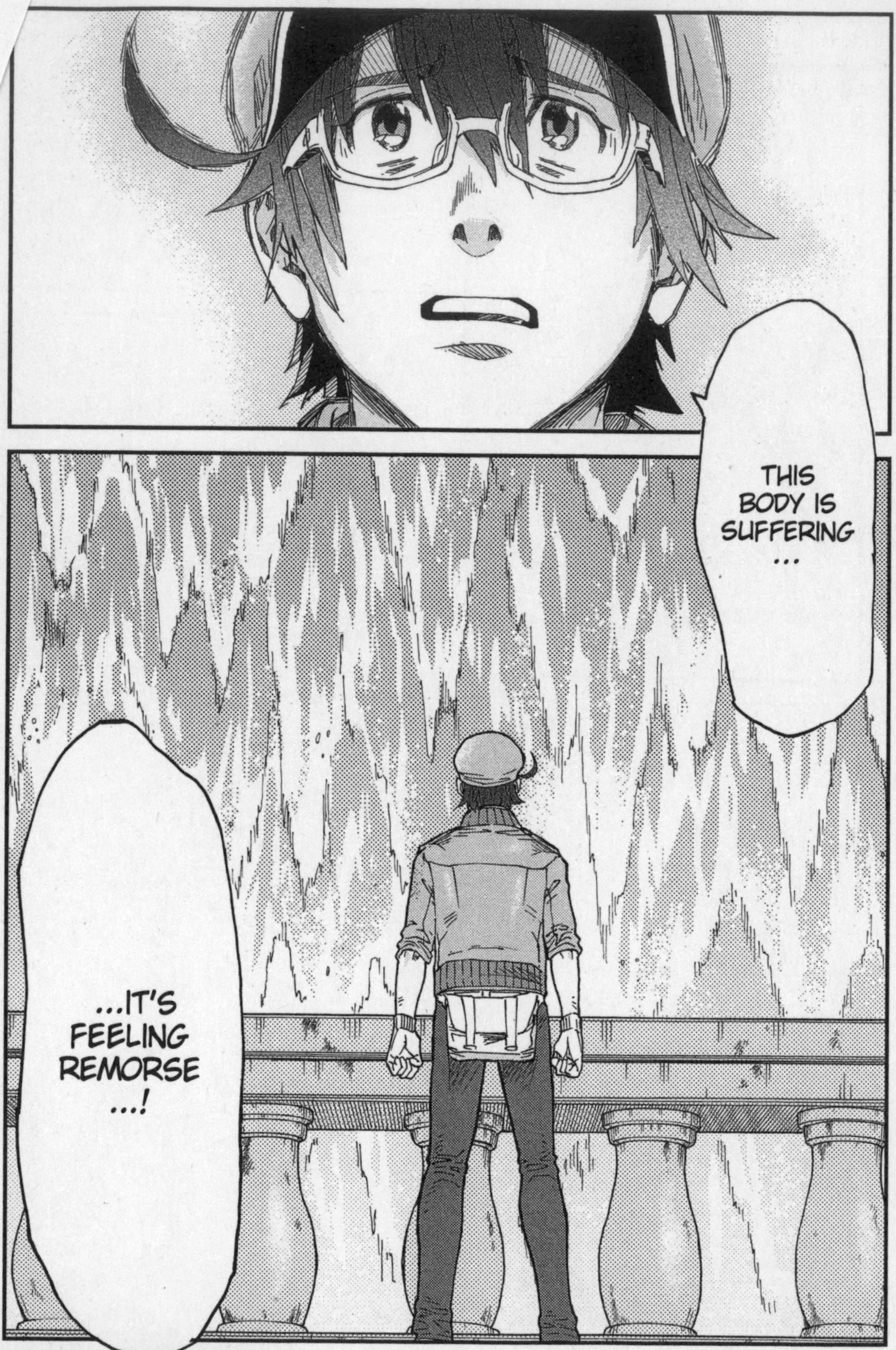
THIS BODY IS SUFFERING...
...IT'S FEELING REMORSE...!

CHAPTER 32 - END

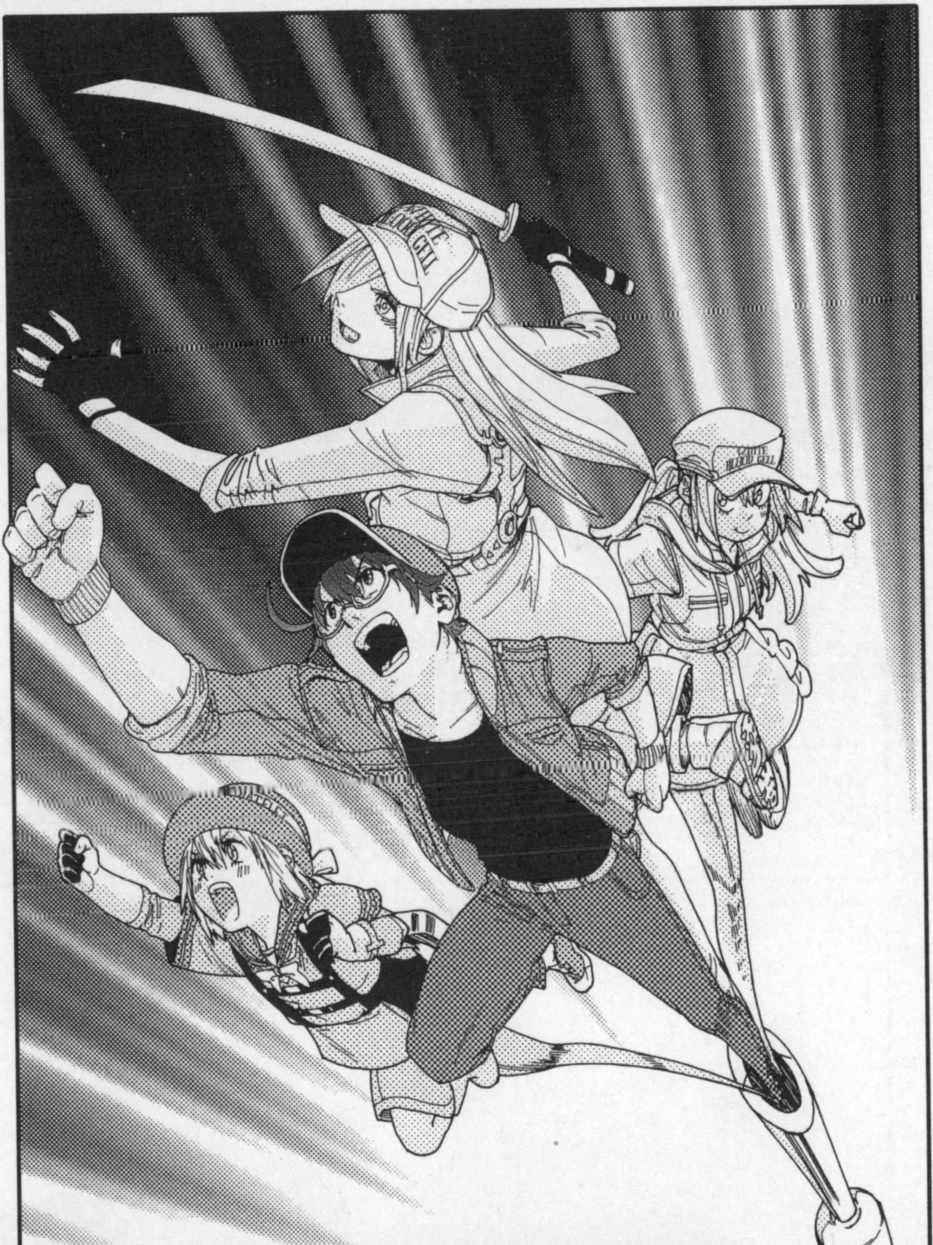

33. THE BRAIN, VITALITY, ATROPHY

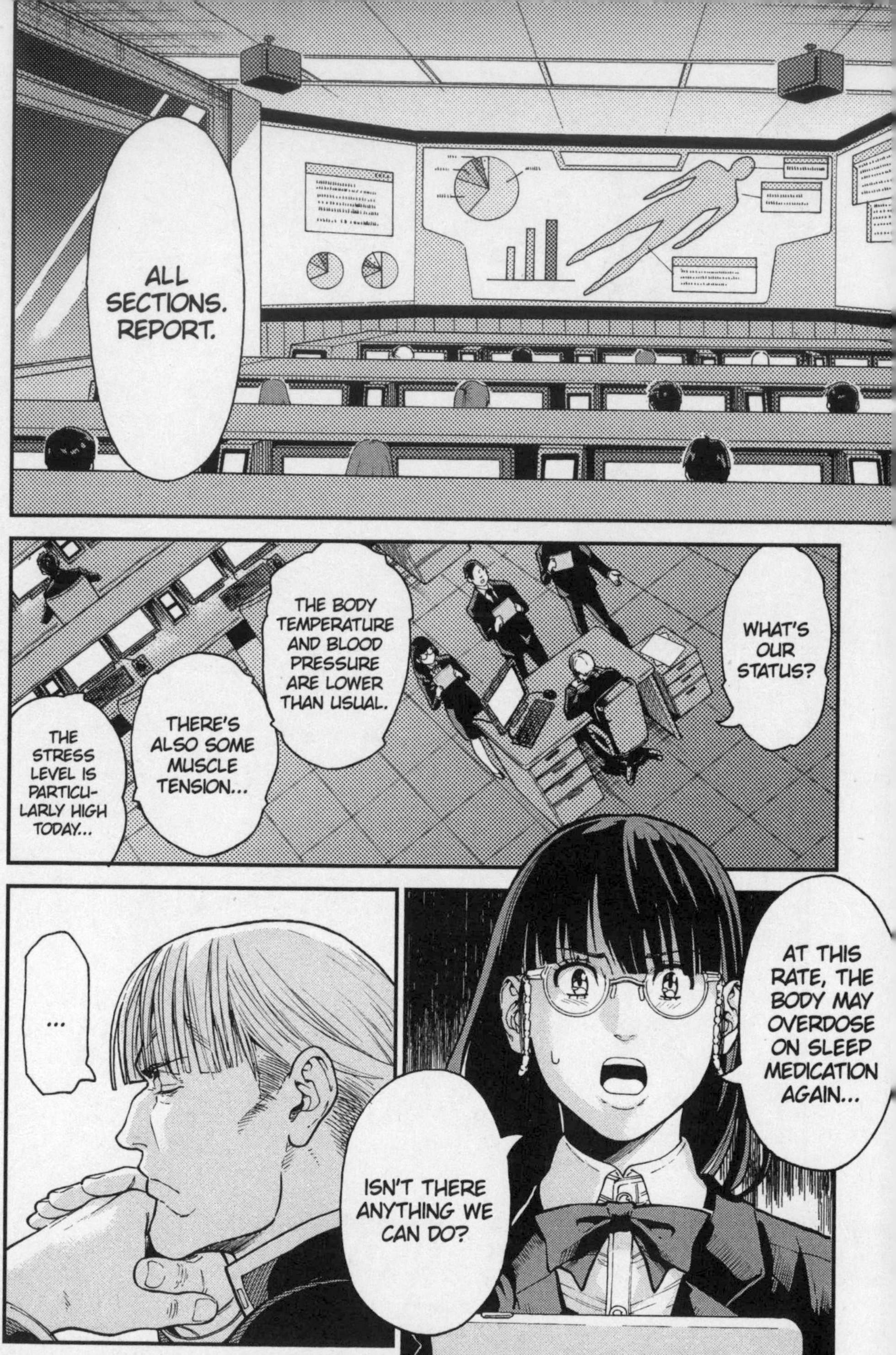
ALL SECTIONS. REPORT.
WHAT'S OUR STATUS?
THE BODY TEMPERATURE AND BLOOD PRESSURE ARE LOWER THAN USUAL.
THERE'S ALSO SOME MUSCLE TENSION...
THE STRESS LEVEL IS PARTICULARLY HIGH TODAY...
AT THIS RATE, THE BODY MAY OVERDOSE ON SLEEP MEDICATION AGAIN...
ISN'T THERE ANYTHING WE CAN DO?
...

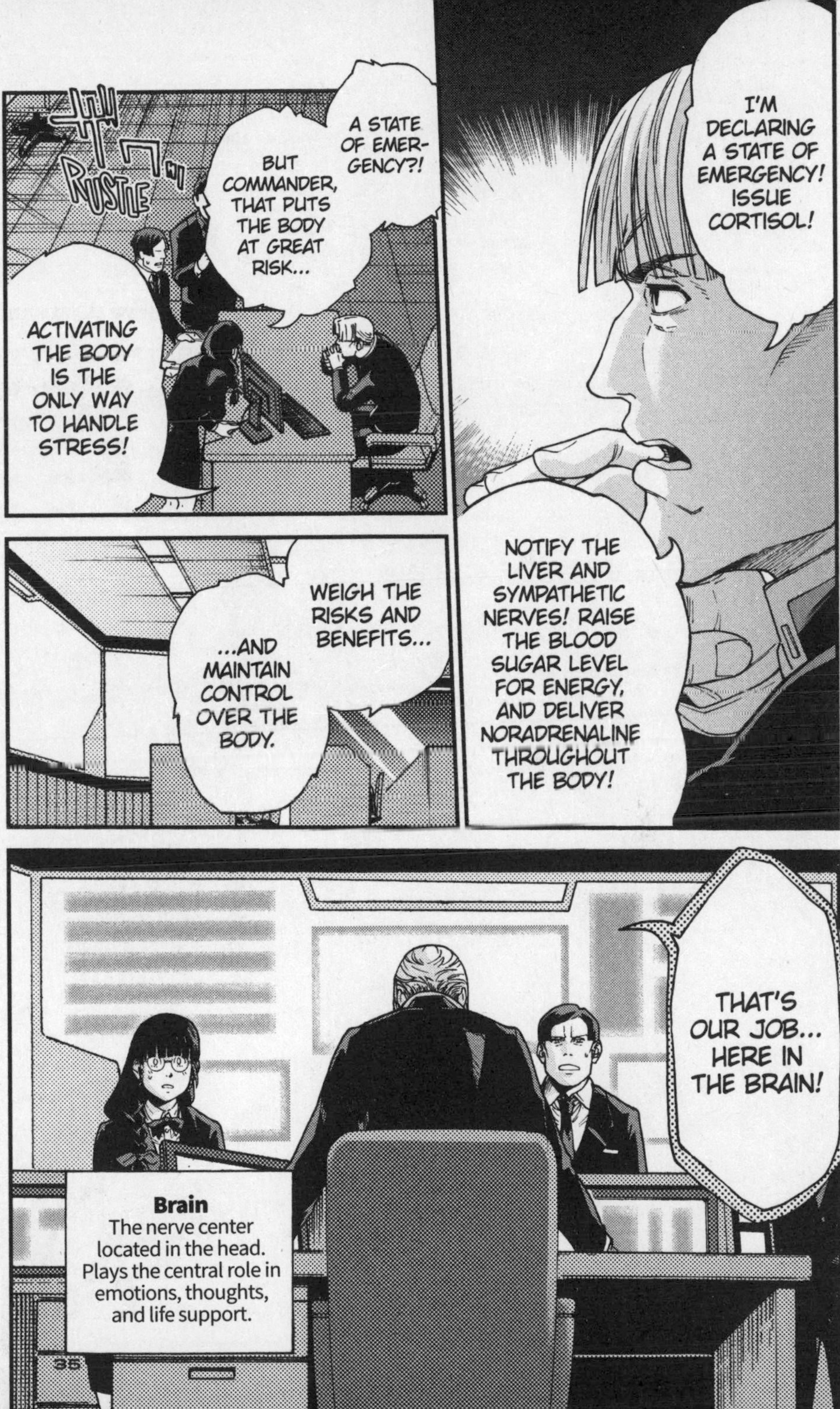
I'M DECLARING A STATE OF EMERGENCY! ISSUE CORTISOL!
NOTIFY THE LIVER AND SYMPATHETIC NERVES! RAISE THE BLOOD SUGAR LEVEL FOR ENERGY, AND DELIVER NORADRENALINE THROUGHOUT THE BODY!
A STATE OF EMERGENCY?!
BUT COMMANDER, THAT PUTS THE BODY AT GREAT RISK...
RUSTLE
ACTIVATING THE BODY IS THE ONLY WAY TO HANDLE STRESS!
WEIGH THE RISKS AND BENEFITS...
...AND MAINTAIN CONTROL OVER THE BODY.
THAT'S OUR JOB... HERE IN THE BRAIN!
Brain
The nerve center located in the head. Plays the central role in emotions, thoughts, and life support.

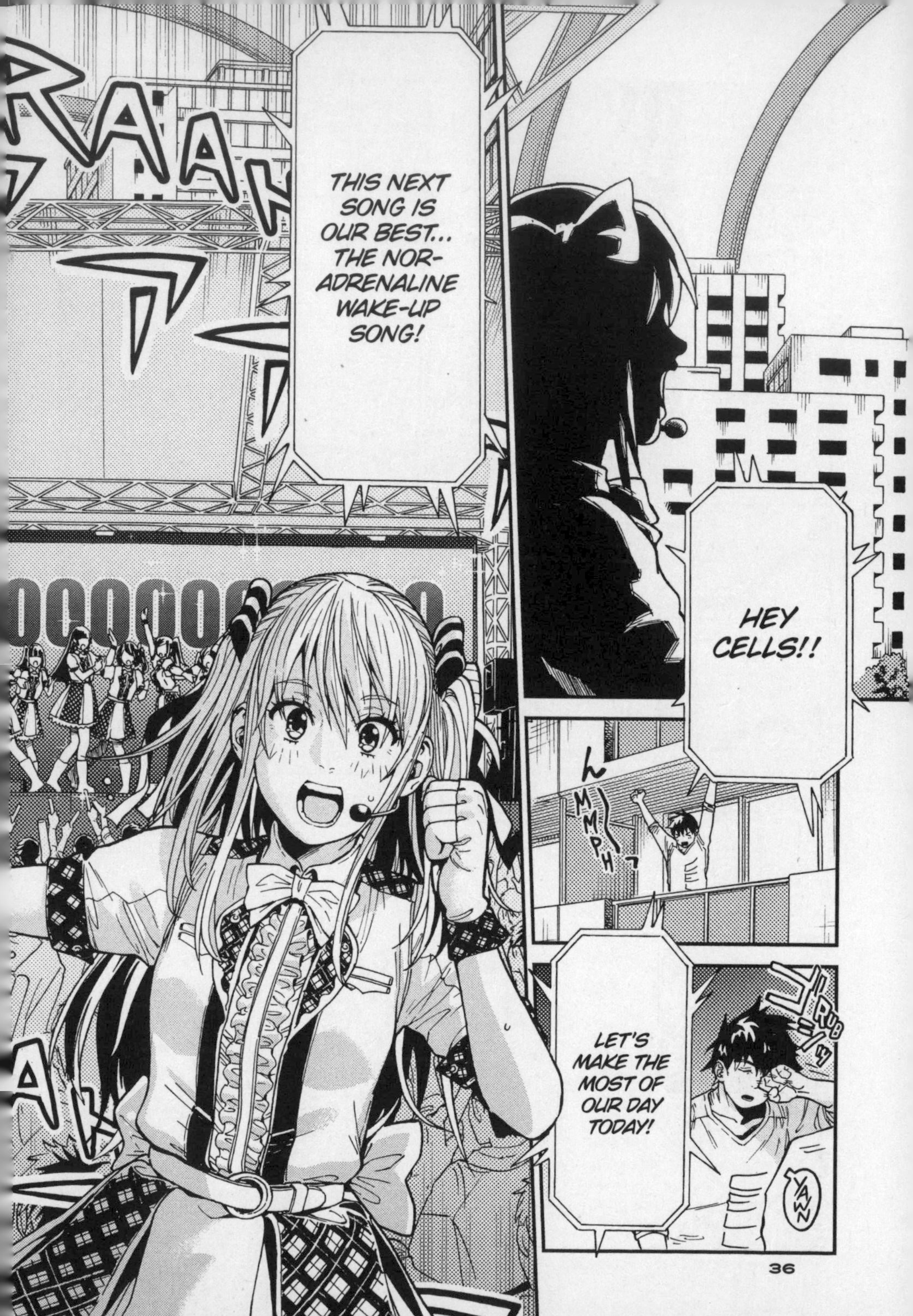
THIS NEXT SONG IS OUR BEST... THE NOR-ADRENALINE WAKE-UP SONG!
HEY CELLS!!
MMMPH
LET'S MAKE THE MOST OF OUR DAY TODAY!
RUB
YAWN
RAAH

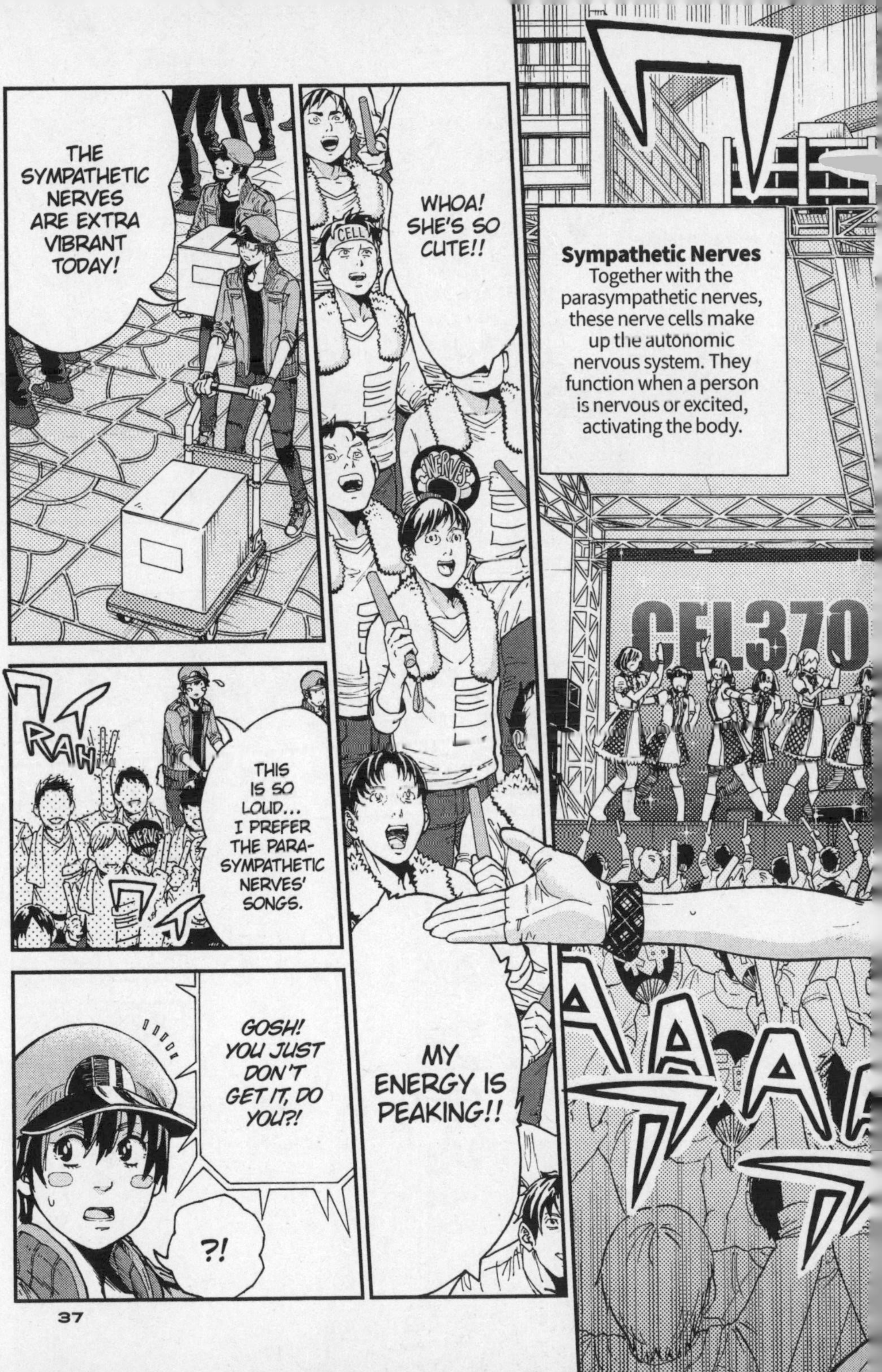
Sympathetic Nerves
Together with the parasympathetic nerves, these nerve cells make up the autonomic nervous system. They function when a person is nervous or excited, activating the body.
CEL370
AAAA
WHOA! SHE'S SO CUTE!!
MY ENERGY IS PEAKING!!
THE SYMPATHETIC NERVES ARE EXTRA VIBRANT TODAY!
RAH
THIS IS SO LOUD... I PREFER THE PARASYMPATHETIC NERVES' SONGS.
GOSH! YOU JUST DON'T GET IT, DO YOU?!
?!

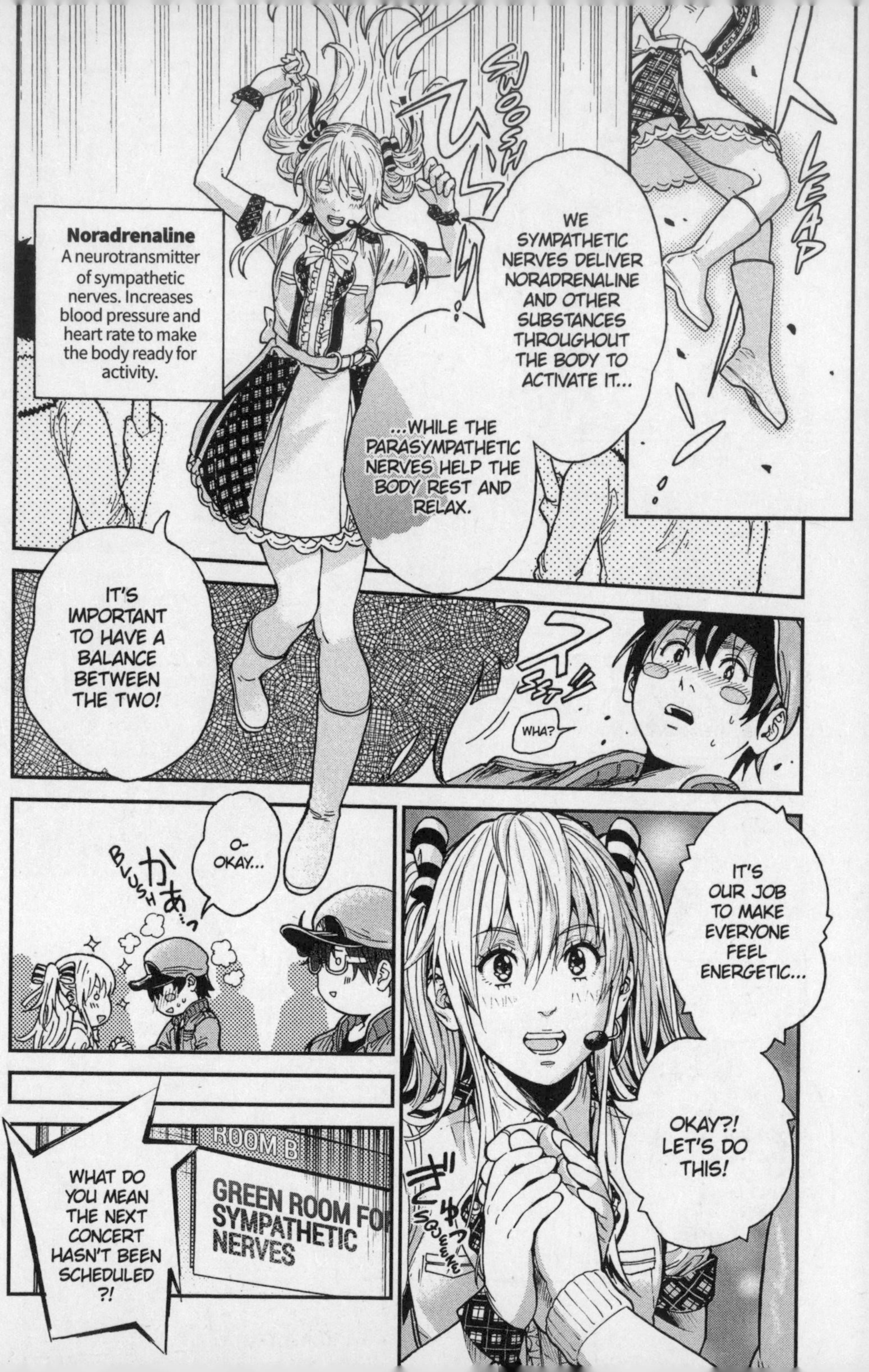
LEAP
SWOOSH
WE SYMPATHETIC NERVES DELIVER NORADRENALINE AND OTHER SUBSTANCES THROUGHOUT THE BODY TO ACTIVATE IT...
...WHILE THE PARASYMPATHETIC NERVES HELP THE BODY REST AND RELAX.
Noradrenaline
A neurotransmitter of sympathetic nerves. Increases blood pressure and heart rate to make the body ready for activity.
IT'S IMPORTANT TO HAVE A BALANCE BETWEEN THE TWO!
WHA?
IT'S OUR JOB TO MAKE EVERYONE FEEL ENERGETIC...
OKAY?! LET'S DO THIS!
O-OKAY...
BLUSH
ROOM B
GREEN ROOM FOR SYMPATHETIC NERVES
WHAT DO YOU MEAN THE NEXT CONCERT HASN'T BEEN SCHEDULED ?!

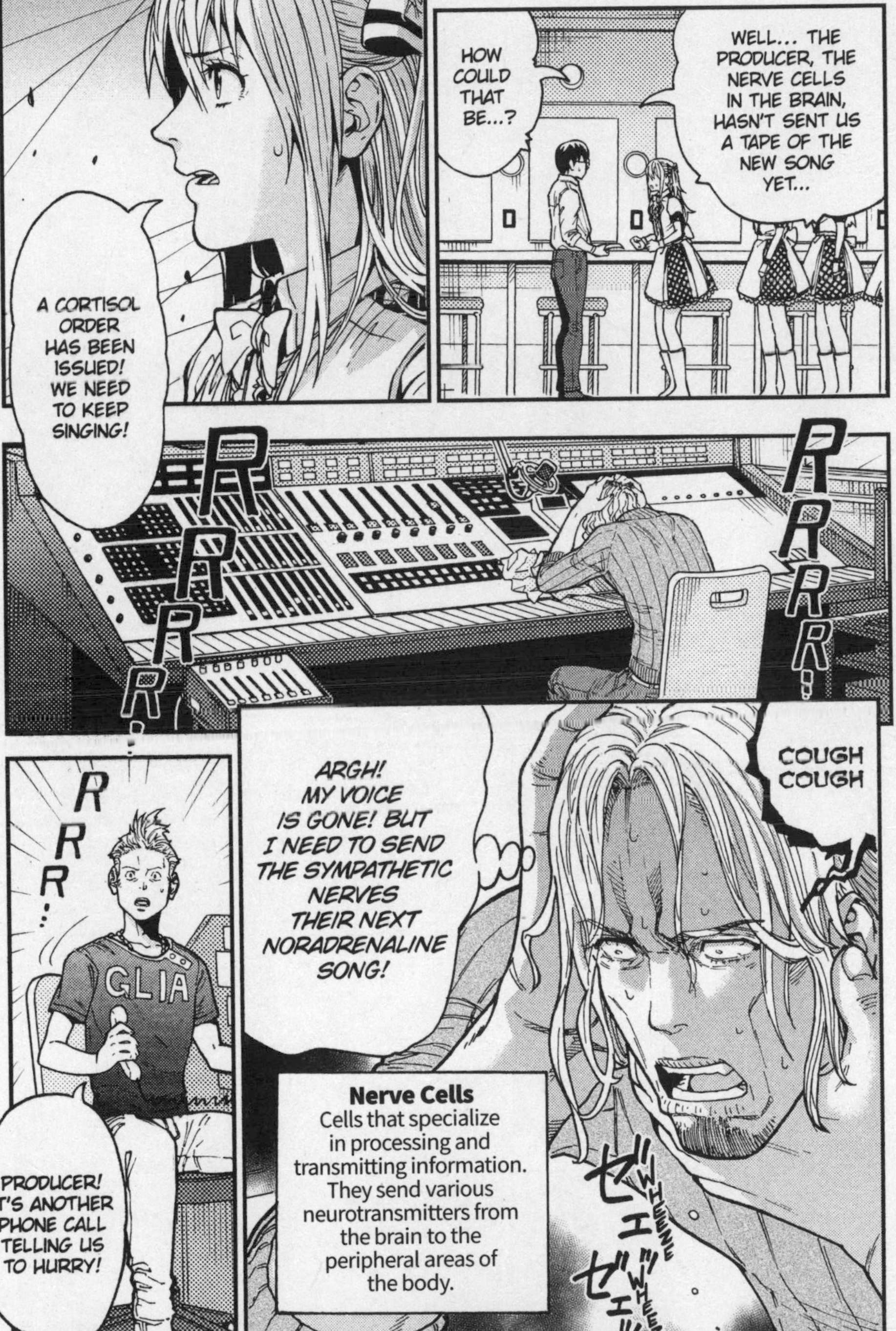
WELL... THE PRODUCER, THE NERVE CELLS IN THE BRAIN, HASN'T SENT US A TAPE OF THE NEW SONG YET...
HOW COULD THAT BE...?
A CORTISOL ORDER HAS BEEN ISSUED! WE NEED TO KEEP SINGING!
RRRR!
RRRR!
COUGH COUGH
ARGH! MY VOICE IS GONE! BUT I NEED TO SEND THE SYMPATHETIC NERVES THEIR NEXT NORADRENALINE SONG!
WHEEZE
WHEEZE
RRR!
PRODUCER! IT'S ANOTHER PHONE CALL TELLING US TO HURRY!

Nerve Cells
Cells that specialize in processing and transmitting information. They send various neurotransmitters from the brain to the peripheral areas of the body.

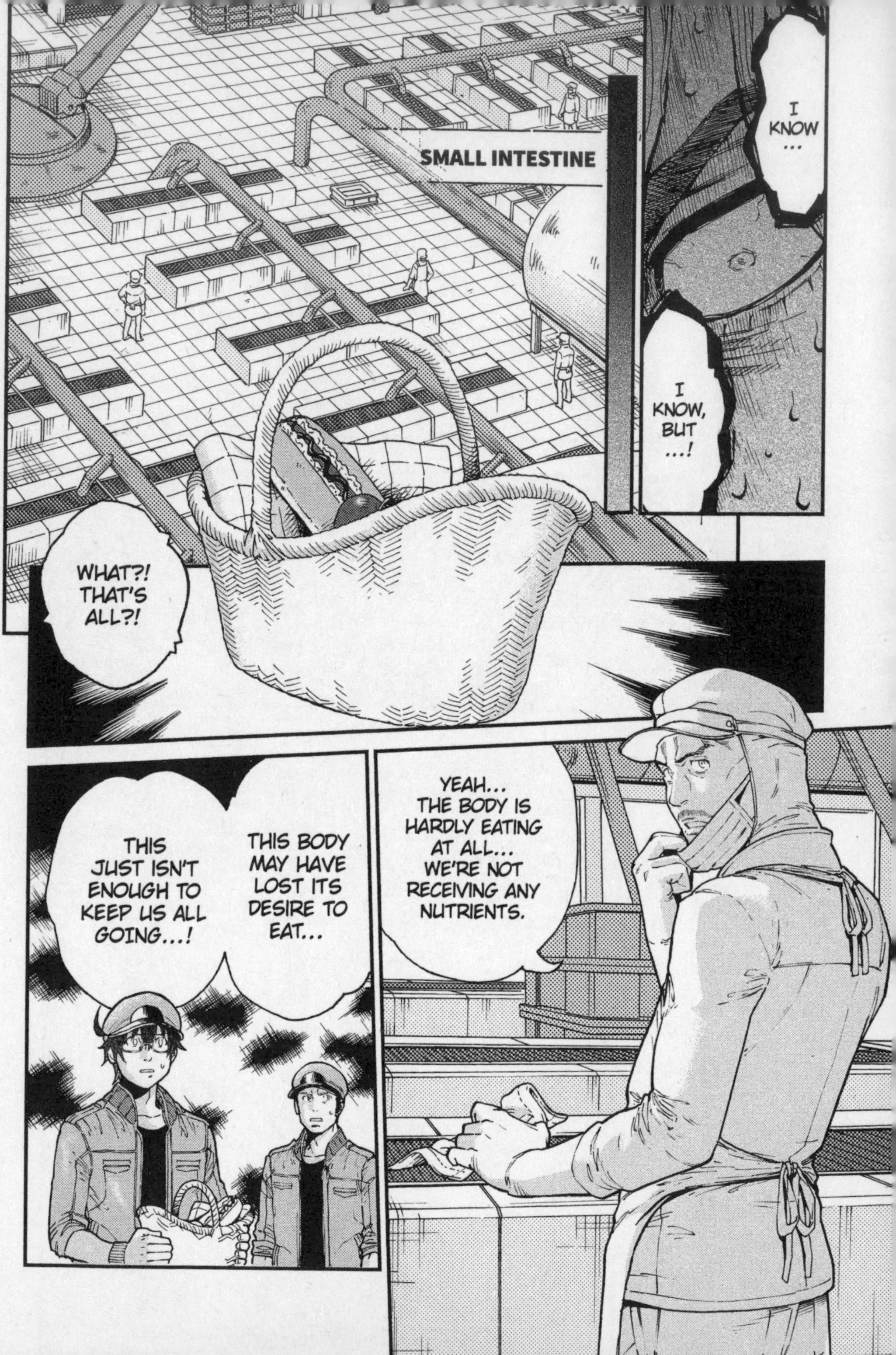

I KNOW...
I KNOW, BUT...!
SMALL INTESTINE
WHAT?! THAT'S ALL?!
YEAH... THE BODY IS HARDLY EATING AT ALL... WE'RE NOT RECEIVING ANY NUTRIENTS.
THIS BODY MAY HAVE LOST ITS DESIRE TO EAT...
THIS JUST ISN'T ENOUGH TO KEEP US ALL GOING...!

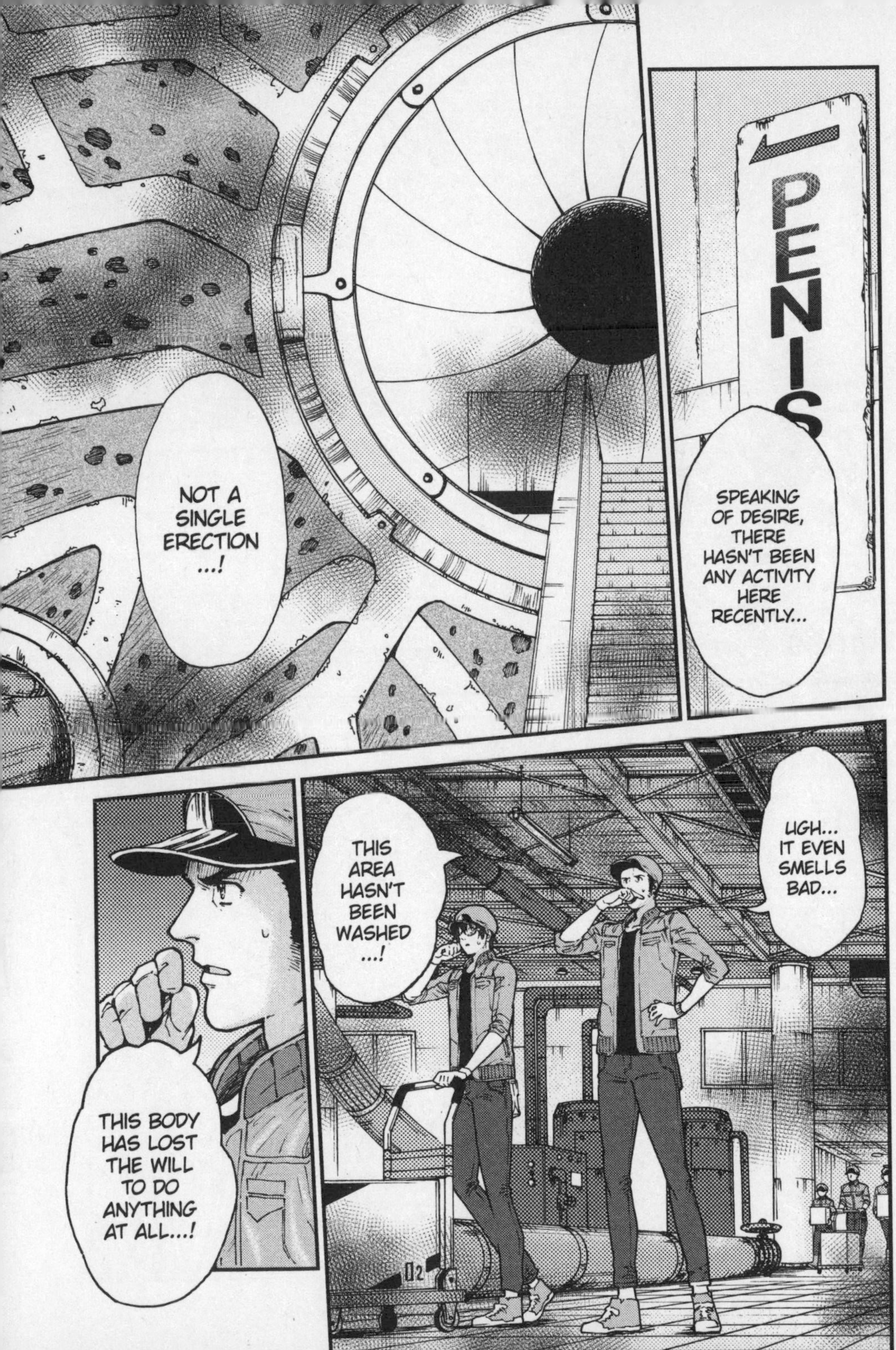
PENIS
SPEAKING OF DESIRE, THERE HASN'T BEEN ANY ACTIVITY HERE RECENTLY...
NOT A SINGLE ERECTION ...!
UGH... IT EVEN SMELLS BAD...
THIS AREA HASN'T BEEN WASHED ...!
THIS BODY HAS LOST THE WILL TO DO ANYTHING AT ALL...!

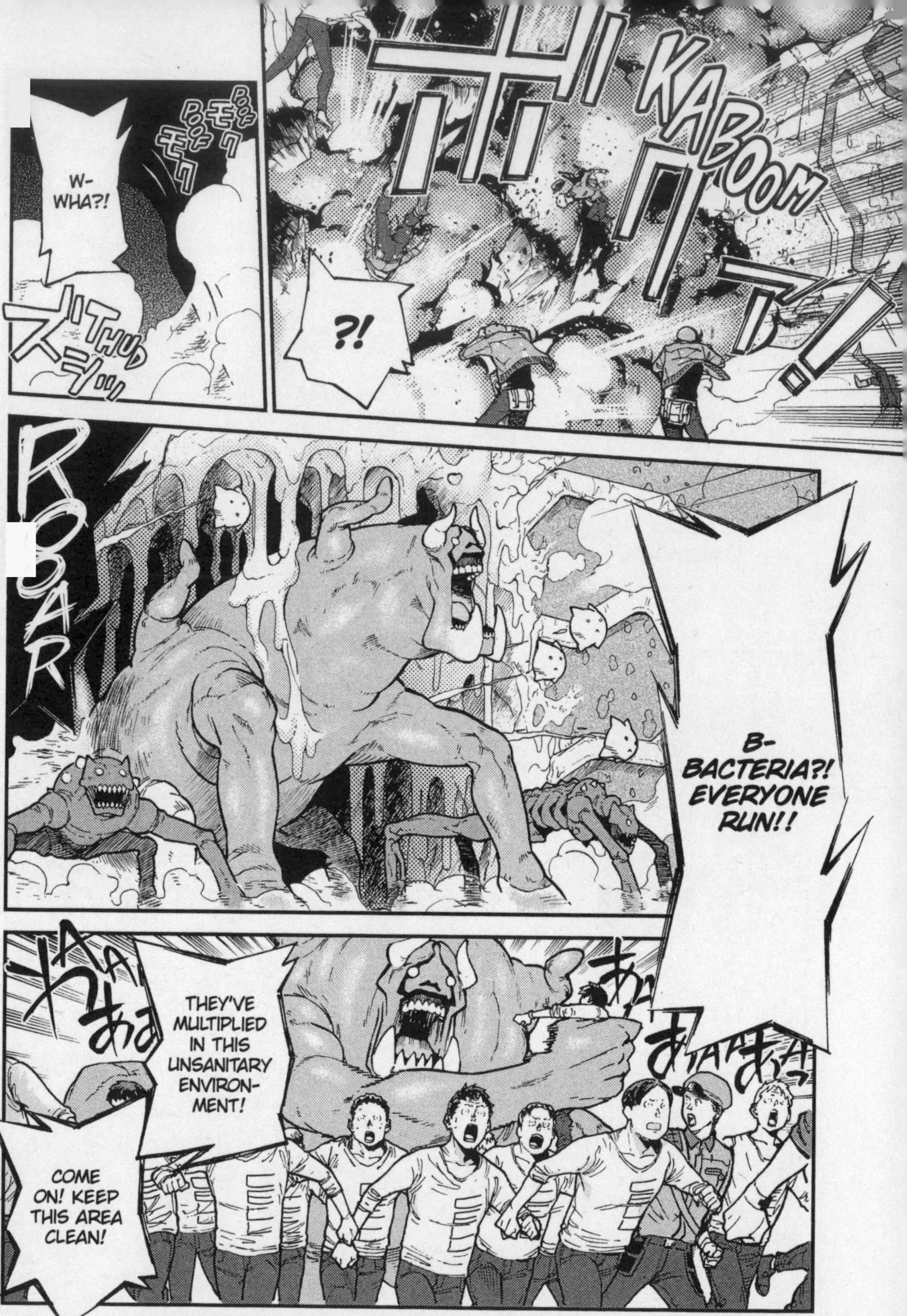
KABOOM
?!
POOF POOF
W-WHA?!
THUD
ROAR
B-BACTERIA?! EVERYONE RUN!!
THEY'VE MULTIPLIED IN THIS UNSANITARY ENVIRON-MENT!
COME ON! KEEP THIS AREA CLEAN!

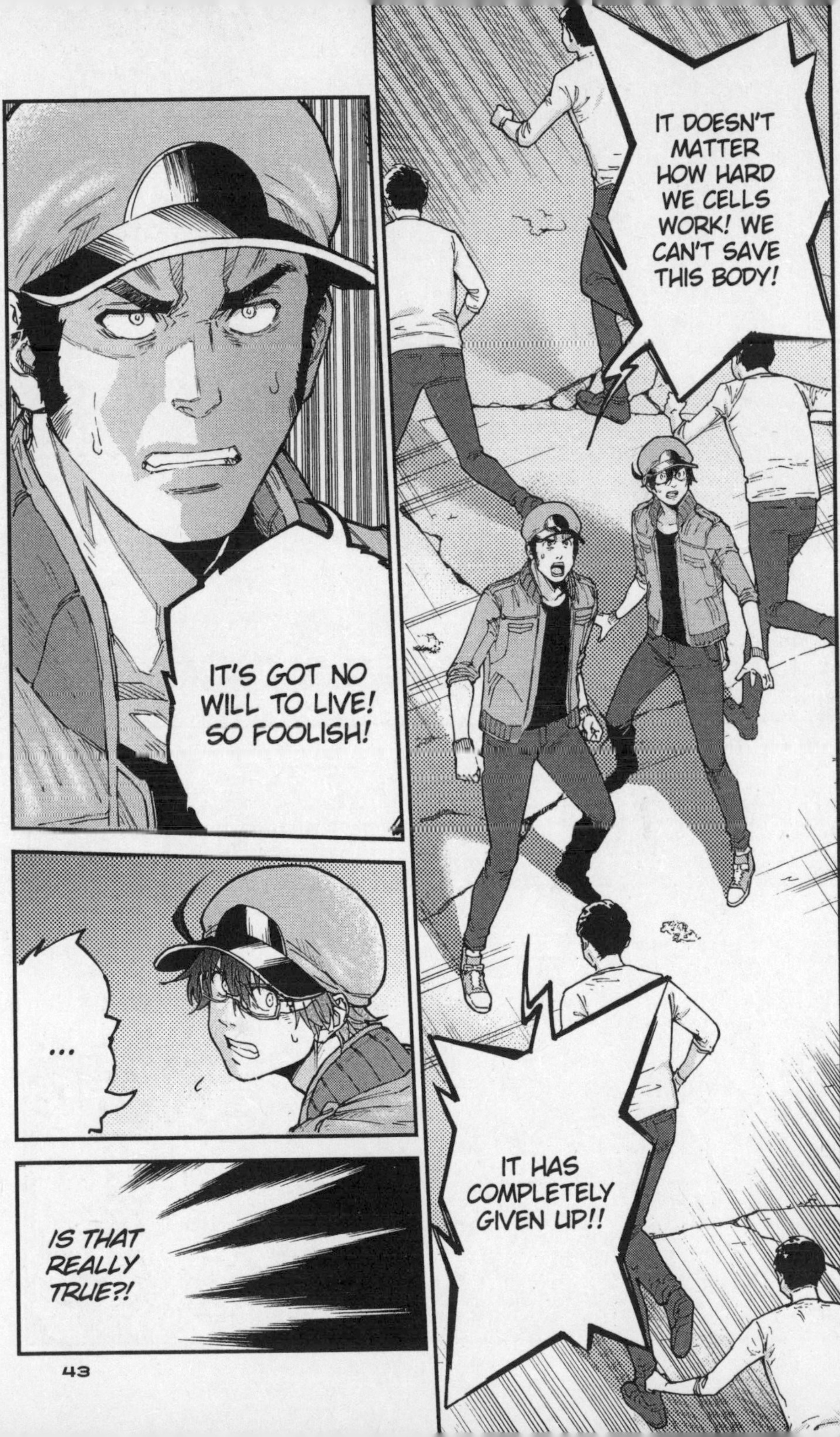
IT DOESN'T MATTER HOW HARD WE CELLS WORK! WE CAN'T SAVE THIS BODY!
IT HAS COMPLETELY GIVEN UP!!
IT'S GOT NO WILL TO LIVE! SO FOOLISH!
...
IS THAT REALLY TRUE?!

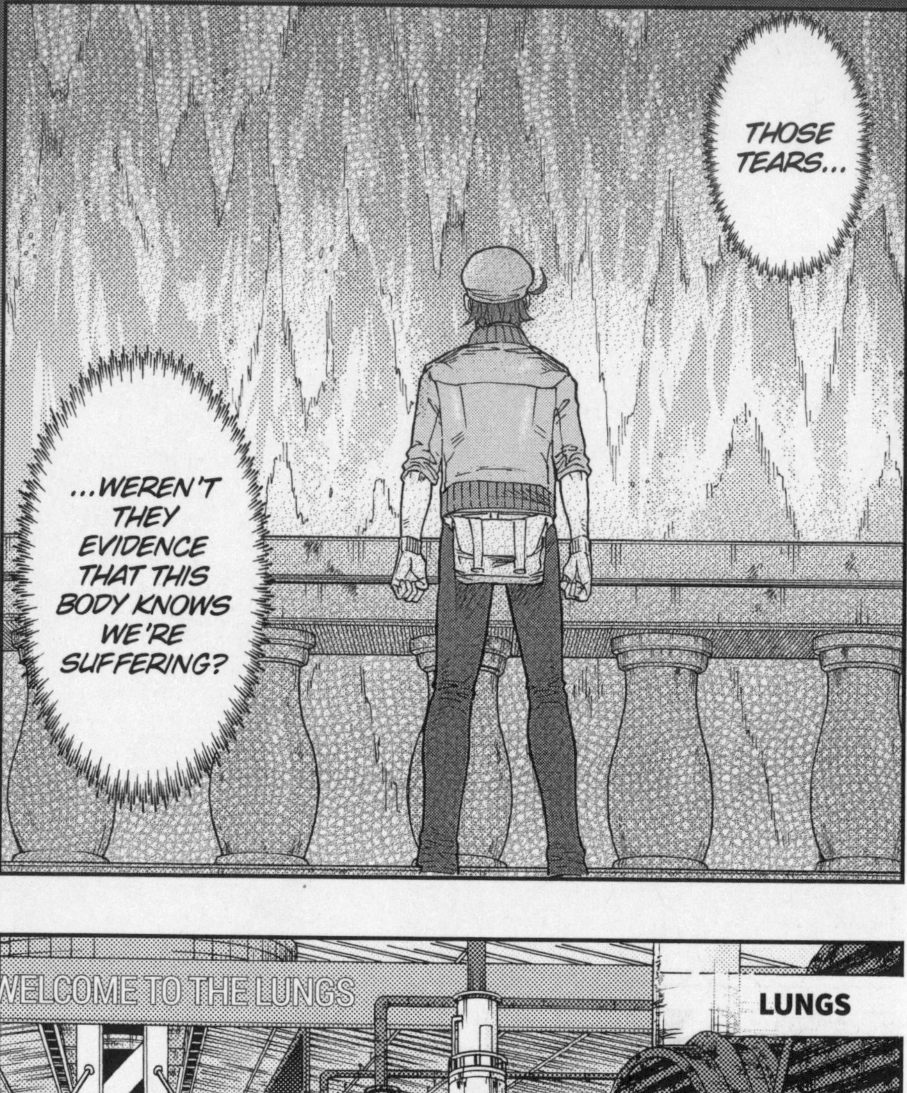
THOSE TEARS...
...WEREN'T THEY EVIDENCE THAT THIS BODY KNOWS WE'RE SUFFERING?

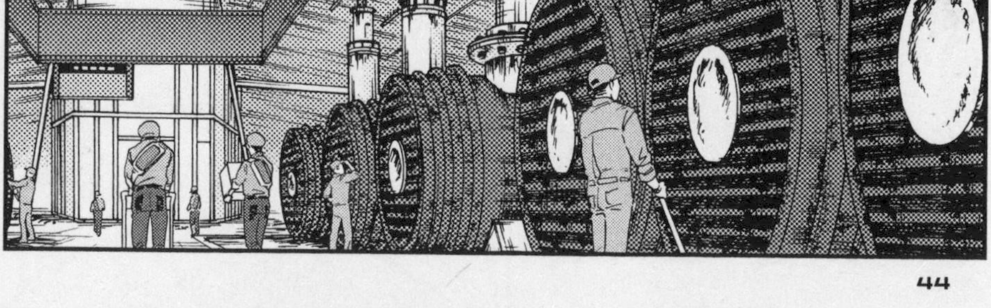
LUNGS
WELCOME TO THE LUNGS

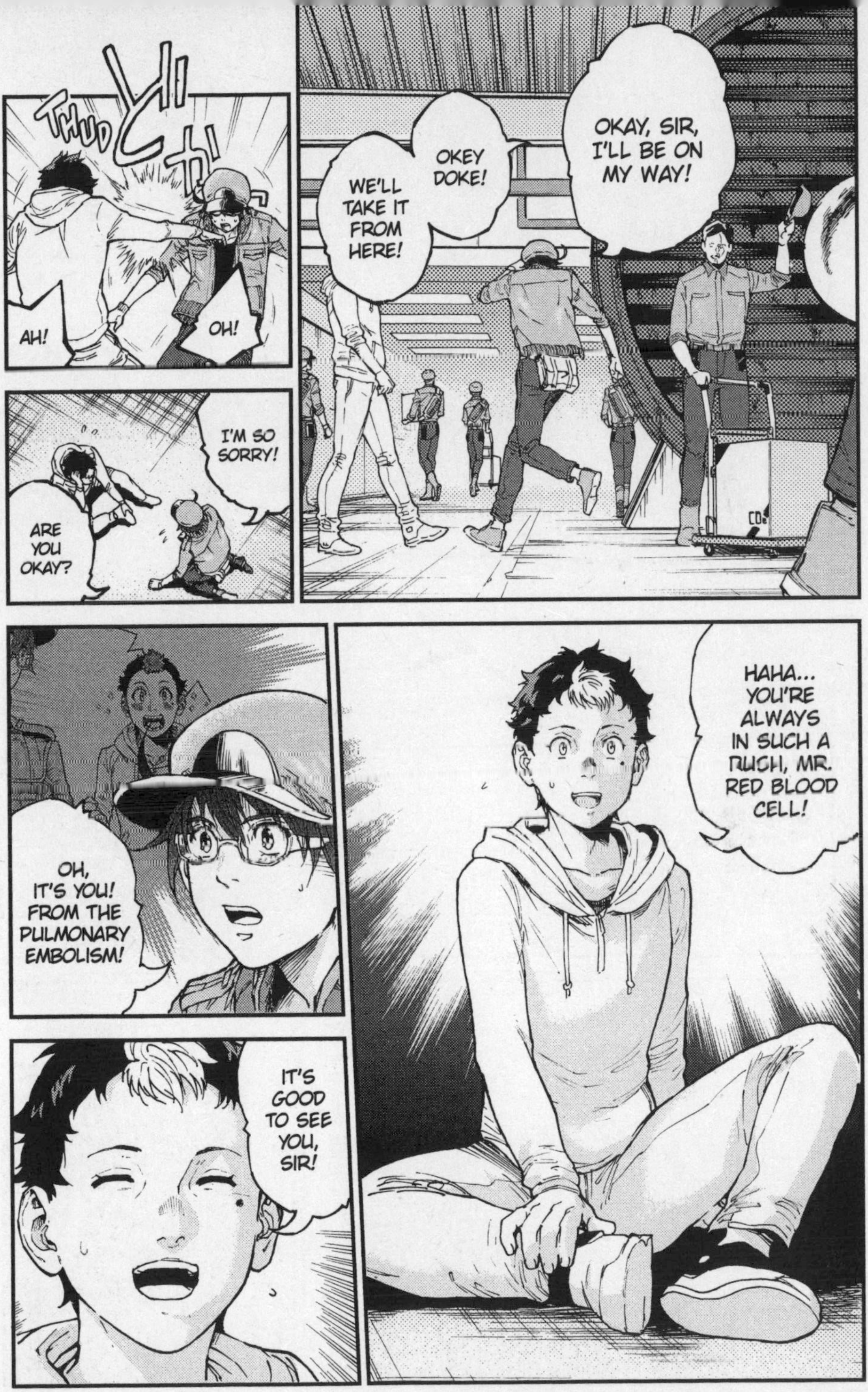
OKAY, SIR, I'LL BE ON MY WAY!
OKEY DOKE!
WE'LL TAKE IT FROM HERE!
THUD
OH!
AH!
I'M SO SORRY!
ARE YOU OKAY?
HAHA... YOU'RE ALWAYS IN SUCH A RUSH, MR. RED BLOOD CELL!
OH, IT'S YOU! FROM THE PULMONARY EMBOLISM!
IT'S GOOD TO SEE YOU, SIR!

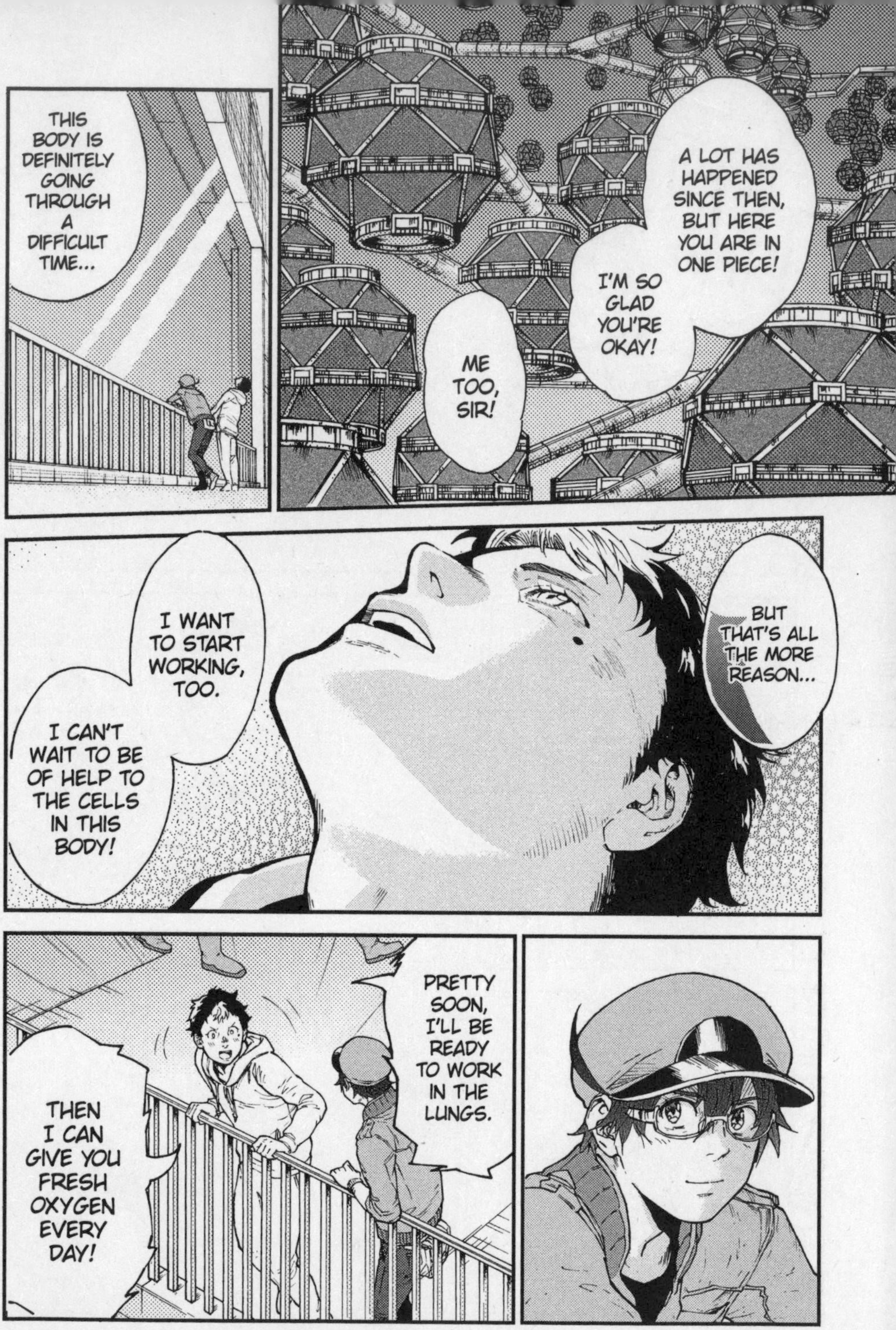
A LOT HAS HAPPENED SINCE THEN, BUT HERE YOU ARE IN ONE PIECE!
I'M SO GLAD YOU'RE OKAY!
ME TOO, SIR!
THIS BODY IS DEFINITELY GOING THROUGH A DIFFICULT TIME...
BUT THAT'S ALL THE MORE REASON...
I WANT TO START WORKING, TOO.
I CAN'T WAIT TO BE OF HELP TO THE CELLS IN THIS BODY!
PRETTY SOON, I'LL BE READY TO WORK IN THE LUNGS.
THEN I CAN GIVE YOU FRESH OXYGEN EVERY DAY!

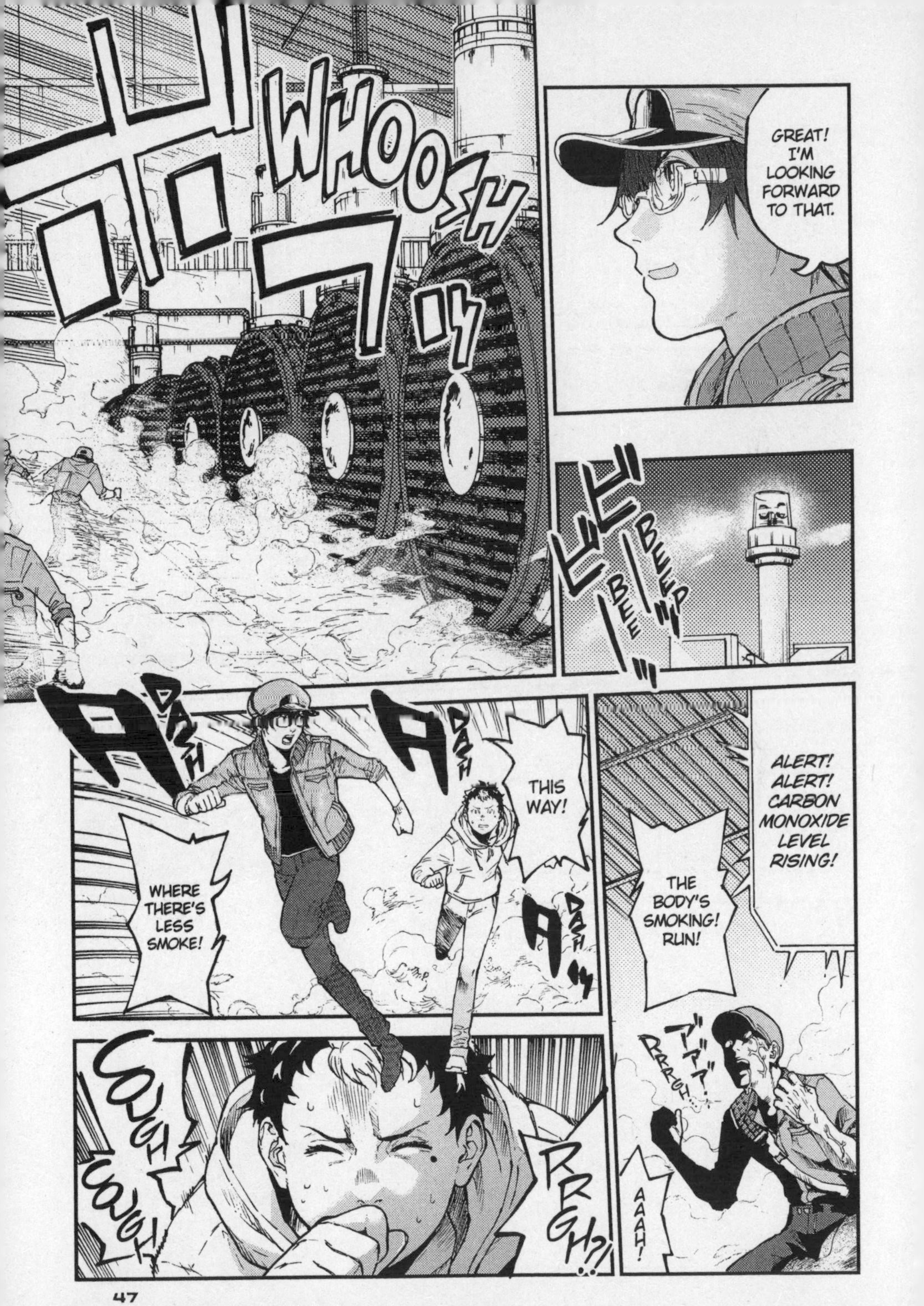

GREAT! I'M LOOKING FORWARD TO THAT.
BEEP
BEE
WHOOSH
ALERT! ALERT! CARBON MONOXIDE LEVEL RISING!
THE BODY'S SMOKING! RUN!
DASH
DASH
THIS WAY!
WHERE THERE'S LESS SMOKE!
DASH
RRRGH...!
AAAH!
RRGH?!
COUGH COUGH

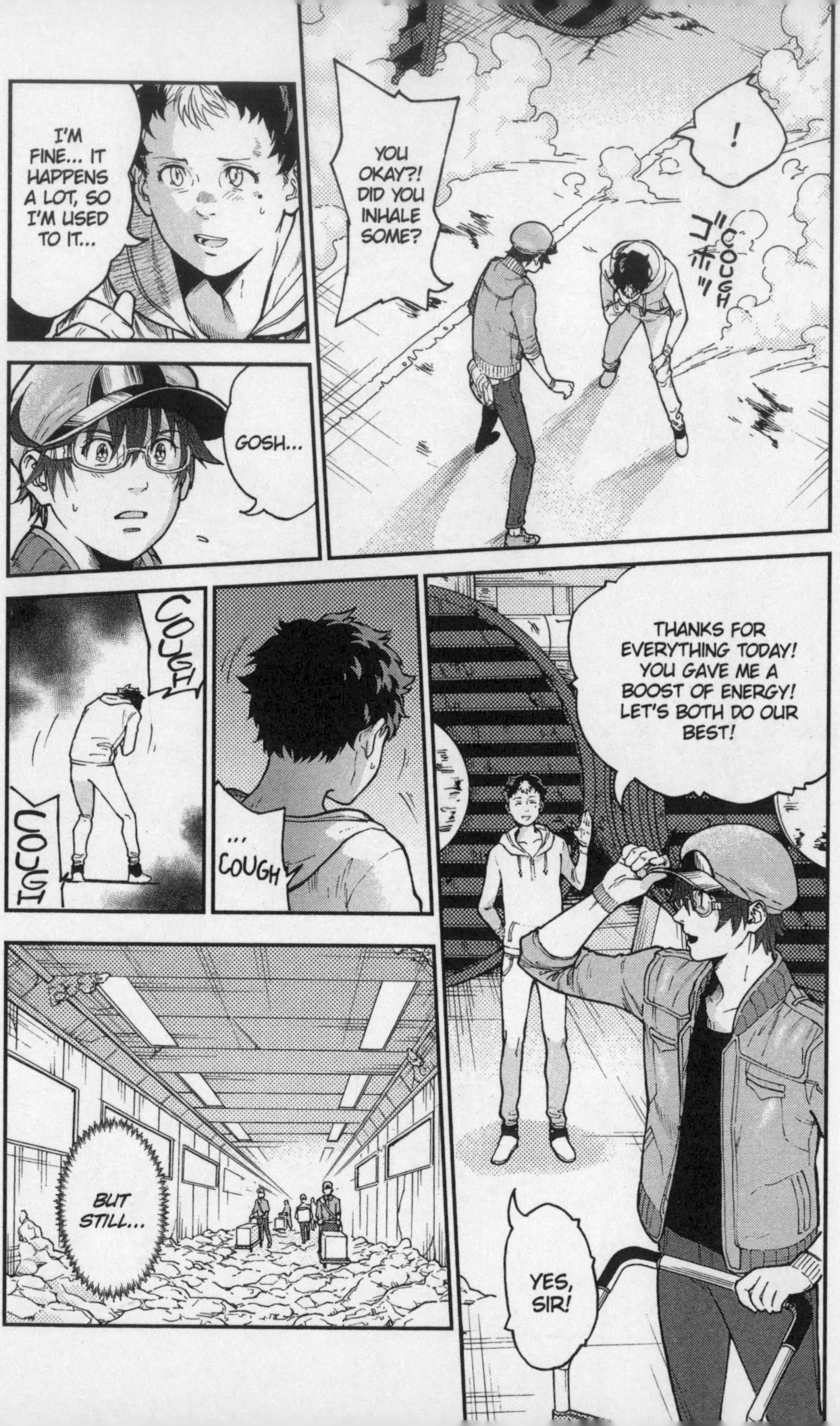
!
ゴホッ
COUGH
YOU OKAY?! DID YOU INHALE SOME?
I'M FINE... IT HAPPENS A LOT, SO I'M USED TO IT...
GOSH...
THANKS FOR EVERYTHING TODAY! YOU GAVE ME A BOOST OF ENERGY! LET'S BOTH DO OUR BEST!
YES, SIR!
... COUGH
COUGH
COUGH
BUT STILL...

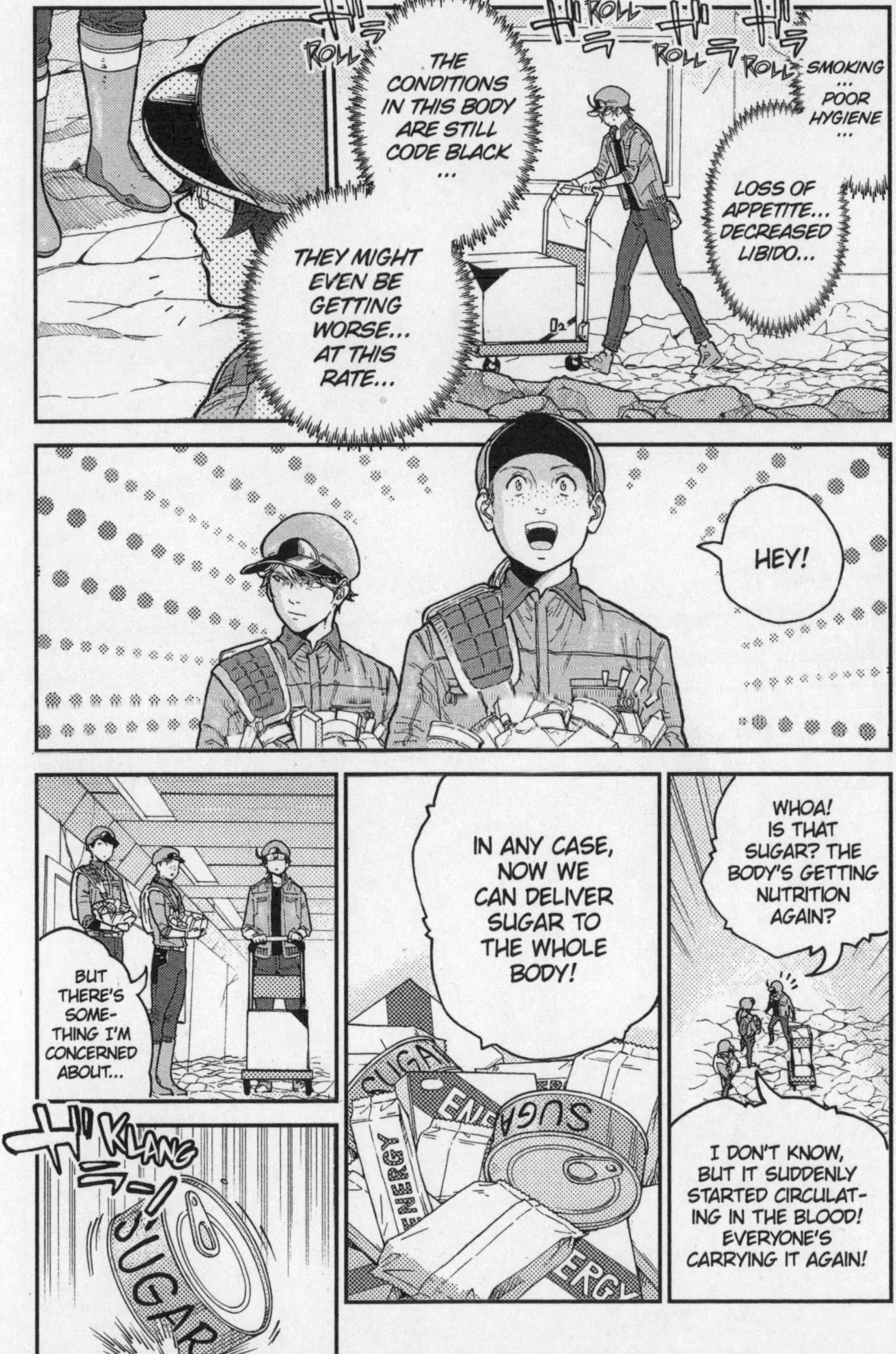
ROLL
ROLL
ROLL
ROLL
SMOKING ... POOR HYGIENE ...
LOSS OF APPETITE... DECREASED LIBIDO...
THE CONDITIONS IN THIS BODY ARE STILL CODE BLACK ...
THEY MIGHT EVEN BE GETTING WORSE... AT THIS RATE...
HEY!
WHOA! IS THAT SUGAR? THE BODY'S GETTING NUTRITION AGAIN?
I DON'T KNOW, BUT IT SUDDENLY STARTED CIRCULATING IN THE BLOOD! EVERYONE'S CARRYING IT AGAIN!
IN ANY CASE, NOW WE CAN DELIVER SUGAR TO THE WHOLE BODY!
SUGAR
ENERGY
SUGAR
ENERGY
ENERGY
BUT THERE'S SOMETHING I'M CONCERNED ABOUT...
KLANG
SUGAR

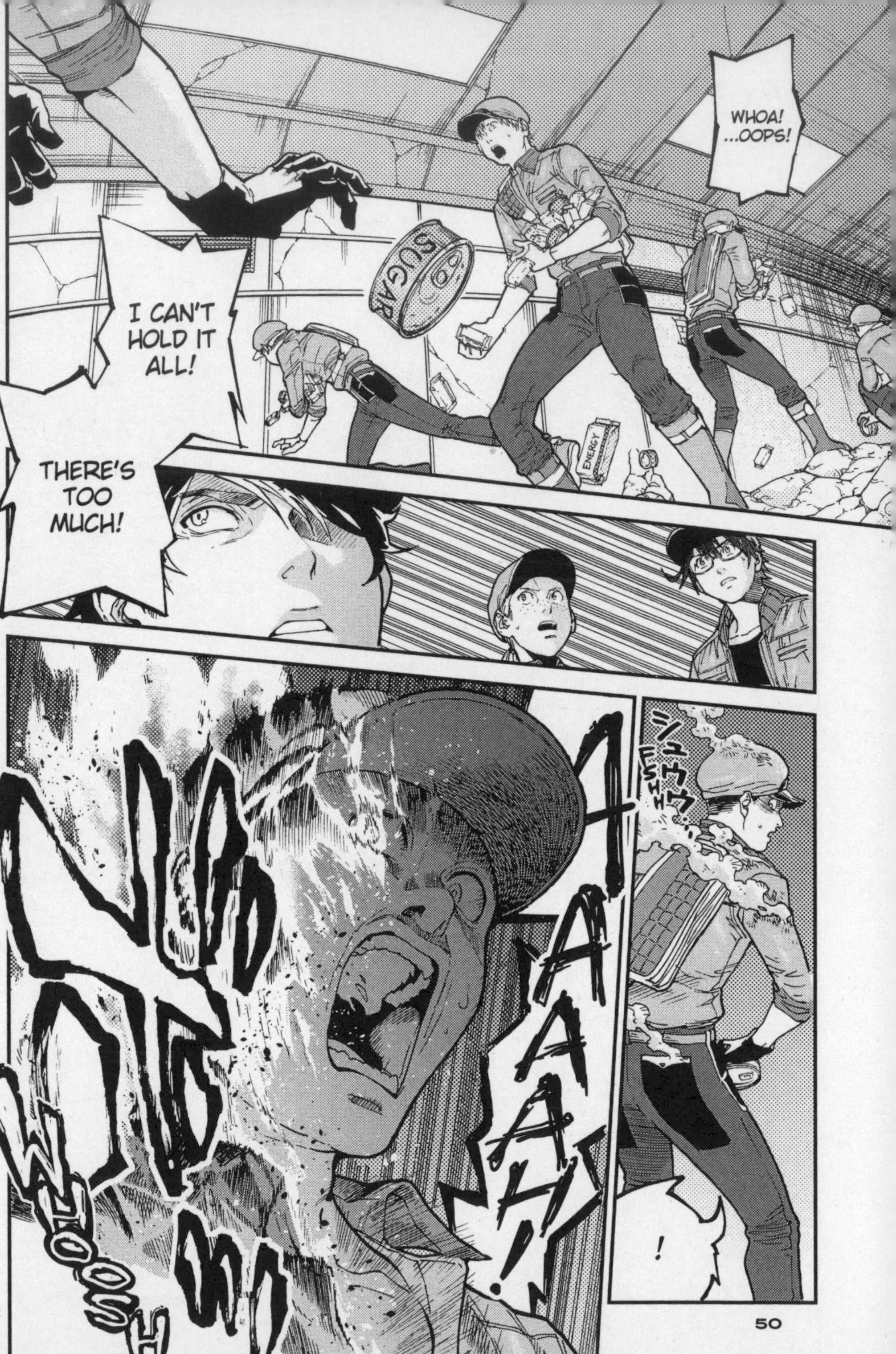
WHOA! ...OOPS!
I CAN'T HOLD IT ALL!
THERE'S TOO MUCH!
シュウウ
FSHHH
!
AAAAH!
WHOOSH

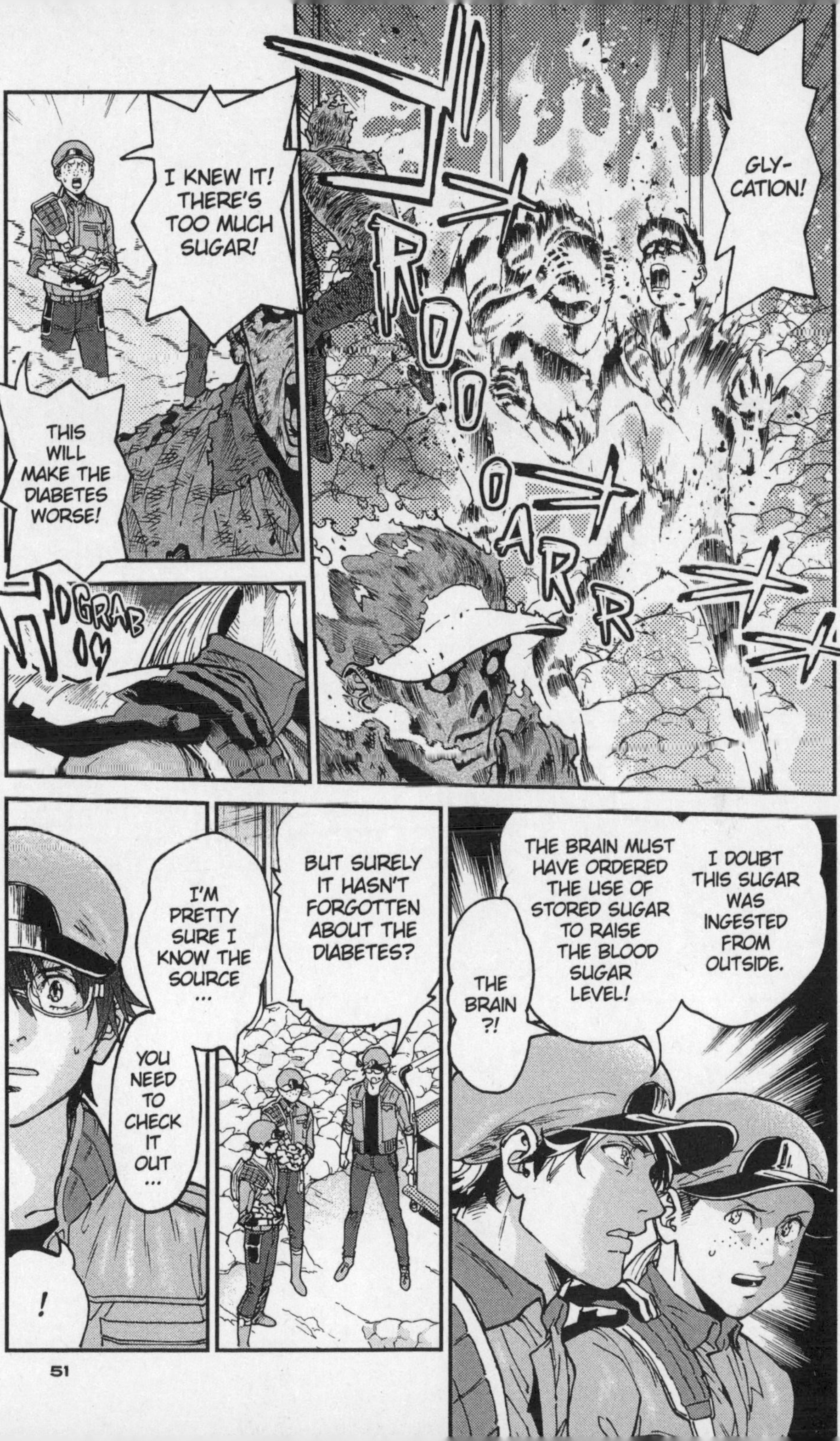
GLY-CATION!
ROOOARRR
I KNEW IT! THERE'S TOO MUCH SUGAR!
THIS WILL MAKE THE DIABETES WORSE!
GRAB
I DOUBT THIS SUGAR WAS INGESTED FROM OUTSIDE.
THE BRAIN MUST HAVE ORDERED THE USE OF STORED SUGAR TO RAISE THE BLOOD SUGAR LEVEL!
THE BRAIN?!
BUT SURELY IT HASN'T FORGOTTEN ABOUT THE DIABETES?
I'M PRETTY SURE I KNOW THE SOURCE...
YOU NEED TO CHECK IT OUT...
!

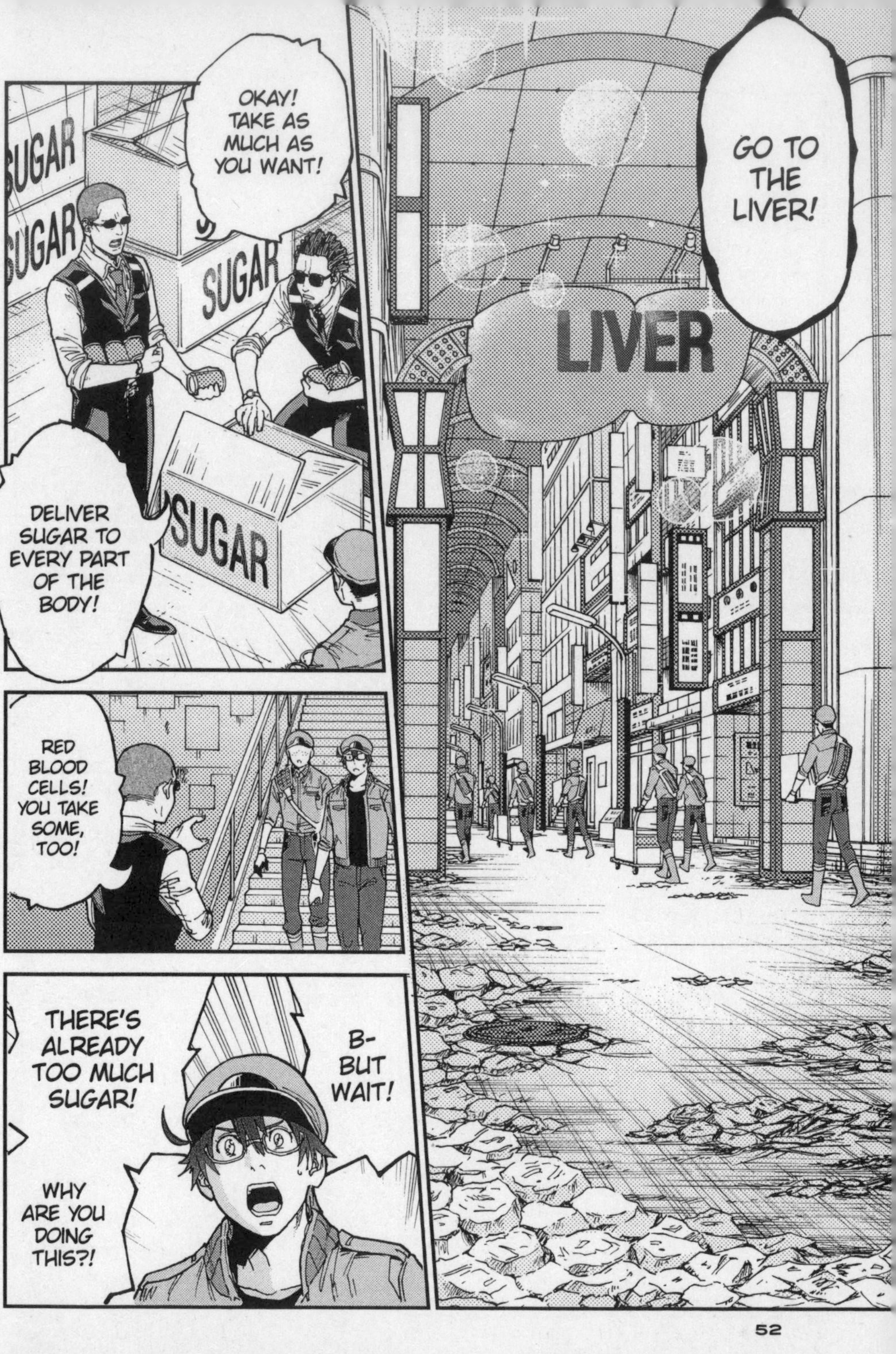
GO TO THE LIVER!
LIVER
OKAY! TAKE AS MUCH AS YOU WANT!
SUGAR
SUGAR
SUGAR
DELIVER SUGAR TO EVERY PART OF THE BODY!
SUGAR
RED BLOOD CELLS! YOU TAKE SOME, TOO!
B- BUT WAIT!
THERE'S ALREADY TOO MUCH SUGAR!
WHY ARE YOU DOING THIS?!

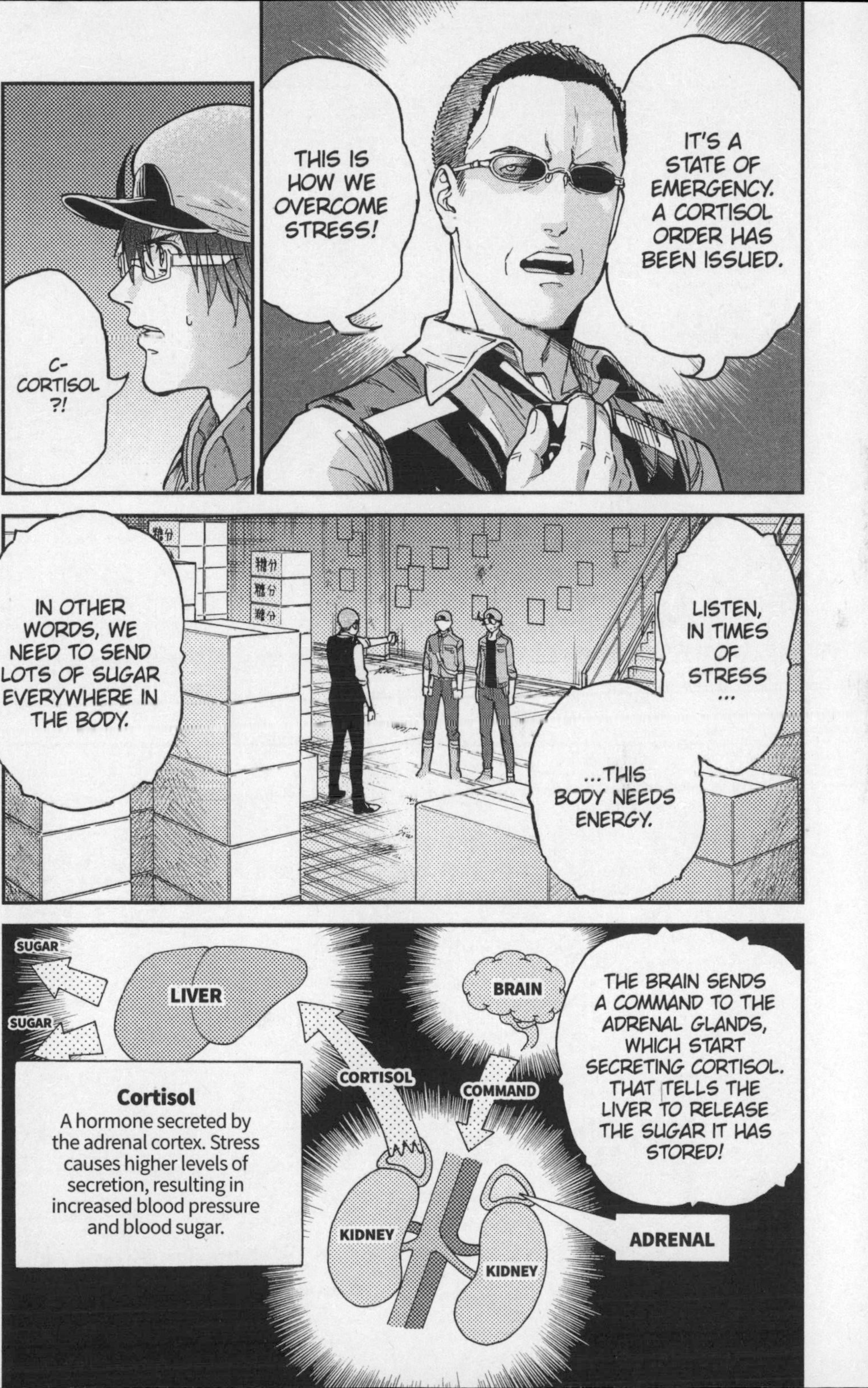
IT'S A STATE OF EMERGENCY. A CORTISOL ORDER HAS BEEN ISSUED.
THIS IS HOW WE OVERCOME STRESS!
C-CORTISOL?!
LISTEN, IN TIMES OF STRESS...
...THIS BODY NEEDS ENERGY.
IN OTHER WORDS, WE NEED TO SEND LOTS OF SUGAR EVERYWHERE IN THE BODY.
THE BRAIN SENDS A COMMAND TO THE ADRENAL GLANDS, WHICH START SECRETING CORTISOL. THAT TELLS THE LIVER TO RELEASE THE SUGAR IT HAS STORED!
BRAIN
COMMAND
CORTISOL
LIVER
SUGAR
SUGAR
ADRENAL
KIDNEY
KIDNEY
Cortisol
A hormone secreted by the adrenal cortex. Stress causes higher levels of secretion, resulting in increased blood pressure and blood sugar.

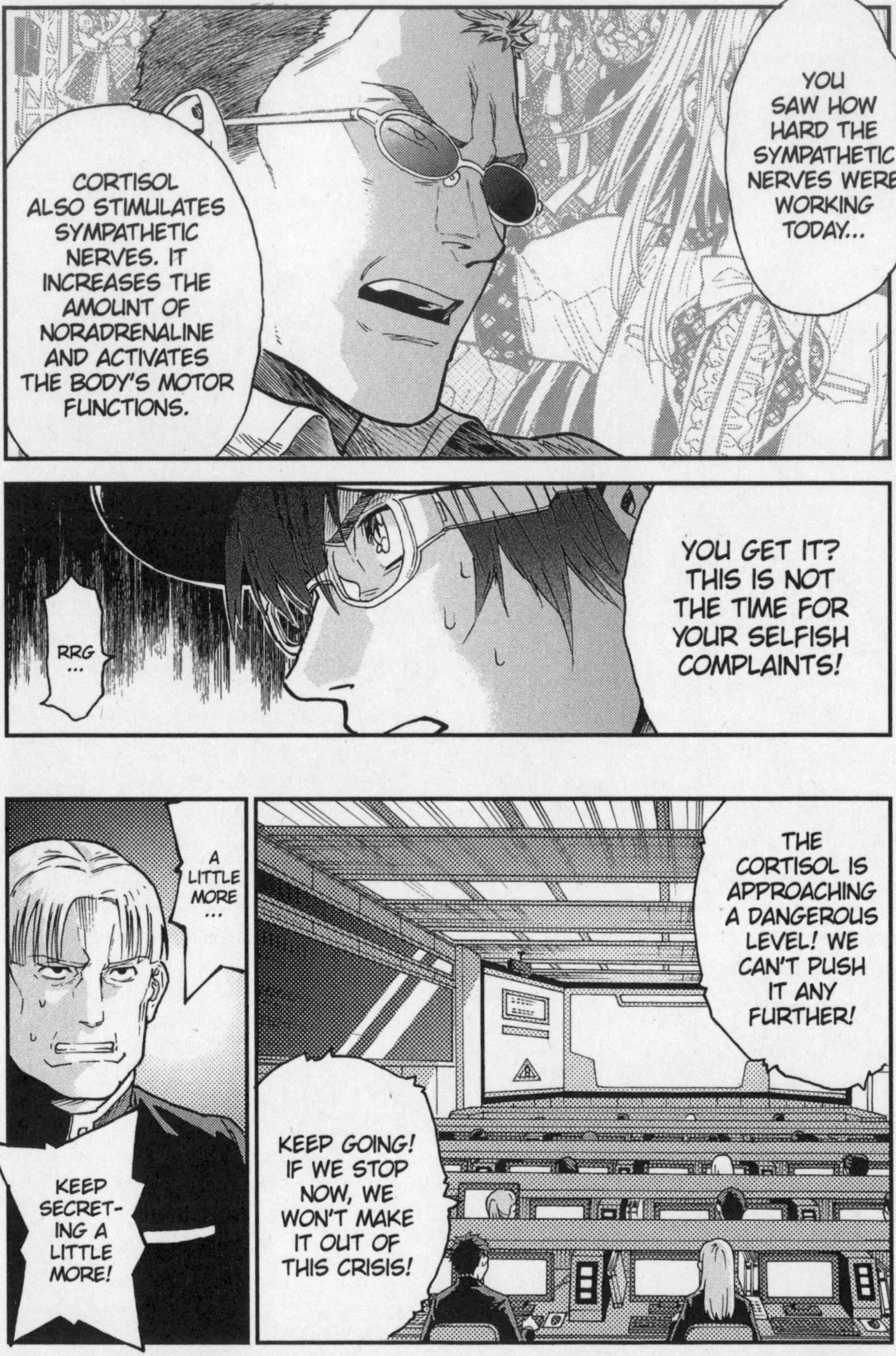
YOU SAW HOW HARD THE SYMPATHETIC NERVES WERE WORKING TODAY...
CORTISOL ALSO STIMULATES SYMPATHETIC NERVES. IT INCREASES THE AMOUNT OF NORADRENALINE AND ACTIVATES THE BODY'S MOTOR FUNCTIONS.
YOU GET IT? THIS IS NOT THE TIME FOR YOUR SELFISH COMPLAINTS!
RRG...
THE CORTISOL IS APPROACHING A DANGEROUS LEVEL! WE CAN'T PUSH IT ANY FURTHER!
KEEP GOING! IF WE STOP NOW, WE WON'T MAKE IT OUT OF THIS CRISIS!
A LITTLE MORE...
KEEP SECRET-ING A LITTLE MORE!

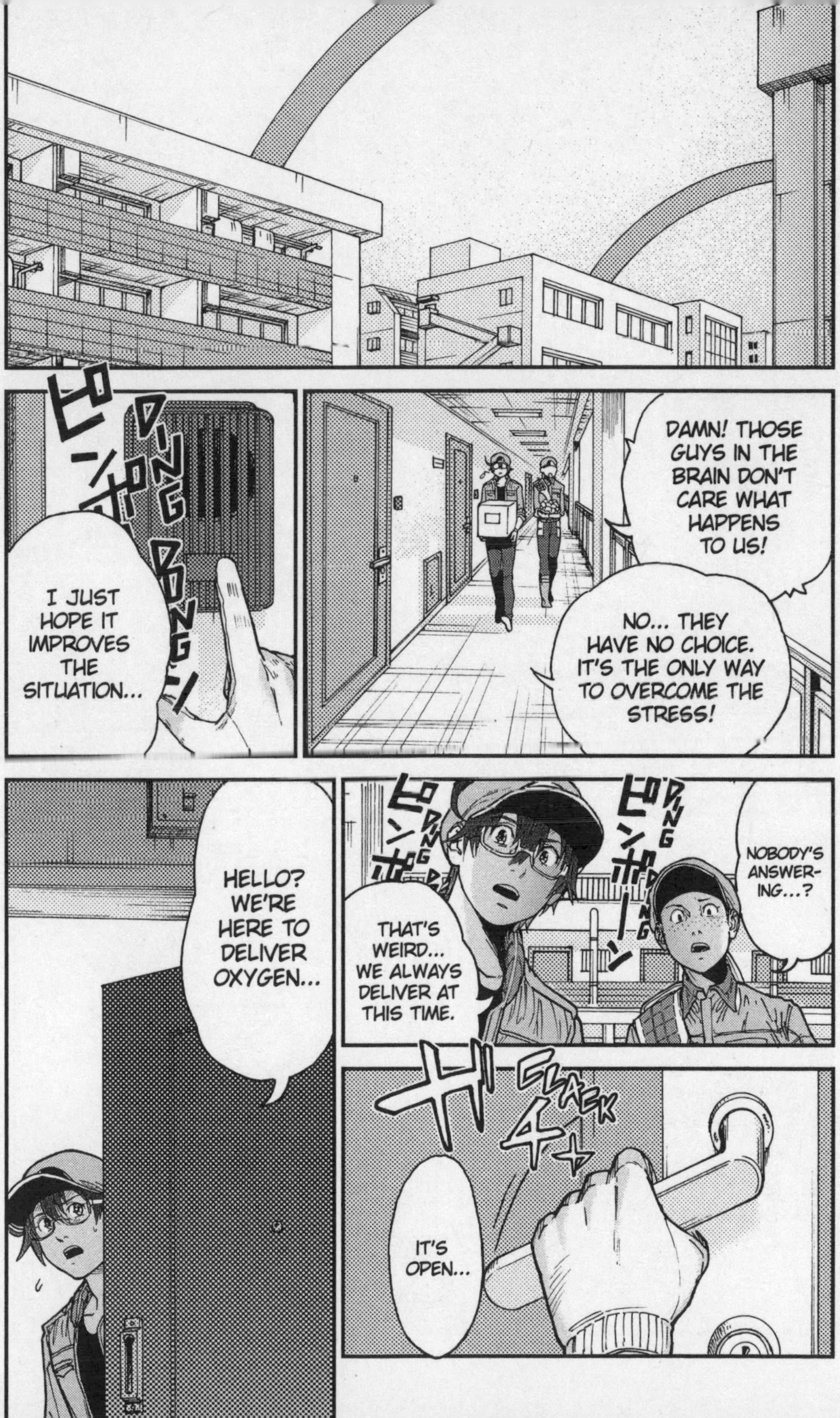
DAMN! THOSE GUYS IN THE BRAIN DON'T CARE WHAT HAPPENS TO US!
NO... THEY HAVE NO CHOICE. IT'S THE ONLY WAY TO OVERCOME THE STRESS!
DING BONG
I JUST HOPE IT IMPROVES THE SITUATION...
NOBODY'S ANSWER-ING...?
DING DONG
DING DONG
THAT'S WEIRD... WE ALWAYS DELIVER AT THIS TIME.
CLACK
IT'S OPEN...
HELLO? WE'RE HERE TO DELIVER OXYGEN...

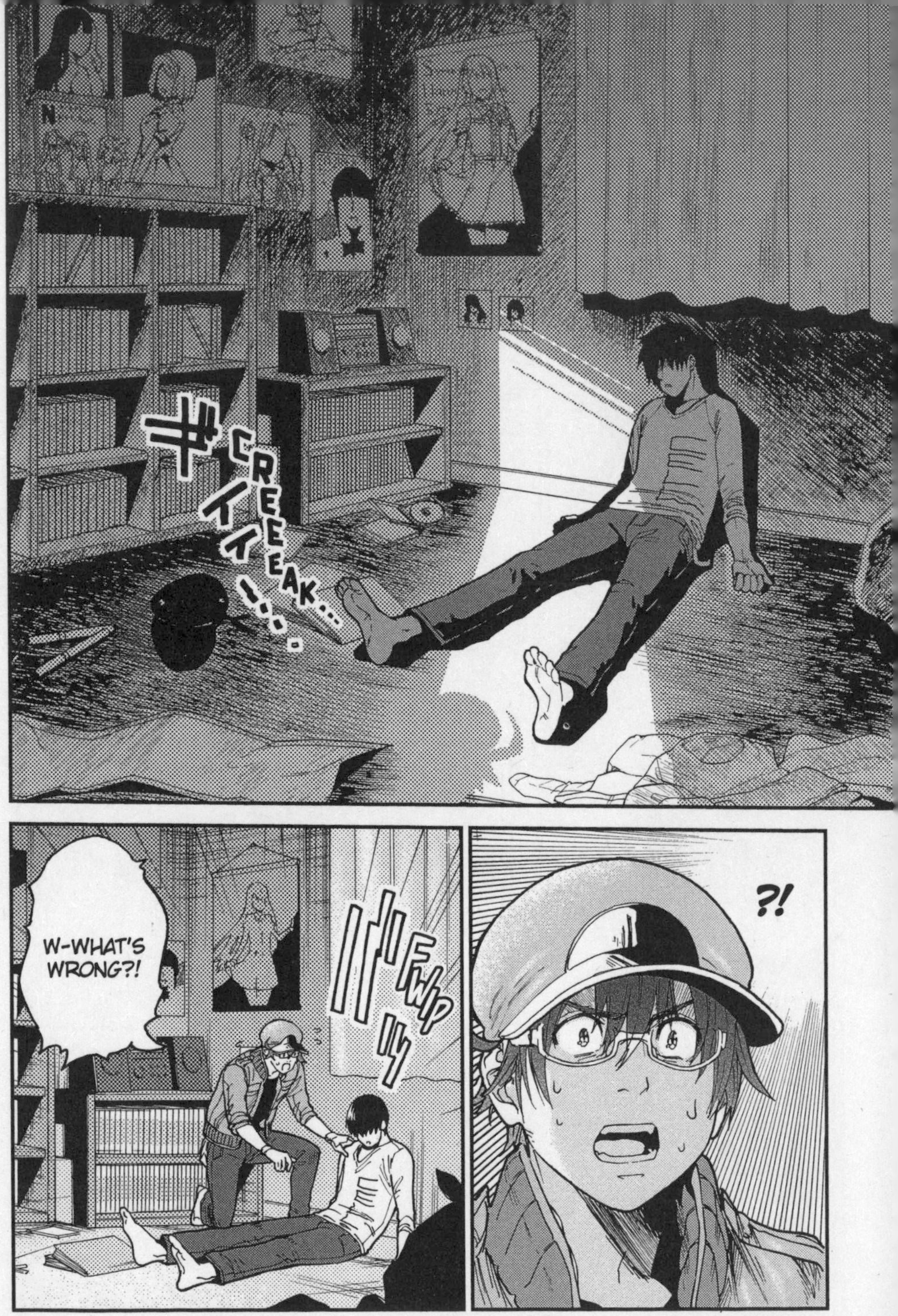
ギイイ…
CREEEAK...
?!
FWIP
W-WHAT'S WRONG?!

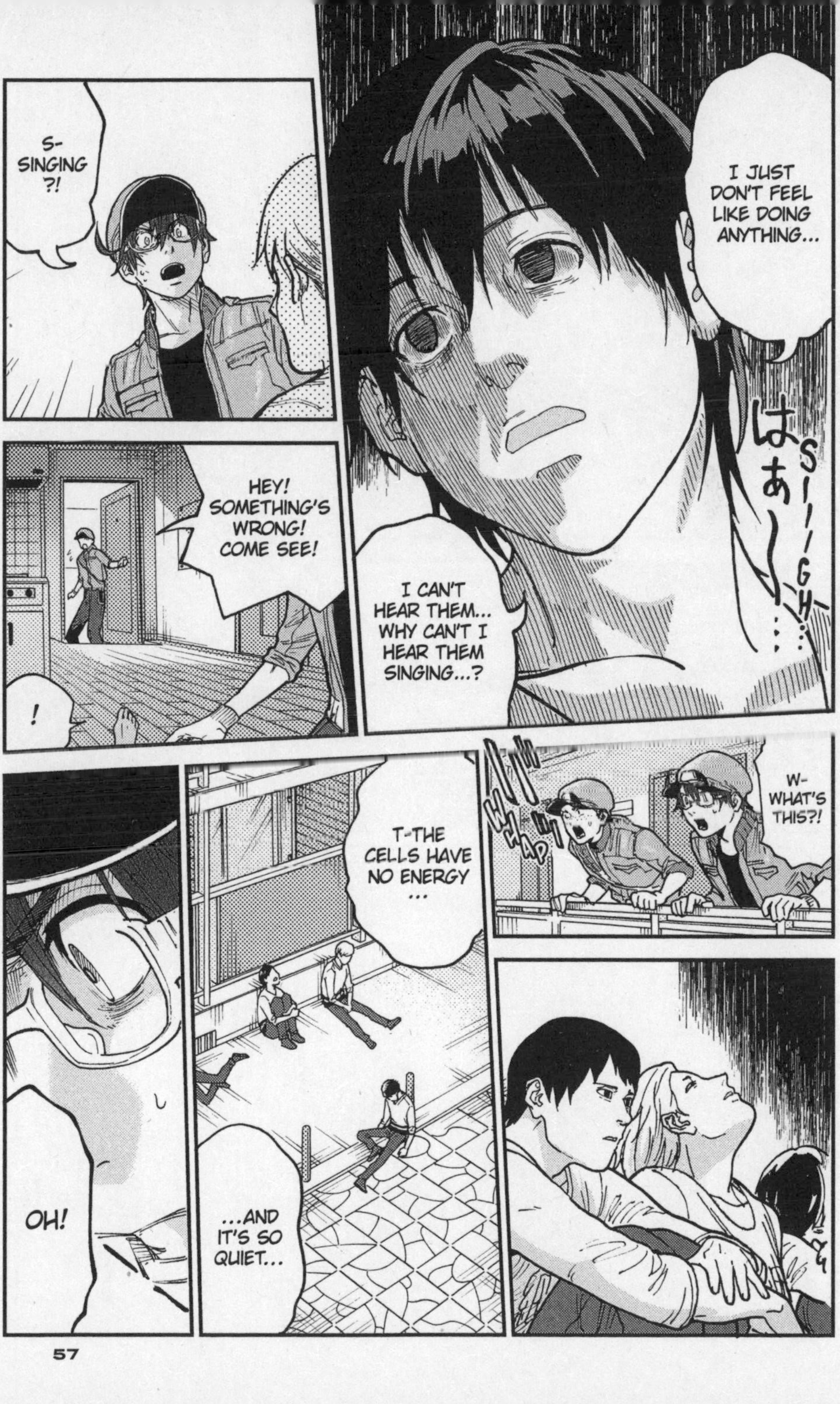
I JUST DON'T FEEL LIKE DOING ANYTHING...
はあ~
S-I-I-GH...
I CAN'T HEAR THEM... WHY CAN'T I HEAR THEM SINGING...?
S-SINGING ?!
HEY! SOMETHING'S WRONG! COME SEE!
!
W- WHAT'S THIS?!
WHAP
T-THE CELLS HAVE NO ENERGY...
...AND IT'S SO QUIET...
OH!

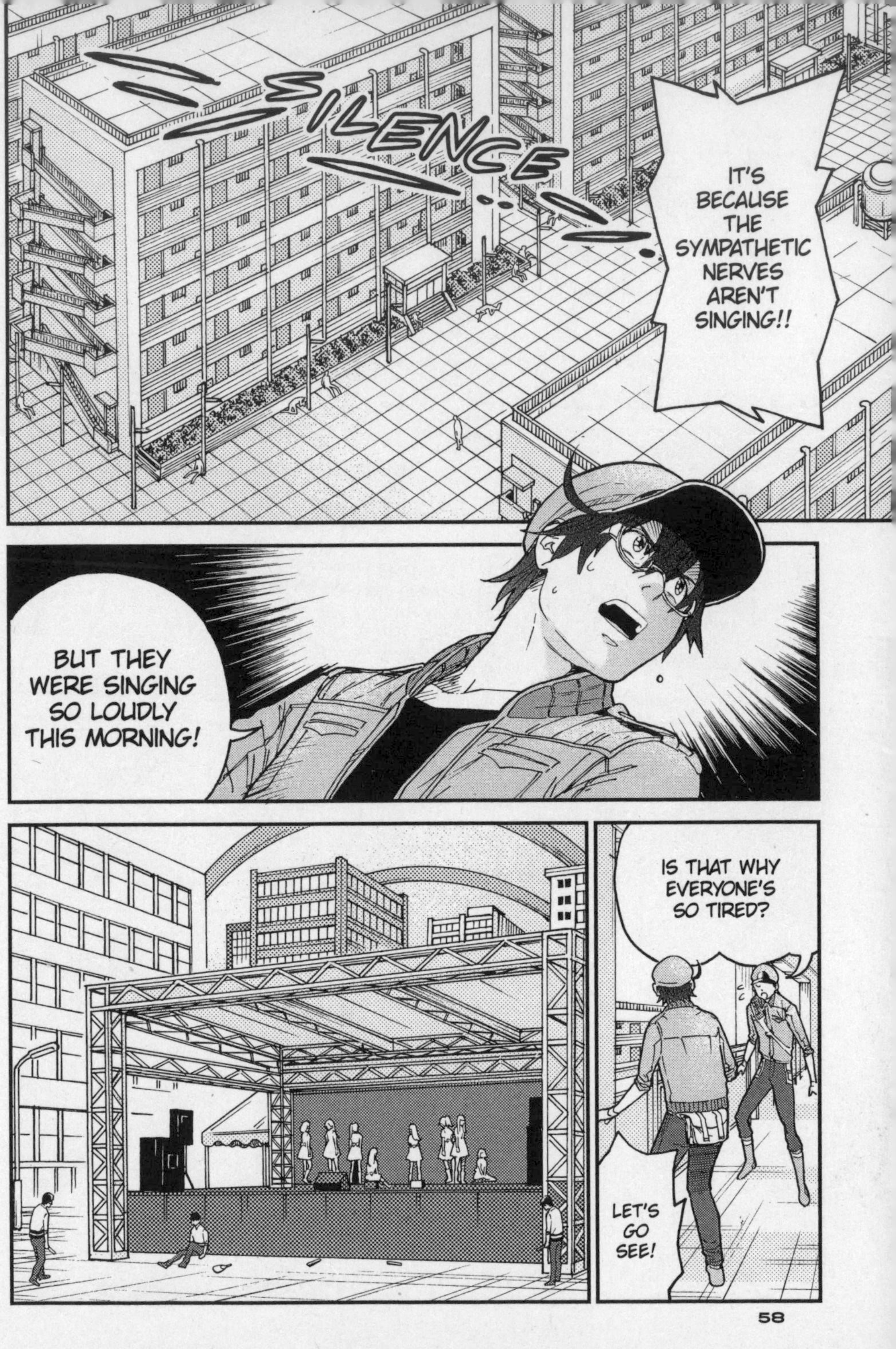
SILENCE...
IT'S BECAUSE THE SYMPATHETIC NERVES AREN'T SINGING!!
BUT THEY WERE SINGING SO LOUDLY THIS MORNING!
IS THAT WHY EVERYONE'S SO TIRED?
LET'S GO SEE!

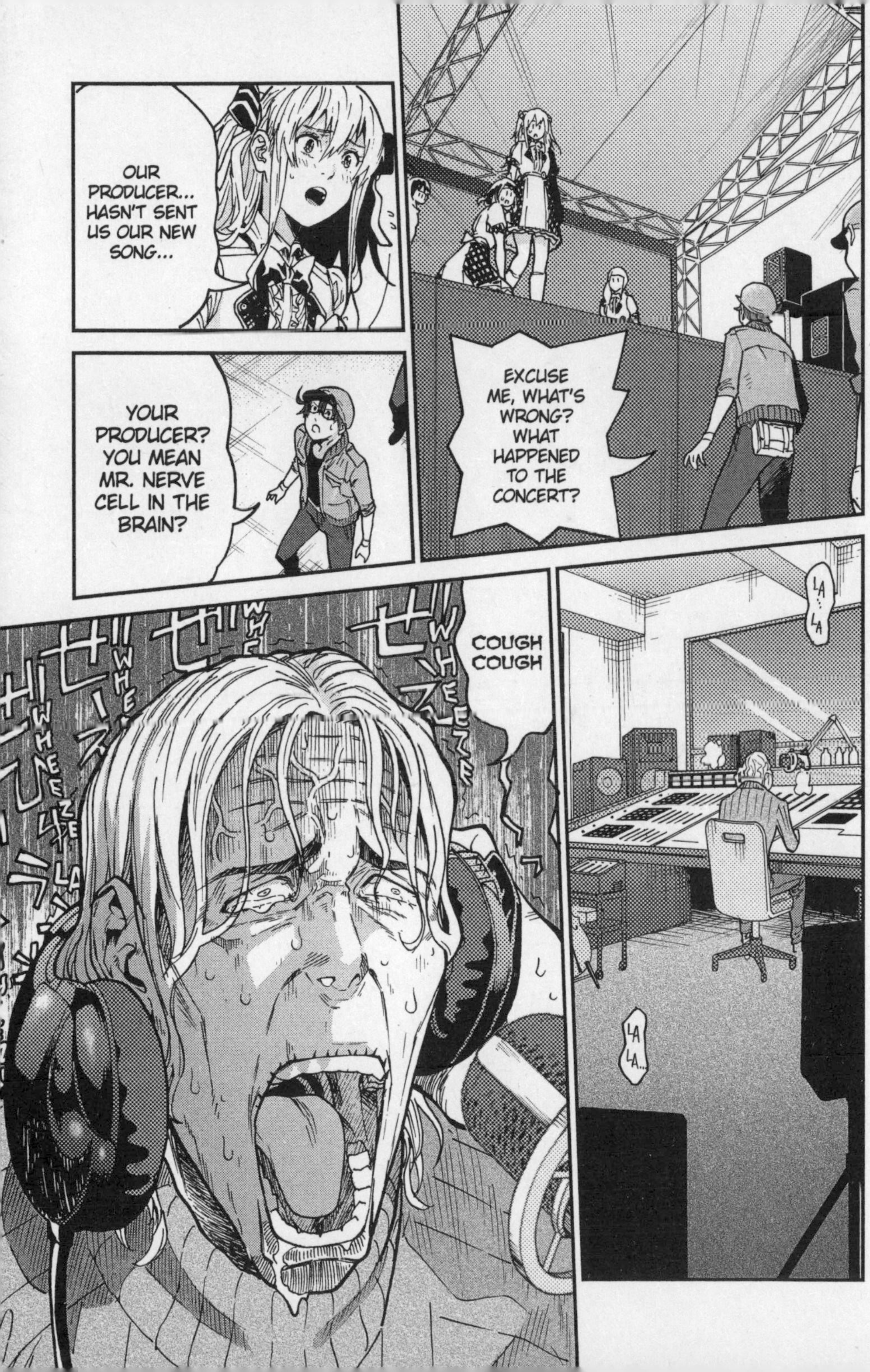
EXCUSE ME, WHAT'S WRONG? WHAT HAPPENED TO THE CONCERT?
OUR PRODUCER... HASN'T SENT US OUR NEW SONG...
YOUR PRODUCER? YOU MEAN MR. NERVE CELL IN THE BRAIN?
LA LA
LA LA...
COUGH COUGH
WHEEZE

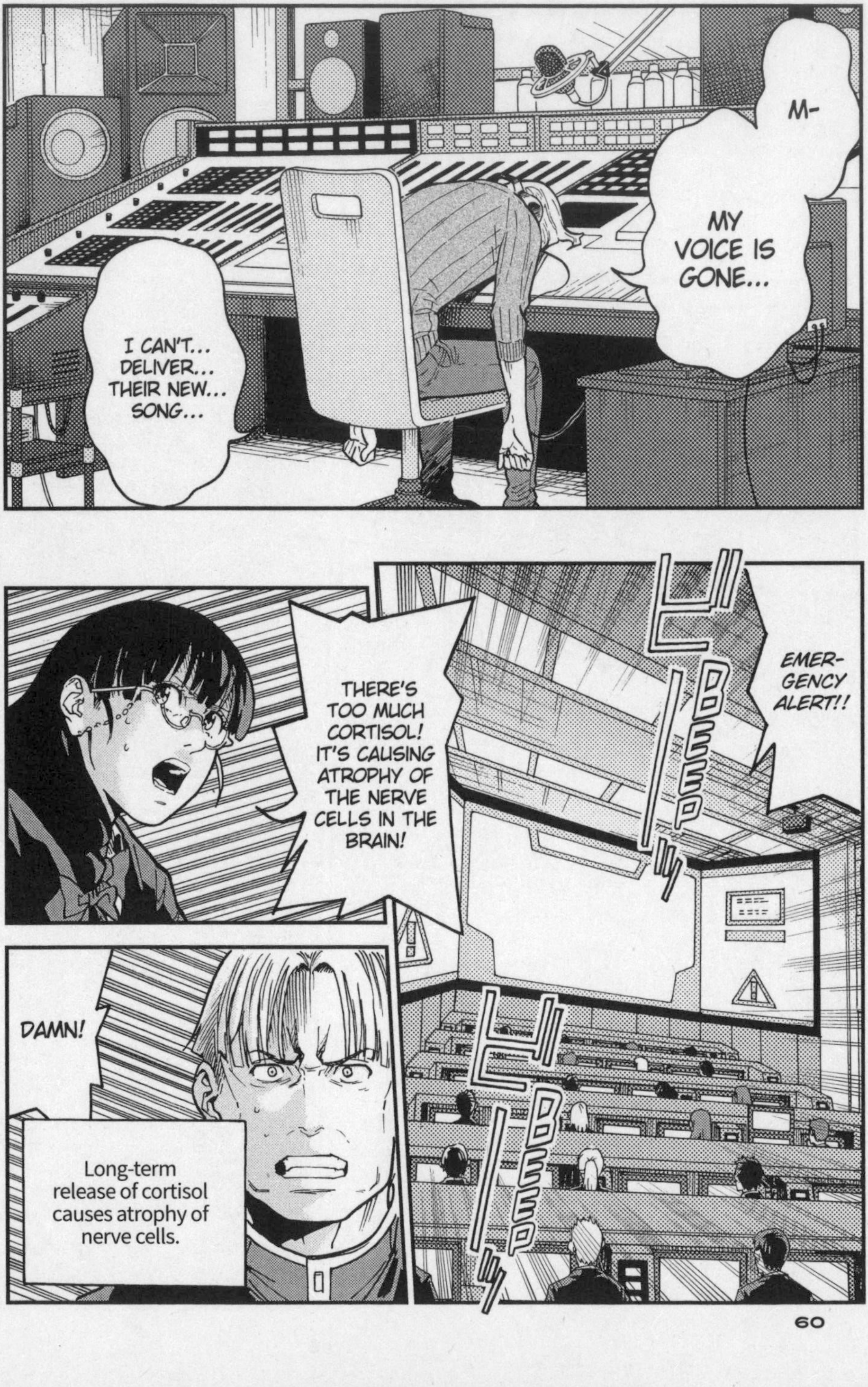
M-
MY VOICE IS GONE...
I CAN'T... DELIVER... THEIR NEW... SONG...
EMER-GENCY ALERT!!
BEEP
BEEP
THERE'S TOO MUCH CORTISOL! IT'S CAUSING ATROPHY OF THE NERVE CELLS IN THE BRAIN!
DAMN!
Long-term release of cortisol causes atrophy of nerve cells.

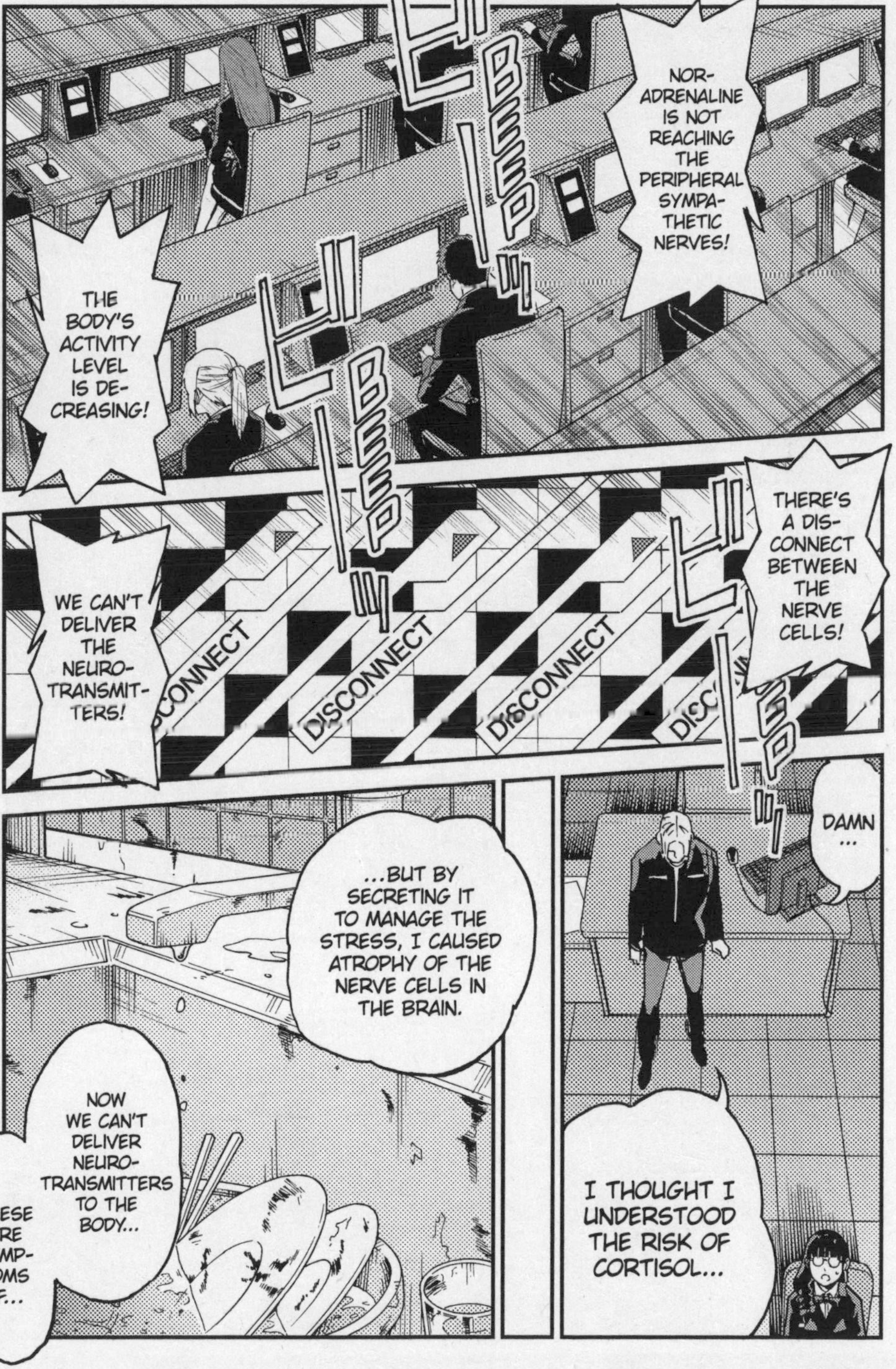
BEEP
BEEP
NOR-ADRENALINE IS NOT REACHING THE PERIPHERAL SYMPATHETIC NERVES!
THE BODY'S ACTIVITY LEVEL IS DECREASING!
BEEP
THERE'S A DISCONNECT BETWEEN THE NERVE CELLS!
DISCONNECT
DISCONNECT
DISCONNECT
WE CAN'T DELIVER THE NEUROTRANSMITTERS!
DAMN...
I THOUGHT I UNDERSTOOD THE RISK OF CORTISOL...
...BUT BY SECRETING IT TO MANAGE THE STRESS, I CAUSED ATROPHY OF THE NERVE CELLS IN THE BRAIN.
NOW WE CAN'T DELIVER NEUROTRANSMITTERS TO THE BODY...
THESE ARE SYMPTOMS OF...

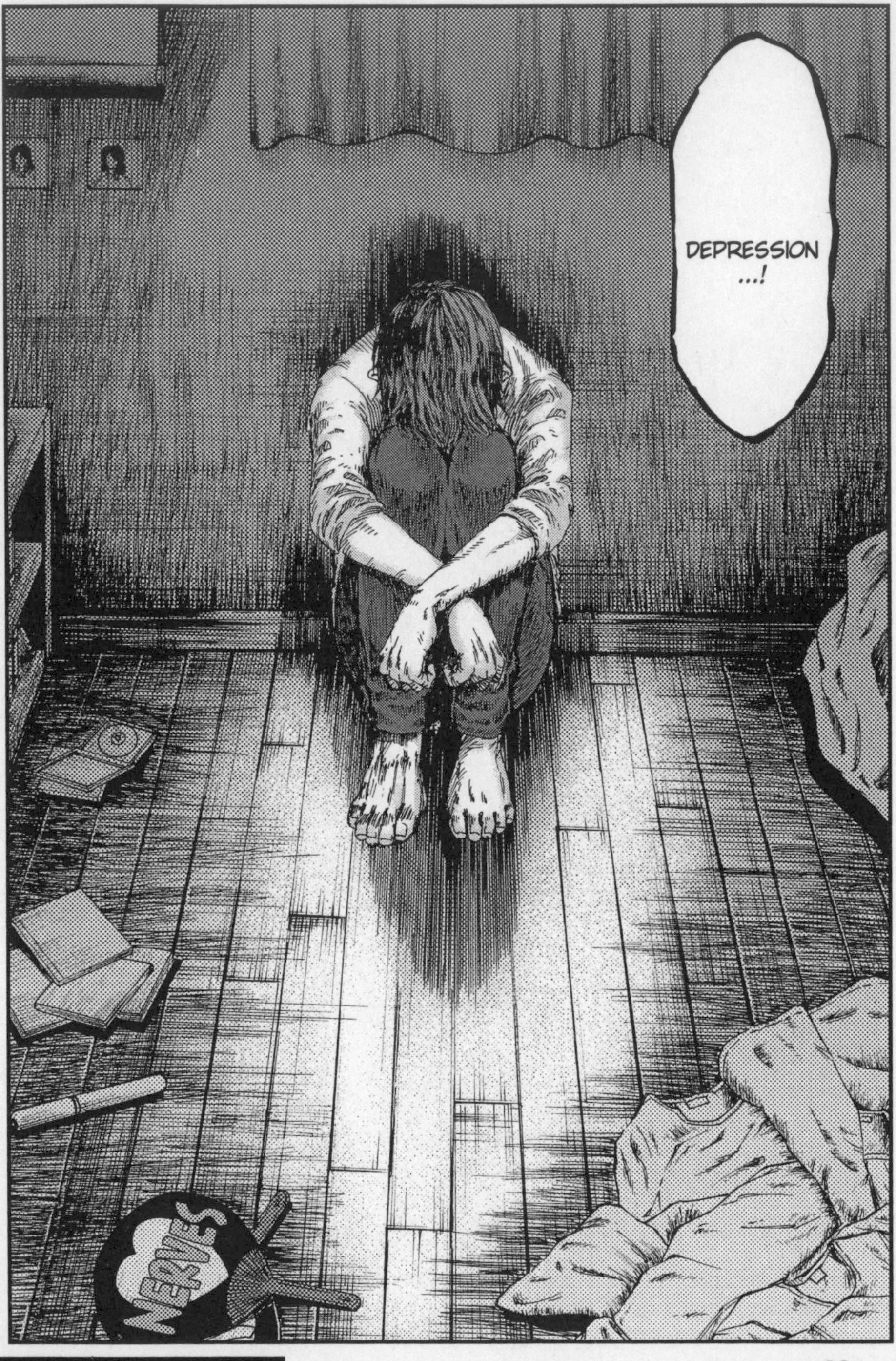
DEPRESSION
...!
MOVIES

CHAPTER 33 - END

34. DEPRESSION, RESOLVE, NO WAY OUT

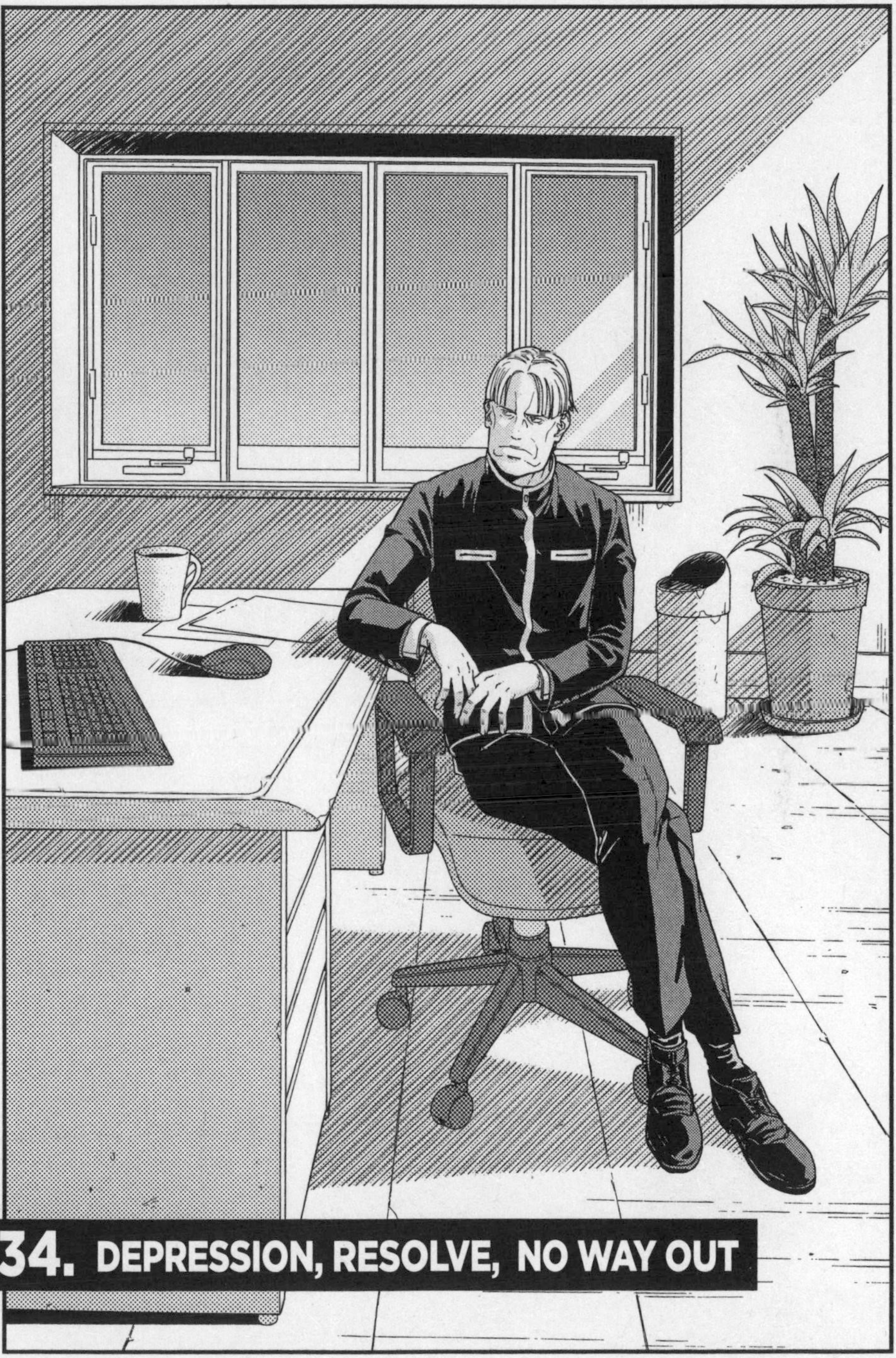

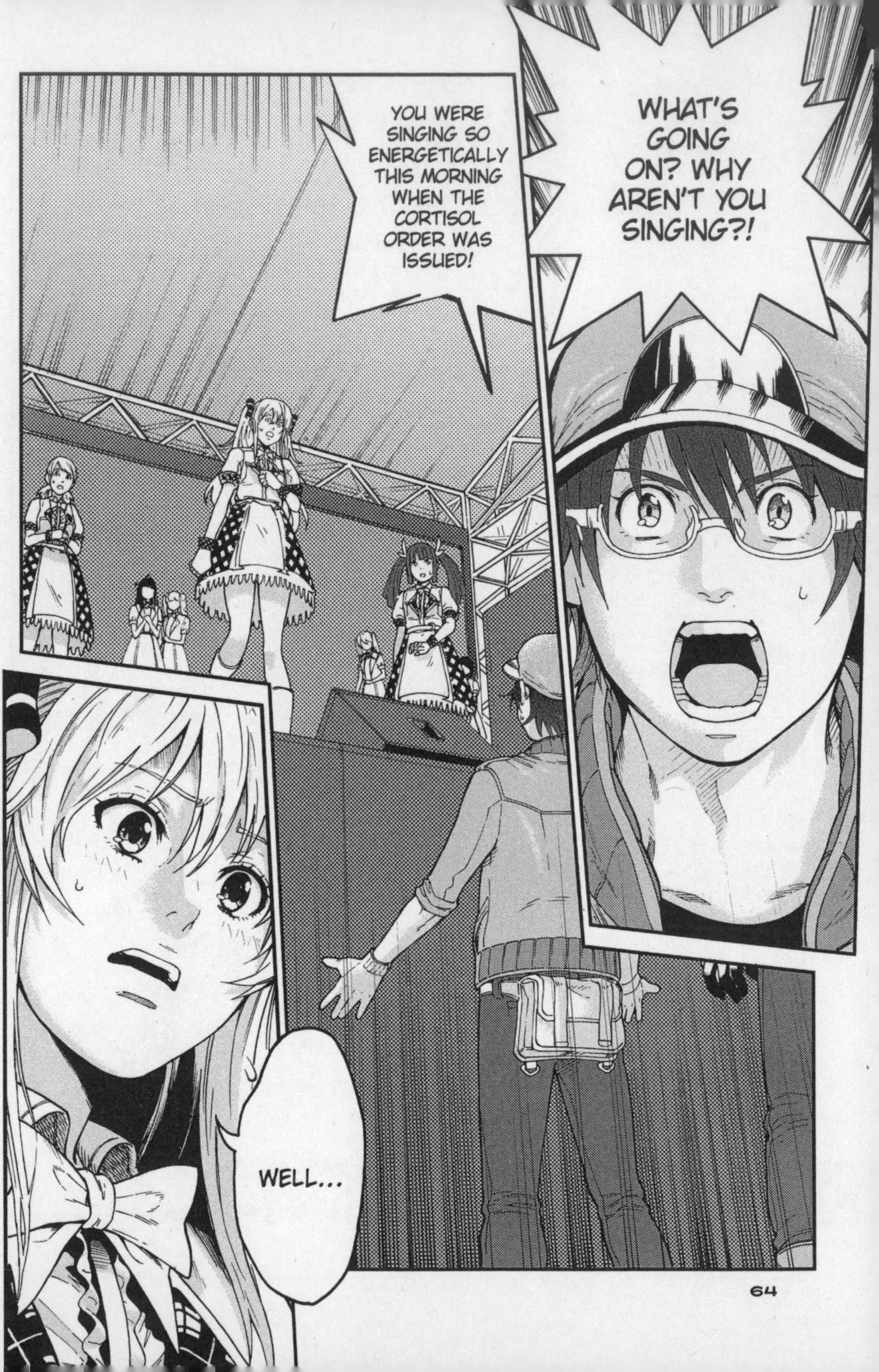
WHAT'S GOING ON? WHY AREN'T YOU SINGING?!
YOU WERE SINGING SO ENERGETICALLY THIS MORNING WHEN THE CORTISOL ORDER WAS ISSUED!
WELL...

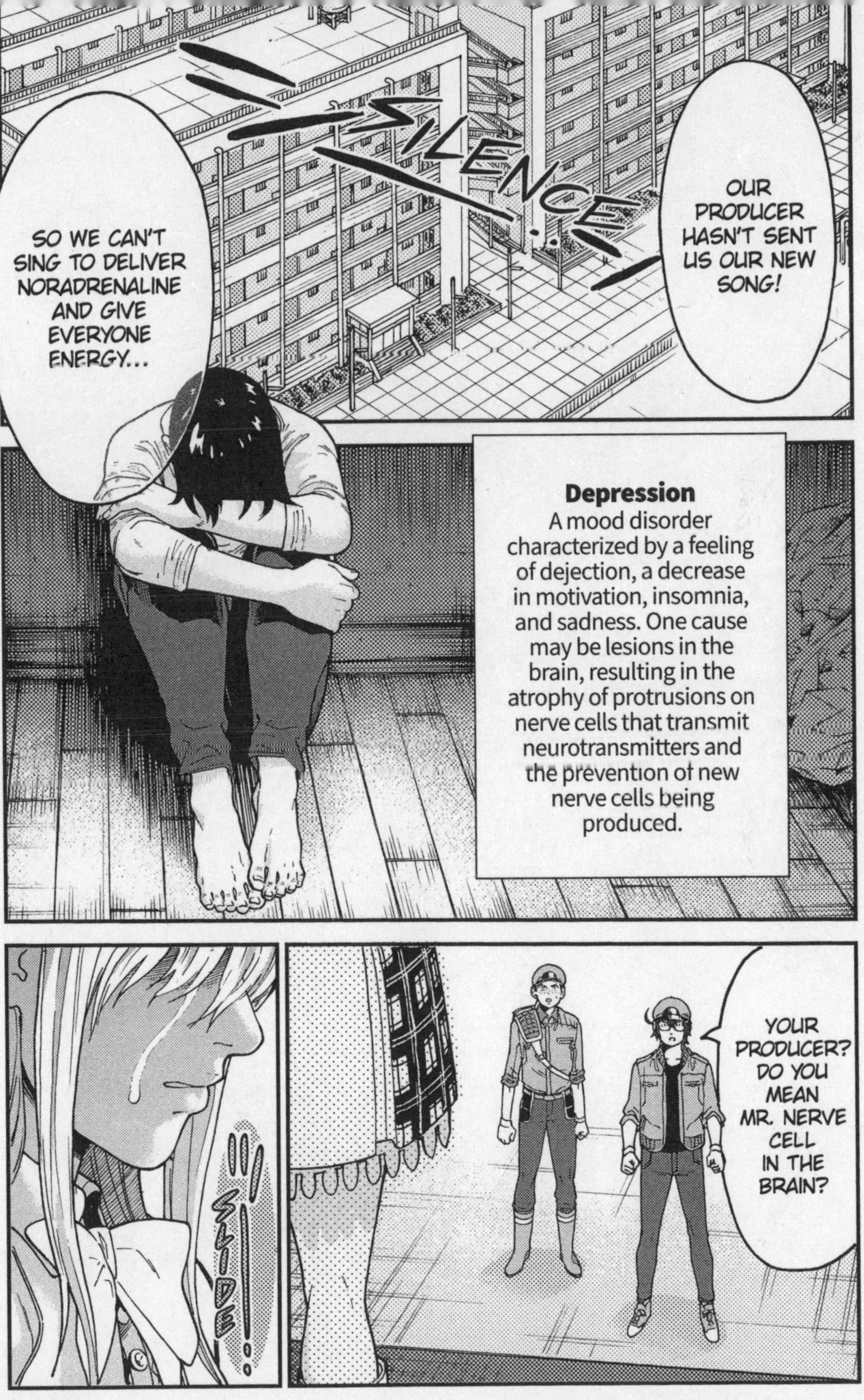
OUR PRODUCER HASN'T SENT US OUR NEW SONG!
SILENCE
SO WE CAN'T SING TO DELIVER NORADRENALINE AND GIVE EVERYONE ENERGY...
Depression
A mood disorder characterized by a feeling of dejection, a decrease in motivation, insomnia, and sadness. One cause may be lesions in the brain, resulting in the atrophy of protrusions on nerve cells that transmit neurotransmitters and the prevention of new nerve cells being produced.
YOUR PRODUCER? DO YOU MEAN MR. NERVE CELL IN THE BRAIN?
SLIDE

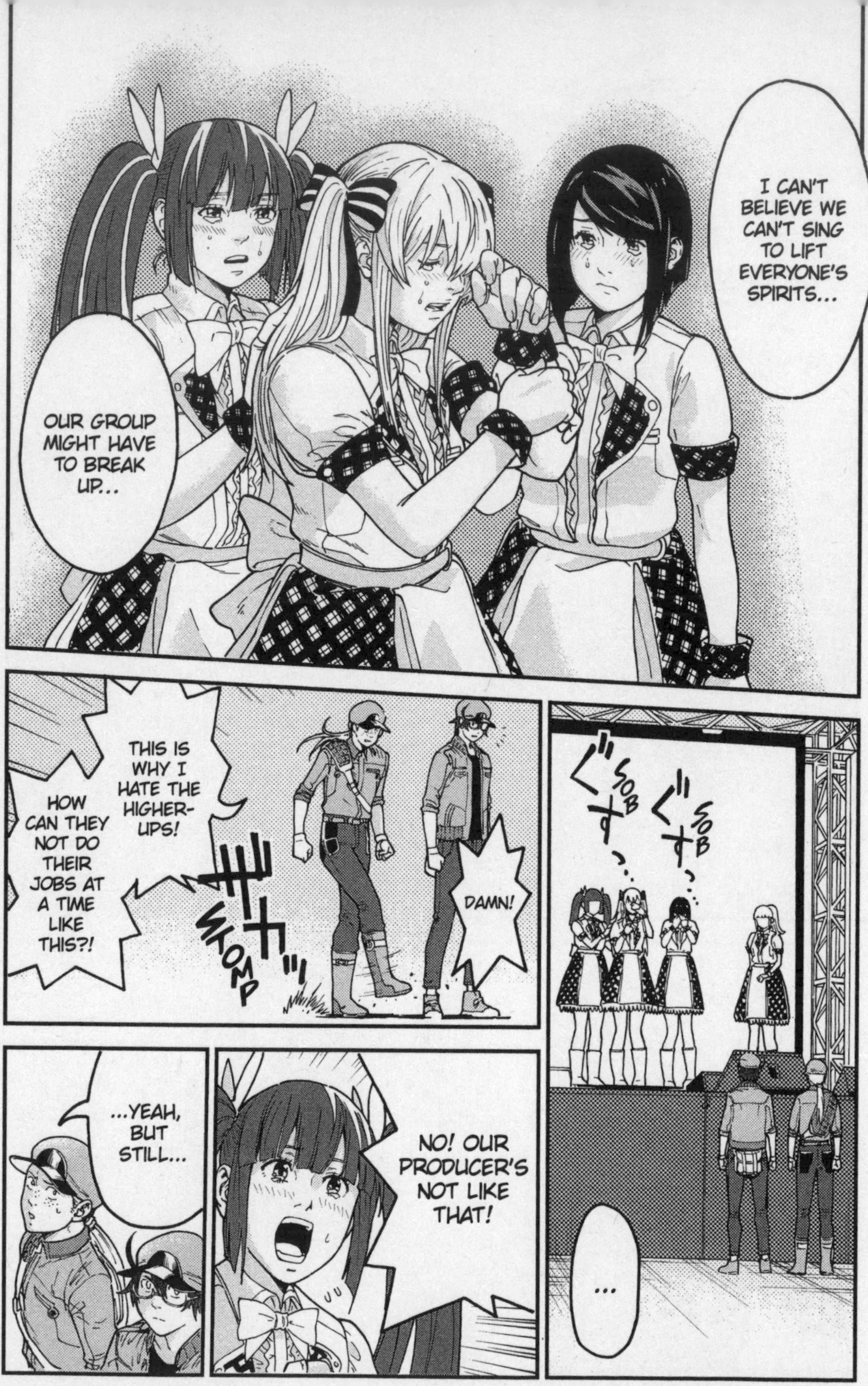
I CAN'T BELIEVE WE CAN'T SING TO LIFT EVERYONE'S SPIRITS...
OUR GROUP MIGHT HAVE TO BREAK UP...
SOB
SOB
...
DAMN!
THIS IS WHY I HATE THE HIGHER-UPS!
HOW CAN THEY NOT DO THEIR JOBS AT A TIME LIKE THIS?!
WKOMP
NO! OUR PRODUCER'S NOT LIKE THAT!
...YEAH, BUT STILL...

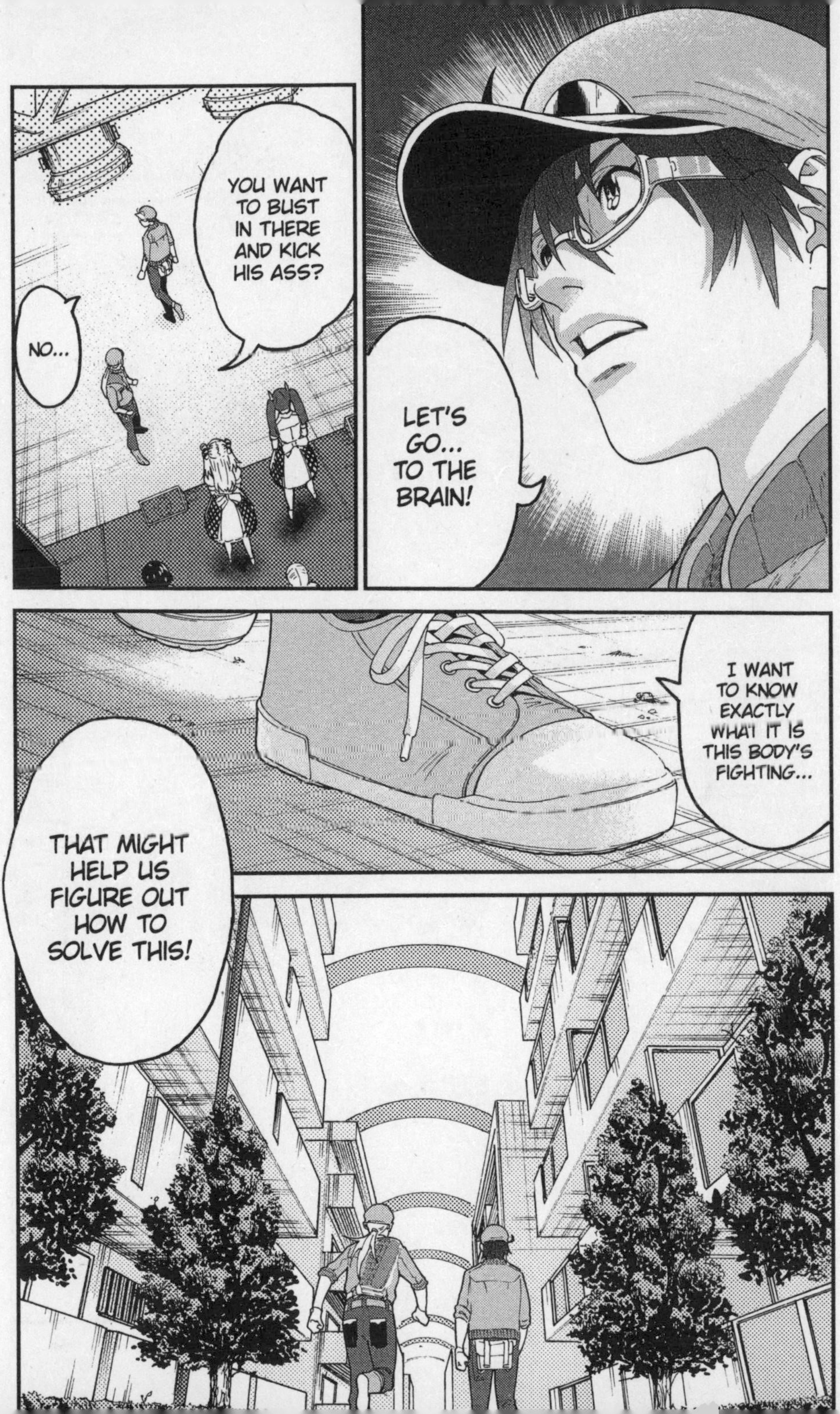
LET'S GO... TO THE BRAIN!
YOU WANT TO BUST IN THERE AND KICK HIS ASS?
NO...
I WANT TO KNOW EXACTLY WHAT IT IS THIS BODY'S FIGHTING...
THAT MIGHT HELP US FIGURE OUT HOW TO SOLVE THIS!

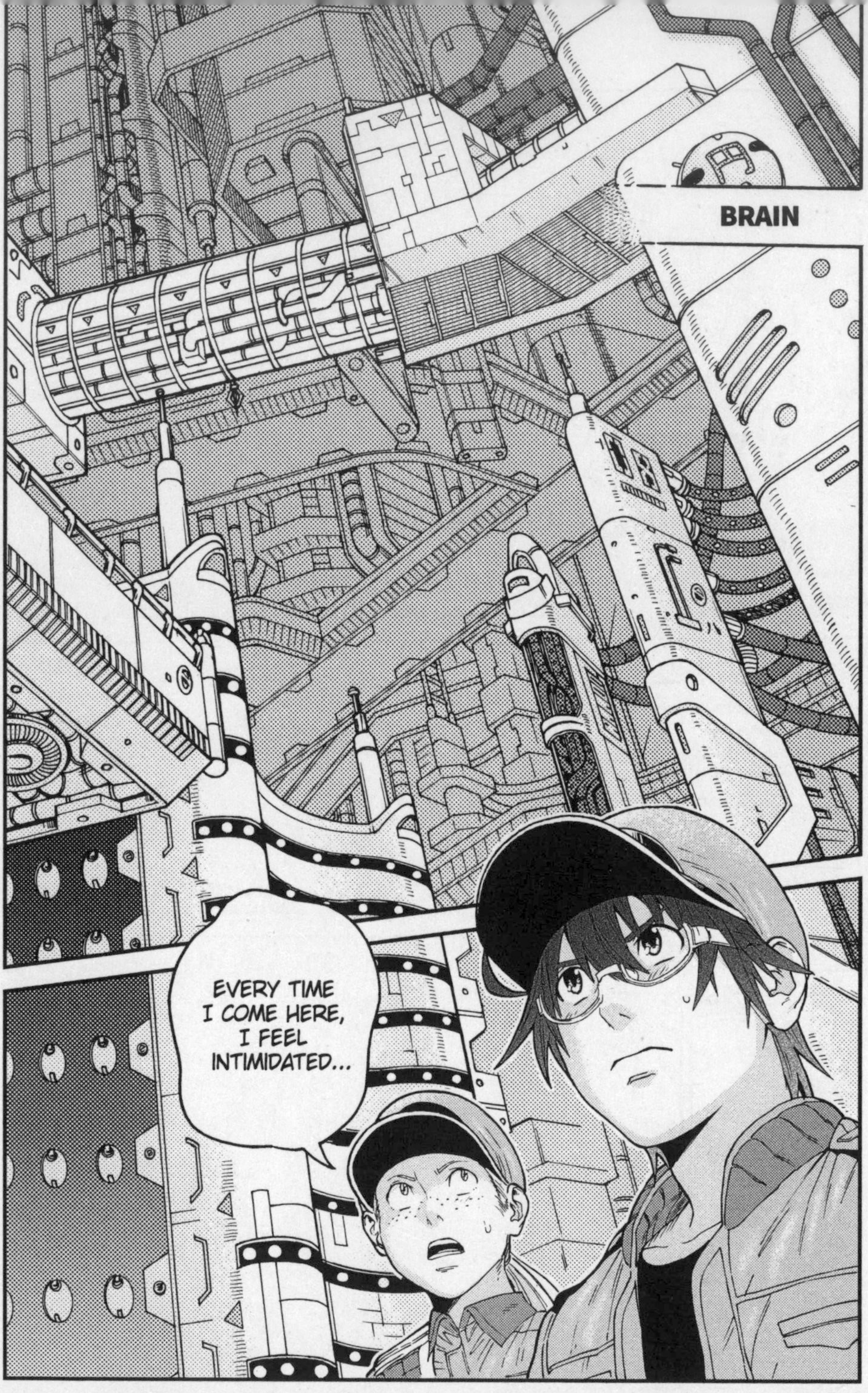
BRAIN
EVERY TIME I COME HERE, I FEEL INTIMIDATED...

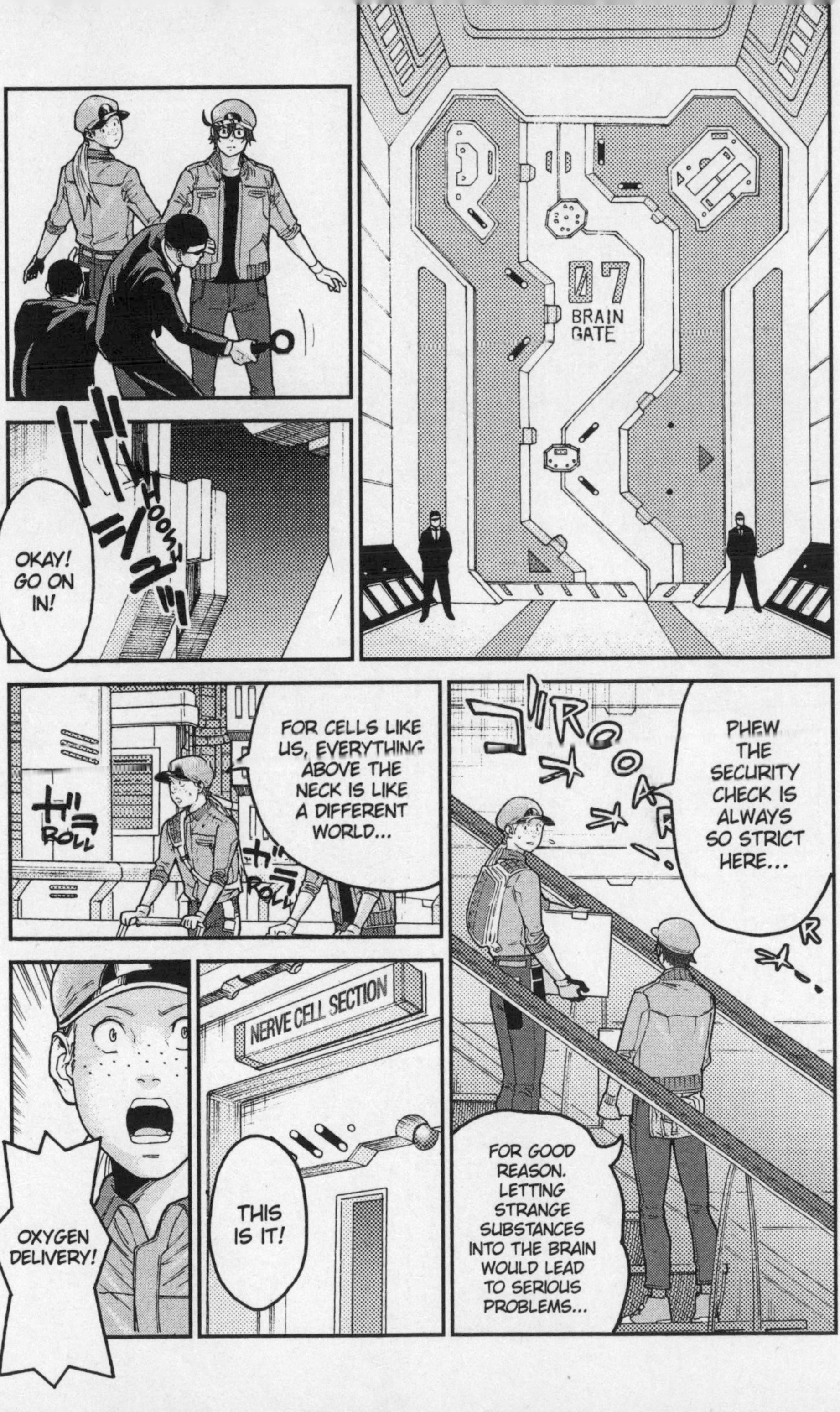
07
BRAIN GATE
WHOOSH
OKAY! GO ON IN!
ROOOAR
PHEW THE SECURITY CHECK IS ALWAYS SO STRICT HERE...
R
FOR GOOD REASON. LETTING STRANGE SUBSTANCES INTO THE BRAIN WOULD LEAD TO SERIOUS PROBLEMS...
ROLL
FOR CELLS LIKE US, EVERYTHING ABOVE THE NECK IS LIKE A DIFFERENT WORLD...
ROLL
NERVE CELL SECTION
THIS IS IT!
OXYGEN DELIVERY!

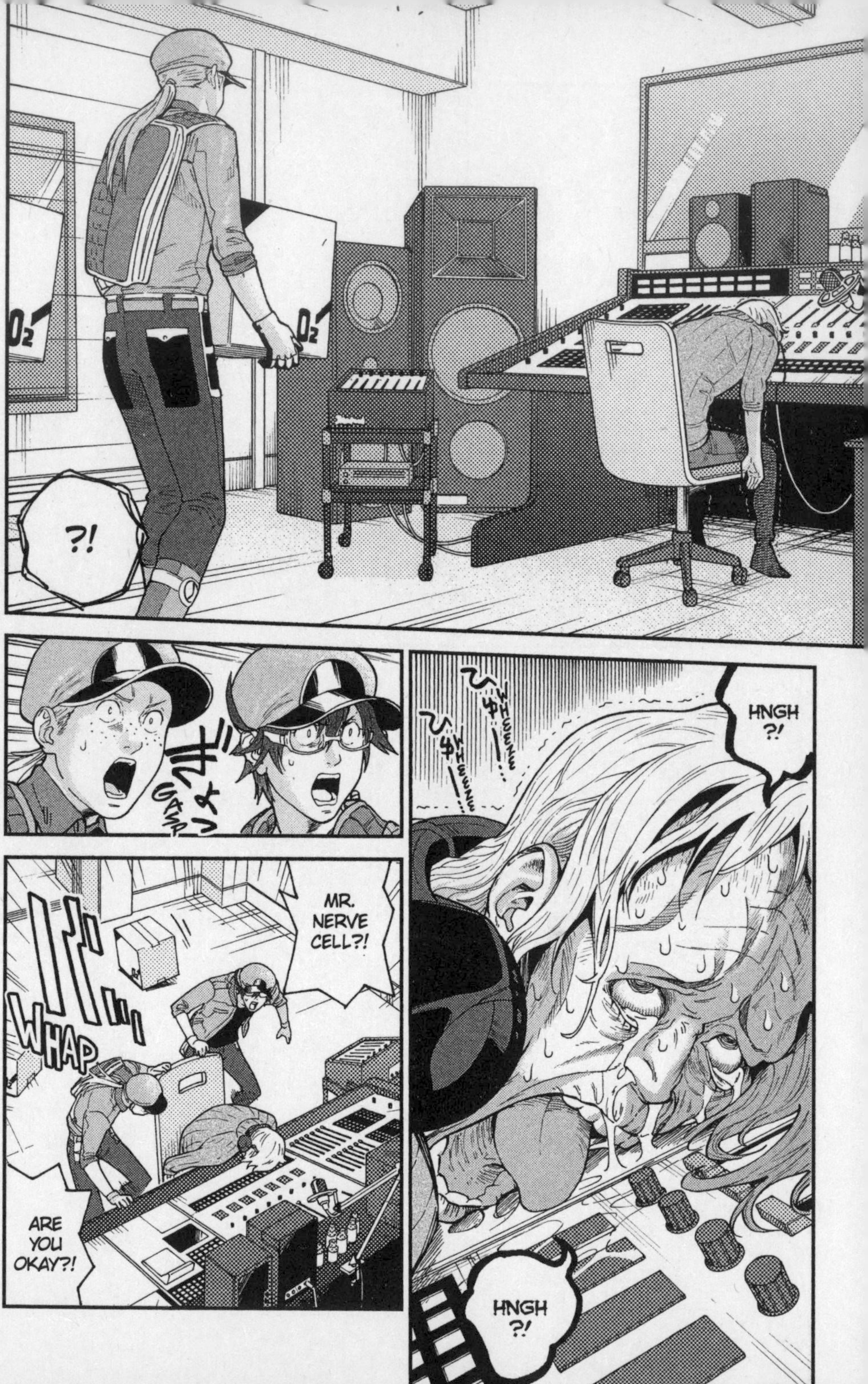
?!
WHEEZE
WHEEZE
HNGH ?!
HNGH ?!
GASP
MR. NERVE CELL?!
WHAP
ARE YOU OKAY?!

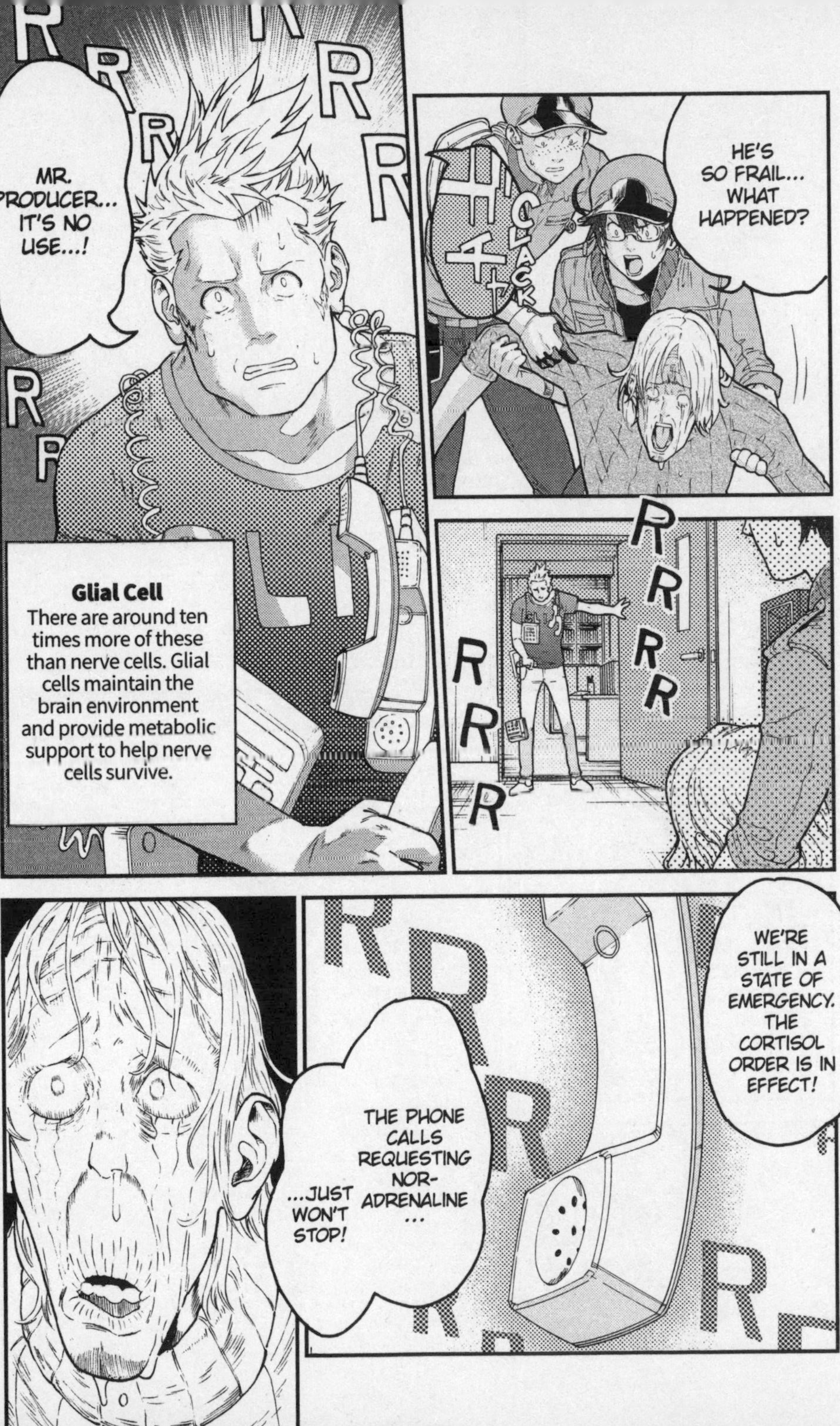
CLACK
HE'S SO FRAIL... WHAT HAPPENED?
RRRR
MR. PRODUCER... IT'S NO USE...!
Glial Cell
There are around ten times more of these than nerve cells. Glial cells maintain the brain environment and provide metabolic support to help nerve cells survive.
WE'RE STILL IN A STATE OF EMERGENCY. THE CORTISOL ORDER IS IN EFFECT!
THE PHONE CALLS REQUESTING NOR-ADRENALINE...
...JUST WON'T STOP!

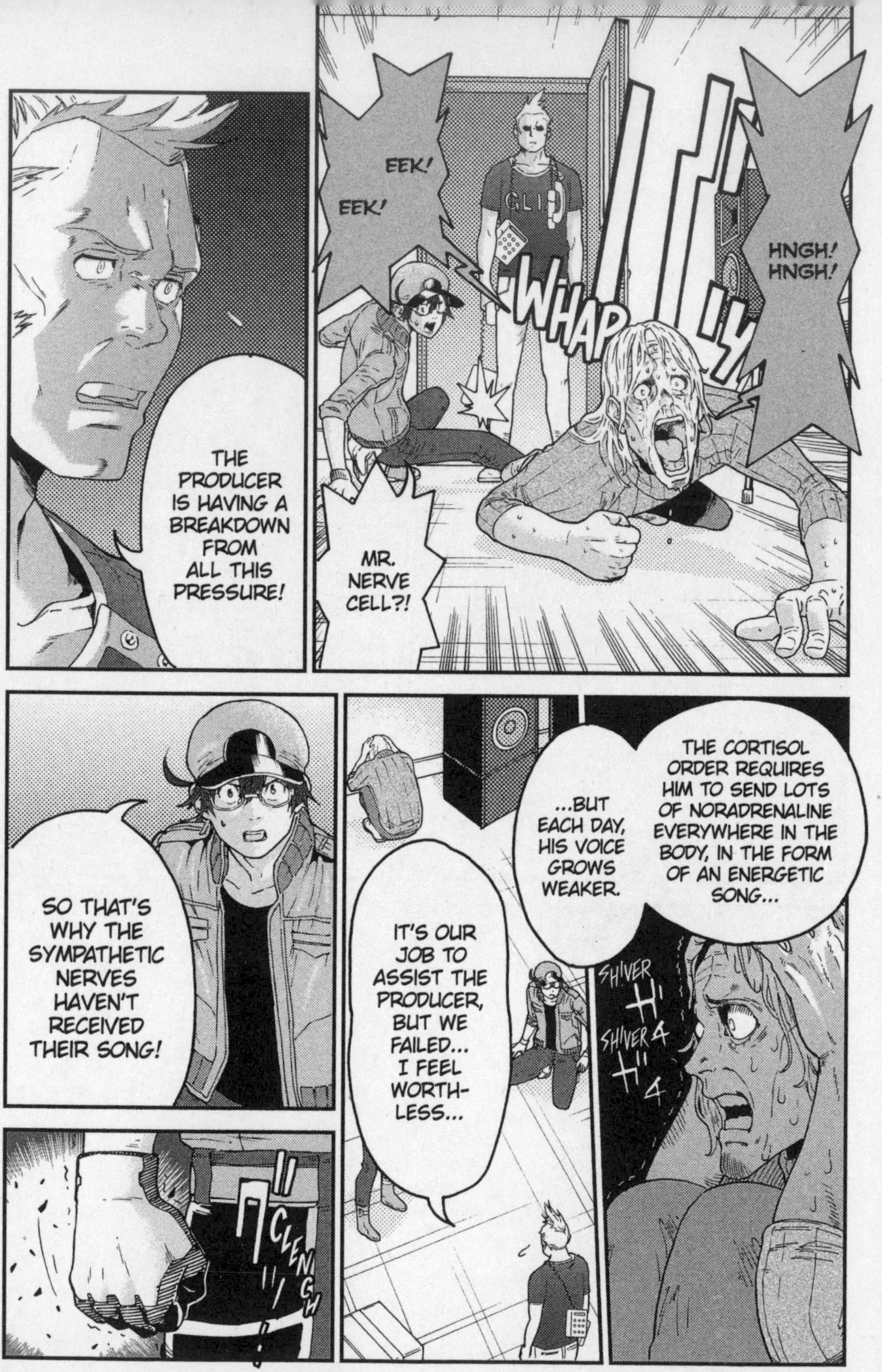
HNGH! HNGH!
EEK!
EEK!
WHAP
MR. NERVE CELL?!
THE PRODUCER IS HAVING A BREAKDOWN FROM ALL THIS PRESSURE!
THE CORTISOL ORDER REQUIRES HIM TO SEND LOTS OF NORADRENALINE EVERYWHERE IN THE BODY, IN THE FORM OF AN ENERGETIC SONG...
SHIVER
SHIVER
...BUT EACH DAY, HIS VOICE GROWS WEAKER.
IT'S OUR JOB TO ASSIST THE PRODUCER, BUT WE FAILED... I FEEL WORTH-LESS...
SO THAT'S WHY THE SYMPATHETIC NERVES HAVEN'T RECEIVED THEIR SONG!
CLENCH

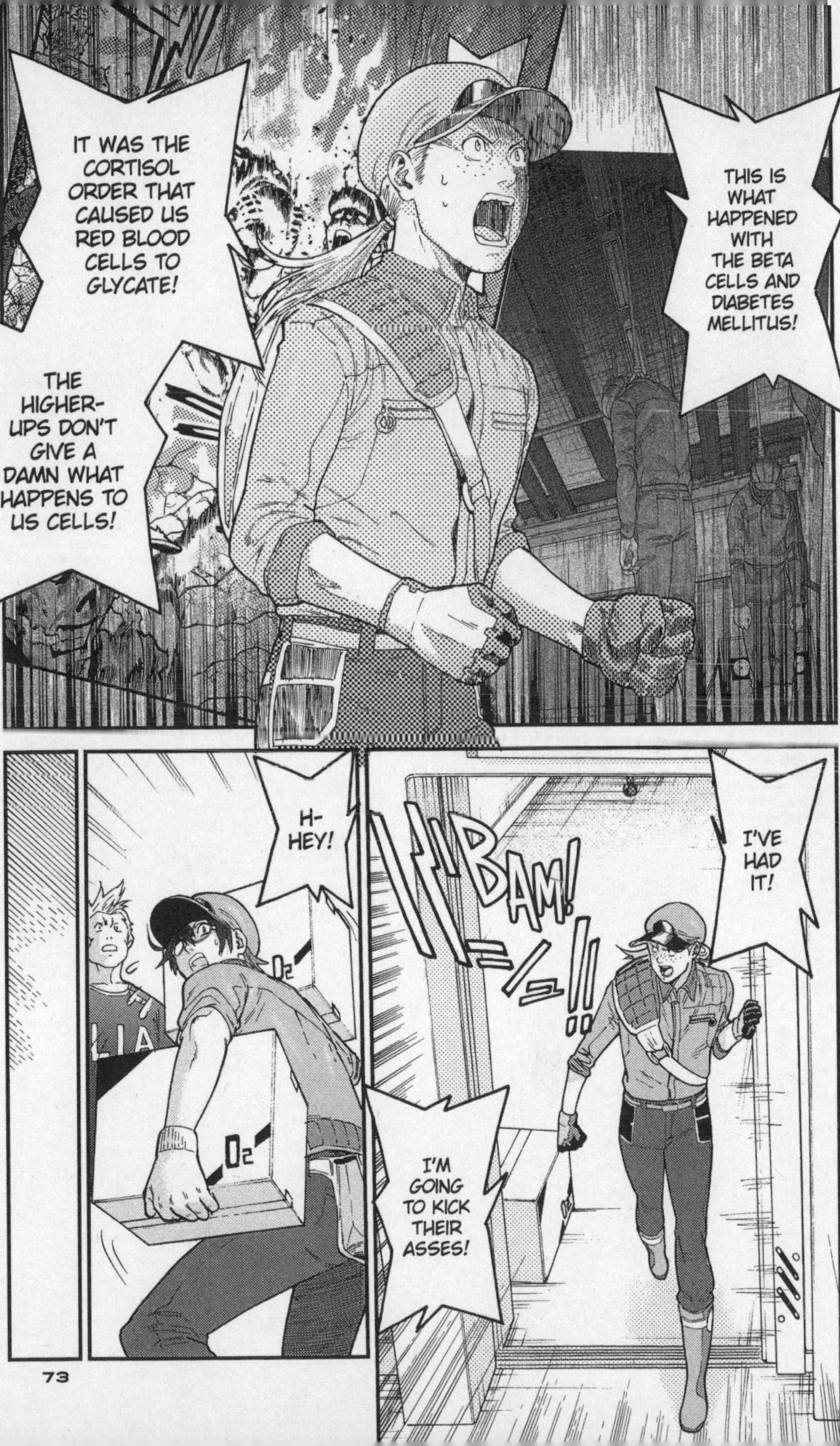
THIS IS WHAT HAPPENED WITH THE BETA CELLS AND DIABETES MELLITUS!
IT WAS THE CORTISOL ORDER THAT CAUSED US RED BLOOD CELLS TO GLYCATE!
THE HIGHER-UPS DON'T GIVE A DAMN WHAT HAPPENS TO US CELLS!
I'VE HAD IT!
BAM!
I'M GOING TO KICK THEIR ASSES!
H-HEY!

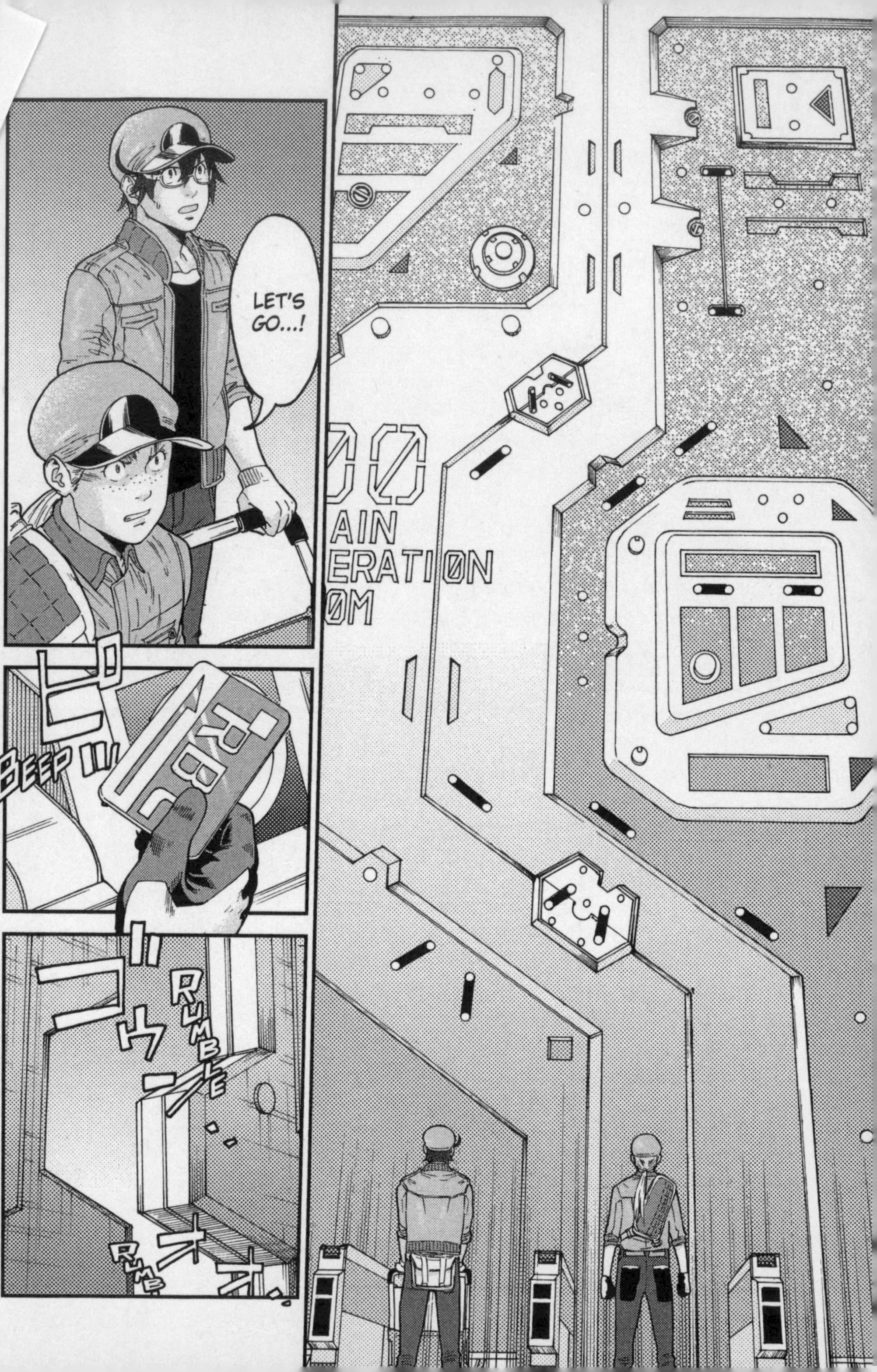

00
AIN
ERATION
ØM
LET'S GO...!
BEEP
RUMBLE
RUMB

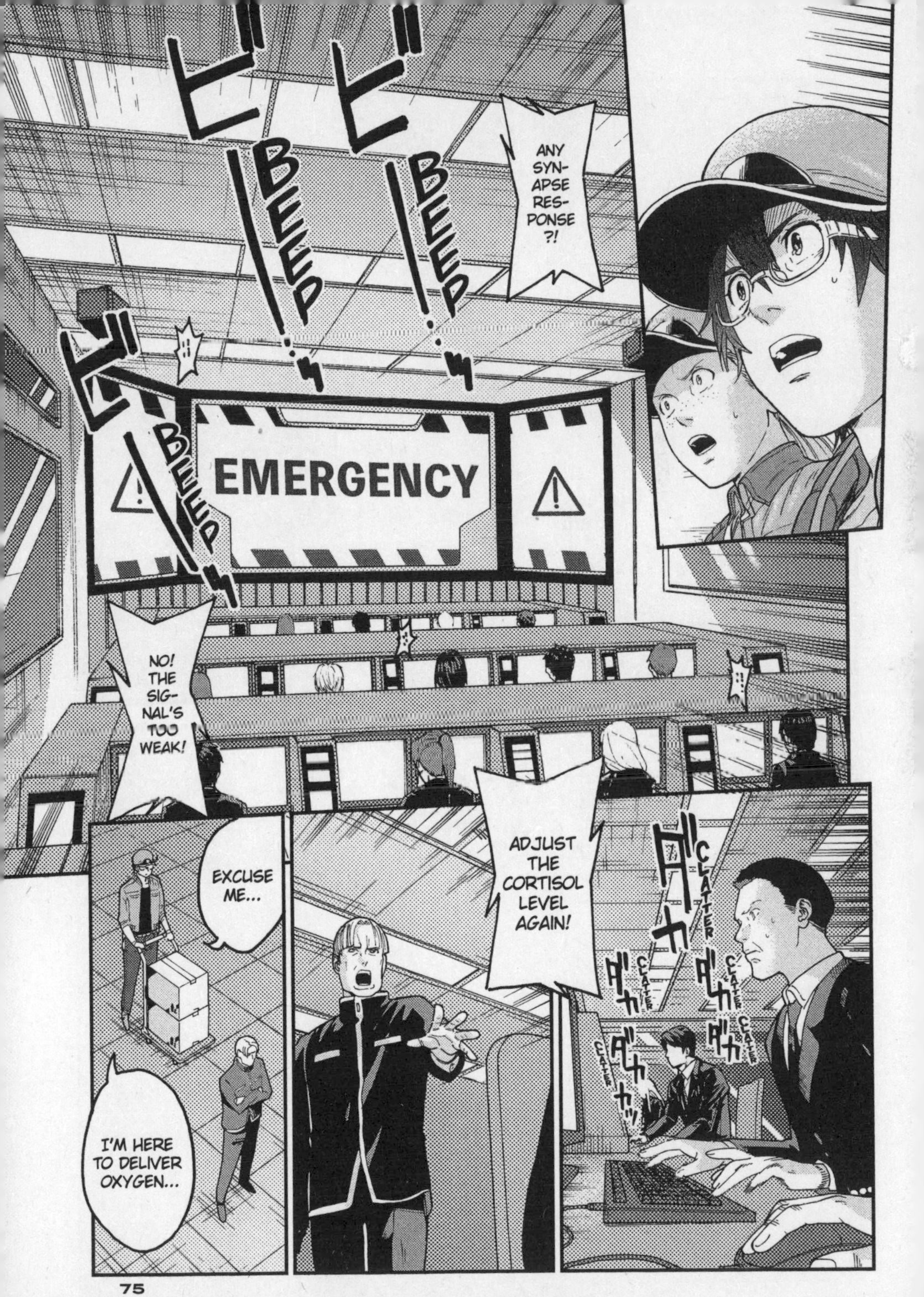
ANY SYNAPSE RESPONSE?!
BEEEP
BEEEP
EMERGENCY
BEEEP
NO! THE SIGNAL'S TOO WEAK!
CLATTER
CLATTER
CLATTER
CLATTER
CLATTER
ADJUST THE CORTISOL LEVEL AGAIN!
EXCUSE ME...
I'M HERE TO DELIVER OXYGEN...

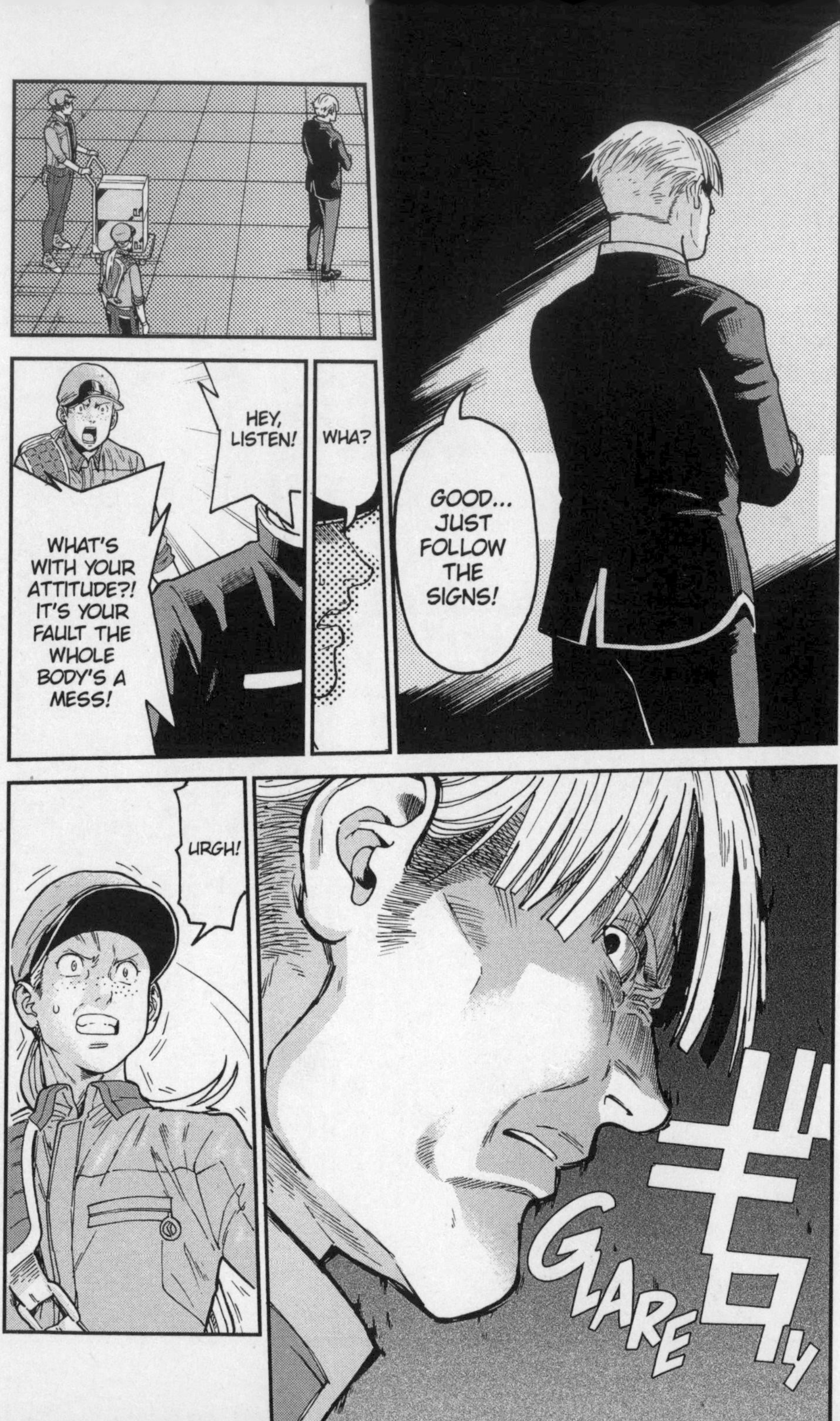
GOOD... JUST FOLLOW THE SIGNS!
WHA?
HEY, LISTEN!
WHAT'S WITH YOUR ATTITUDE?! IT'S YOUR FAULT THE WHOLE BODY'S A MESS!
ギロッ
GLARE
URGH!

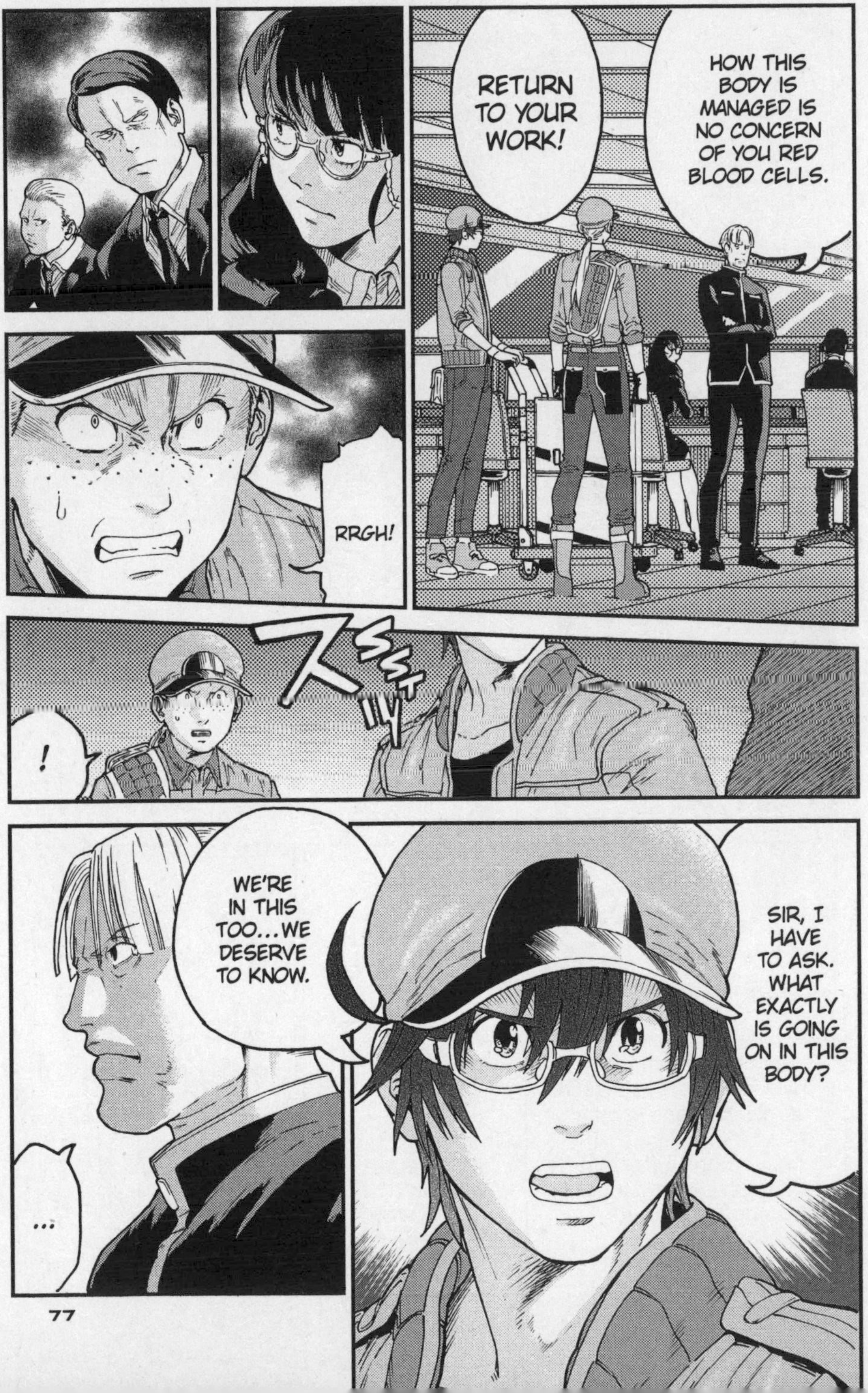
HOW THIS BODY IS MANAGED IS NO CONCERN OF YOU RED BLOOD CELLS.
RETURN TO YOUR WORK!
RRGH!
SSST
!
SIR, I HAVE TO ASK. WHAT EXACTLY IS GOING ON IN THIS BODY?
WE'RE IN THIS TOO...WE DESERVE TO KNOW.
...

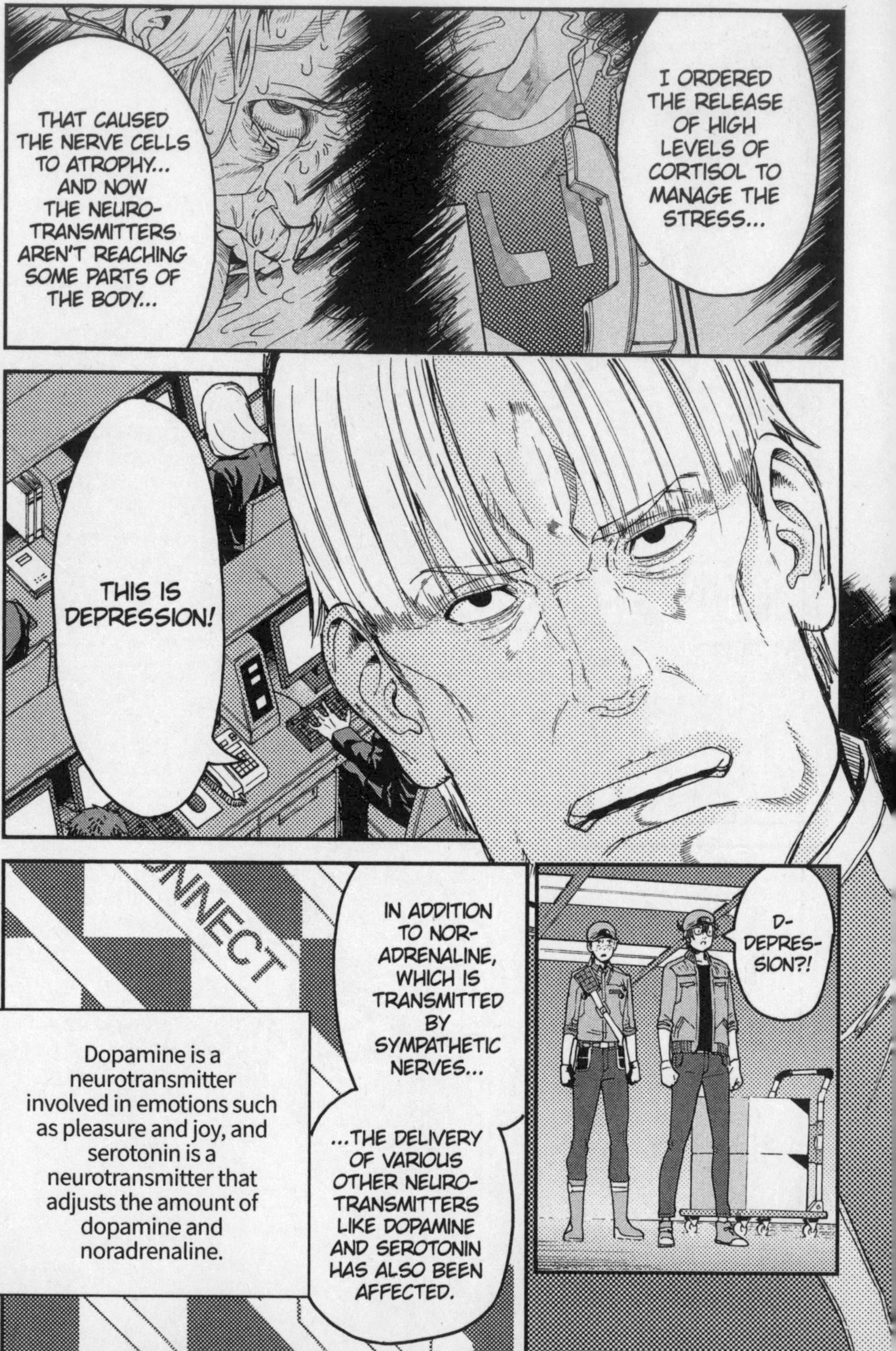
I ORDERED THE RELEASE OF HIGH LEVELS OF CORTISOL TO MANAGE THE STRESS...
THAT CAUSED THE NERVE CELLS TO ATROPHY... AND NOW THE NEURO-TRANSMITTERS AREN'T REACHING SOME PARTS OF THE BODY...
THIS IS DEPRESSION!
D-DEPRES-SION?!
IN ADDITION TO NOR-ADRENALINE, WHICH IS TRANSMITTED BY SYMPATHETIC NERVES...
...THE DELIVERY OF VARIOUS OTHER NEURO-TRANSMITTERS LIKE DOPAMINE AND SEROTONIN HAS ALSO BEEN AFFECTED.
Dopamine is a neurotransmitter involved in emotions such as pleasure and joy, and serotonin is a neurotransmitter that adjusts the amount of dopamine and noradrenaline.
UNNECT

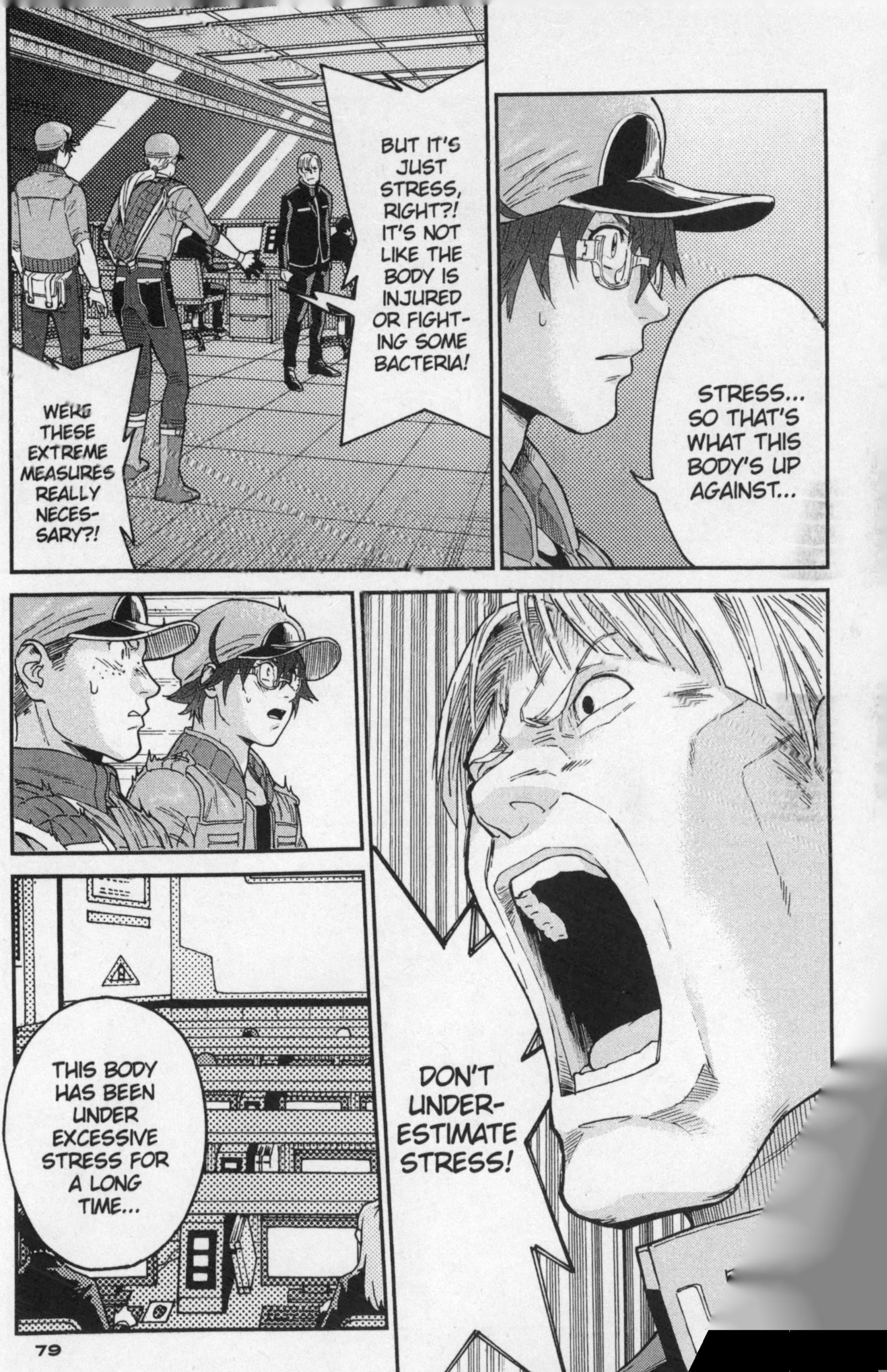
STRESS... SO THAT'S WHAT THIS BODY'S UP AGAINST...
BUT IT'S JUST STRESS, RIGHT?! IT'S NOT LIKE THE BODY IS INJURED OR FIGHTING SOME BACTERIA!
WERE THESE EXTREME MEASURES REALLY NECESSARY?!
DON'T UNDERESTIMATE STRESS!
THIS BODY HAS BEEN UNDER EXCESSIVE STRESS FOR A LONG TIME...

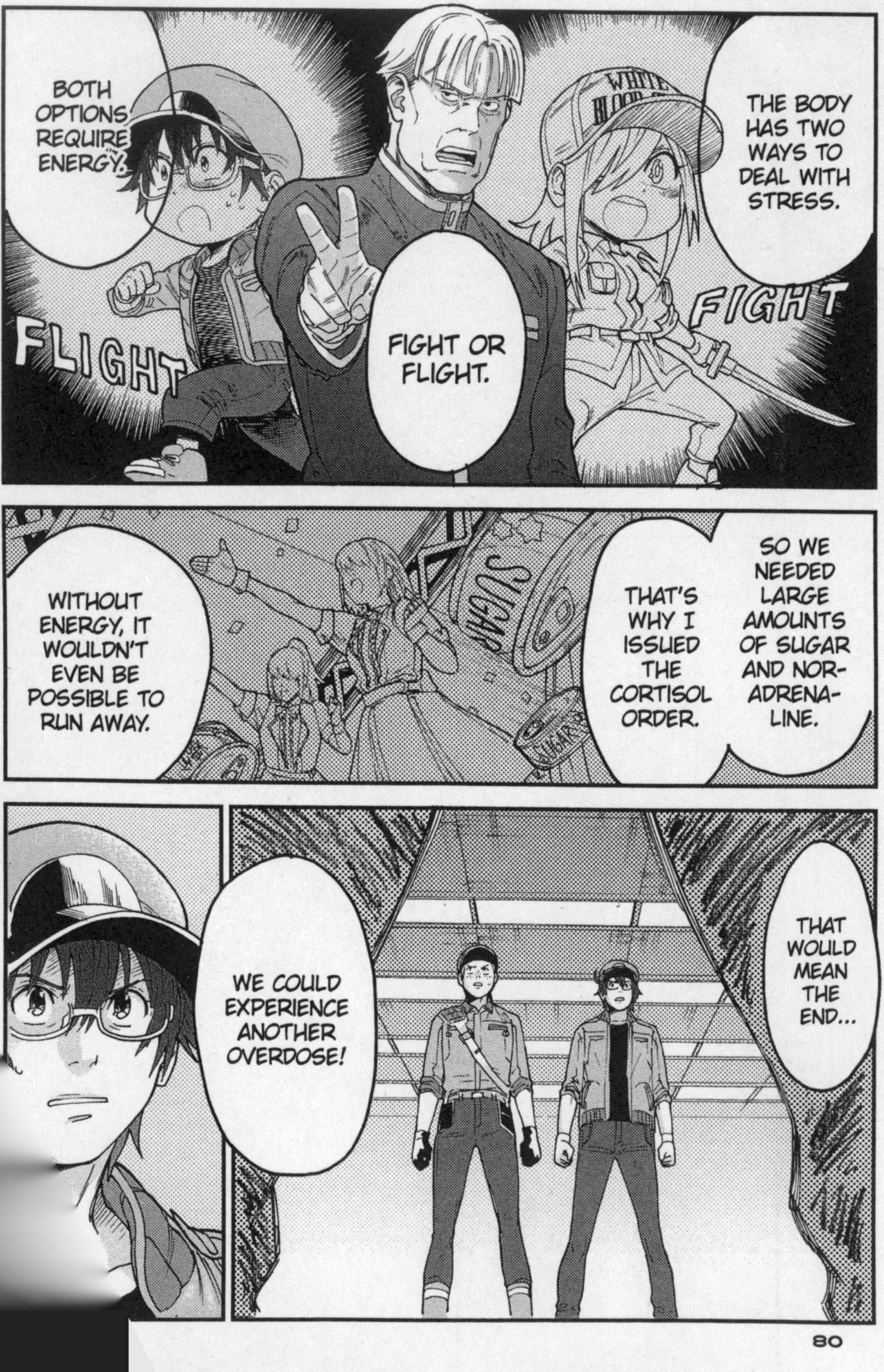
THE BODY HAS TWO WAYS TO DEAL WITH STRESS.
FIGHT OR FLIGHT.
BOTH OPTIONS REQUIRE ENERGY.
FIGHT
FLIGHT
SO WE NEEDED LARGE AMOUNTS OF SUGAR AND NOR-ADRENALINE.
THAT'S WHY I ISSUED THE CORTISOL ORDER.
SUGAR
WITHOUT ENERGY, IT WOULDN'T EVEN BE POSSIBLE TO RUN AWAY.
THAT WOULD MEAN THE END...
WE COULD EXPERIENCE ANOTHER OVERDOSE!

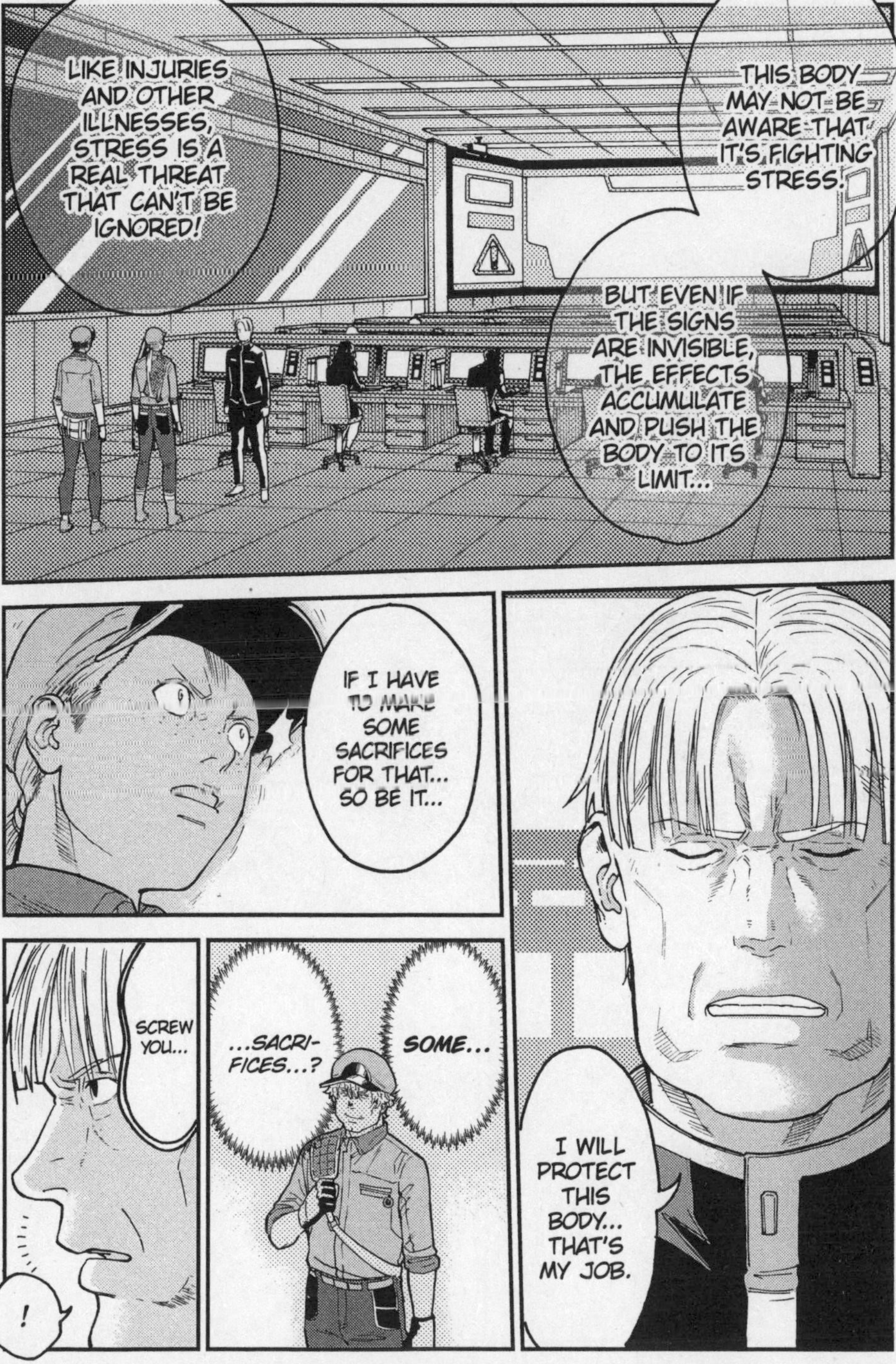
THIS BODY MAY NOT BE AWARE THAT IT'S FIGHTING STRESS.
LIKE INJURIES AND OTHER ILLNESSES, STRESS IS A REAL THREAT THAT CAN'T BE IGNORED!
BUT EVEN IF THE SIGNS ARE INVISIBLE, THE EFFECTS ACCUMULATE AND PUSH THE BODY TO ITS LIMIT...
I WILL PROTECT THIS BODY... THAT'S MY JOB.
IF I HAVE TO MAKE SOME SACRIFICES FOR THAT... SO BE IT...
SOME...
...SACRI-FICES...?
SCREW YOU...
!

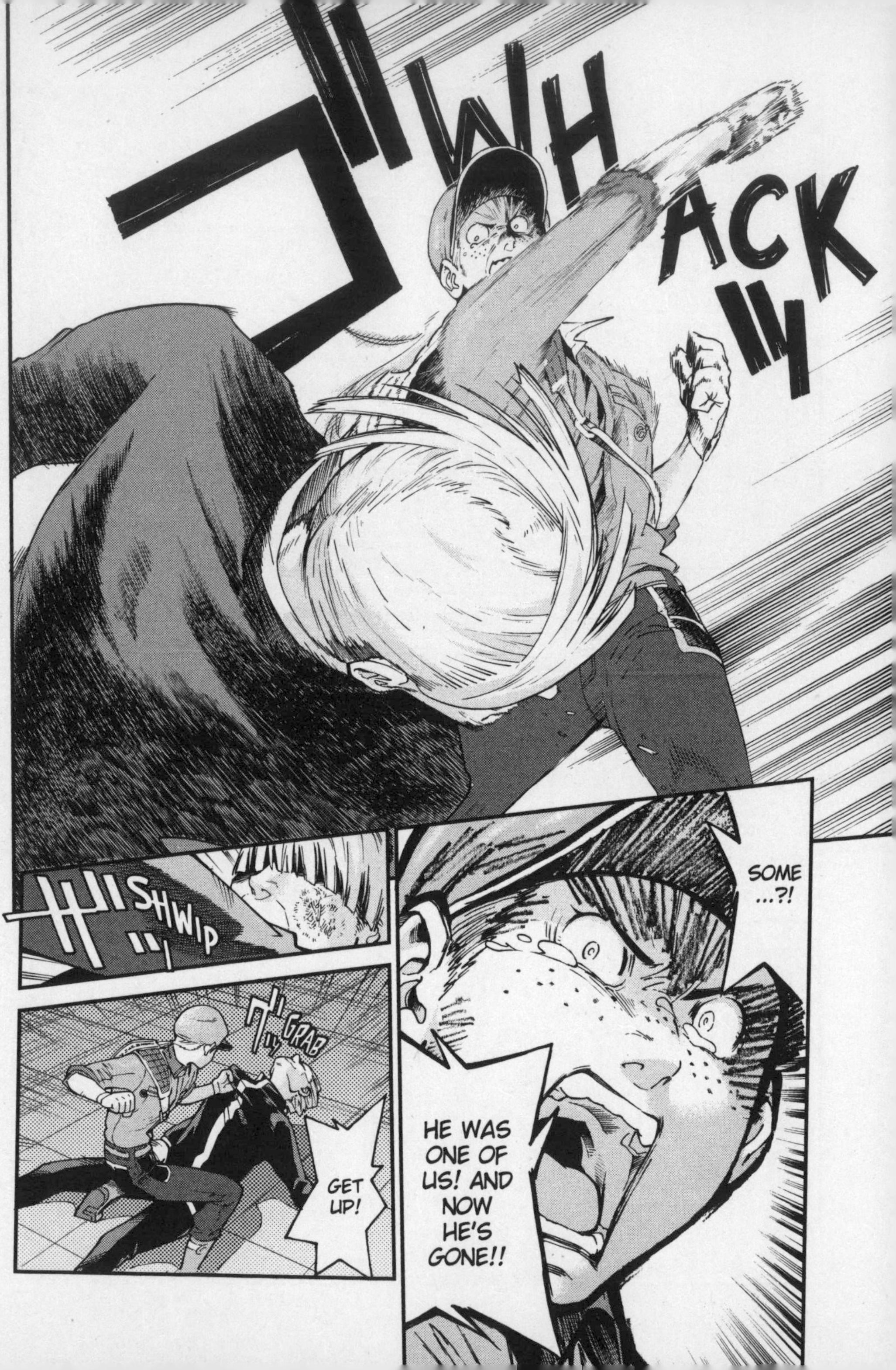
WHACK
SOME ...?!
HE WAS ONE OF US! AND NOW HE'S GONE!!
SHWIP
GRAB
GET UP!

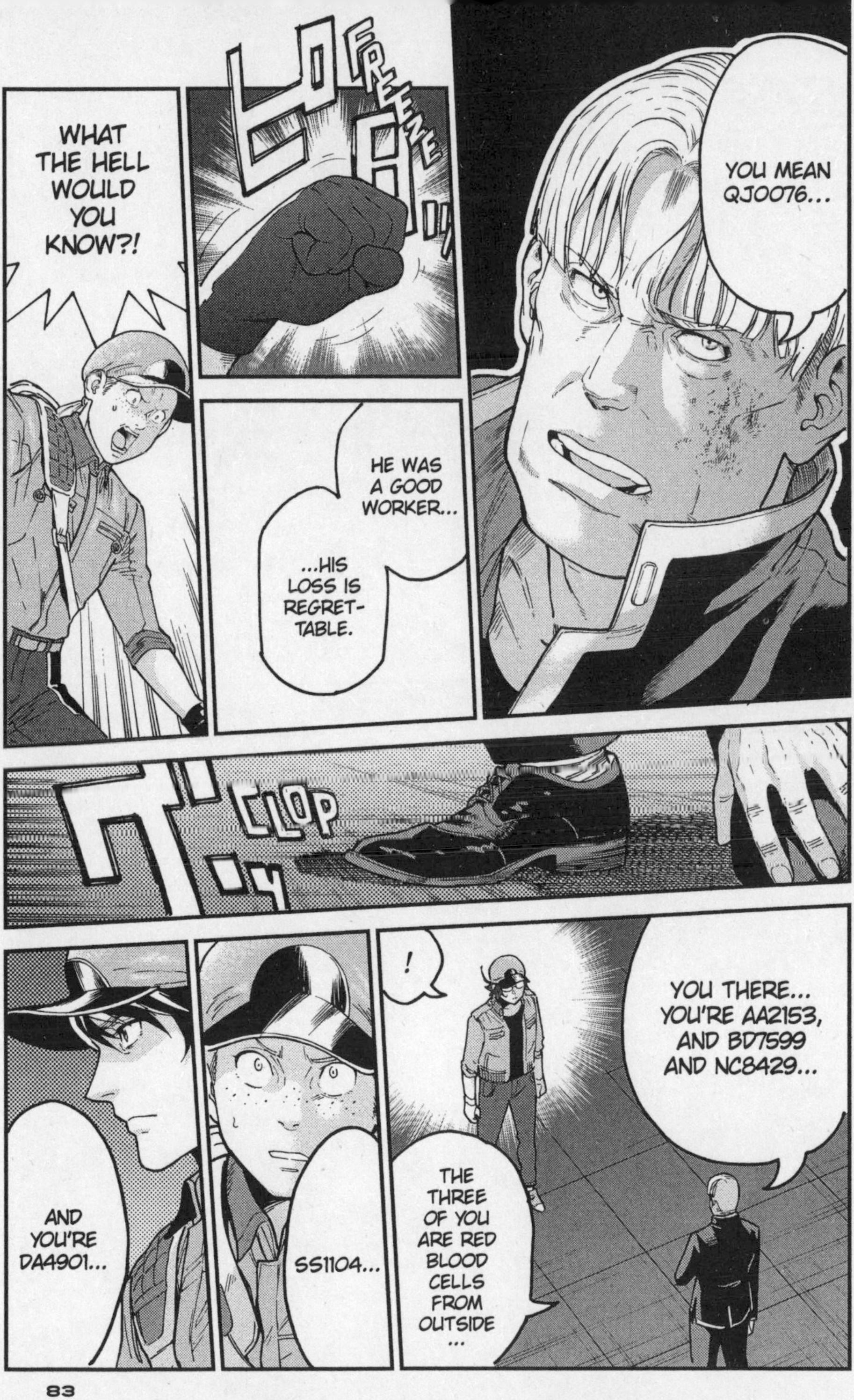
YOU MEAN QJ0076...
FREEZE
HE WAS A GOOD WORKER...
...HIS LOSS IS REGRET-TABLE.
WHAT THE HELL WOULD YOU KNOW?!
CLOP
YOU THERE... YOU'RE AA2153, AND BD7599 AND NC8429...
!
THE THREE OF YOU ARE RED BLOOD CELLS FROM OUTSIDE ...
SS1104...
AND YOU'RE DA4901...

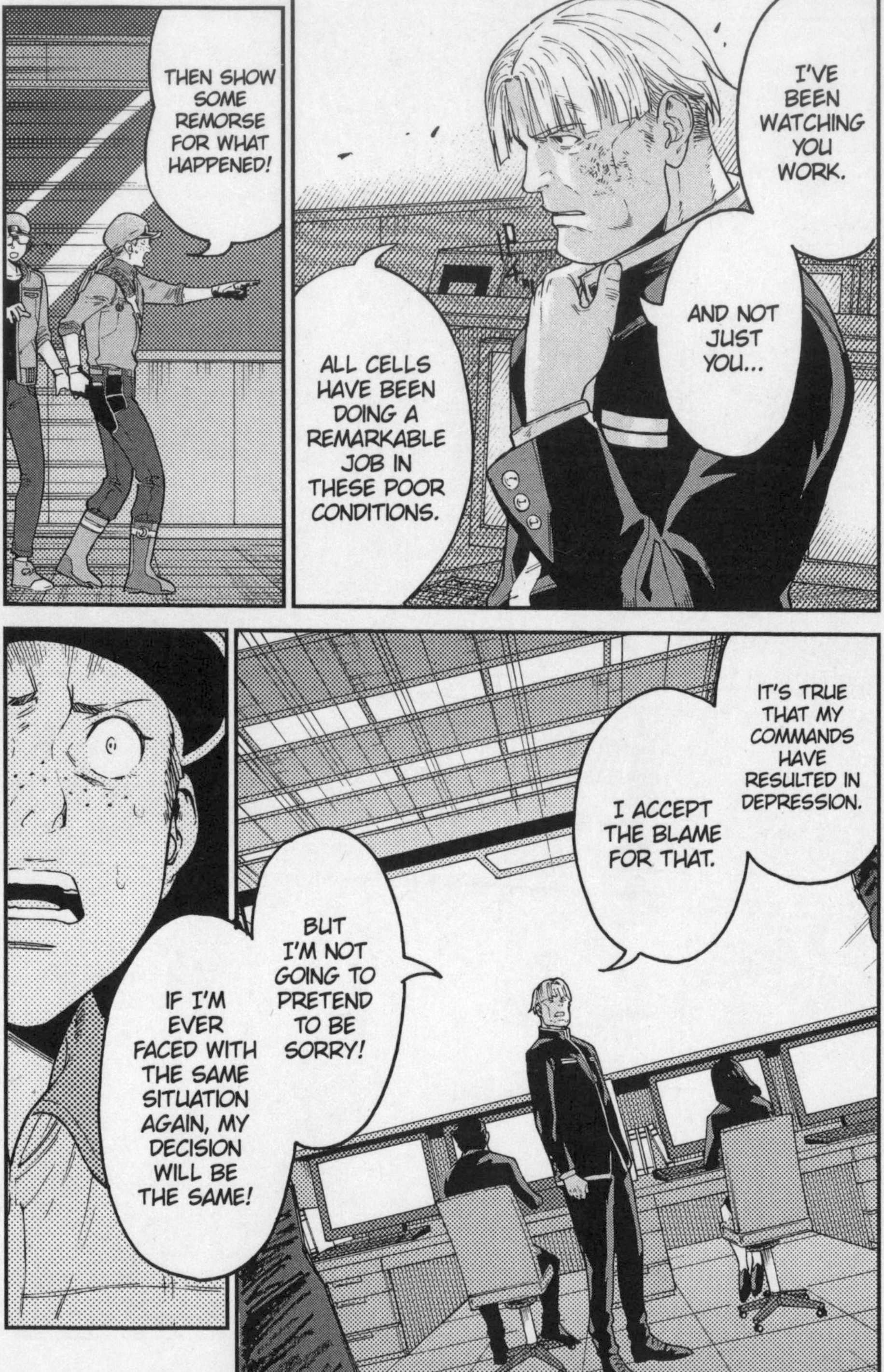
I'VE BEEN WATCHING YOU WORK.
AND NOT JUST YOU...
ALL CELLS HAVE BEEN DOING A REMARKABLE JOB IN THESE POOR CONDITIONS.
THEN SHOW SOME REMORSE FOR WHAT HAPPENED!
IT'S TRUE THAT MY COMMANDS HAVE RESULTED IN DEPRESSION.
I ACCEPT THE BLAME FOR THAT.
BUT I'M NOT GOING TO PRETEND TO BE SORRY!
IF I'M EVER FACED WITH THE SAME SITUATION AGAIN, MY DECISION WILL BE THE SAME!

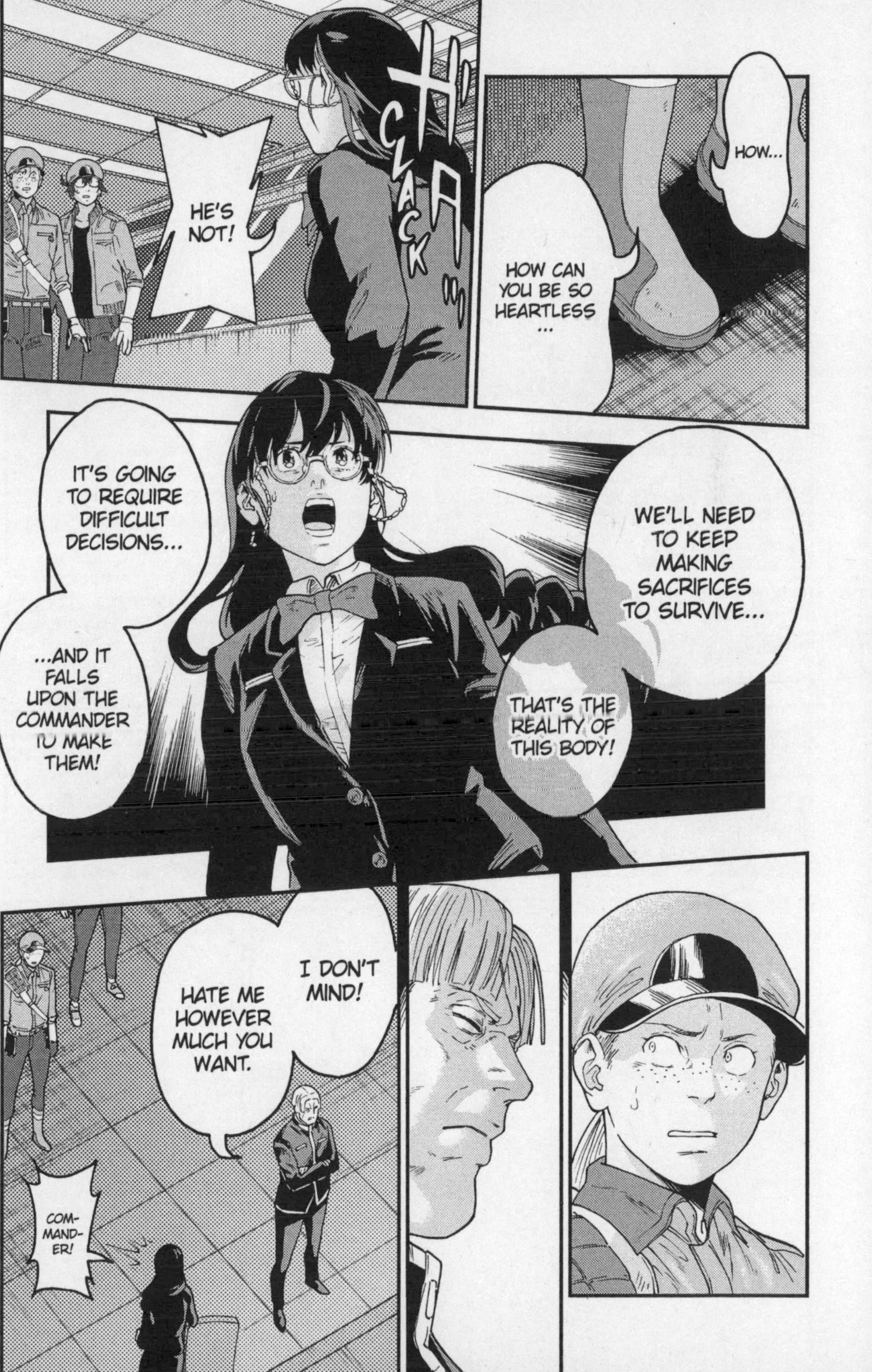
HOW...
HOW CAN YOU BE SO HEARTLESS...
CLACK
HE'S NOT!
WE'LL NEED TO KEEP MAKING SACRIFICES TO SURVIVE...
IT'S GOING TO REQUIRE DIFFICULT DECISIONS...
THAT'S THE REALITY OF THIS BODY!
...AND IT FALLS UPON THE COMMANDER TO MAKE THEM!
I DON'T MIND!
HATE ME HOWEVER MUCH YOU WANT.
COMMANDER!

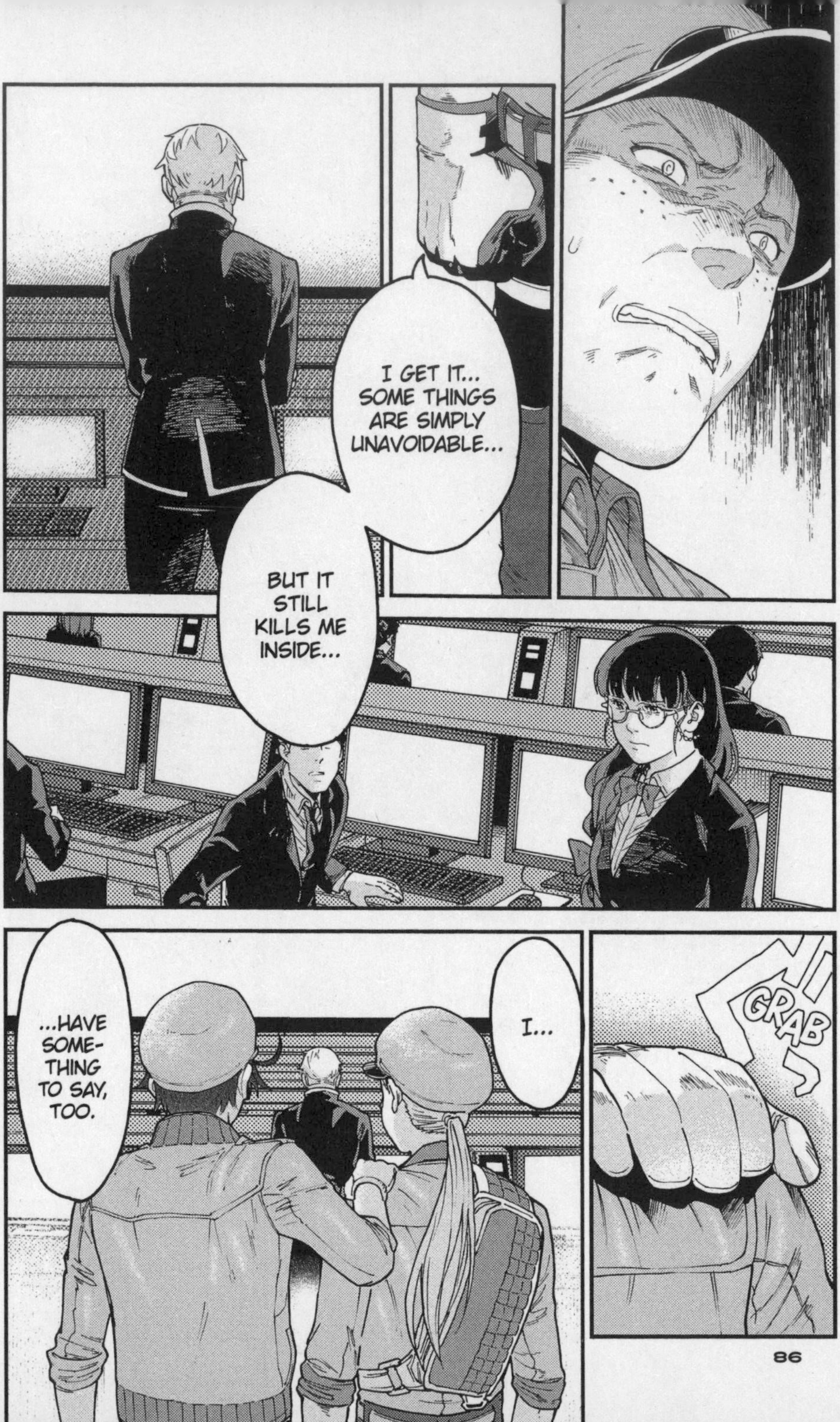
I GET IT... SOME THINGS ARE SIMPLY UNAVOIDABLE...
BUT IT STILL KILLS ME INSIDE...
GRAB
I...
...HAVE SOME-THING TO SAY, TOO.

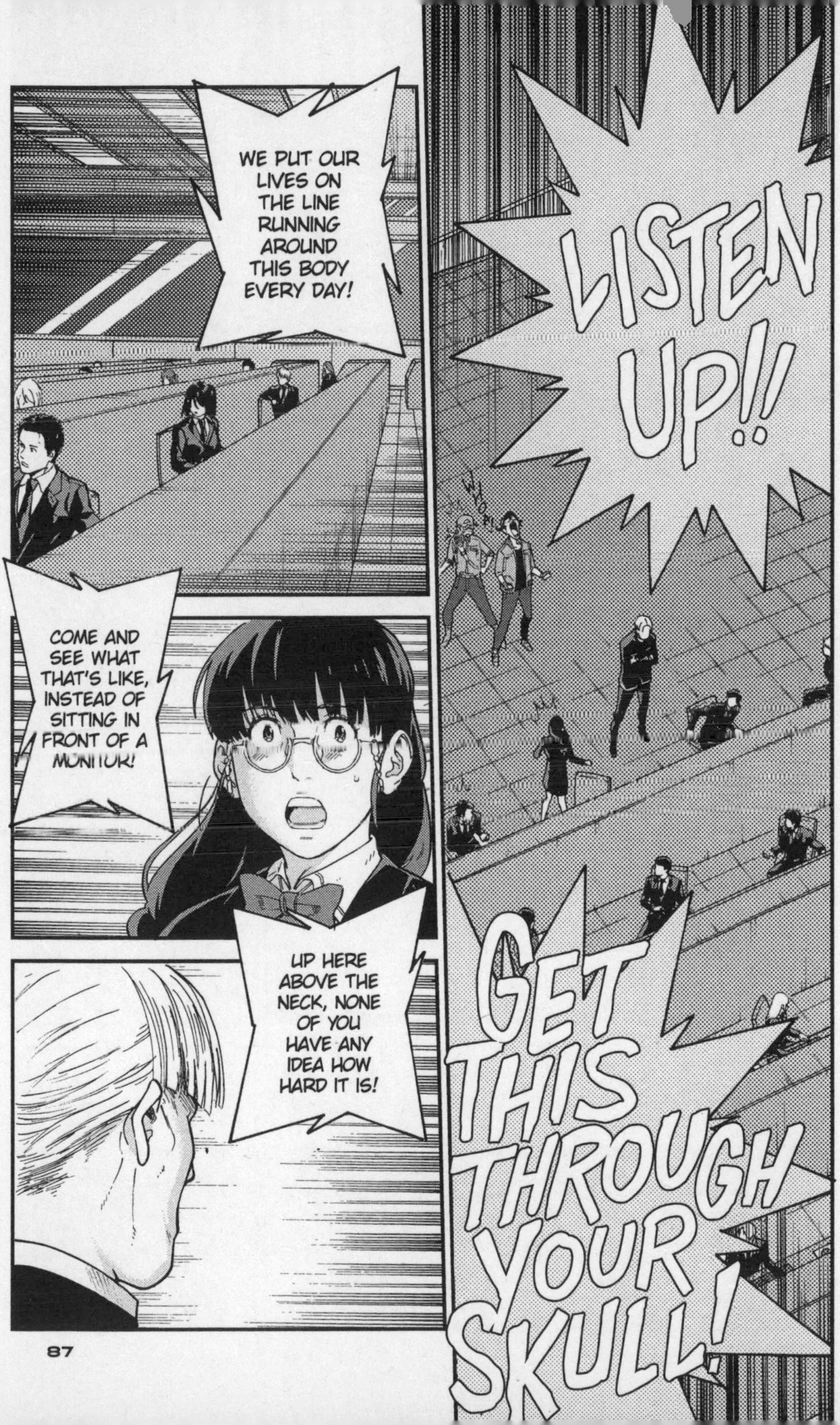
LISTEN UP!!
GET THIS THROUGH YOUR SKULL!
WE PUT OUR LIVES ON THE LINE RUNNING AROUND THIS BODY EVERY DAY!
COME AND SEE WHAT THAT'S LIKE, INSTEAD OF SITTING IN FRONT OF A MONITOR!
UP HERE ABOVE THE NECK, NONE OF YOU HAVE ANY IDEA HOW HARD IT IS!

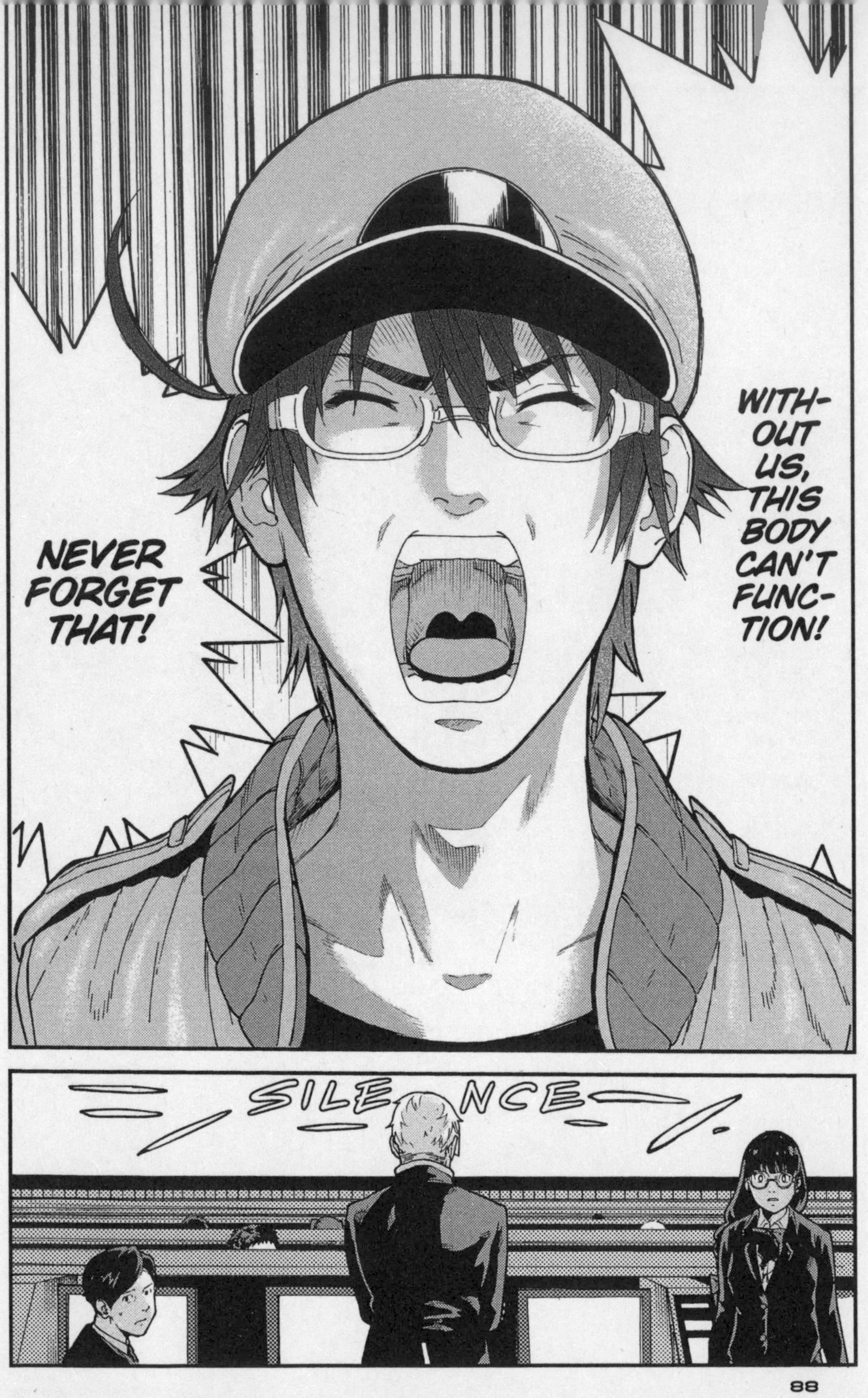
WITH-OUT US, THIS BODY CAN'T FUNC-TION!
NEVER FORGET THAT!
SILENCE

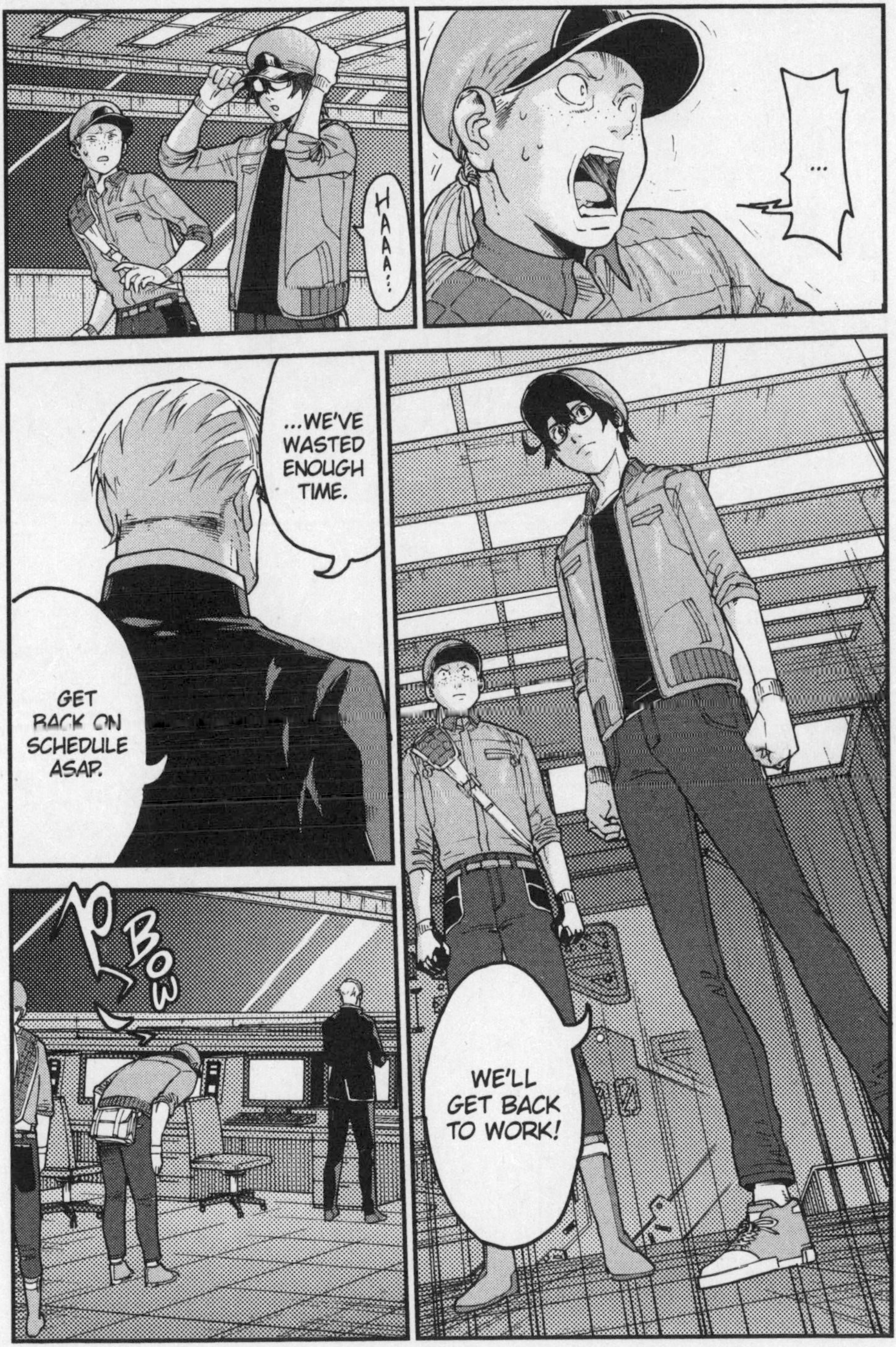
...
HAAAA?!
WE'LL GET BACK TO WORK!
...WE'VE WASTED ENOUGH TIME.
GET BACK ON SCHEDULE ASAP.
BOW

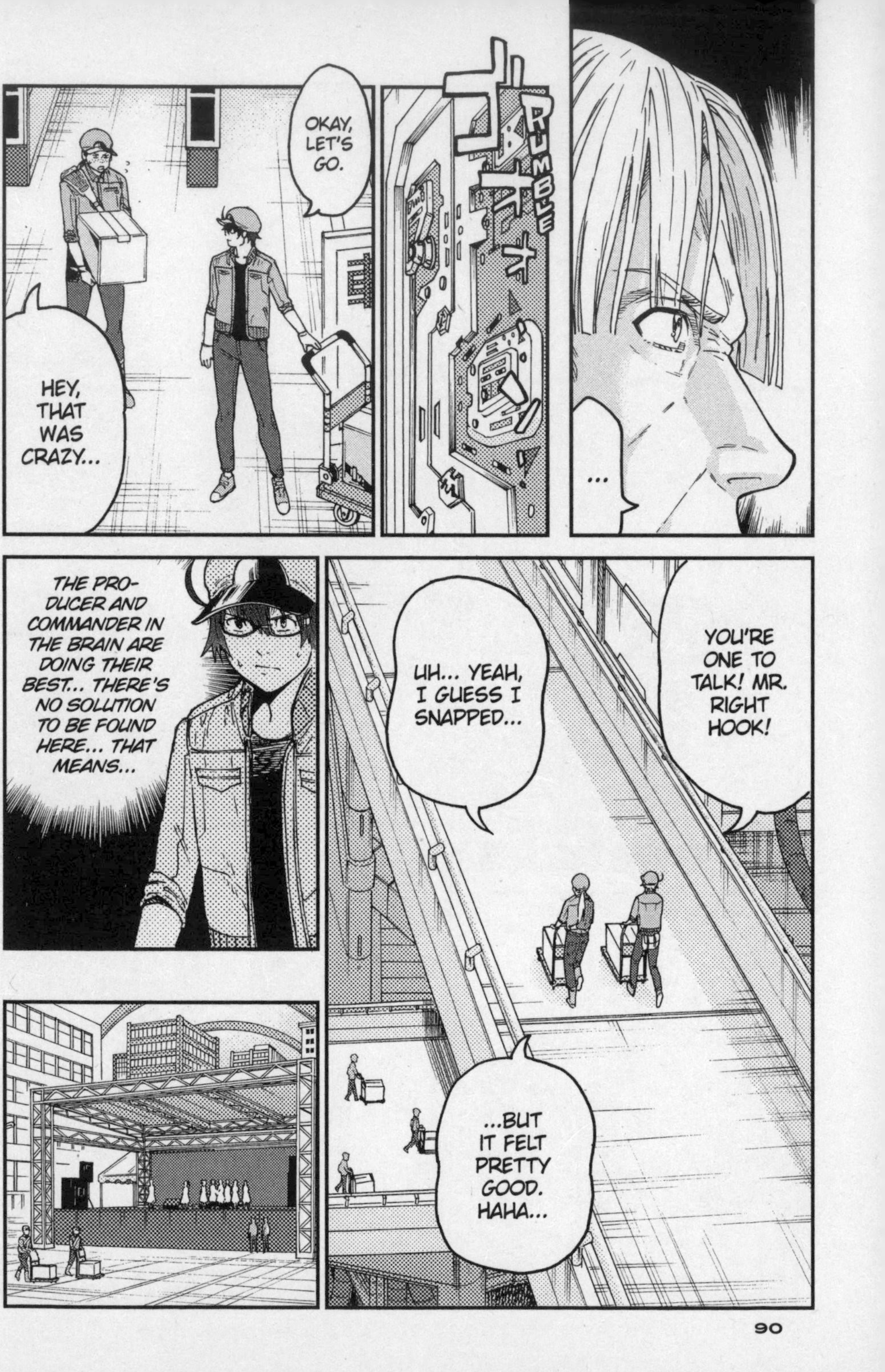
...
RUMBLE
OKAY, LET'S GO.
HEY, THAT WAS CRAZY...
YOU'RE ONE TO TALK! MR. RIGHT HOOK!
UH... YEAH, I GUESS I SNAPPED...
...BUT IT FELT PRETTY GOOD. HAHA...
THE PRO-DUCER AND COMMANDER IN THE BRAIN ARE DOING THEIR BEST... THERE'S NO SOLUTION TO BE FOUND HERE... THAT MEANS...

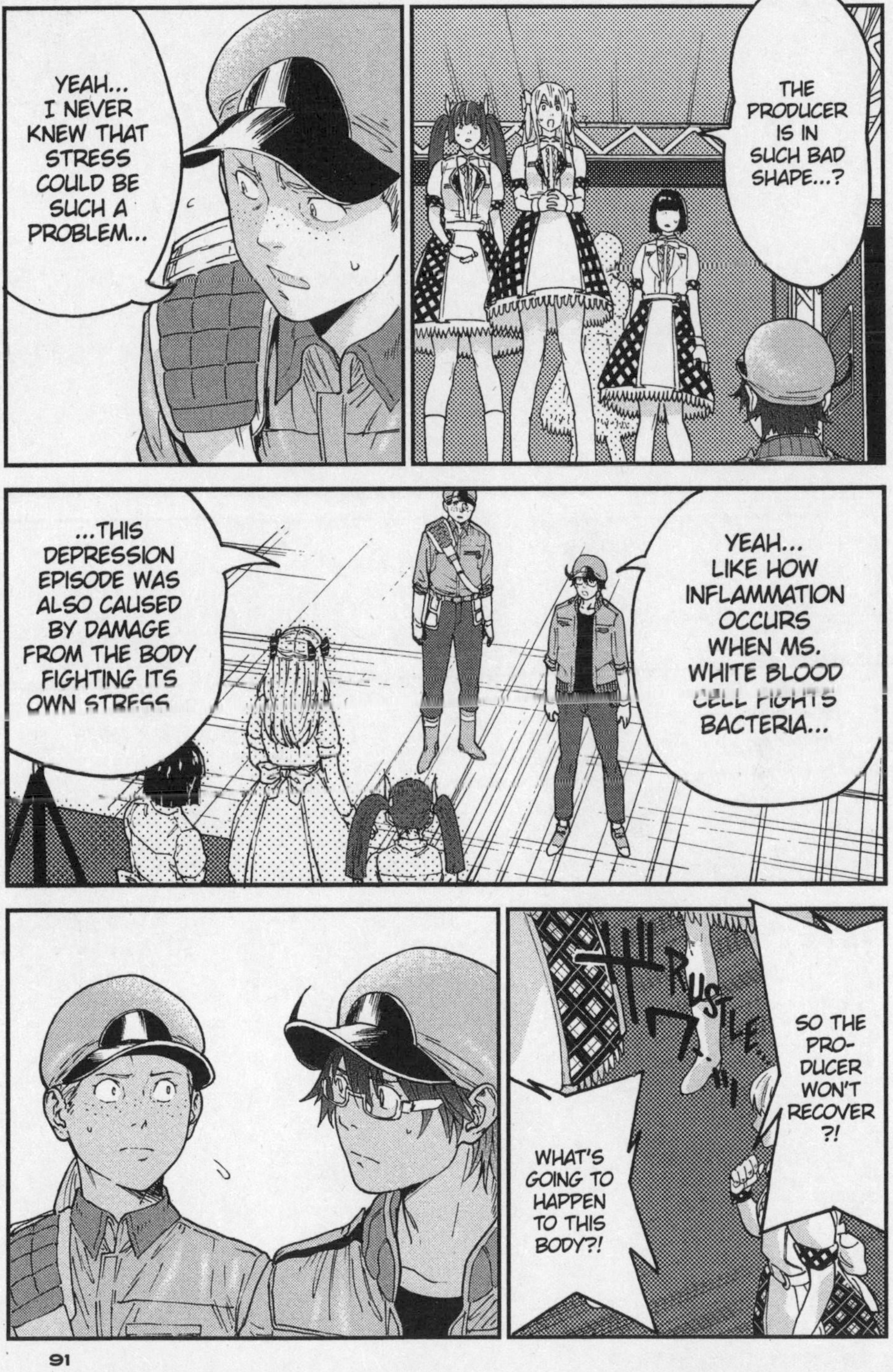
THE PRODUCER IS IN SUCH BAD SHAPE...?
YEAH... I NEVER KNEW THAT STRESS COULD BE SUCH A PROBLEM...
YEAH... LIKE HOW INFLAMMATION OCCURS WHEN MS. WHITE BLOOD CELL FIGHTS BACTERIA...
...THIS DEPRESSION EPISODE WAS ALSO CAUSED BY DAMAGE FROM THE BODY FIGHTING ITS OWN STRESS
RUSTLE...
SO THE PRO-DUCER WON'T RECOVER?!
WHAT'S GOING TO HAPPEN TO THIS BODY?!

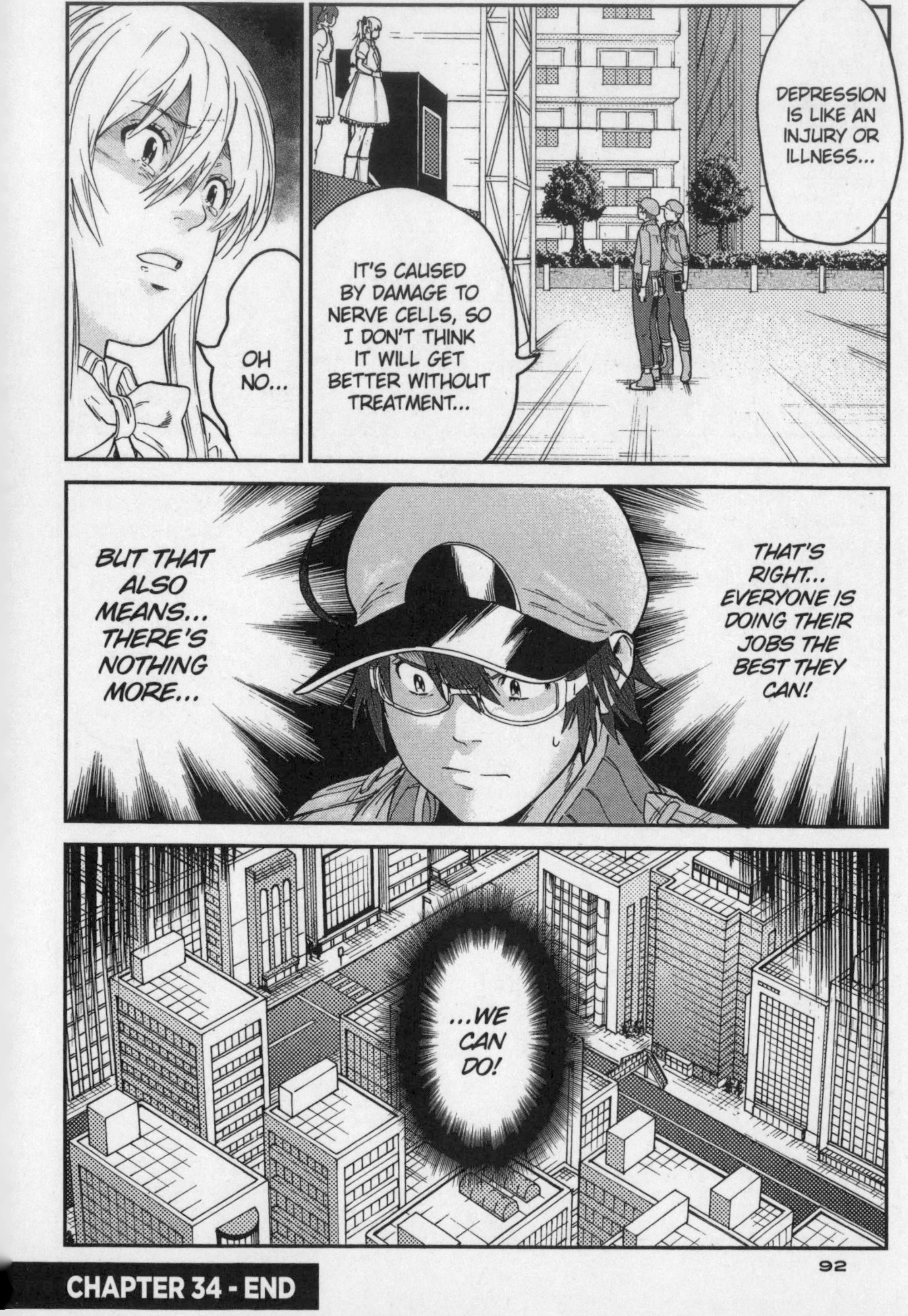
DEPRESSION IS LIKE AN INJURY OR ILLNESS...
IT'S CAUSED BY DAMAGE TO NERVE CELLS, SO I DON'T THINK IT WILL GET BETTER WITHOUT TREATMENT...
OH NO...
THAT'S RIGHT... EVERYONE IS DOING THEIR JOBS THE BEST THEY CAN!
BUT THAT ALSO MEANS... THERE'S NOTHING MORE...
...WE CAN DO!

CHAPTER 34 - END

35. DRUGS, QUITTING SMOKING, FEAR

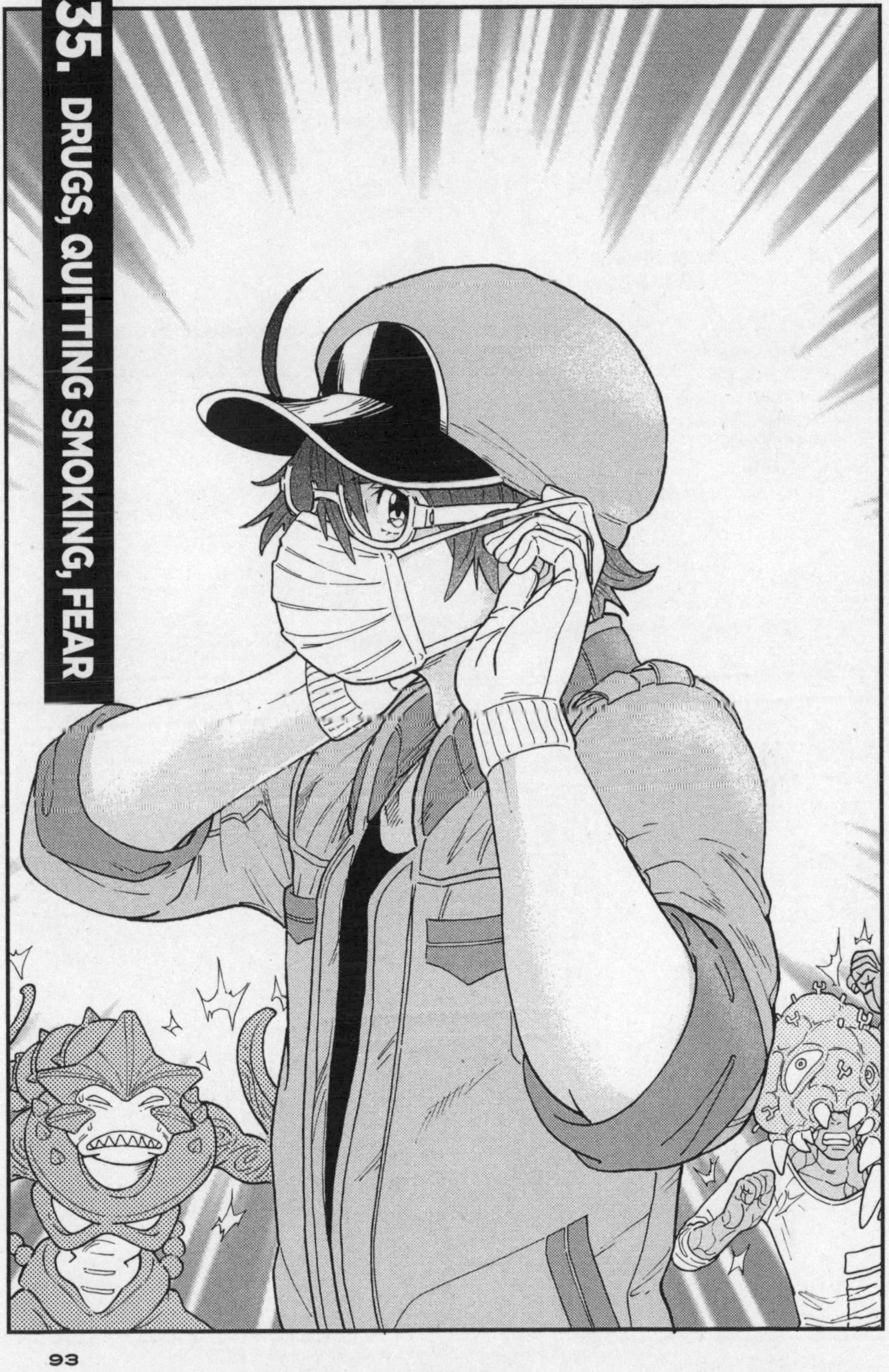

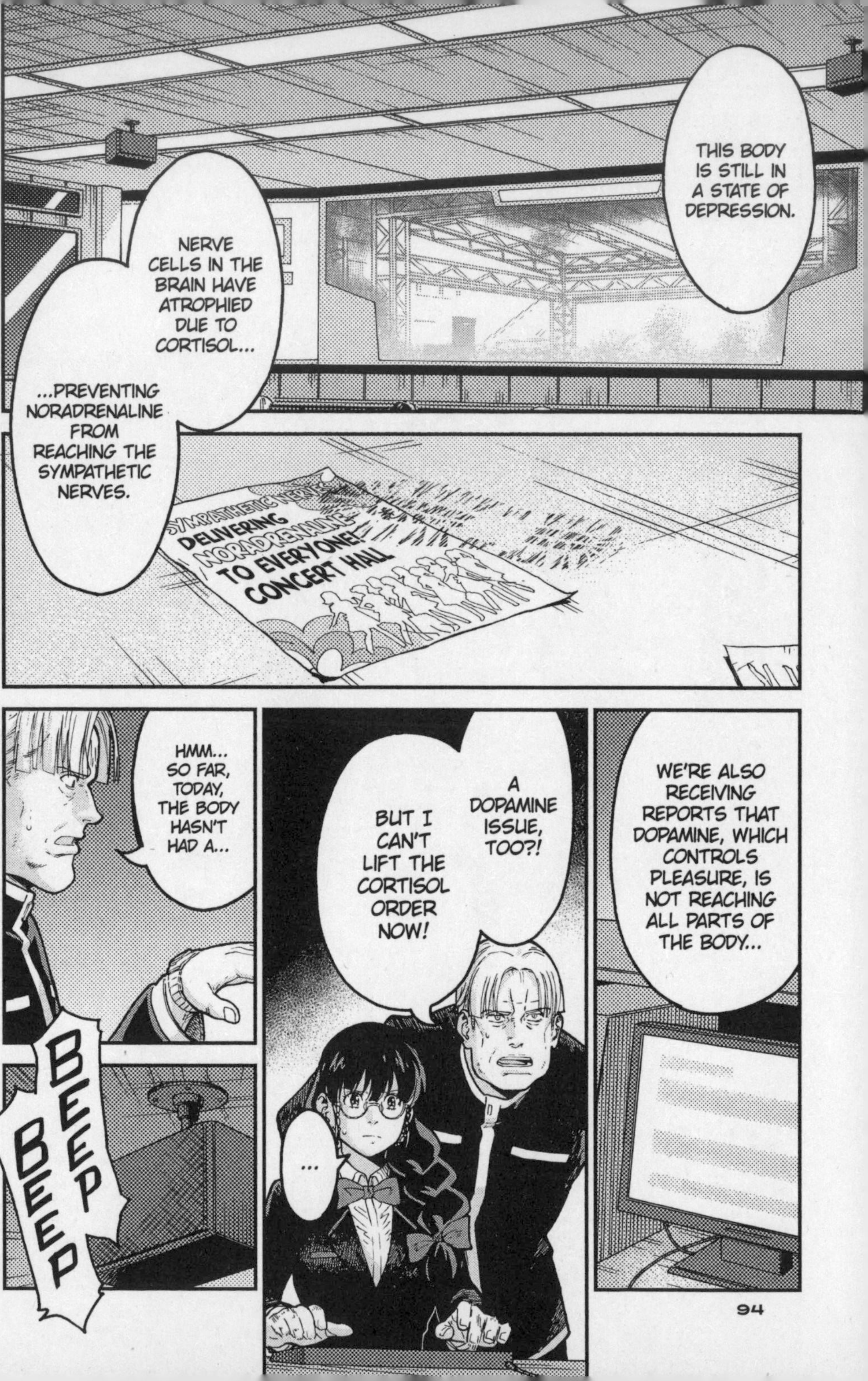
THIS BODY IS STILL IN A STATE OF DEPRESSION.
NERVE CELLS IN THE BRAIN HAVE ATROPHIED DUE TO CORTISOL...
...PREVENTING NORADRENALINE FROM REACHING THE SYMPATHETIC NERVES.
SYMPATHETIC NERVES DELIVERING NORADRENALINE TO EVERYONE! CONCERT HALL
WE'RE ALSO RECEIVING REPORTS THAT DOPAMINE, WHICH CONTROLS PLEASURE, IS NOT REACHING ALL PARTS OF THE BODY...
A DOPAMINE ISSUE, TOO?!
BUT I CAN'T LIFT THE CORTISOL ORDER NOW!
...
HMM... SO FAR, TODAY, THE BODY HASN'T HAD A...
BEEP BEEP

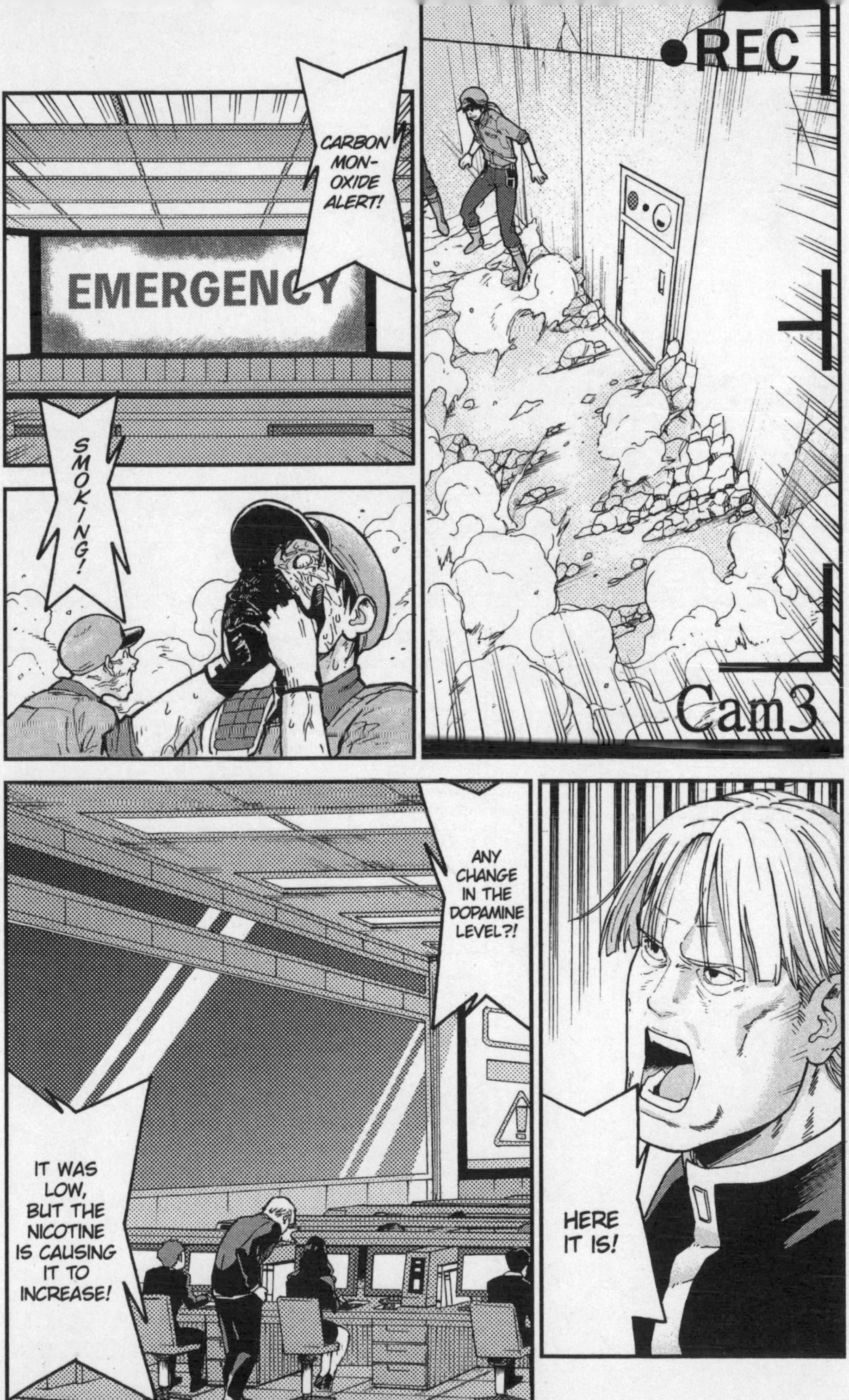
●REC
Cam3
CARBON MON-OXIDE ALERT!
EMERGENCY
SMOKING!
ANY CHANGE IN THE DOPAMINE LEVEL?!
HERE IT IS!
IT WAS LOW, BUT THE NICOTINE IS CAUSING IT TO INCREASE!

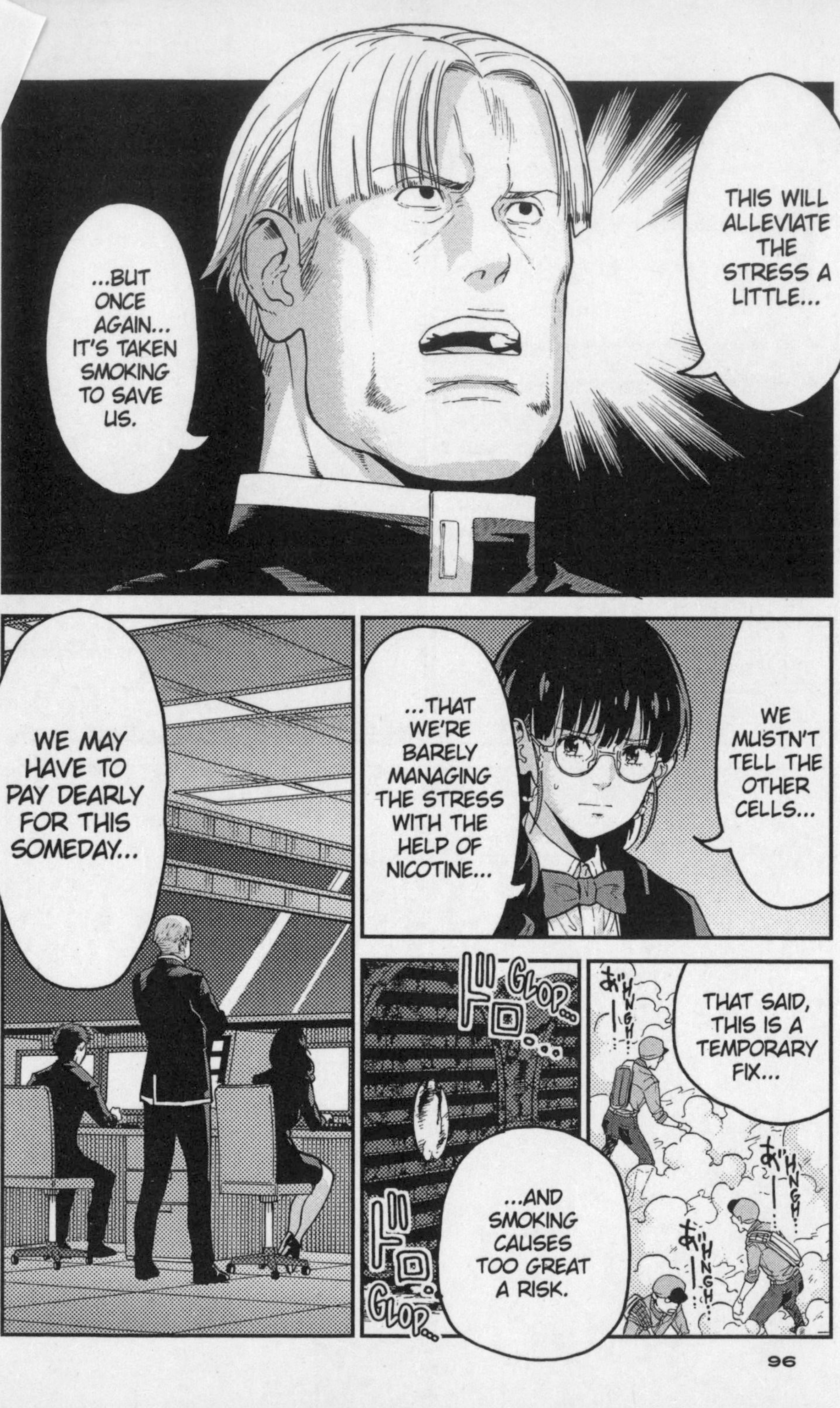
THIS WILL ALLEVIATE THE STRESS A LITTLE...
...BUT ONCE AGAIN... IT'S TAKEN SMOKING TO SAVE US.
WE MUSTN'T TELL THE OTHER CELLS...
...THAT WE'RE BARELY MANAGING THE STRESS WITH THE HELP OF NICOTINE...
HNGH...
THAT SAID, THIS IS A TEMPORARY FIX...
HNGH...
HNGH...
GLOP...
GLOP...
...AND SMOKING CAUSES TOO GREAT A RISK.
WE MAY HAVE TO PAY DEARLY FOR THIS SOMEDAY...

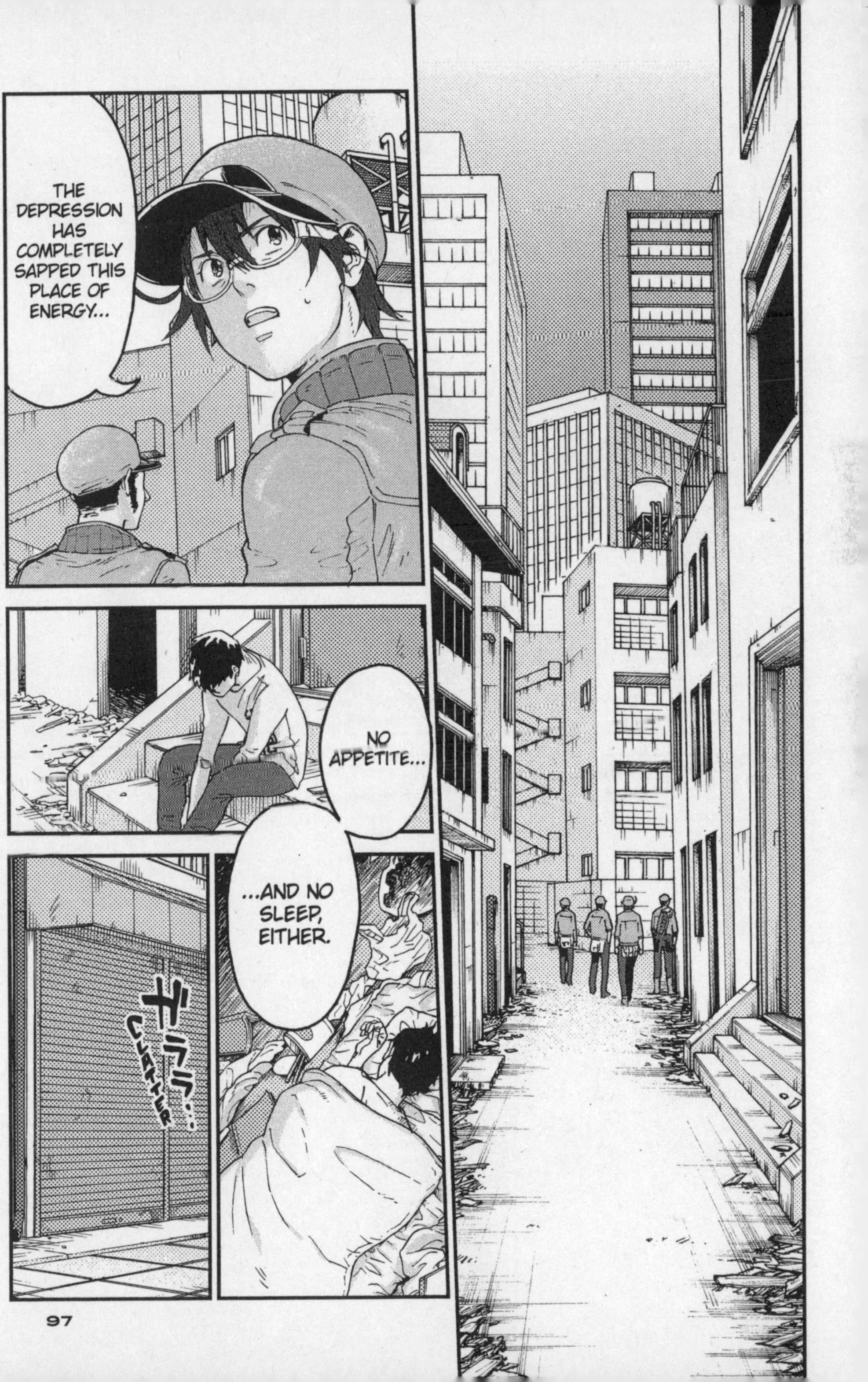
THE DEPRESSION HAS COMPLETELY SAPPED THIS PLACE OF ENERGY...
NO APPETITE...
...AND NO SLEEP, EITHER.
ザララ...
CLATTER

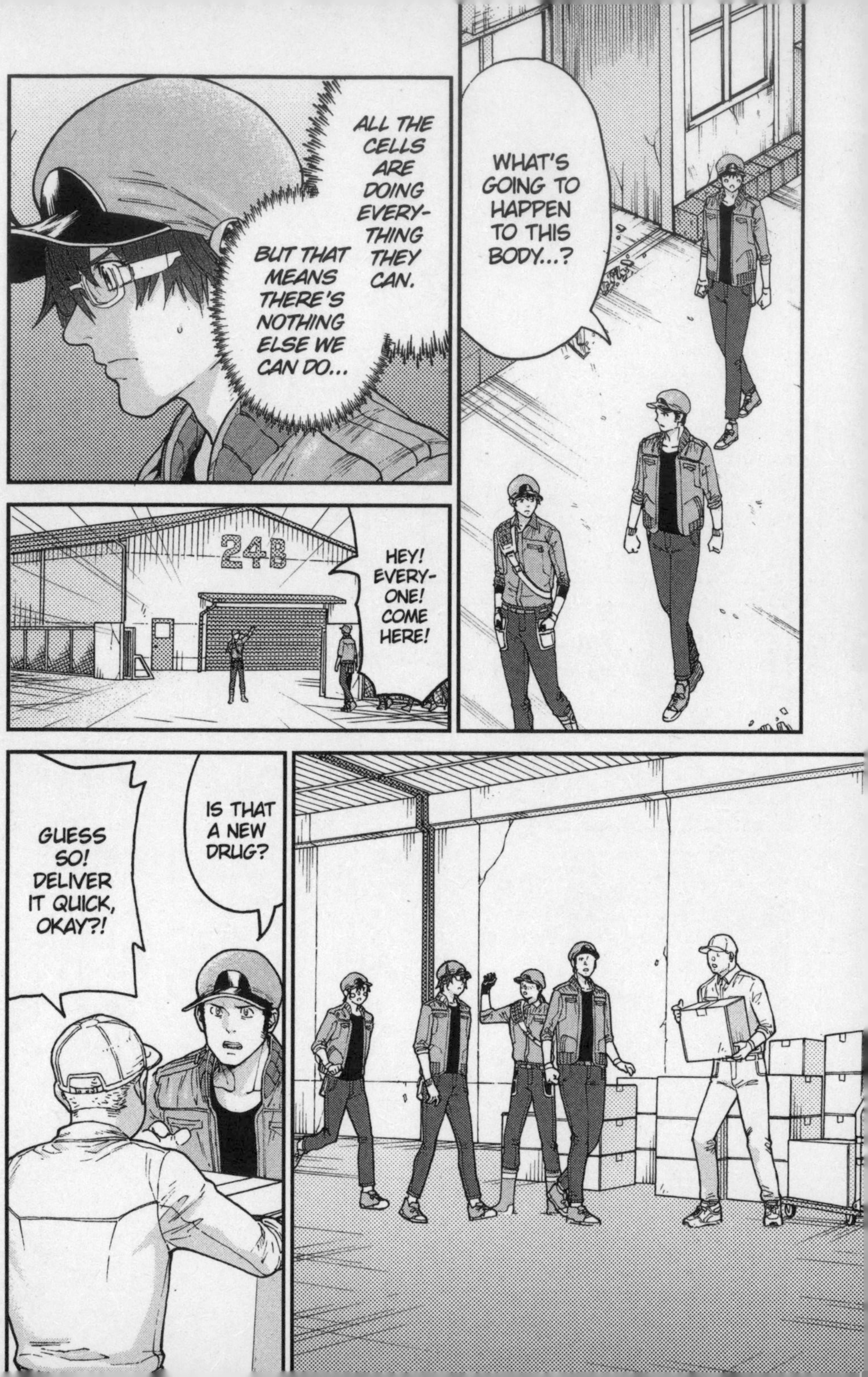
WHAT'S GOING TO HAPPEN TO THIS BODY...?
ALL THE CELLS ARE DOING EVERY-THING THEY CAN.
BUT THAT MEANS THERE'S NOTHING ELSE WE CAN DO...
HEY! EVERY-ONE! COME HERE!
IS THAT A NEW DRUG?
GUESS SO! DELIVER IT QUICK, OKAY?!

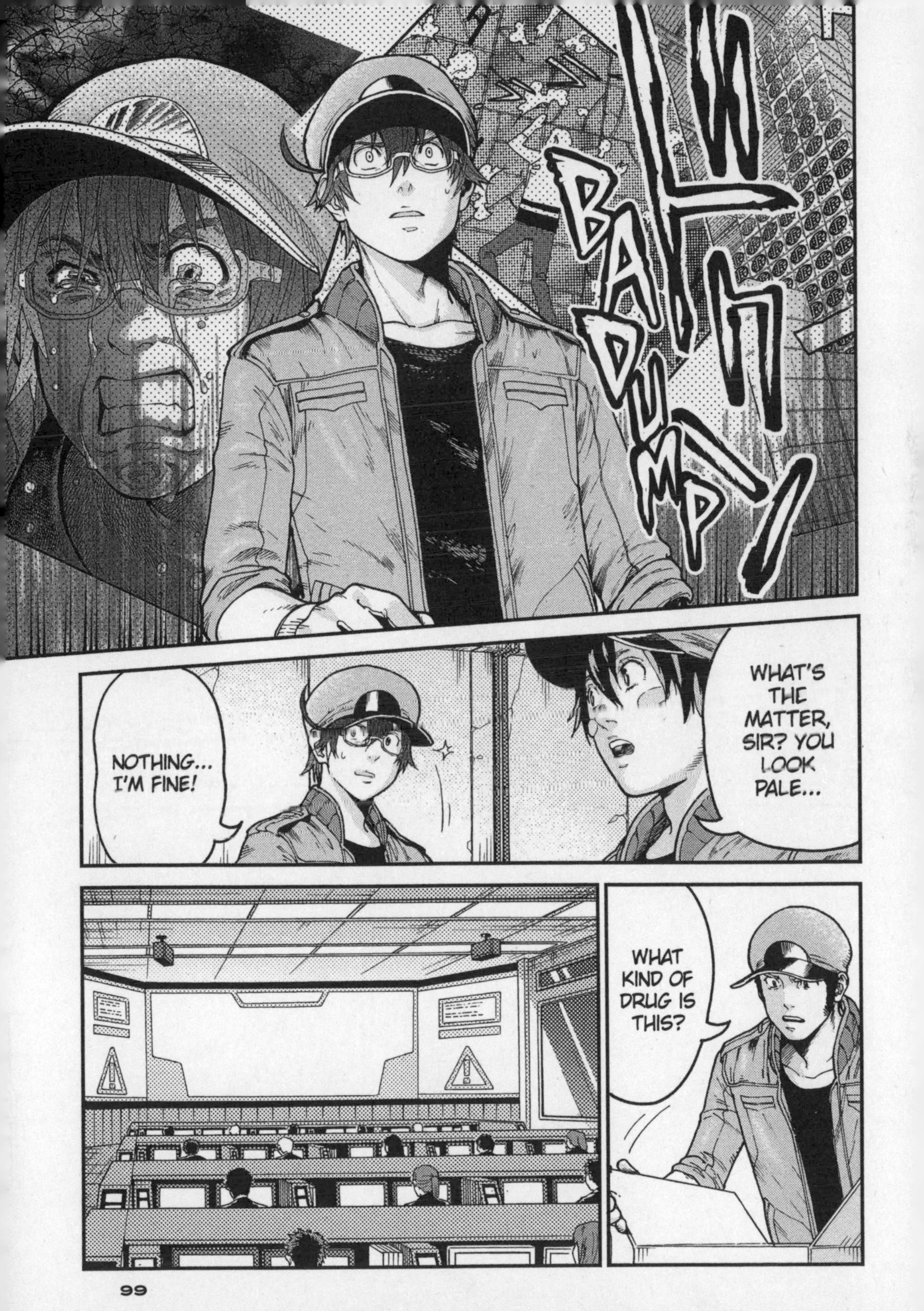
BADUMP!
WHAT'S THE MATTER, SIR? YOU LOOK PALE...
NOTHING... I'M FINE!
WHAT KIND OF DRUG IS THIS?

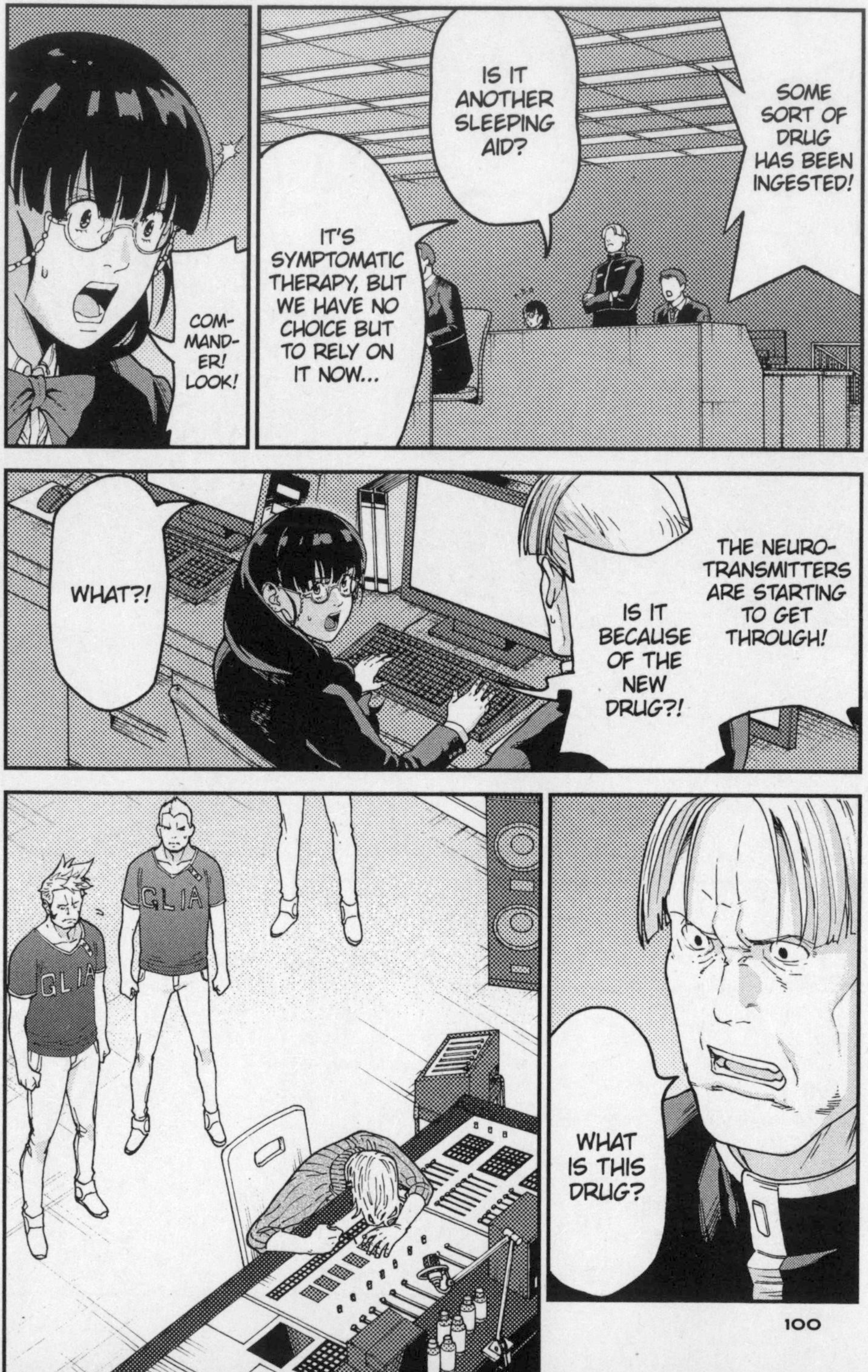
SOME SORT OF DRUG HAS BEEN INGESTED!
IS IT ANOTHER SLEEPING AID?
IT'S SYMPTOMATIC THERAPY, BUT WE HAVE NO CHOICE BUT TO RELY ON IT NOW...
COM-MAND-ER! LOOK!
THE NEURO-TRANSMITTERS ARE STARTING TO GET THROUGH!
IS IT BECAUSE OF THE NEW DRUG?!
WHAT?!
WHAT IS THIS DRUG?
GLIA
GLIA

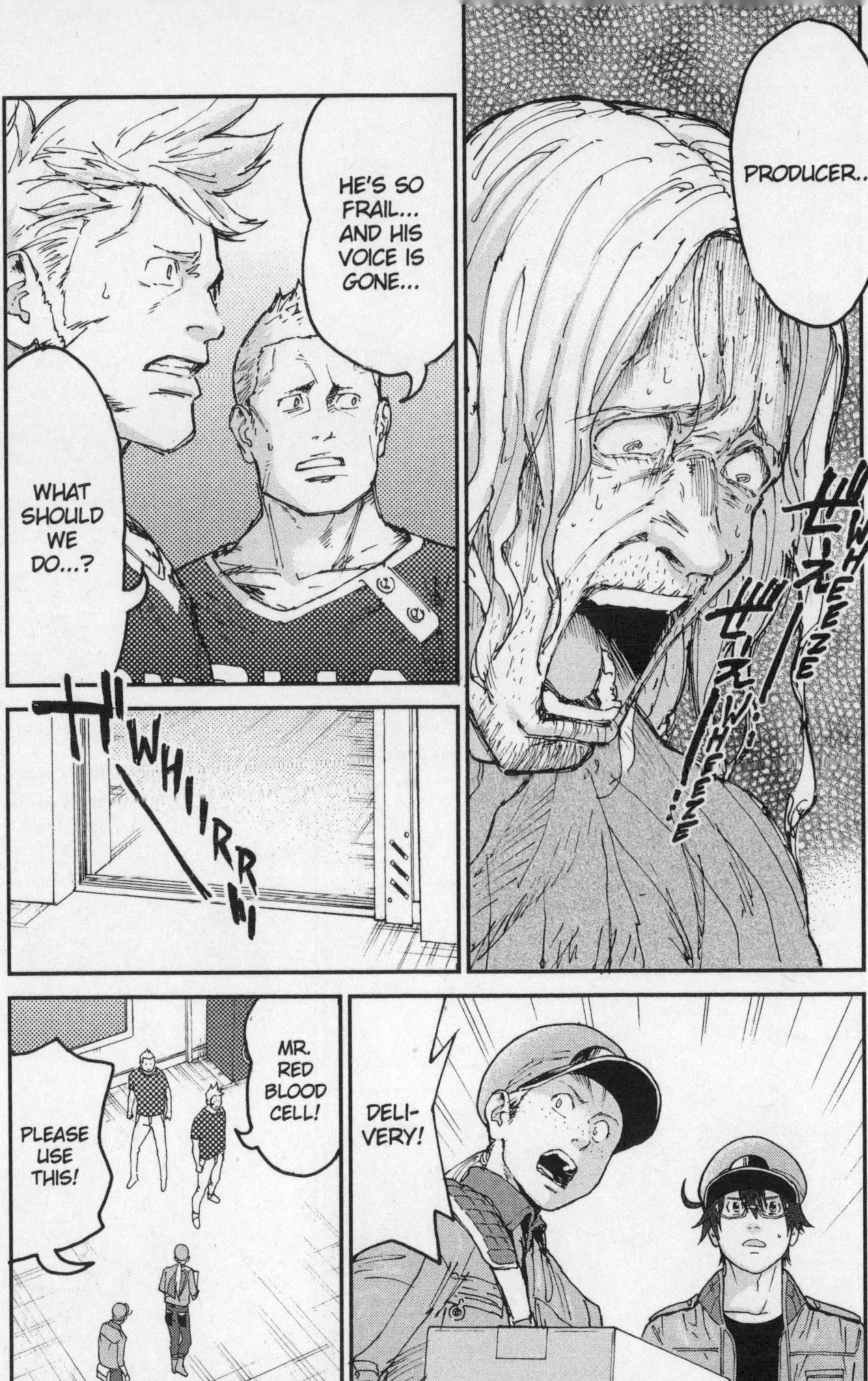
PRODUCER...
WHEEZE
WHEEZE
HE'S SO FRAIL... AND HIS VOICE IS GONE...
WHAT SHOULD WE DO...?
WHIIRRR
DELI-VERY!
MR. RED BLOOD CELL!
PLEASE USE THIS!

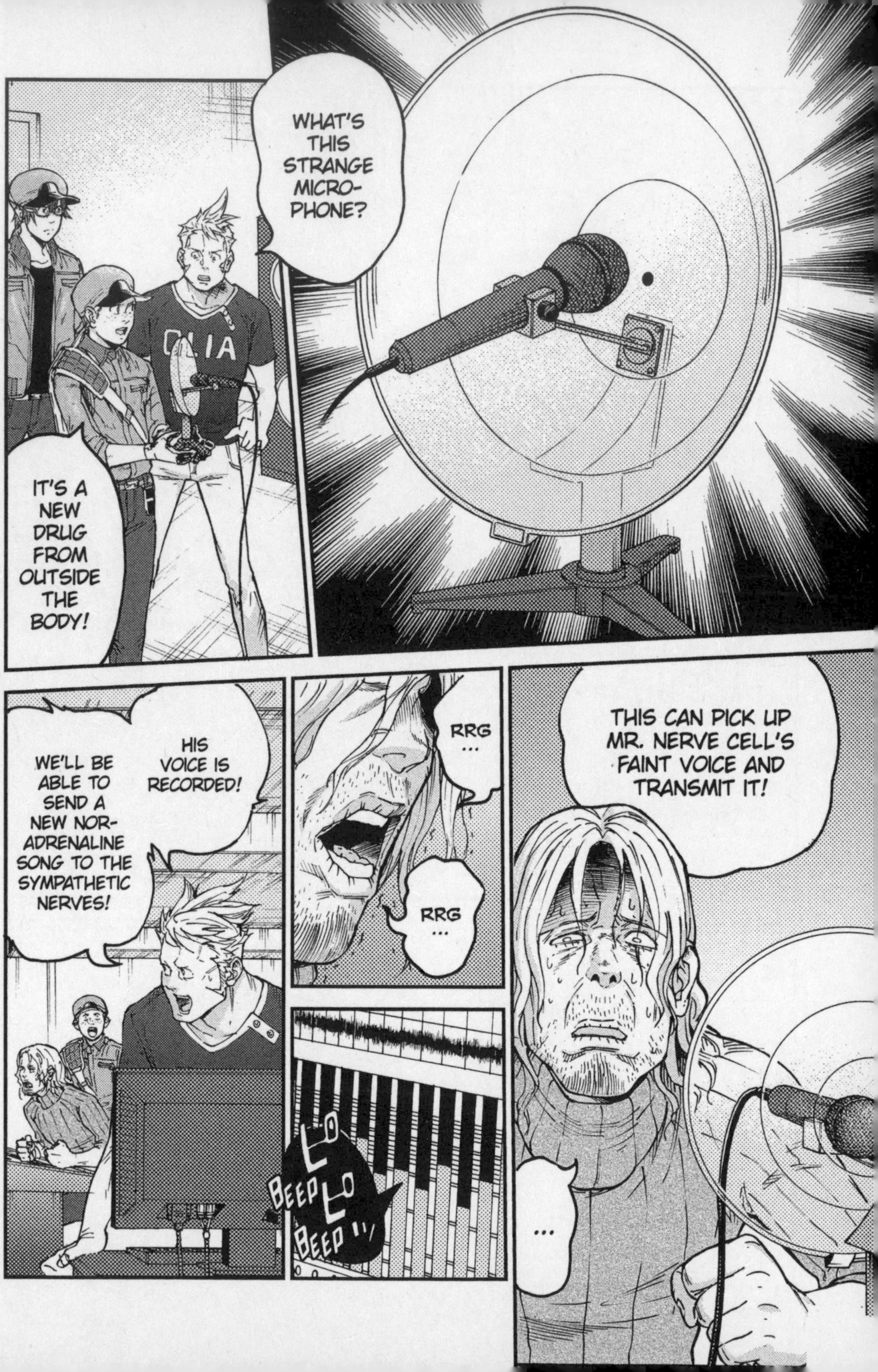
WHAT'S THIS STRANGE MICRO-PHONE?
IT'S A NEW DRUG FROM OUTSIDE THE BODY!
THIS CAN PICK UP MR. NERVE CELL'S FAINT VOICE AND TRANSMIT IT!
...
RRG ...
RRG ...
ピロ BEEP ピロ BEEP
HIS VOICE IS RECORDED!
WE'LL BE ABLE TO SEND A NEW NOR-ADRENALINE SONG TO THE SYMPATHETIC NERVES!

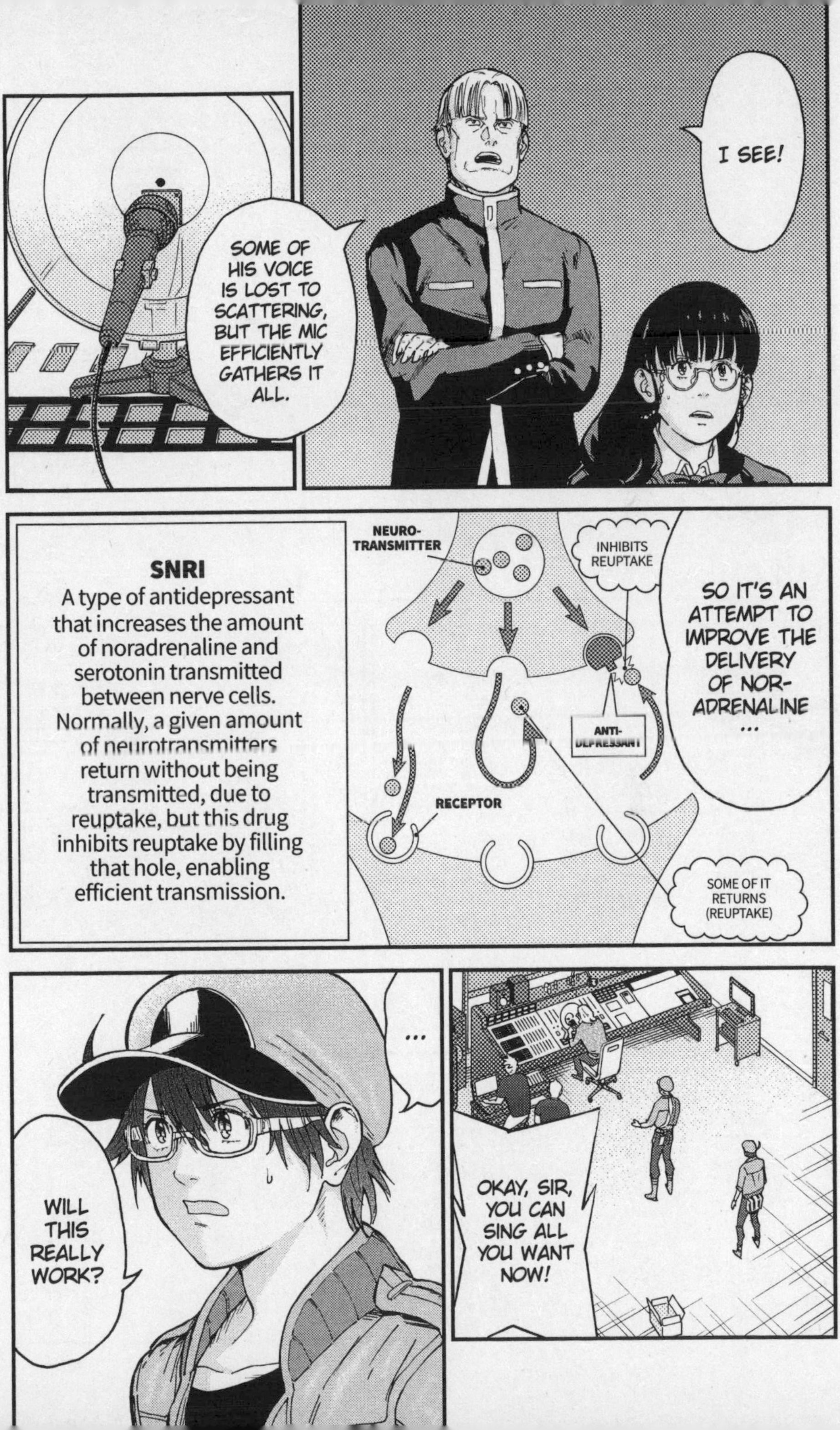
I SEE!
SOME OF HIS VOICE IS LOST TO SCATTERING, BUT THE MIC EFFICIENTLY GATHERS IT ALL.
SO IT'S AN ATTEMPT TO IMPROVE THE DELIVERY OF NOR-ADRENALINE ...
INHIBITS REUPTAKE
NEURO-TRANSMITTER
SNRI
A type of antidepressant that increases the amount of noradrenaline and serotonin transmitted between nerve cells. Normally, a given amount of neurotransmitters return without being transmitted, due to reuptake, but this drug inhibits reuptake by filling that hole, enabling efficient transmission.
ANTI-DEPRESSANT
SOME OF IT RETURNS (REUPTAKE)
RECEPTOR
OKAY, SIR, YOU CAN SING ALL YOU WANT NOW!
...
WILL THIS REALLY WORK?

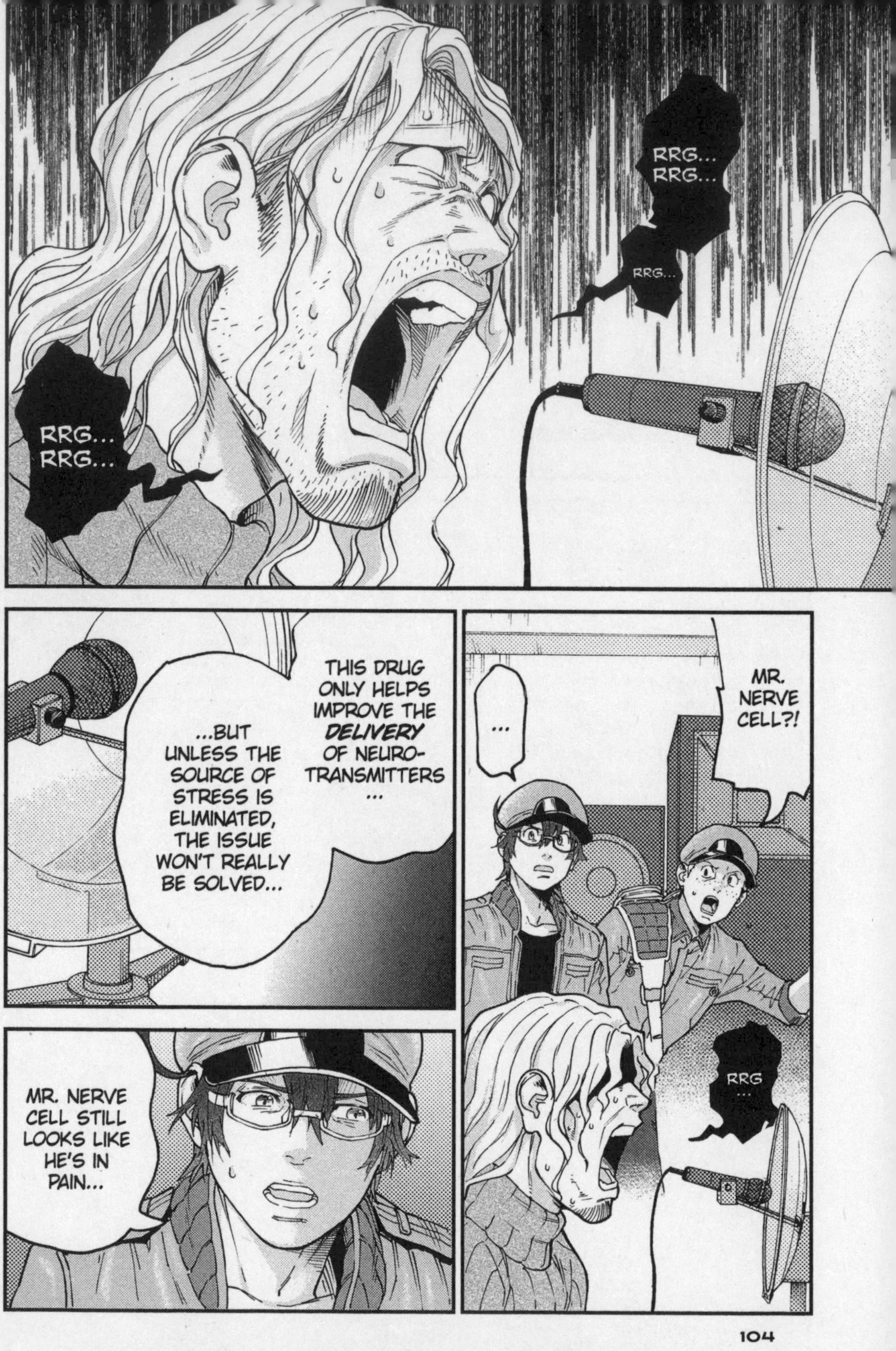
RRG... RRG...
RRG...
RRG... RRG...
MR. NERVE CELL?!
...
RRG ...
THIS DRUG ONLY HELPS IMPROVE THE DELIVERY OF NEURO-TRANSMITTERS ...
...BUT UNLESS THE SOURCE OF STRESS IS ELIMINATED, THE ISSUE WON'T REALLY BE SOLVED...
MR. NERVE CELL STILL LOOKS LIKE HE'S IN PAIN...

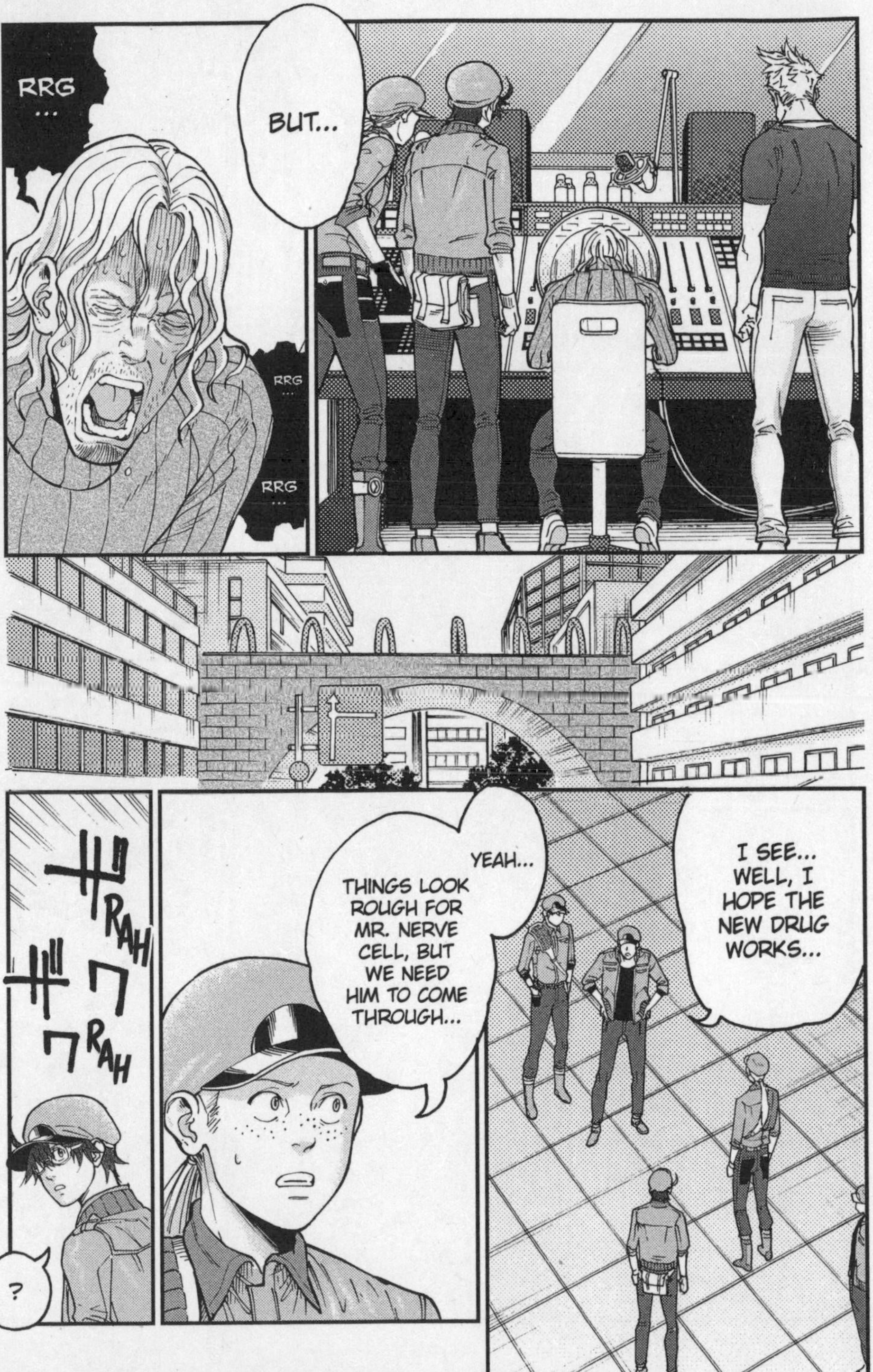
BUT...
RRG...
RRG...
RRG...
I SEE... WELL, I HOPE THE NEW DRUG WORKS...
YEAH...
THINGS LOOK ROUGH FOR MR. NERVE CELL, BUT WE NEED HIM TO COME THROUGH...
RAH
RAH
?

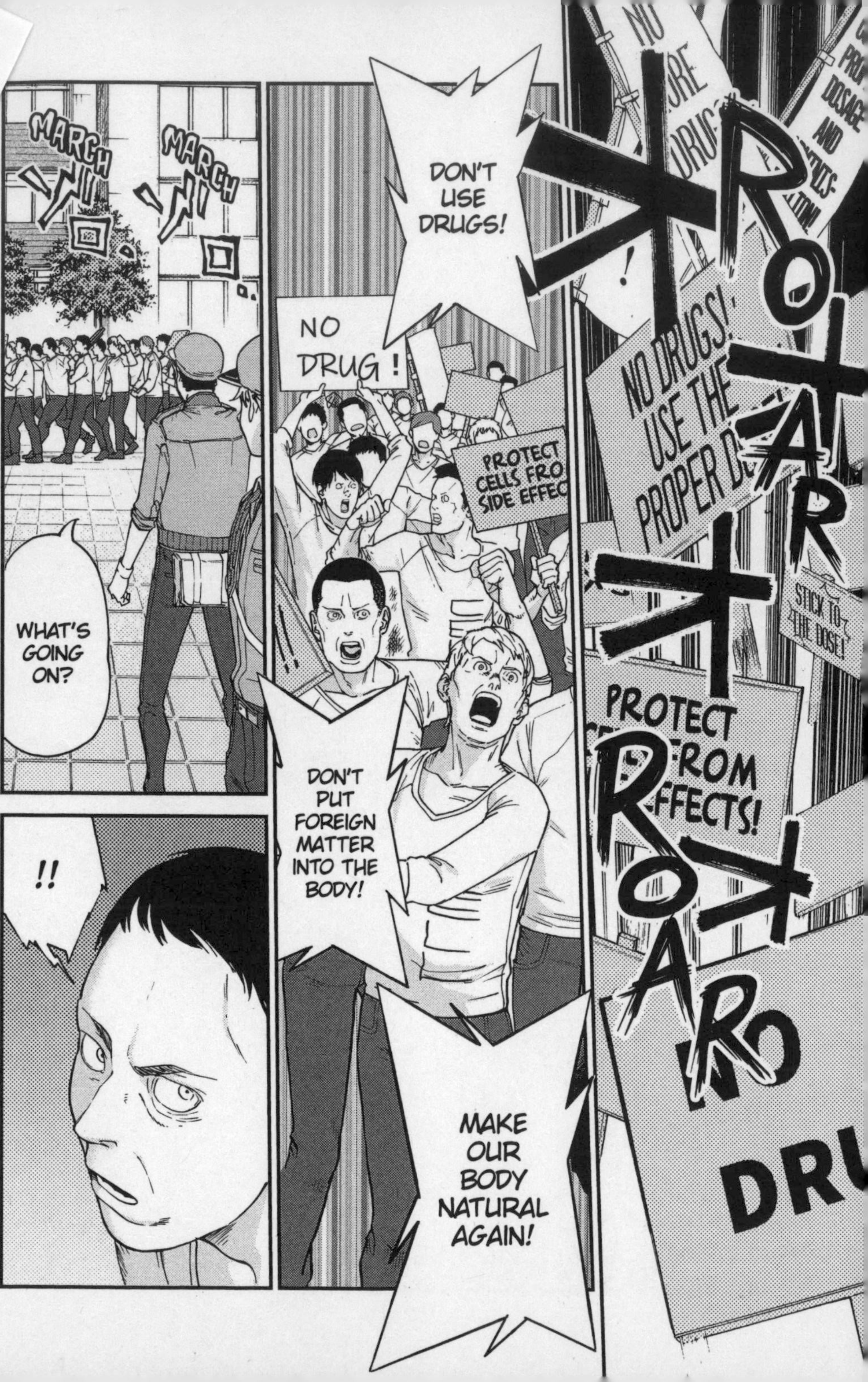
NO DRUGS! USE THE PROPER D
STICK TO THE DOSE!
PROTECT FROM EFFECTS!
ROAR
ROAR
ROAR
DRU
DON'T USE DRUGS!
NO DRUG !
PROTECT CELLS FRO SIDE EFFEC
DON'T PUT FOREIGN MATTER INTO THE BODY!
MAKE OUR BODY NATURAL AGAIN!
MARCH
MARCH
WHAT'S GOING ON?
!!

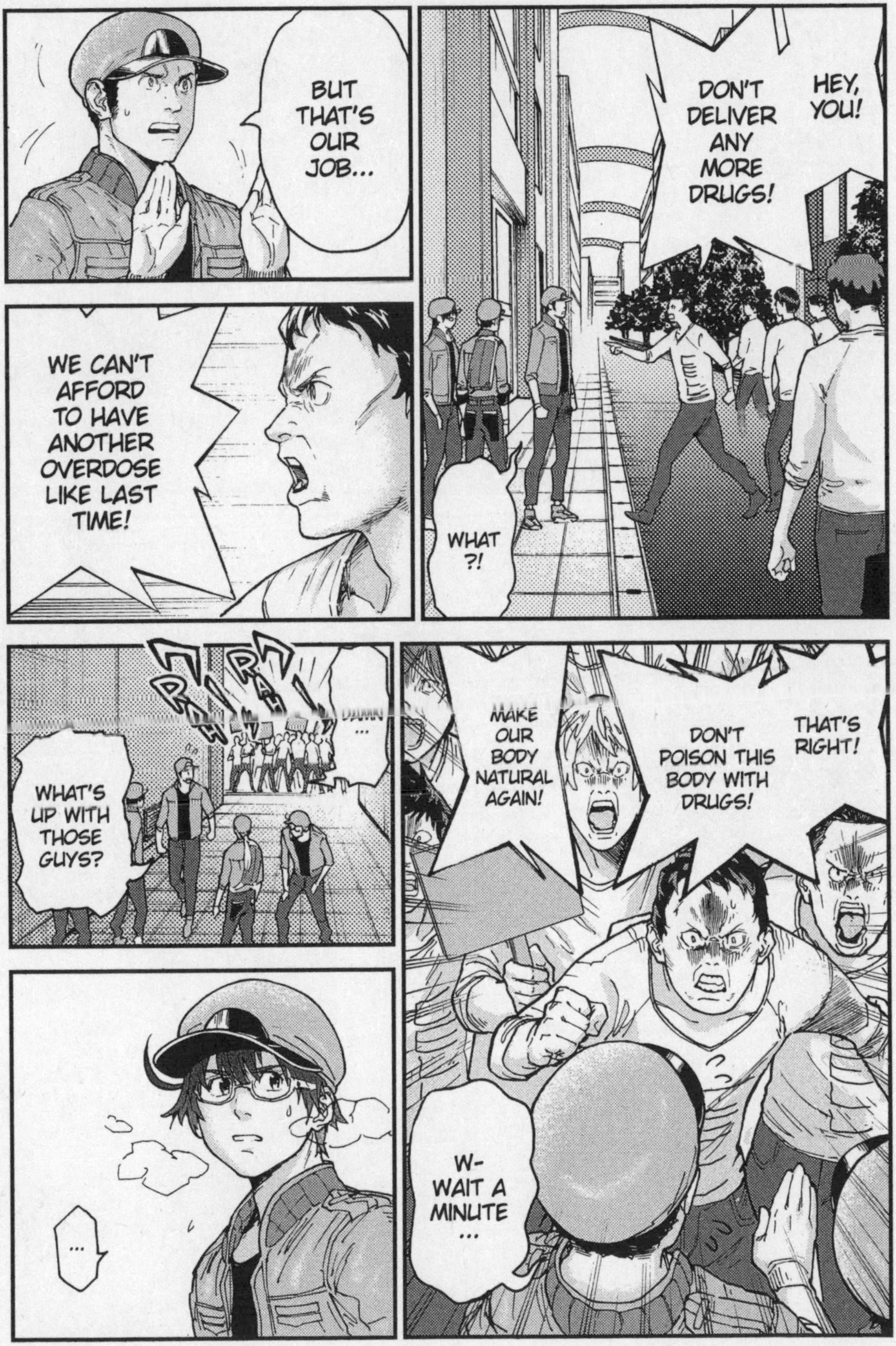
HEY, YOU!
DON'T DELIVER ANY MORE DRUGS!
WHAT ?!
BUT THAT'S OUR JOB...
WE CAN'T AFFORD TO HAVE ANOTHER OVERDOSE LIKE LAST TIME!
THAT'S RIGHT!
DON'T POISON THIS BODY WITH DRUGS!
MAKE OUR BODY NATURAL AGAIN!
W- WAIT A MINUTE ...
RAH
RAH
DAMN ...
WHAT'S UP WITH THOSE GUYS?
...

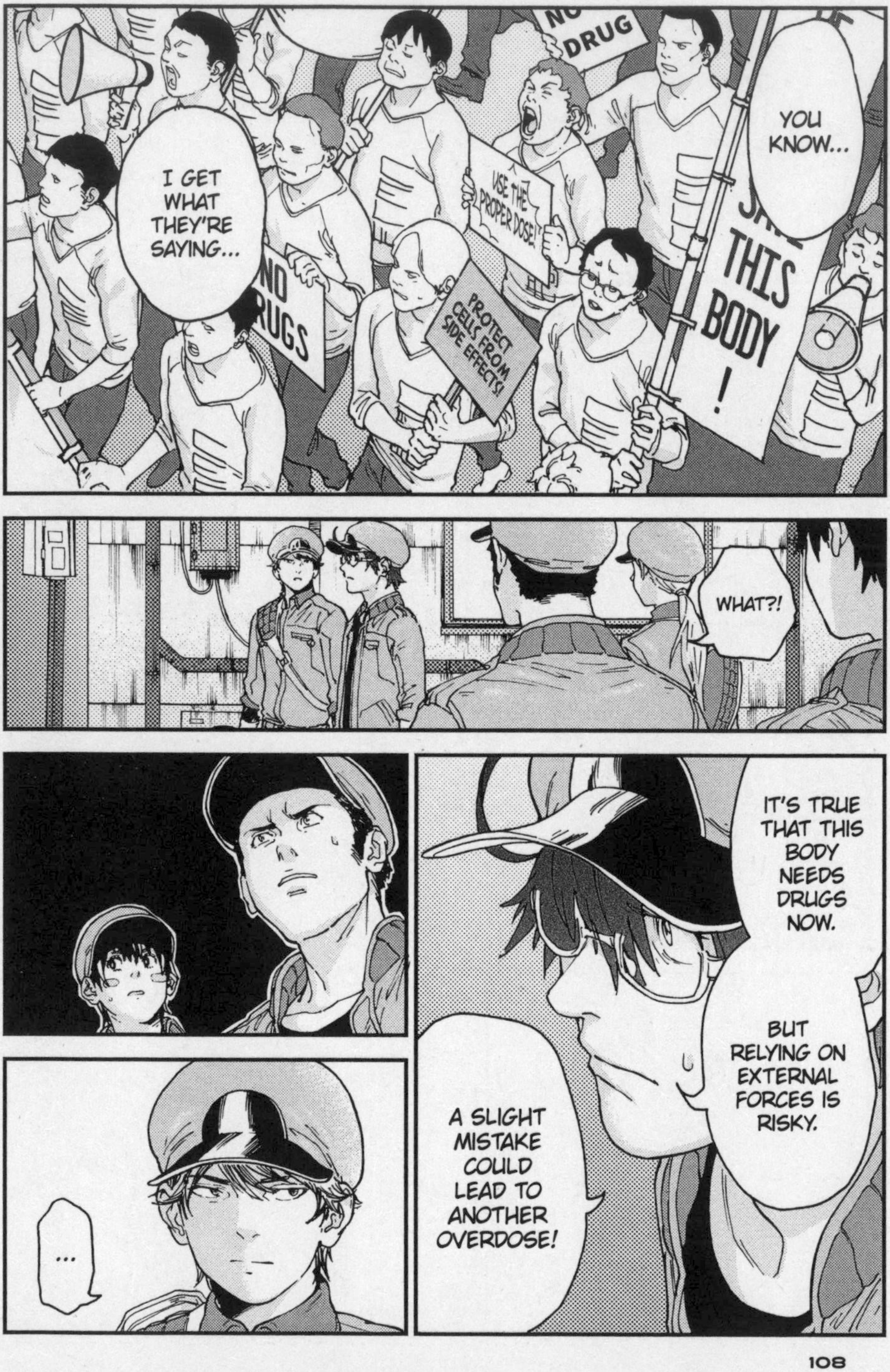
YOU KNOW...
NO DRUG
THIS BODY !
USE THE PROPER DOSE!
PROTECT CELLS FROM SIDE EFFECTS!
NO DRUGS
I GET WHAT THEY'RE SAYING...
WHAT?!
IT'S TRUE THAT THIS BODY NEEDS DRUGS NOW.
BUT RELYING ON EXTERNAL FORCES IS RISKY.
A SLIGHT MISTAKE COULD LEAD TO ANOTHER OVERDOSE!
...

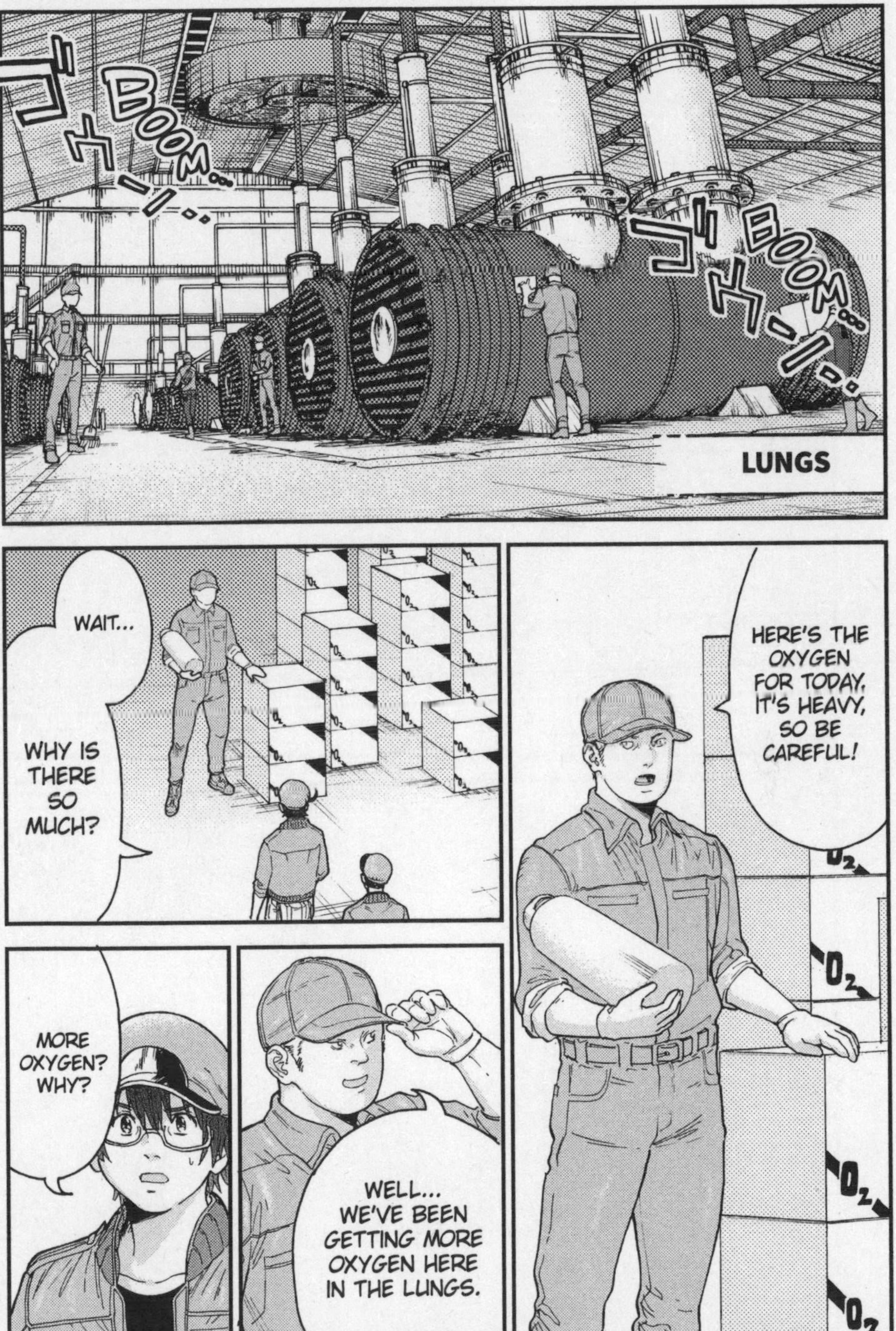
ゴウーン‥ BOOM...
ゴウーン‥ BOOM...
LUNGS
HERE'S THE OXYGEN FOR TODAY. IT'S HEAVY, SO BE CAREFUL!
WAIT...
WHY IS THERE SO MUCH?
WELL... WE'VE BEEN GETTING MORE OXYGEN HERE IN THE LUNGS.
MORE OXYGEN? WHY?

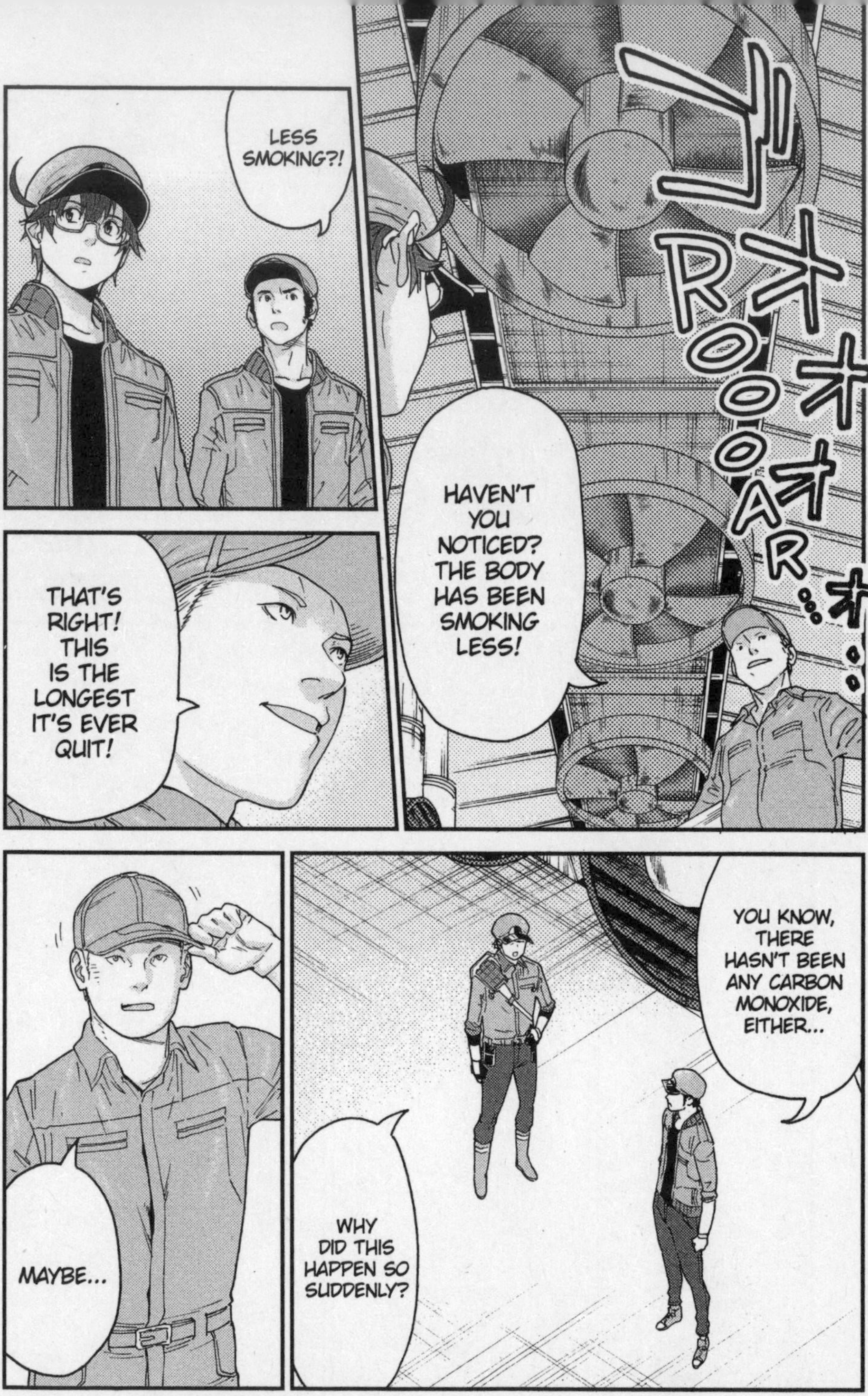
ROOOAR...
HAVEN'T YOU NOTICED? THE BODY HAS BEEN SMOKING LESS!
LESS SMOKING?!
THAT'S RIGHT! THIS IS THE LONGEST IT'S EVER QUIT!
YOU KNOW, THERE HASN'T BEEN ANY CARBON MONOXIDE, EITHER...
WHY DID THIS HAPPEN SO SUDDENLY?
MAYBE...

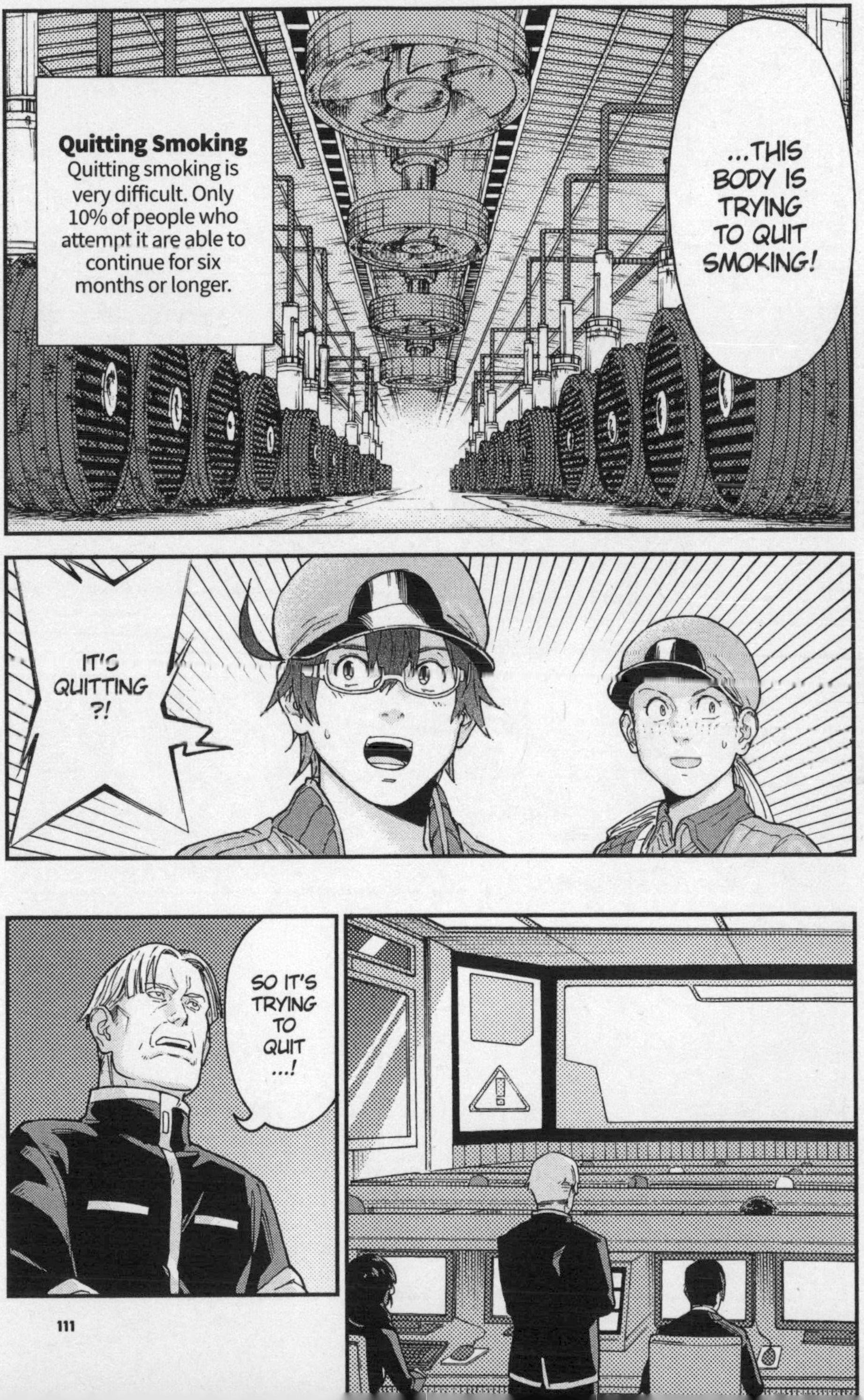
...THIS BODY IS TRYING TO QUIT SMOKING!
Quitting Smoking
Quitting smoking is very difficult. Only 10% of people who attempt it are able to continue for six months or longer.
IT'S QUITTING ?!
SO IT'S TRYING TO QUIT ...!

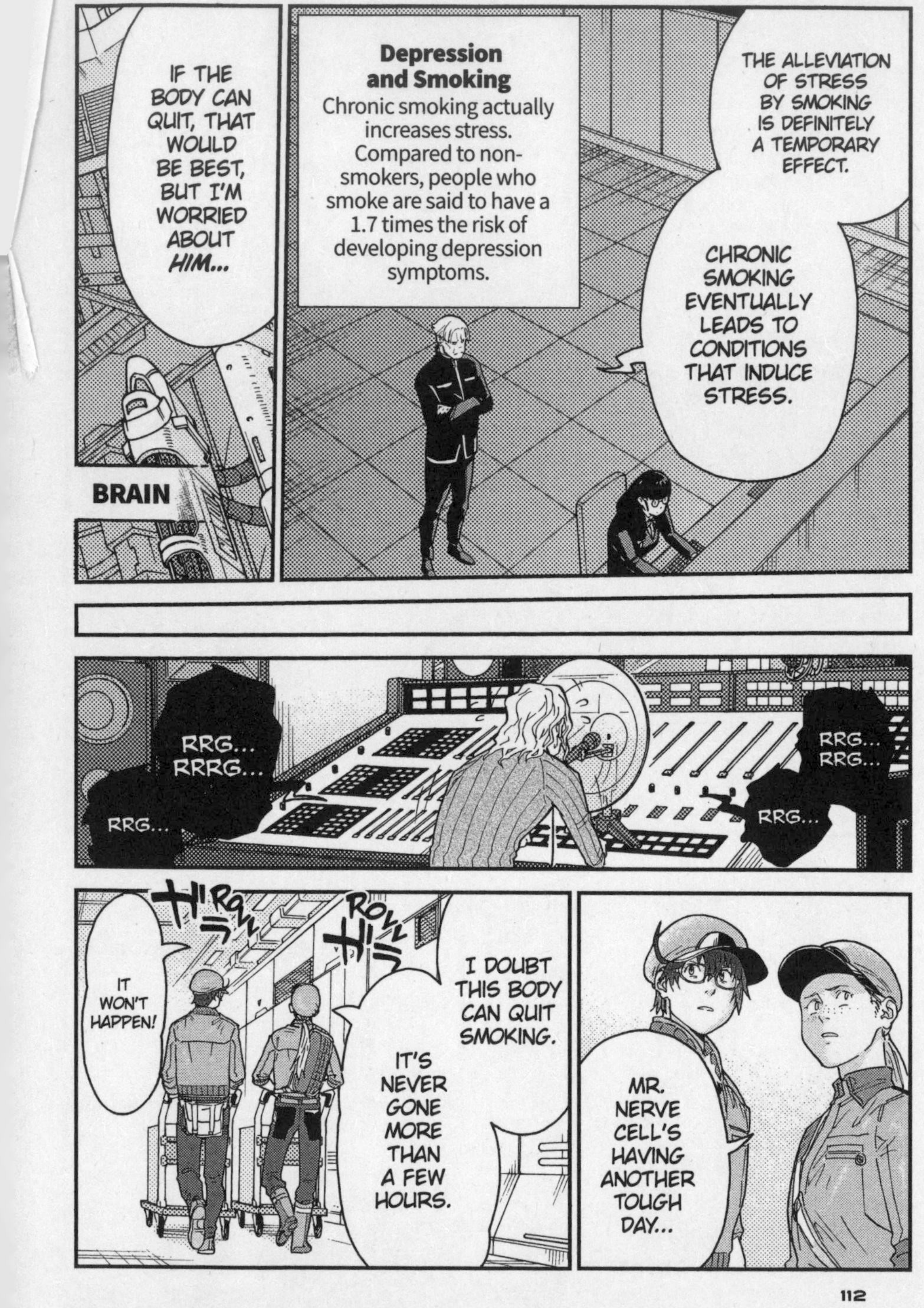
THE ALLEVIATION OF STRESS BY SMOKING IS DEFINITELY A TEMPORARY EFFECT.
CHRONIC SMOKING EVENTUALLY LEADS TO CONDITIONS THAT INDUCE STRESS.
Depression and Smoking
Chronic smoking actually increases stress. Compared to non-smokers, people who smoke are said to have a 1.7 times the risk of developing depression symptoms.
IF THE BODY CAN QUIT, THAT WOULD BE BEST, BUT I'M WORRIED ABOUT *HIM*...
BRAIN
RRG... RRG...
RRG...
RRG... RRRG...
RRG...
MR. NERVE CELL'S HAVING ANOTHER TOUGH DAY...
I DOUBT THIS BODY CAN QUIT SMOKING.
IT'S NEVER GONE MORE THAN A FEW HOURS.
IT WON'T HAPPEN!

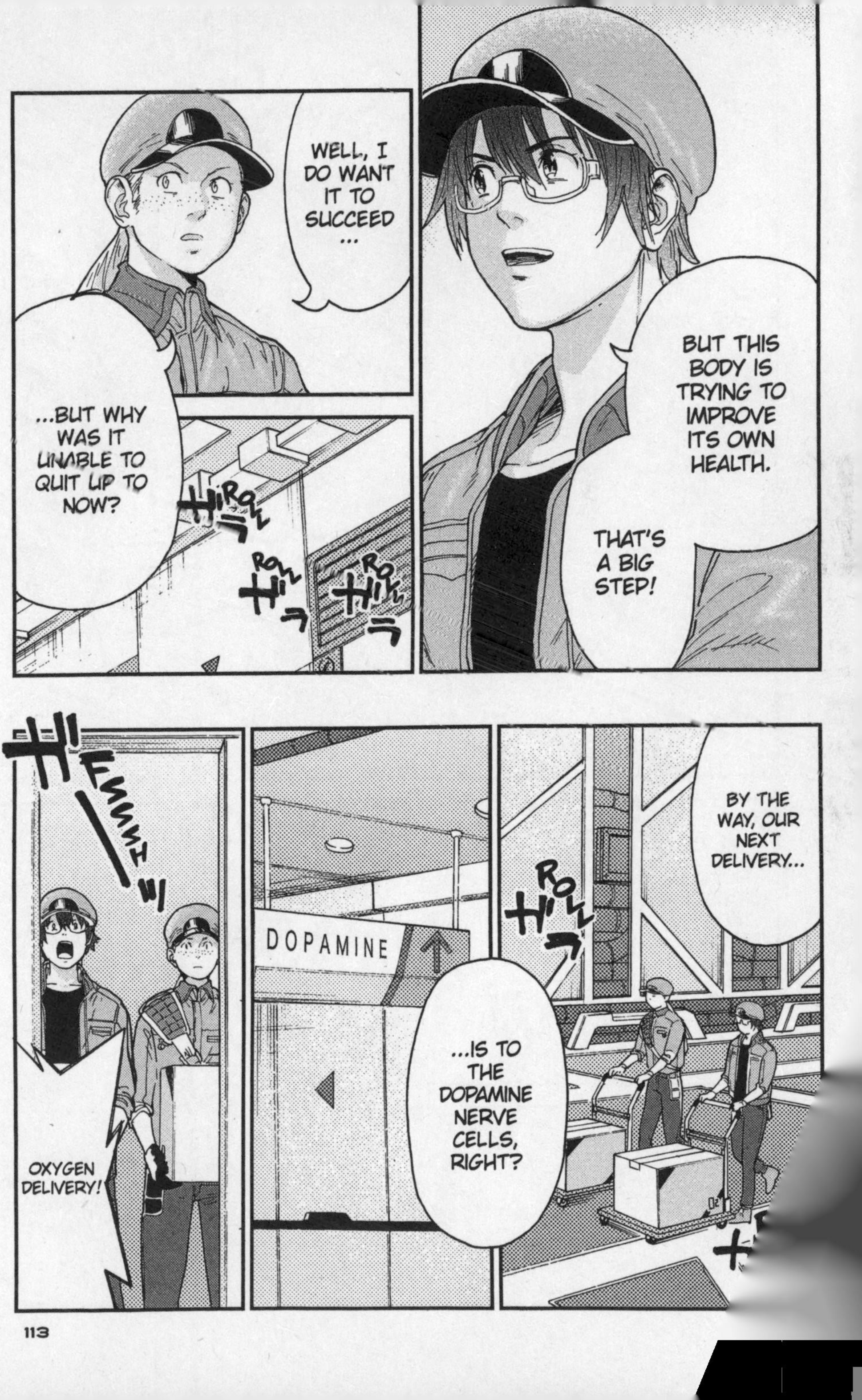
BUT THIS BODY IS TRYING TO IMPROVE ITS OWN HEALTH.
THAT'S A BIG STEP!
WELL, I DO WANT IT TO SUCCEED ...
...BUT WHY WAS IT UNABLE TO QUIT UP TO NOW?
ROLL
ROLL
ROLL
BY THE WAY, OUR NEXT DELIVERY...
ROLL
...IS TO THE DOPAMINE NERVE CELLS, RIGHT?
DOPAMINE
FSSSSH
OXYGEN DELIVERY!

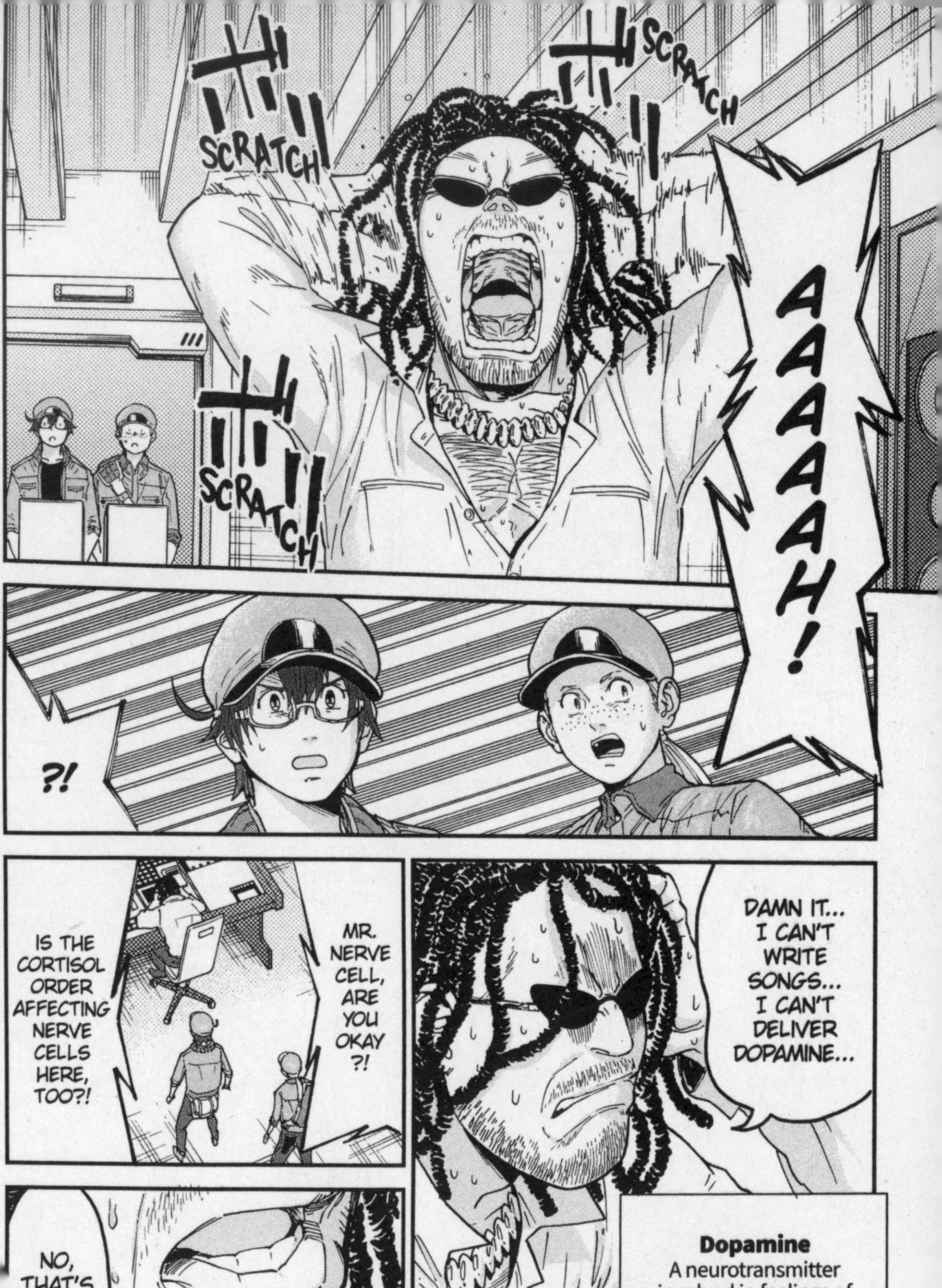
SCRATCH
SCRATCH
SCRATCH
AAAAAH!
?!
DAMN IT... I CAN'T WRITE SONGS... I CAN'T DELIVER DOPAMINE...
Dopamine
A neurotransmitter involved in feelings of pleasure and desire.
MR. NERVE CELL, ARE YOU OKAY?!
IS THE CORTISOL ORDER AFFECTING NERVE CELLS HERE, TOO?!
NO, THAT'S NOT IT...

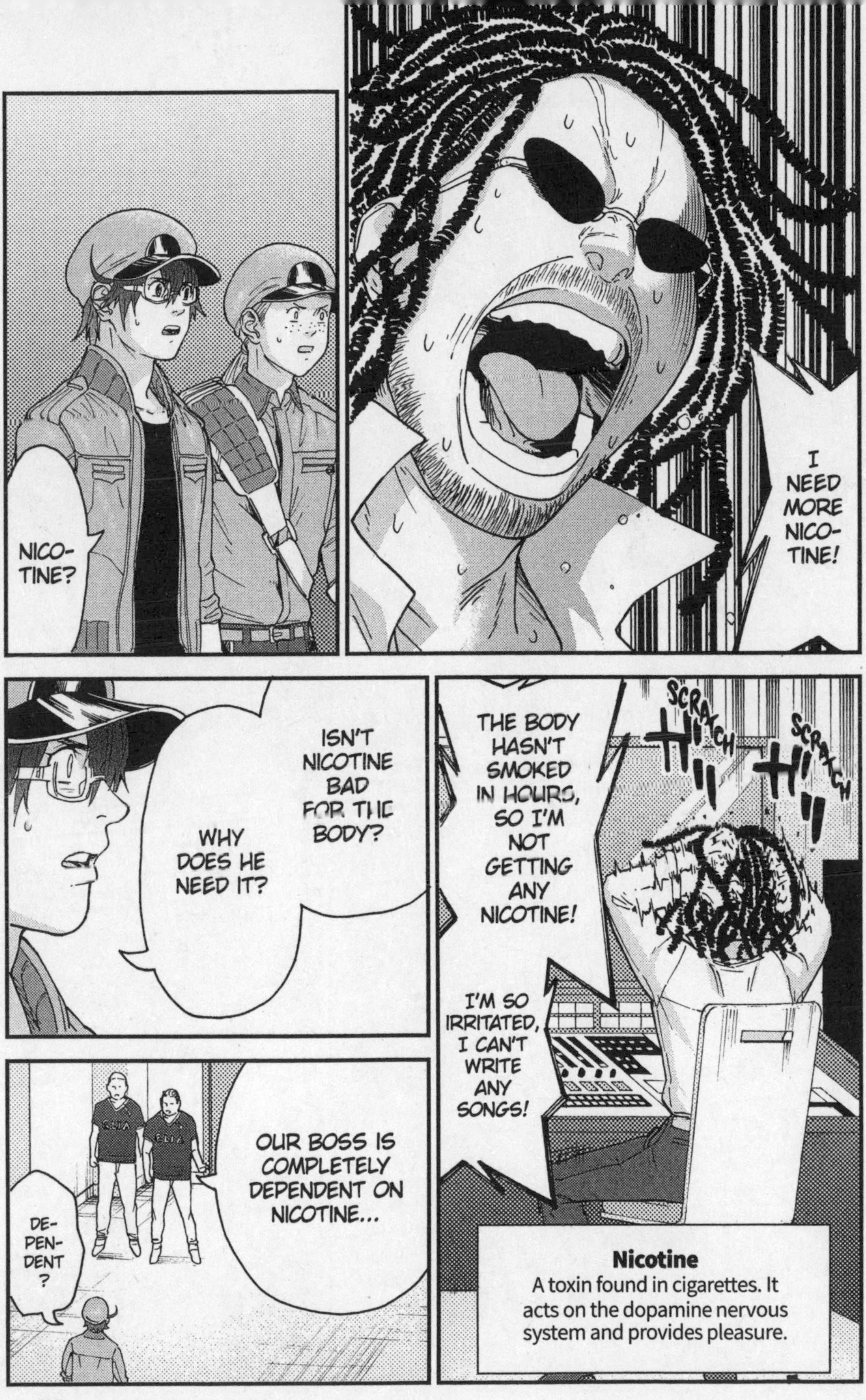
I NEED MORE NICO-TINE!
NICO-TINE?
THE BODY HASN'T SMOKED IN HOURS, SO I'M NOT GETTING ANY NICOTINE!
SCRATCH
SCRATCH
I'M SO IRRITATED, I CAN'T WRITE ANY SONGS!
Nicotine
A toxin found in cigarettes. It acts on the dopamine nervous system and provides pleasure.
ISN'T NICOTINE BAD FOR THE BODY?
WHY DOES HE NEED IT?
OUR BOSS IS COMPLETELY DEPENDENT ON NICOTINE...
DE-PEN-DENT?

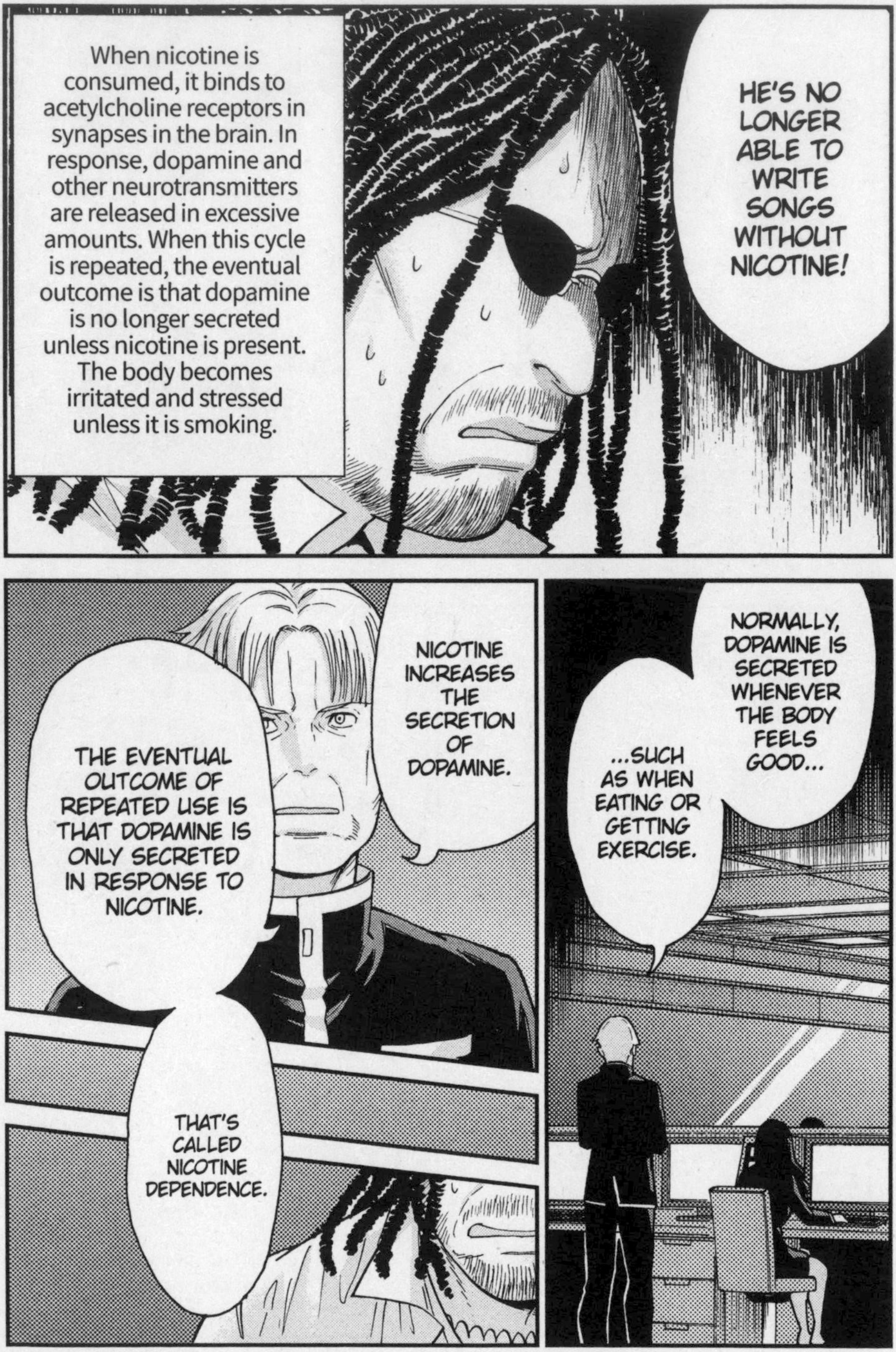
HE'S NO LONGER ABLE TO WRITE SONGS WITHOUT NICOTINE!
When nicotine is consumed, it binds to acetylcholine receptors in synapses in the brain. In response, dopamine and other neurotransmitters are released in excessive amounts. When this cycle is repeated, the eventual outcome is that dopamine is no longer secreted unless nicotine is present. The body becomes irritated and stressed unless it is smoking.
NORMALLY, DOPAMINE IS SECRETED WHENEVER THE BODY FEELS GOOD...
...SUCH AS WHEN EATING OR GETTING EXERCISE.
NICOTINE INCREASES THE SECRETION OF DOPAMINE.
THE EVENTUAL OUTCOME OF REPEATED USE IS THAT DOPAMINE IS ONLY SECRETED IN RESPONSE TO NICOTINE.
THAT'S CALLED NICOTINE DEPENDENCE.

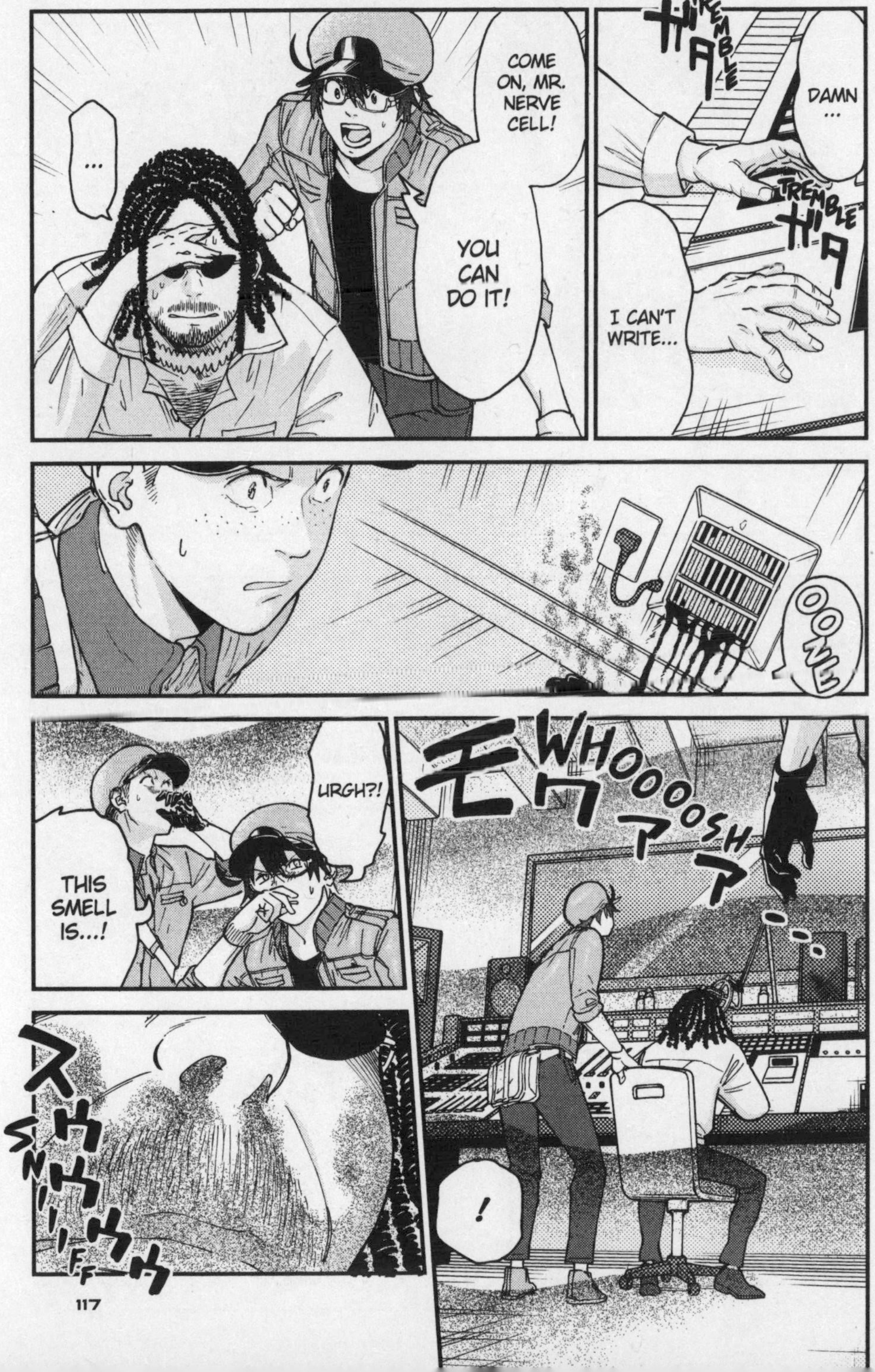
TREMBLE
DAMN ...
TREMBLE
I CAN'T WRITE...
COME ON, MR. NERVE CELL!
YOU CAN DO IT!
...
OOZE
WHOOOOOSH
!
URGH?!
THIS SMELL IS...!
SNIIIFF

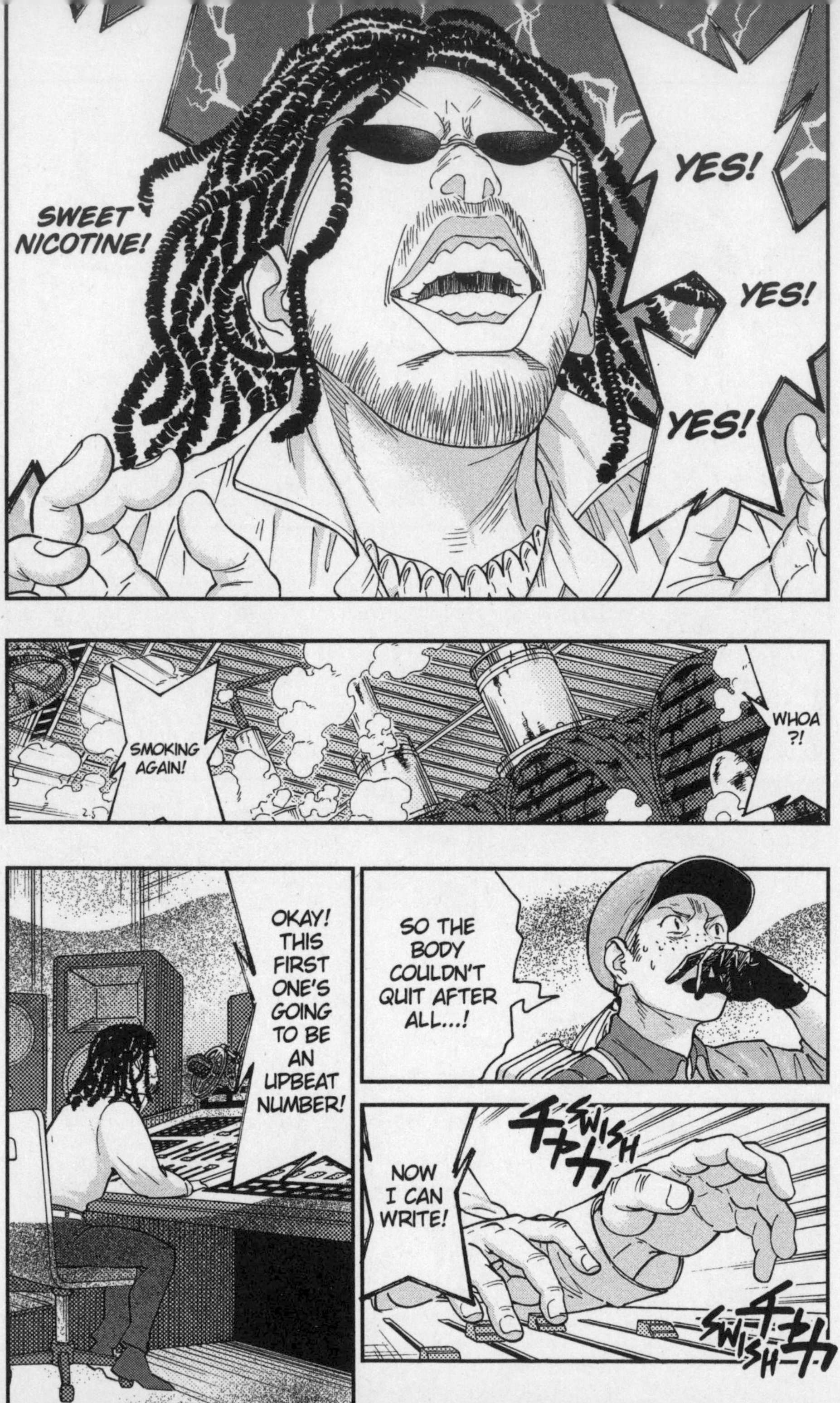
YES!
YES!
YES!
SWEET NICOTINE!
WHOA ?!
SMOKING AGAIN!
SO THE BODY COULDN'T QUIT AFTER ALL...!
SWISH
NOW I CAN WRITE!
SWISH
OKAY! THIS FIRST ONE'S GOING TO BE AN UPBEAT NUMBER!

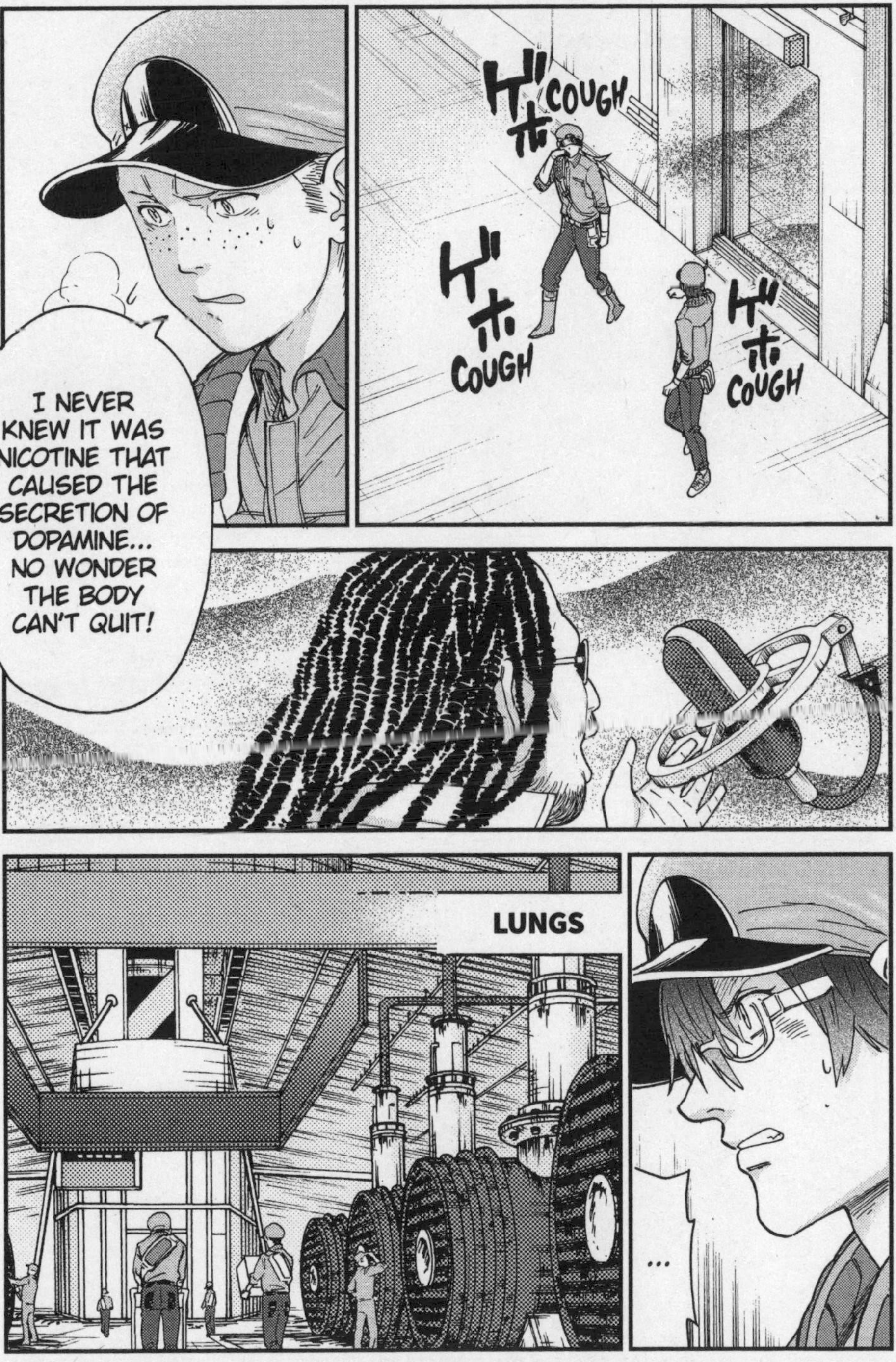

ゲホ COUGH
ゲホ COUGH
ゲホ COUGH
I NEVER KNEW IT WAS NICOTINE THAT CAUSED THE SECRETION OF DOPAMINE... NO WONDER THE BODY CAN'T QUIT!
...
LUNGS

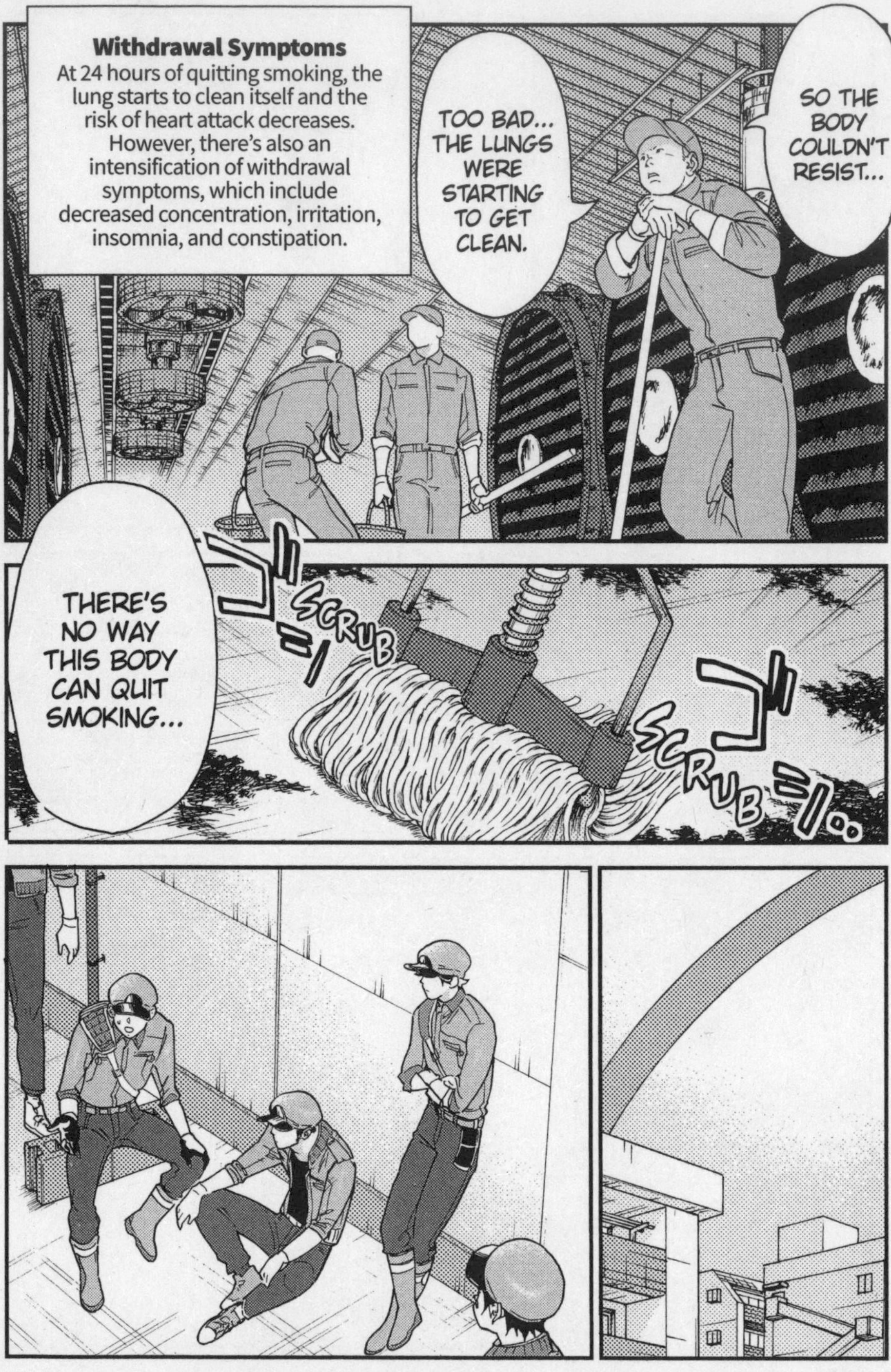
SO THE BODY COULDN'T RESIST...
TOO BAD... THE LUNGS WERE STARTING TO GET CLEAN.
Withdrawal Symptoms
At 24 hours of quitting smoking, the lung starts to clean itself and the risk of heart attack decreases. However, there's also an intensification of withdrawal symptoms, which include decreased concentration, irritation, insomnia, and constipation.
SCRUB
SCRUB
THERE'S NO WAY THIS BODY CAN QUIT SMOKING...

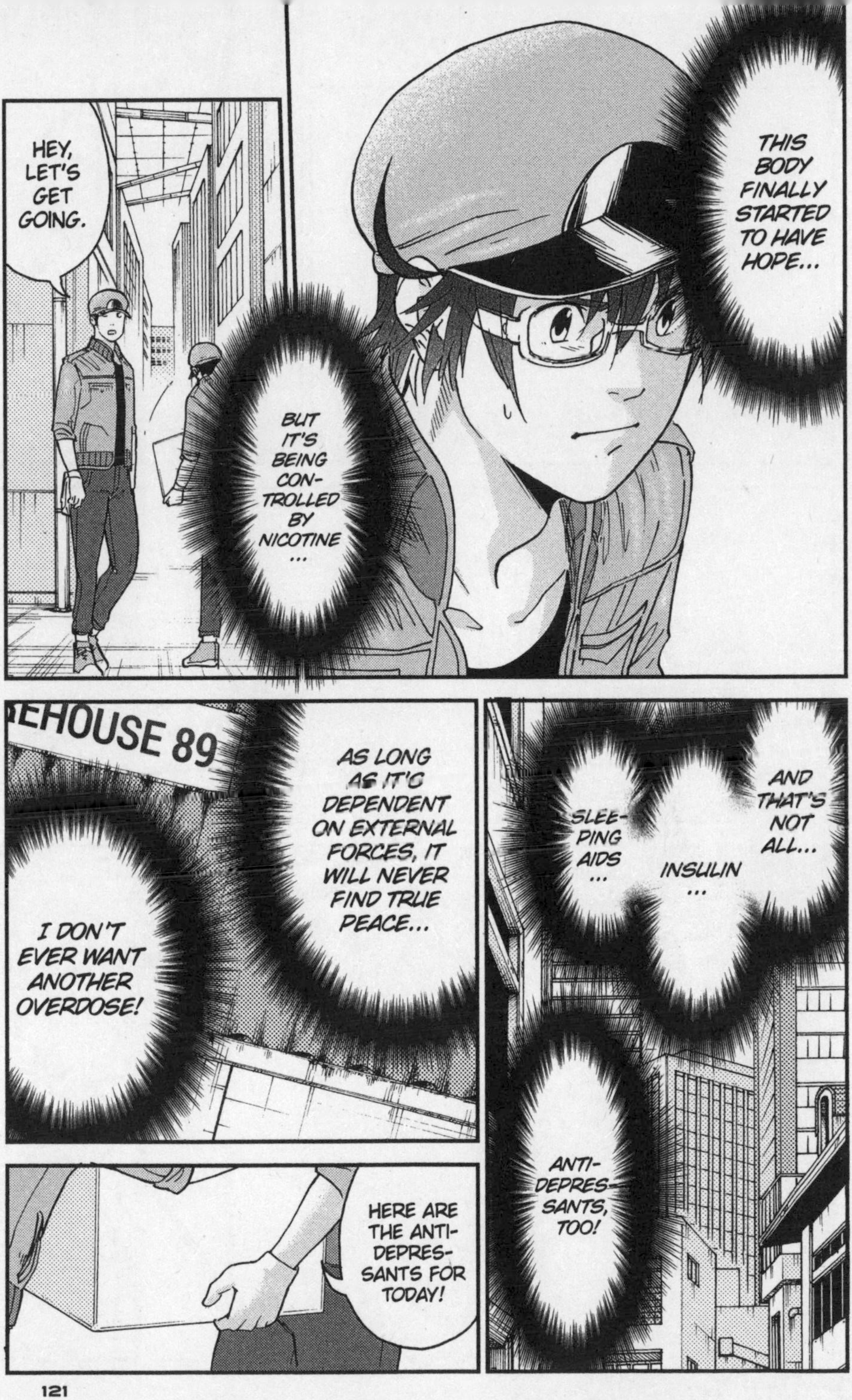
THIS BODY FINALLY STARTED TO HAVE HOPE...
BUT IT'S BEING CON-TROLLED BY NICOTINE ...
HEY, LET'S GET GOING.
AND THAT'S NOT ALL...
INSULIN ...
SLEE-PING AIDS ...
ANTI-DEPRES-SANTS, TOO!
EHOUSE 89
AS LONG AS IT'S DEPENDENT ON EXTERNAL FORCES, IT WILL NEVER FIND TRUE PEACE...
I DON'T EVER WANT ANOTHER OVERDOSE!
HERE ARE THE ANTI-DEPRES-SANTS FOR TODAY!

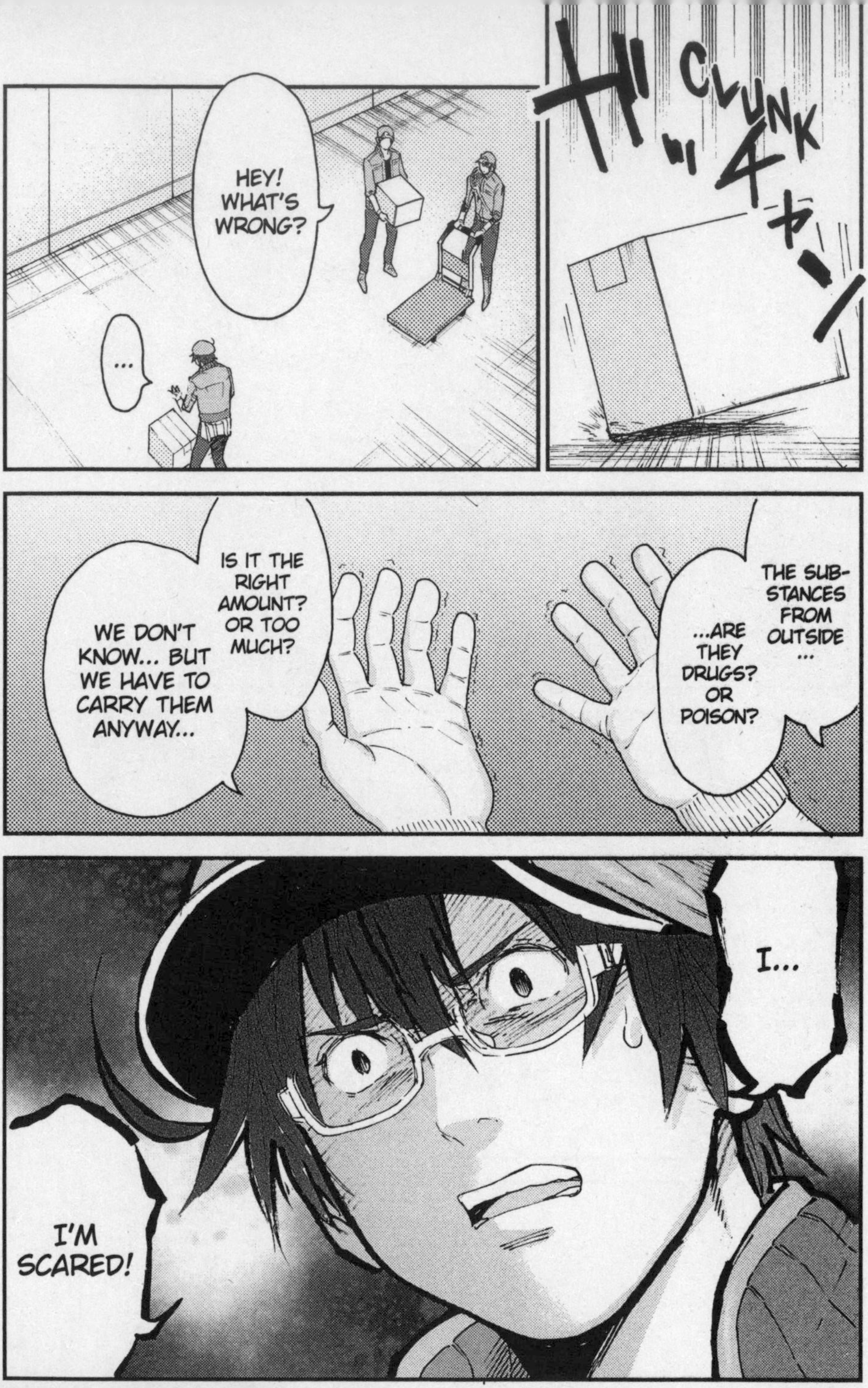
CLUNK
HEY! WHAT'S WRONG?
...
THE SUB- STANCES FROM OUTSIDE ...
...ARE THEY DRUGS? OR POISON?
IS IT THE RIGHT AMOUNT? OR TOO MUCH?
WE DON'T KNOW... BUT WE HAVE TO CARRY THEM ANYWAY...
I...
I'M SCARED!

CHAPTER 35 - END

36. WANDERING, DRUG EFFICACY, MISSION

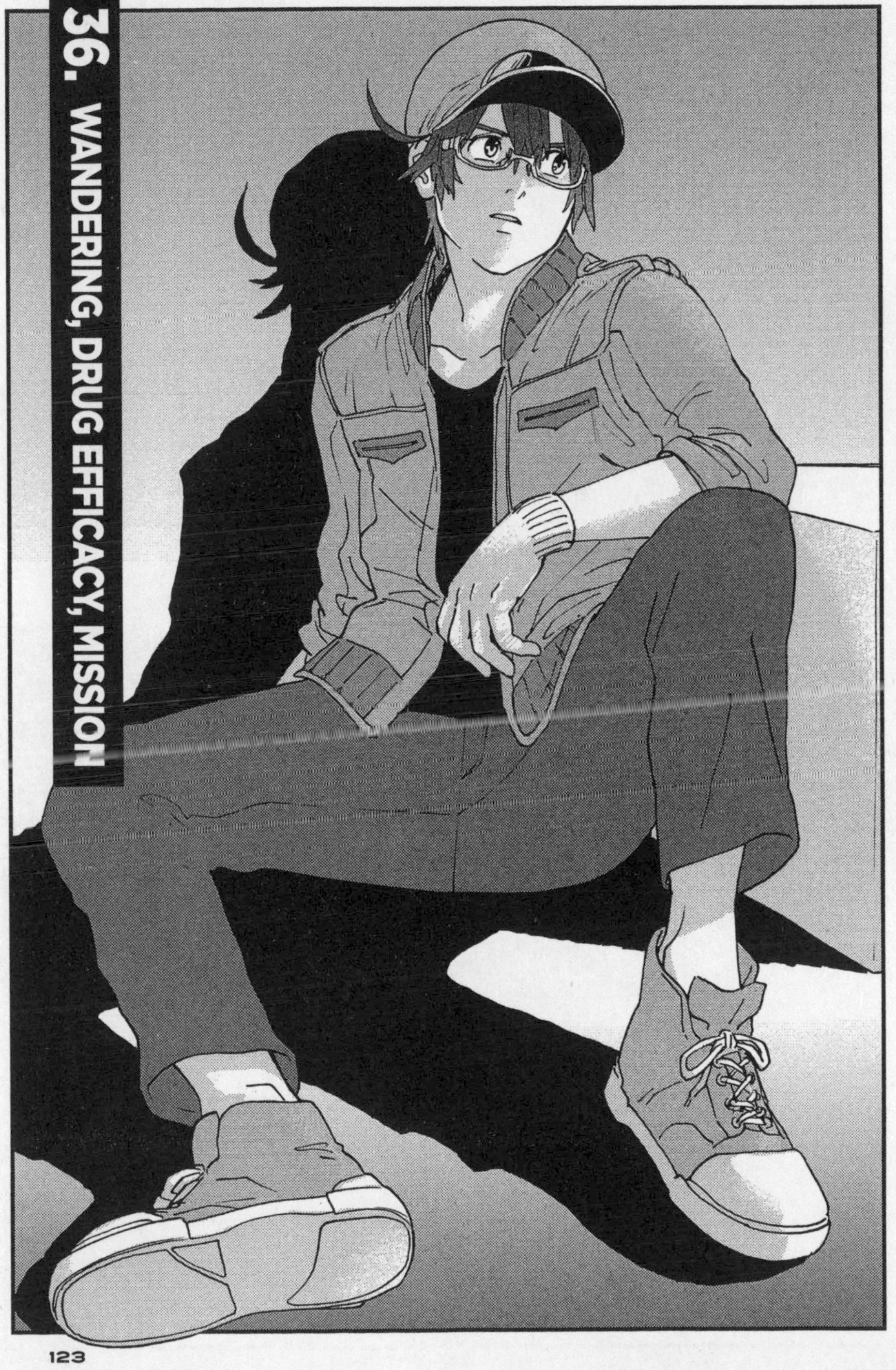

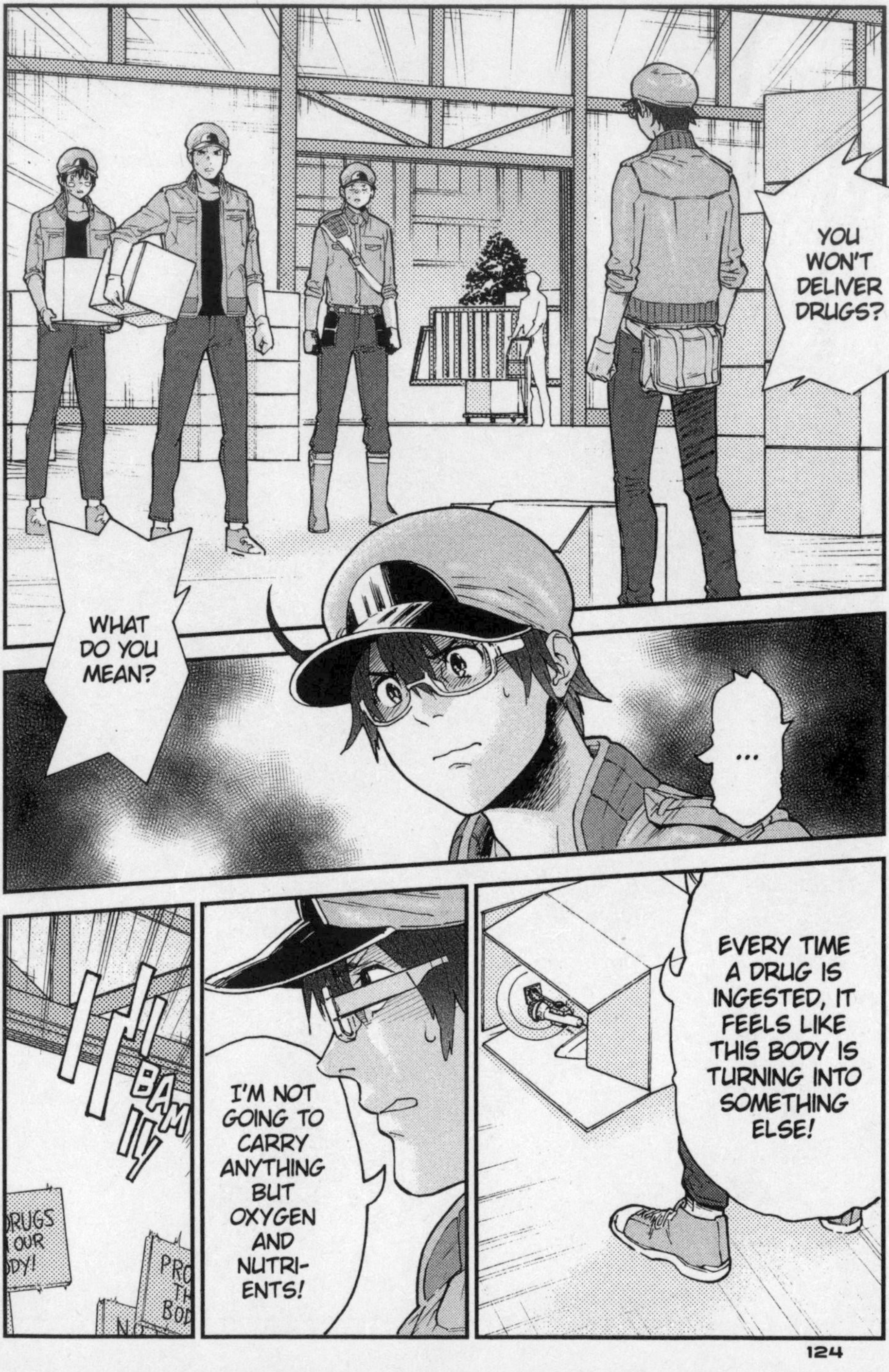
YOU WON'T DELIVER DRUGS?
WHAT DO YOU MEAN?
...
EVERY TIME A DRUG IS INGESTED, IT FEELS LIKE THIS BODY IS TURNING INTO SOMETHING ELSE!
I'M NOT GOING TO CARRY ANYTHING BUT OXYGEN AND NUTRI-ENTS!
BAM

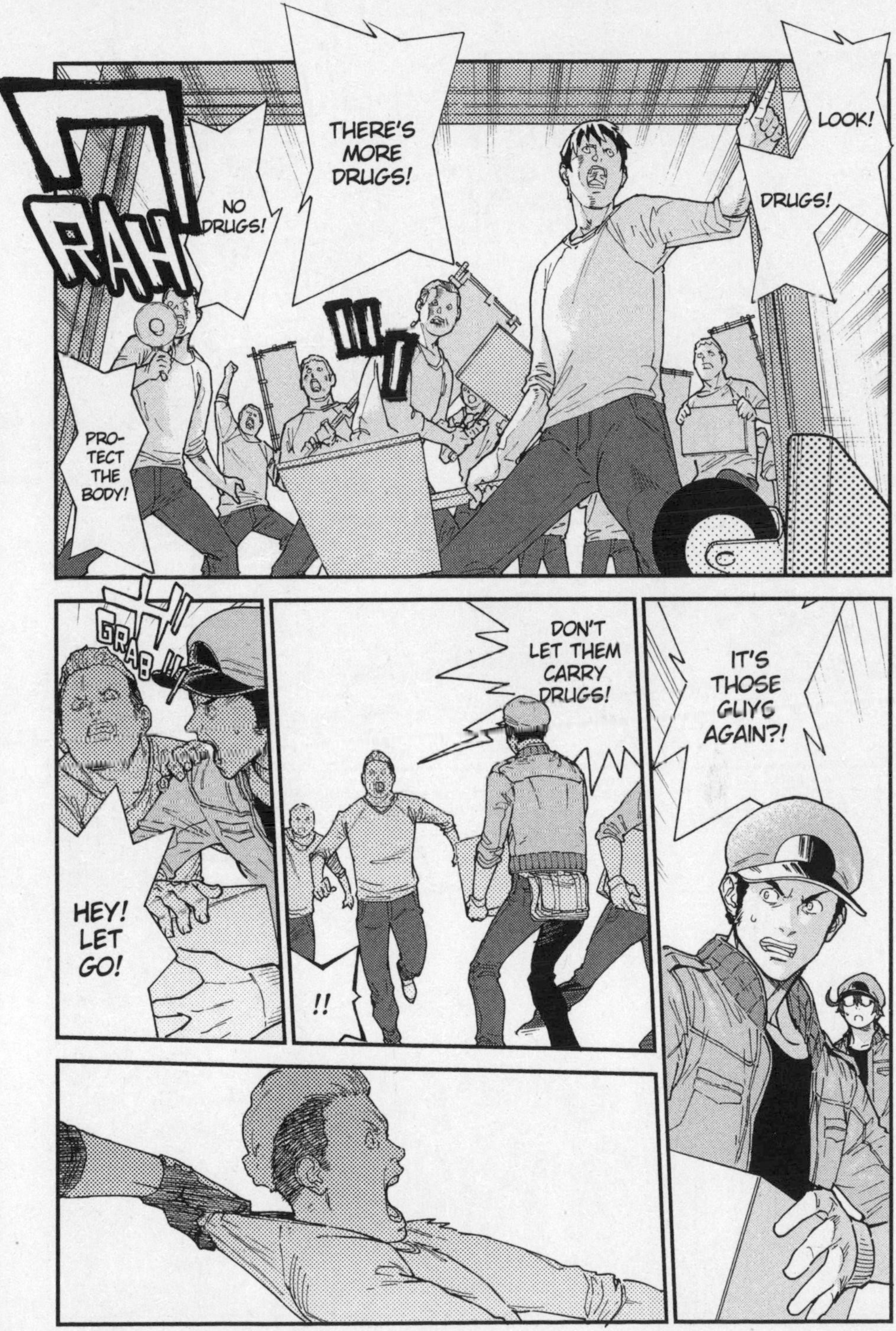
LOOK!
DRUGS!
THERE'S MORE DRUGS!
NO DRUGS!
RAH
PROTECT THE BODY!
IT'S THOSE GUYS AGAIN?!
DON'T LET THEM CARRY DRUGS!
!!
GRAB!!
HEY! LET GO!

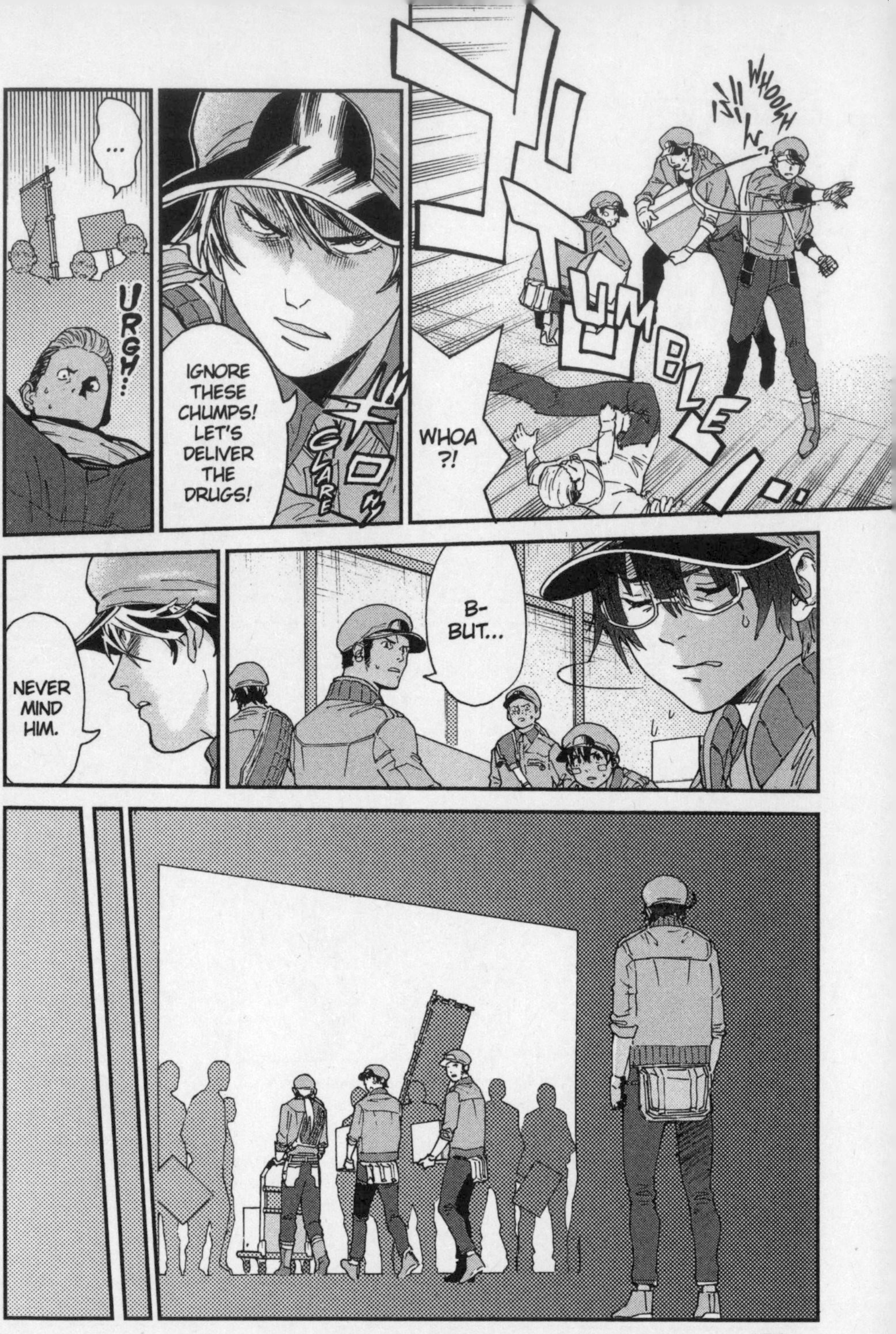
WHOOSH
TUMBLE
WHOA?!
GLARE
IGNORE THESE CHUMPS! LET'S DELIVER THE DRUGS!
...
URGH...
B-BUT...
NEVER MIND HIM.

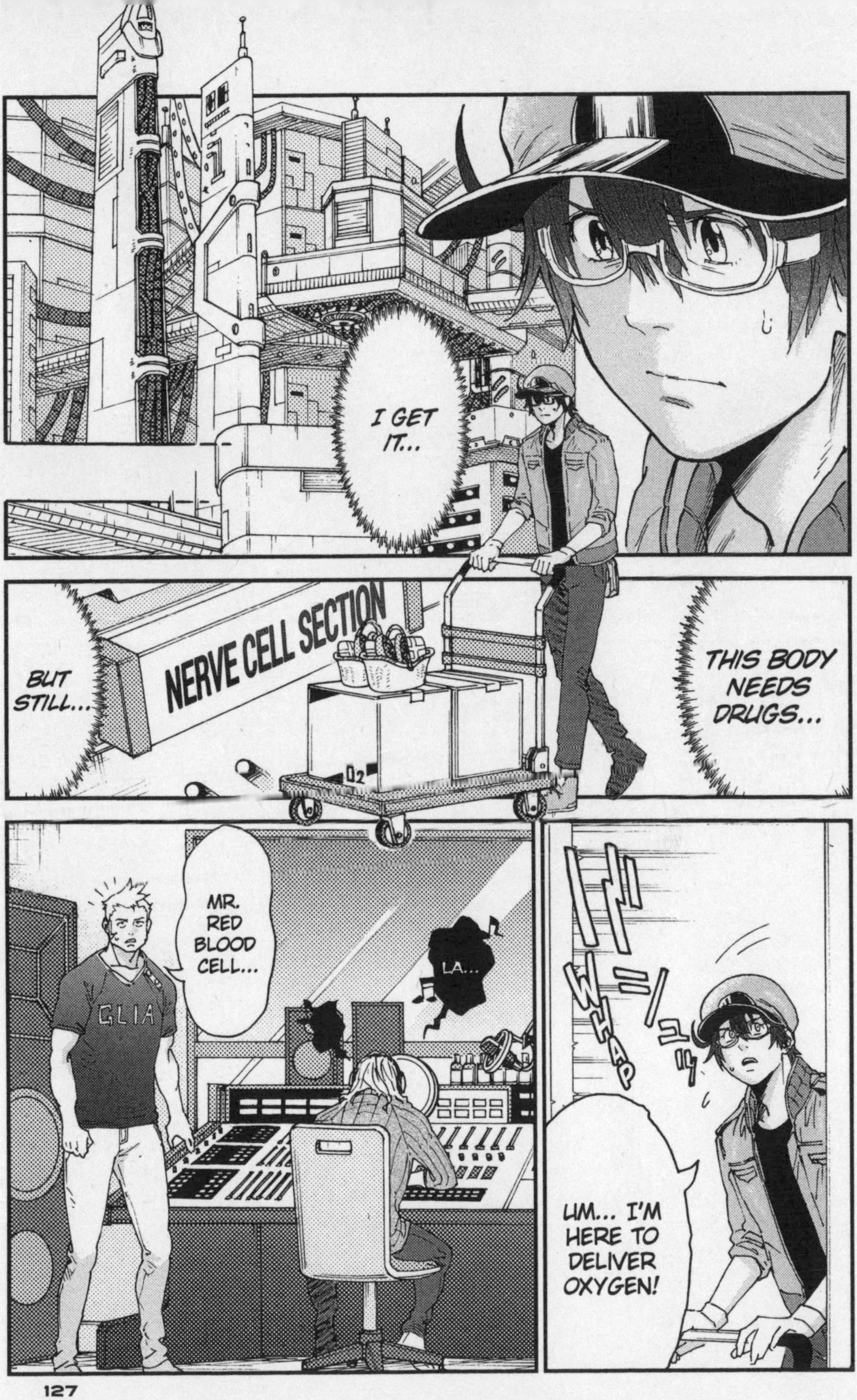
I GET IT...
THIS BODY NEEDS DRUGS...
NERVE CELL SECTION
BUT STILL...
WHHAP
UM... I'M HERE TO DELIVER OXYGEN!
MR. RED BLOOD CELL...
LA...
GLIA

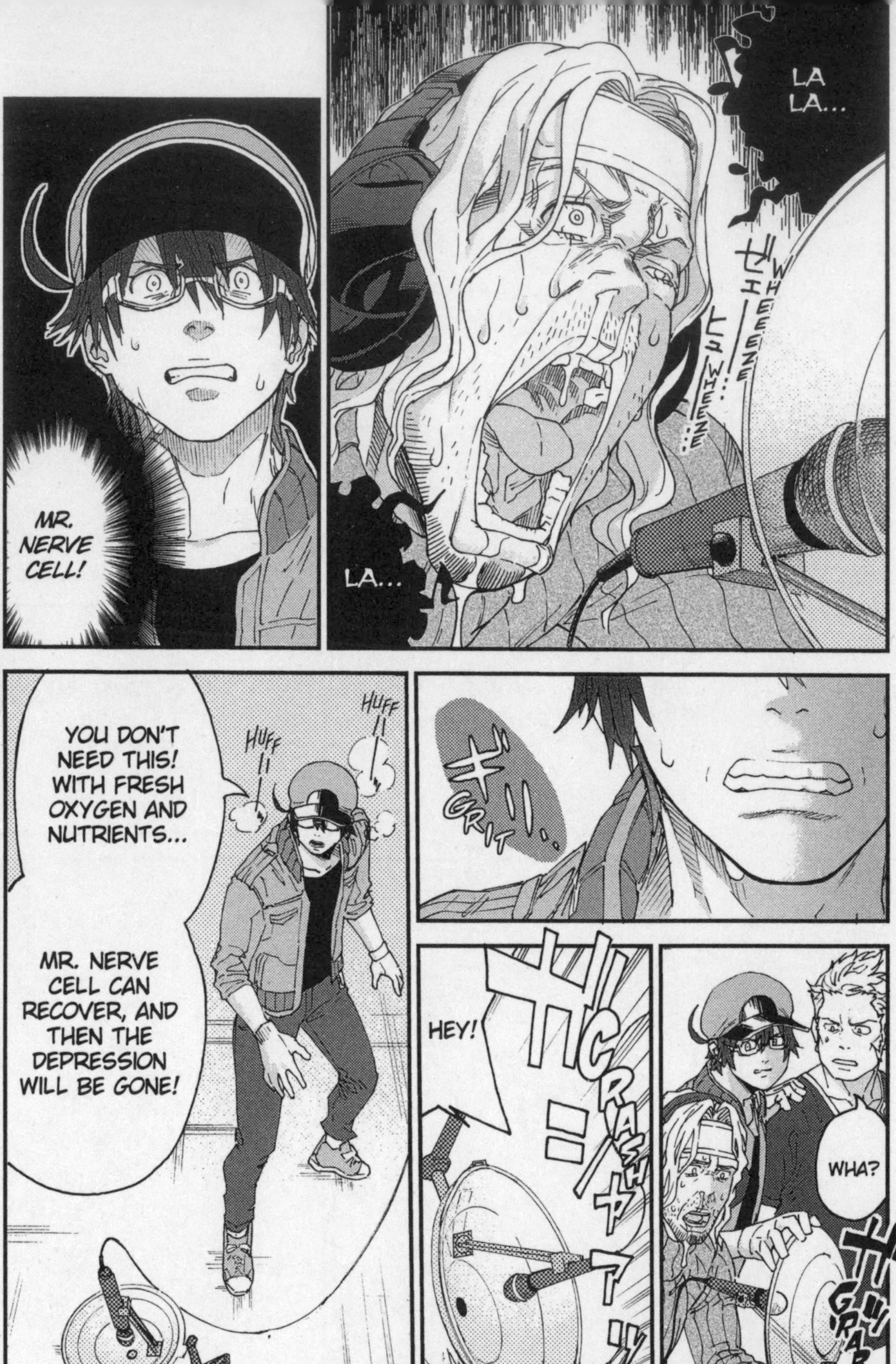
LA LA...
WHEEZE... WHEEZE...
LA...
MR. NERVE CELL!
GRIT
WHA?
GRAB
HEY!
CRASH
HUFF HUFF
YOU DON'T NEED THIS! WITH FRESH OXYGEN AND NUTRIENTS...
MR. NERVE CELL CAN RECOVER, AND THEN THE DEPRESSION WILL BE GONE!

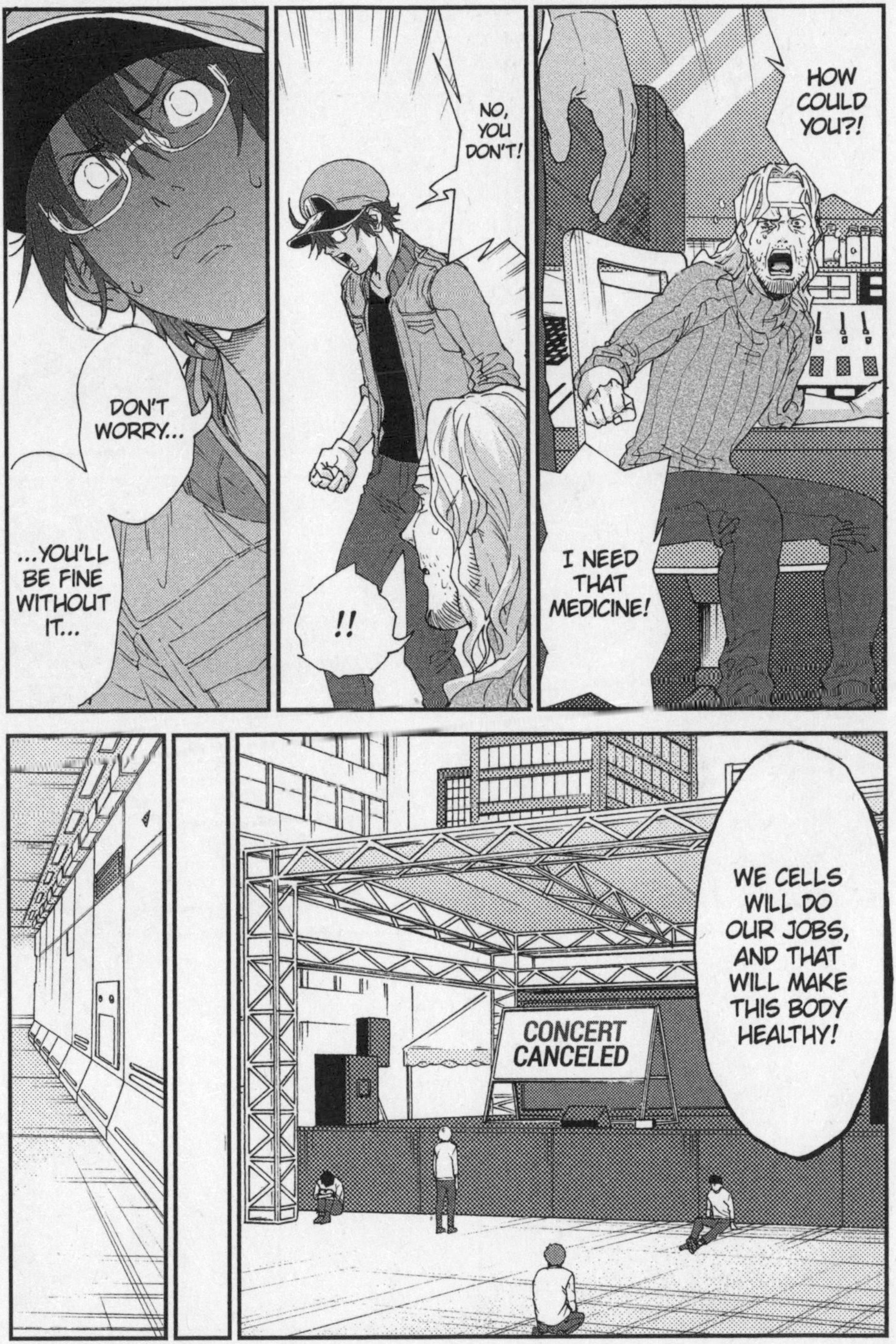
HOW COULD YOU?!
I NEED THAT MEDICINE!
NO, YOU DON'T!
!!
DON'T WORRY...
...YOU'LL BE FINE WITHOUT IT...
WE CELLS WILL DO OUR JOBS, AND THAT WILL MAKE THIS BODY HEALTHY!
CONCERT CANCELED

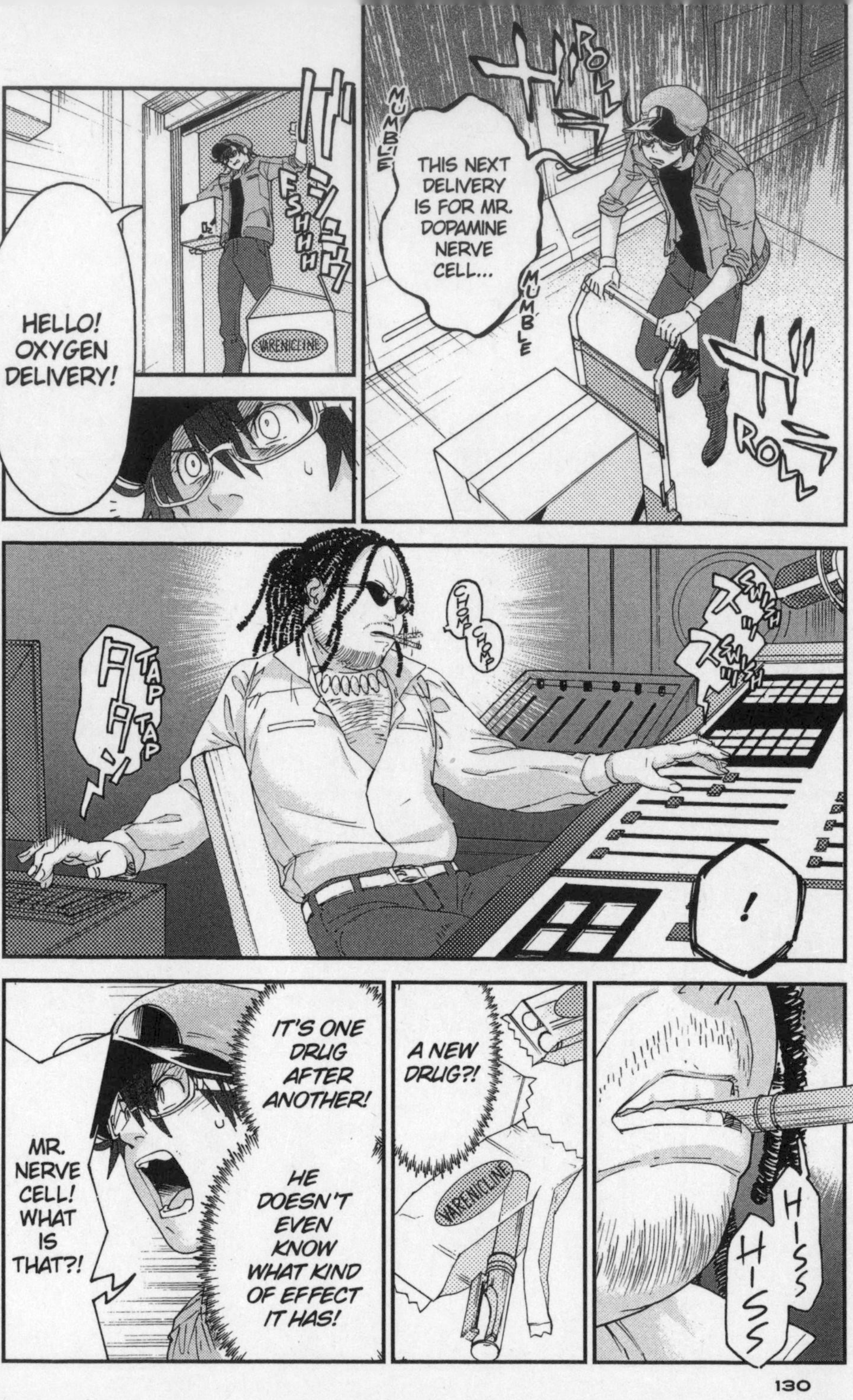
ROLL
MUMBLE
THIS NEXT DELIVERY IS FOR MR. DOPAMINE NERVE CELL...
MUMBLE
ROLL
FSHHH
VARENICLINE
HELLO! OXYGEN DELIVERY!
SWISH
SWISH
CHOMP CHOMP
TAP TAP
!
HISS HISS
QUIT
A NEW DRUG?!
VARENICLINE
IT'S ONE DRUG AFTER ANOTHER!
HE DOESN'T EVEN KNOW WHAT KIND OF EFFECT IT HAS!
MR. NERVE CELL! WHAT IS THAT?!

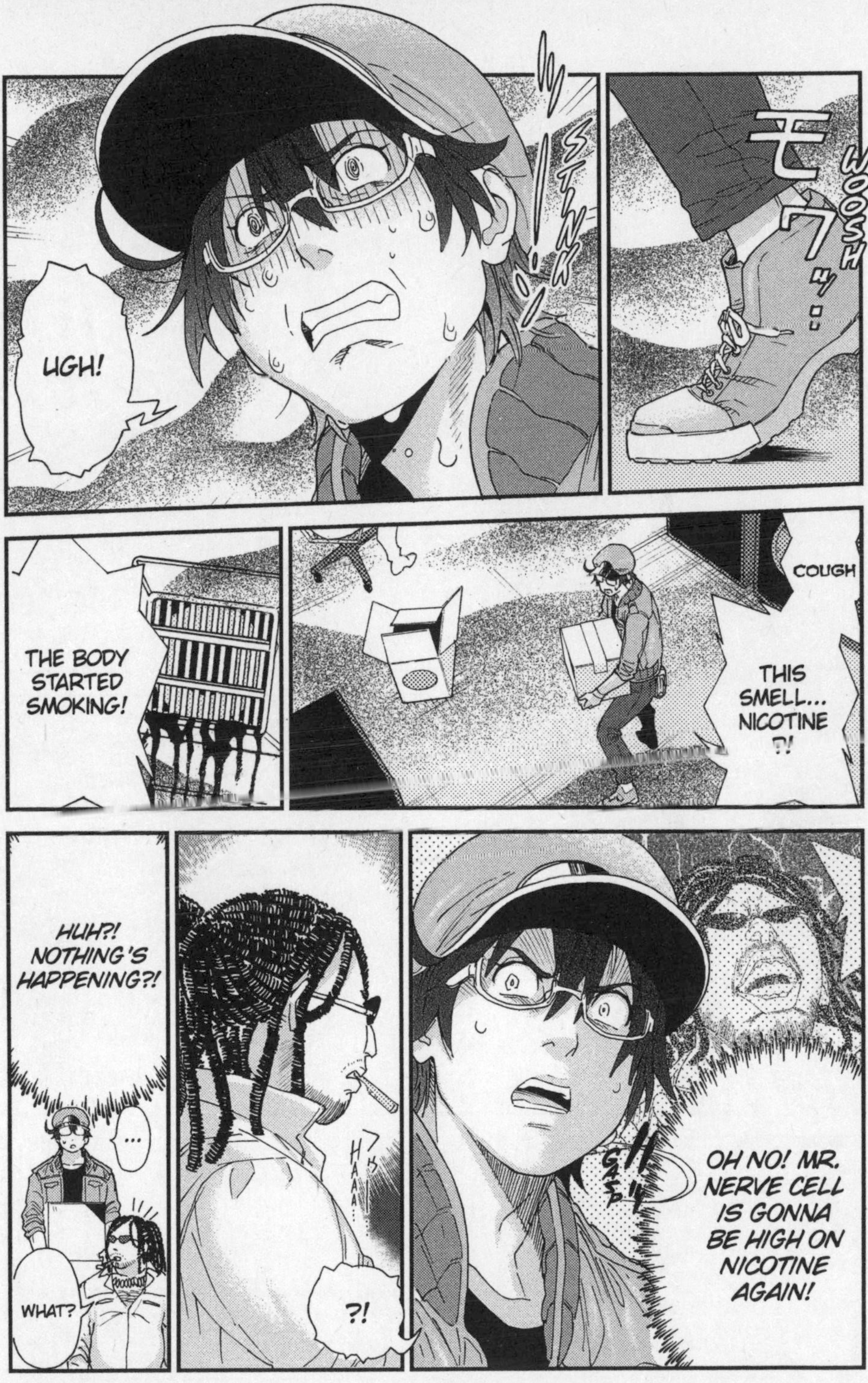

WOOSH
モワッ
STINK
UGH!
COUGH
THIS SMELL... NICOTINE ?!
THE BODY STARTED SMOKING!
GASP
OH NO! MR. NERVE CELL IS GONNA BE HIGH ON NICOTINE AGAIN!
HAAA...
?!
HUH?! NOTHING'S HAPPENING?!
...
WHAT?

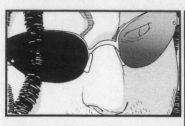

MR. NERVE CELL! WHY AREN'T YOU AFFECTED BY THE NICOTINE?!

...?

I GUESS IT'S THIS NEW DRUG...

WHAT?

WHEN I USE THIS...

NICOTINE DOESN'T MAKE ME FEEL HIGH...

COMMANDER! THE SMOKING IS NOT CAUSING DOPAMINE TO INCREASE!

WHAT?!

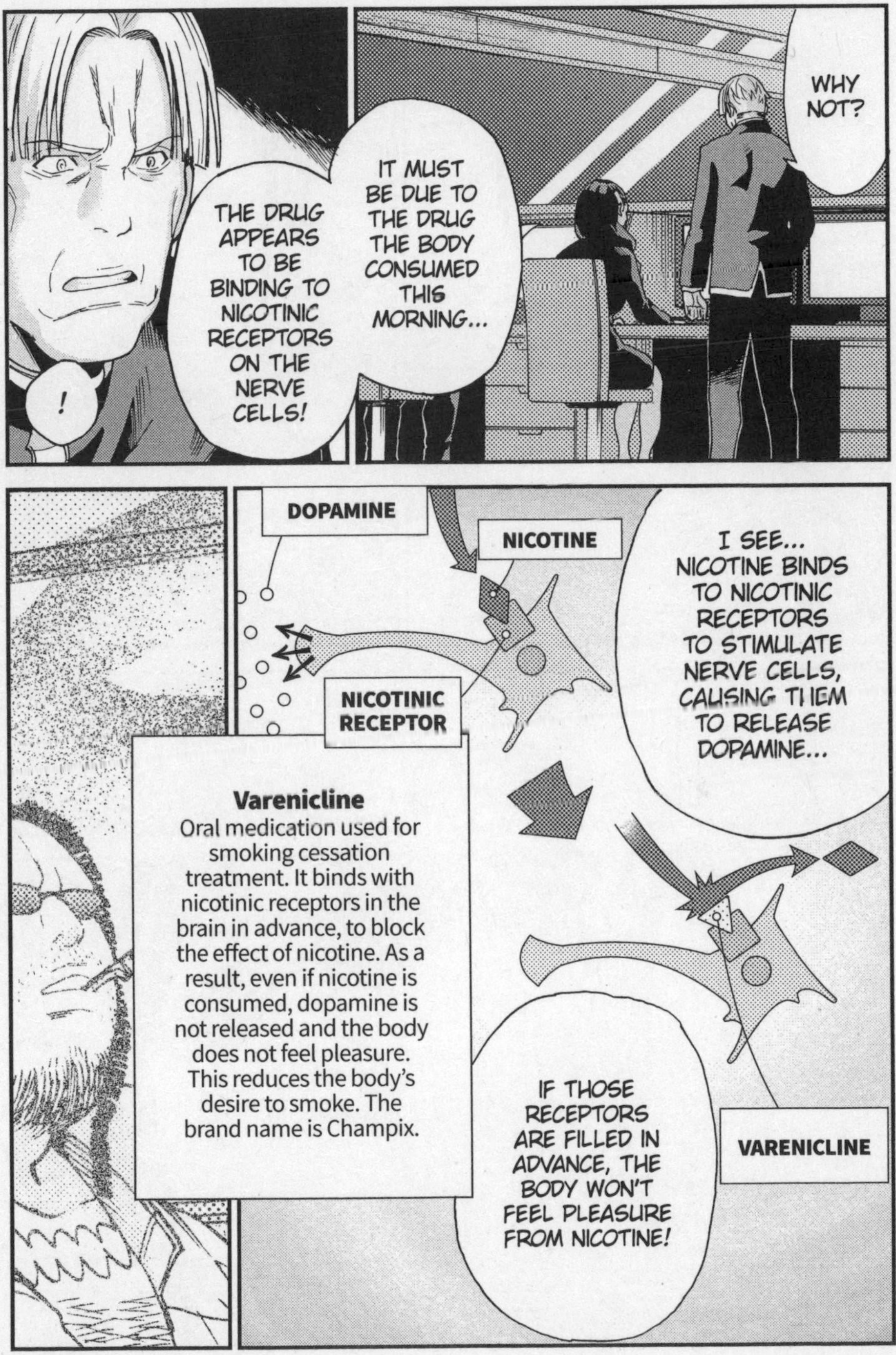
WHY NOT?
IT MUST BE DUE TO THE DRUG THE BODY CONSUMED THIS MORNING...
THE DRUG APPEARS TO BE BINDING TO NICOTINIC RECEPTORS ON THE NERVE CELLS!
!
I SEE... NICOTINE BINDS TO NICOTINIC RECEPTORS TO STIMULATE NERVE CELLS, CAUSING THEM TO RELEASE DOPAMINE...
NICOTINE
DOPAMINE
NICOTINIC RECEPTOR
IF THOSE RECEPTORS ARE FILLED IN ADVANCE, THE BODY WON'T FEEL PLEASURE FROM NICOTINE!
VARENICLINE
Varenicline
Oral medication used for smoking cessation treatment. It binds with nicotinic receptors in the brain in advance, to block the effect of nicotine. As a result, even if nicotine is consumed, dopamine is not released and the body does not feel pleasure. This reduces the body's desire to smoke. The brand name is Champix.

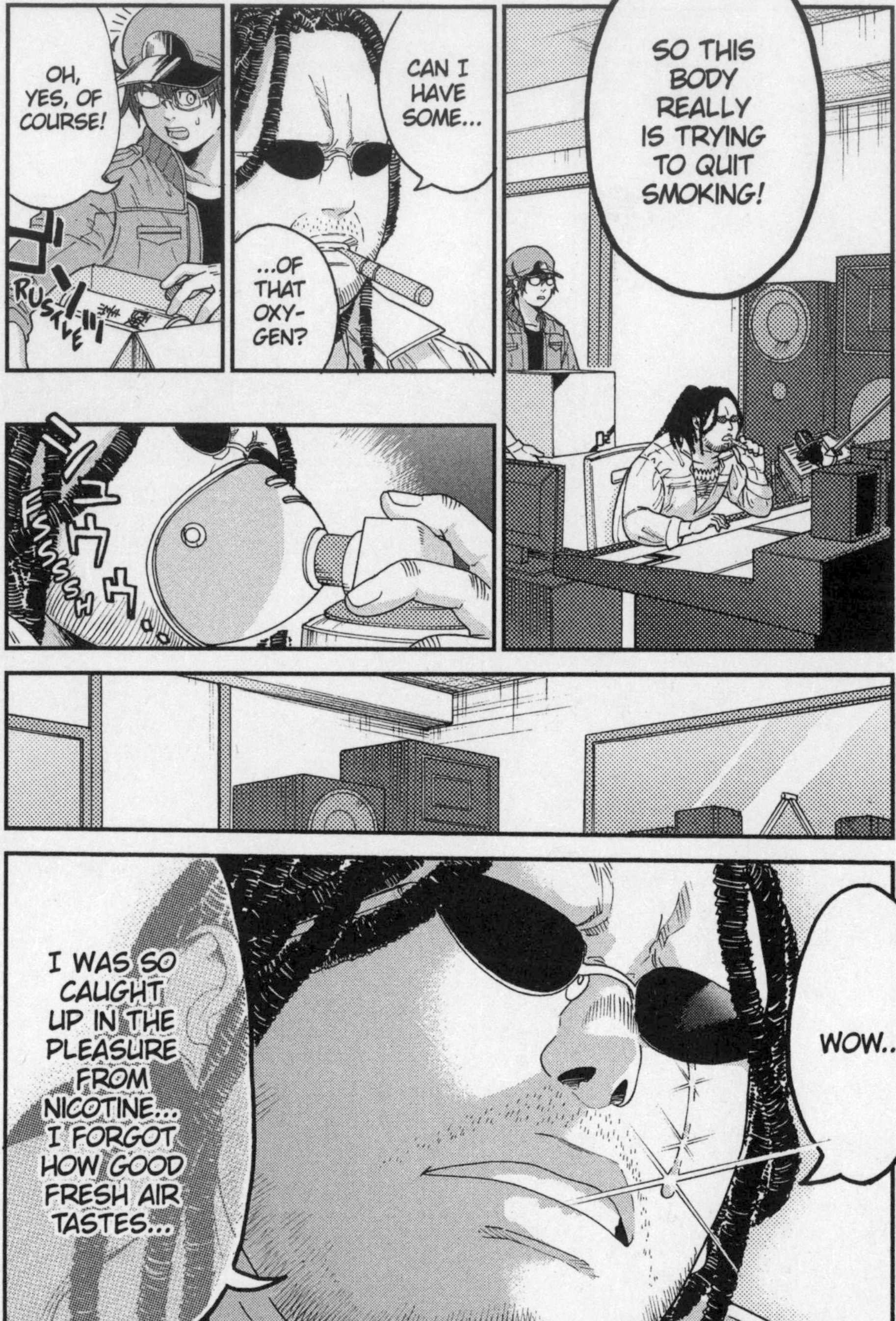
SO THIS BODY REALLY IS TRYING TO QUIT SMOKING!
CAN I HAVE SOME...
...OF THAT OXYGEN?
OH, YES, OF COURSE!
RUSTLE
FSSSSH
WOW...
I WAS SO CAUGHT UP IN THE PLEASURE FROM NICOTINE... I FORGOT HOW GOOD FRESH AIR TASTES...

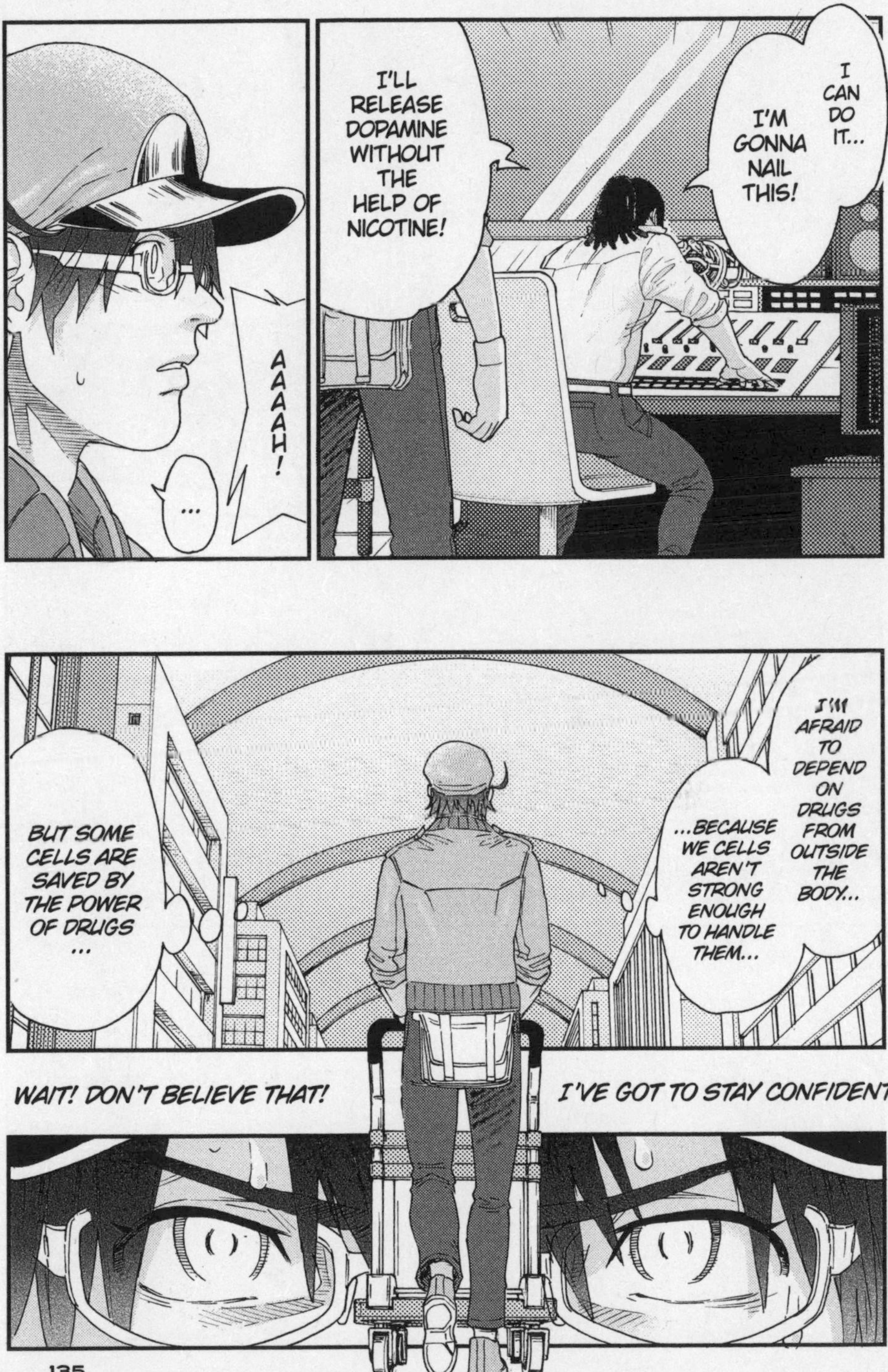
I CAN DO IT...
I'M GONNA NAIL THIS!
I'LL RELEASE DOPAMINE WITHOUT THE HELP OF NICOTINE!
AAAAH!
...
I'M AFRAID TO DEPEND ON DRUGS FROM OUTSIDE THE BODY...
...BECAUSE WE CELLS AREN'T STRONG ENOUGH TO HANDLE THEM...
BUT SOME CELLS ARE SAVED BY THE POWER OF DRUGS ...
I'VE GOT TO STAY CONFIDENT!
WAIT! DON'T BELIEVE THAT!

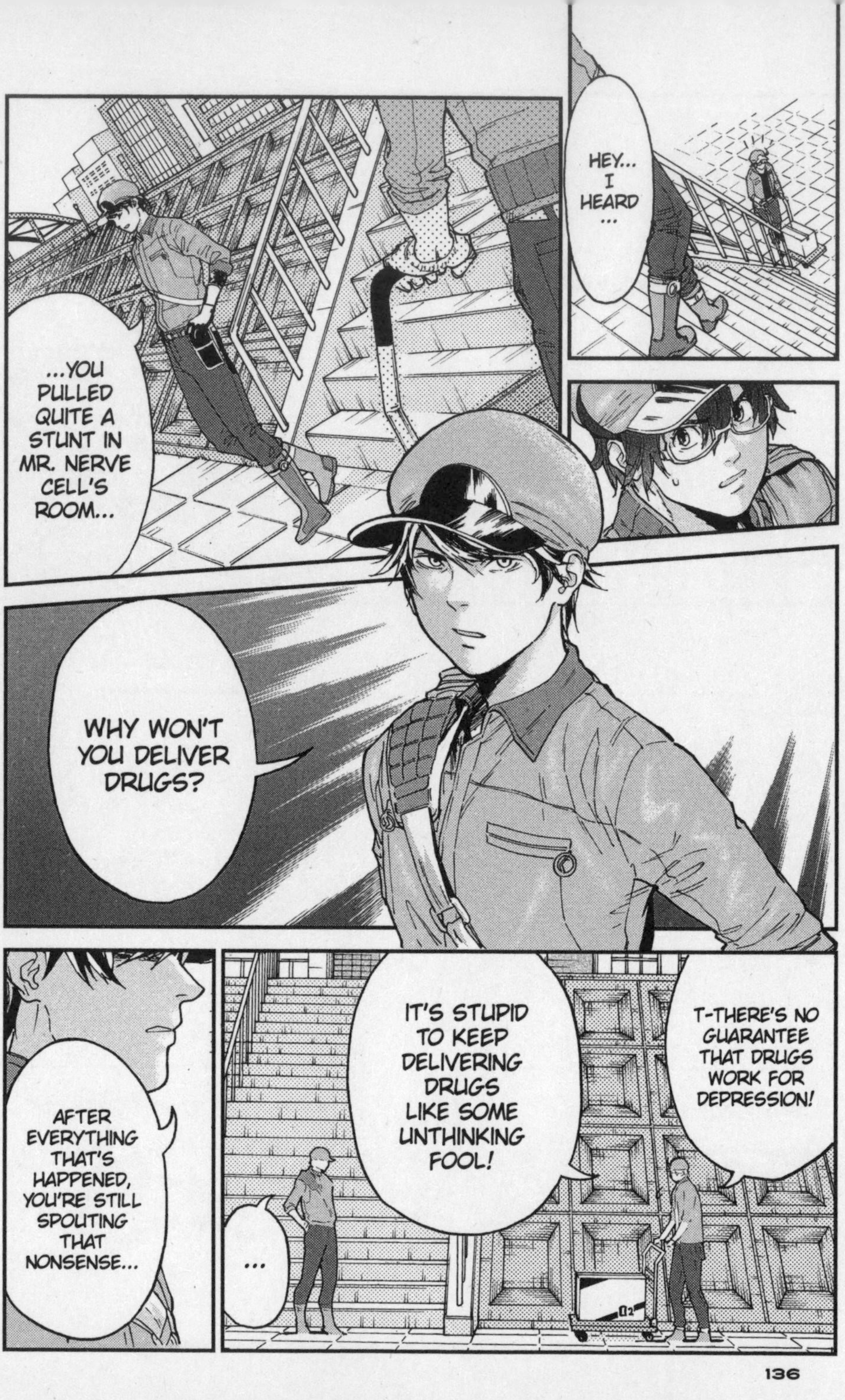
HEY... I HEARD...
...YOU PULLED QUITE A STUNT IN MR. NERVE CELL'S ROOM...
WHY WON'T YOU DELIVER DRUGS?
T-THERE'S NO GUARANTEE THAT DRUGS WORK FOR DEPRESSION!
IT'S STUPID TO KEEP DELIVERING DRUGS LIKE SOME UNTHINKING FOOL!
...
AFTER EVERYTHING THAT'S HAPPENED, YOU'RE STILL SPOUTING THAT NONSENSE...

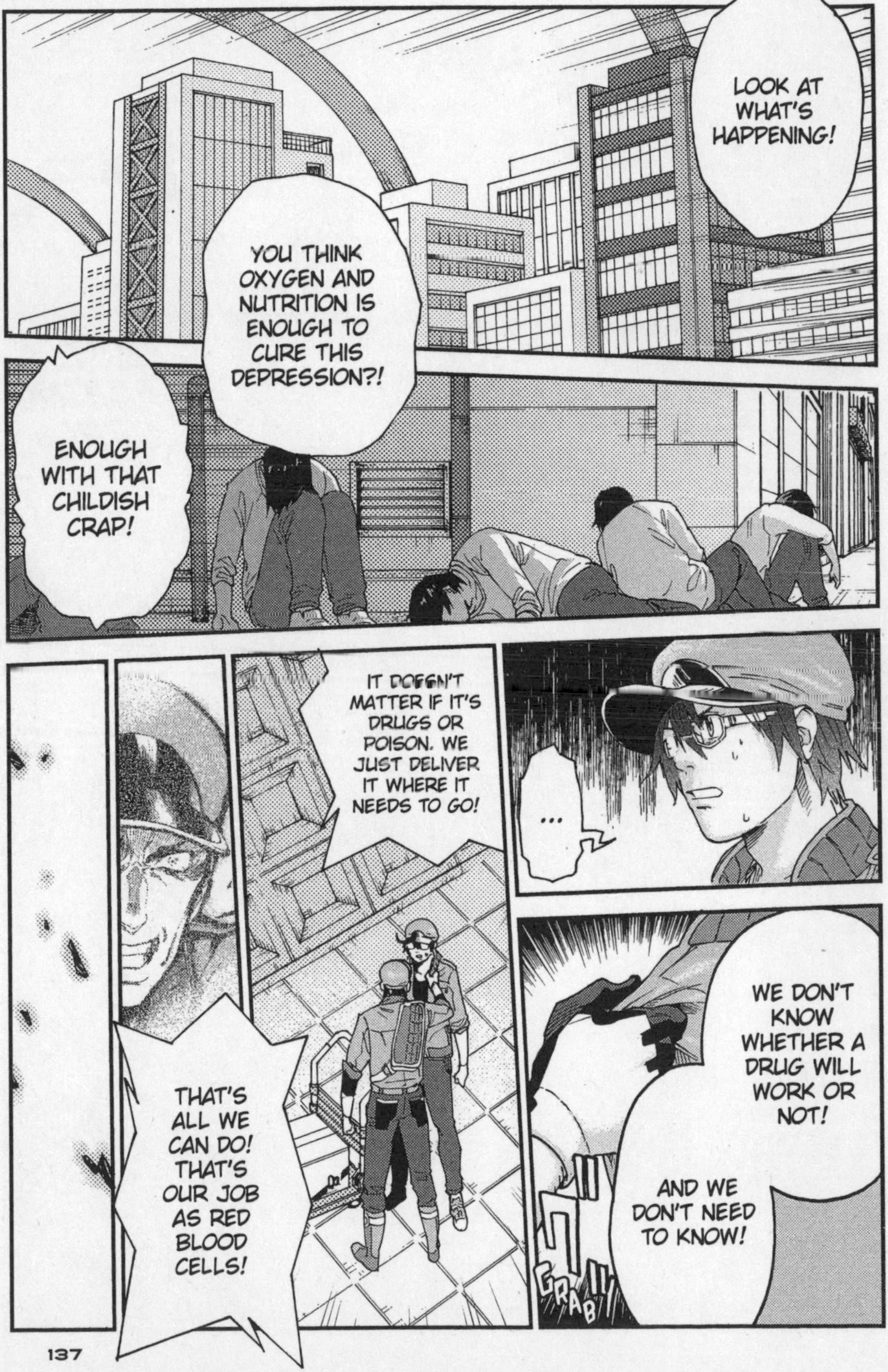
LOOK AT WHAT'S HAPPENING!
YOU THINK OXYGEN AND NUTRITION IS ENOUGH TO CURE THIS DEPRESSION?!
ENOUGH WITH THAT CHILDISH CRAP!
...
WE DON'T KNOW WHETHER A DRUG WILL WORK OR NOT!
AND WE DON'T NEED TO KNOW!
GRAB
IT DOESN'T MATTER IF IT'S DRUGS OR POISON. WE JUST DELIVER IT WHERE IT NEEDS TO GO!
THAT'S ALL WE CAN DO! THAT'S OUR JOB AS RED BLOOD CELLS!

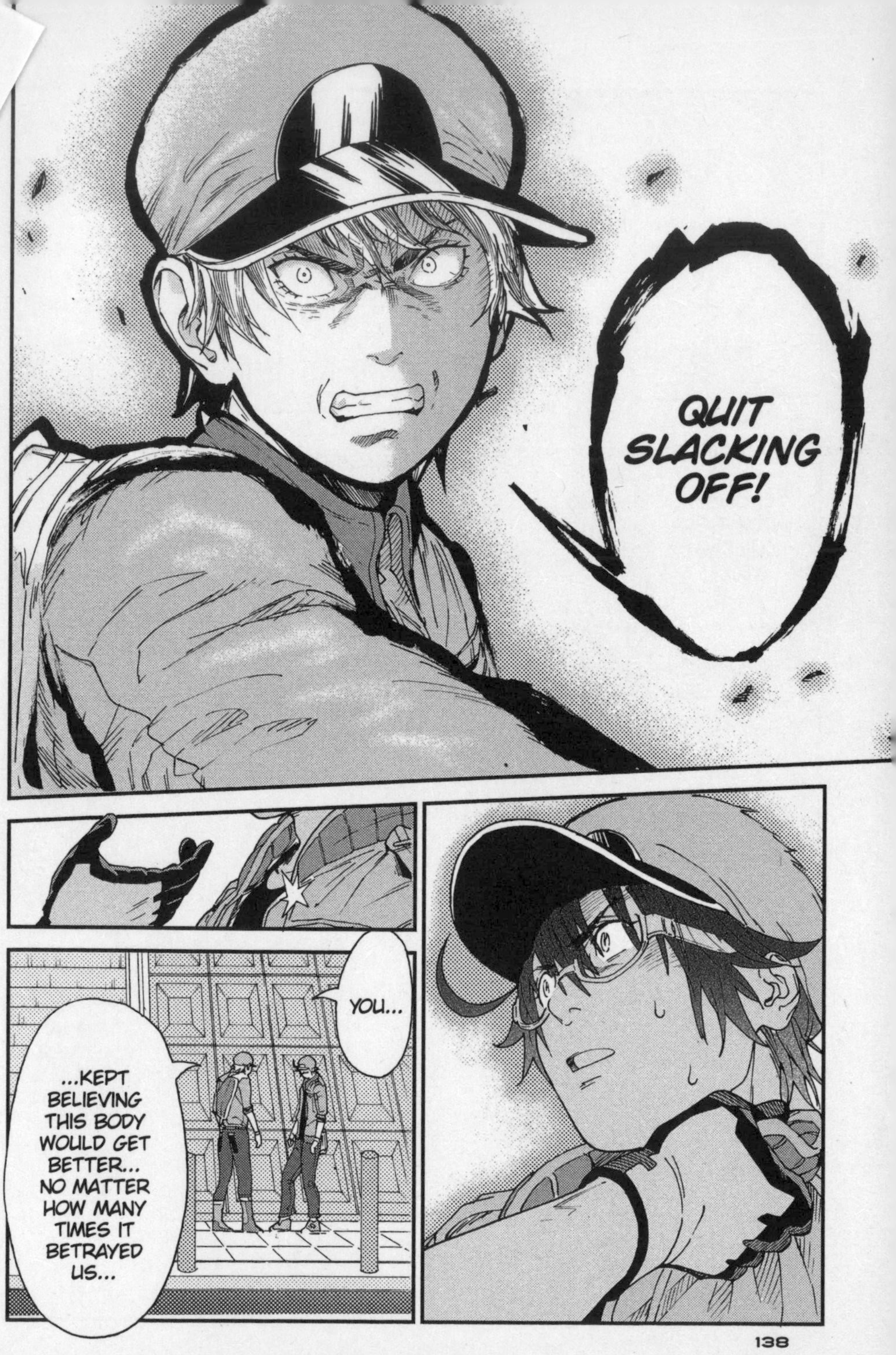
QUIT SLACKING OFF!
YOU...
...KEPT BELIEVING THIS BODY WOULD GET BETTER... NO MATTER HOW MANY TIMES IT BETRAYED US...

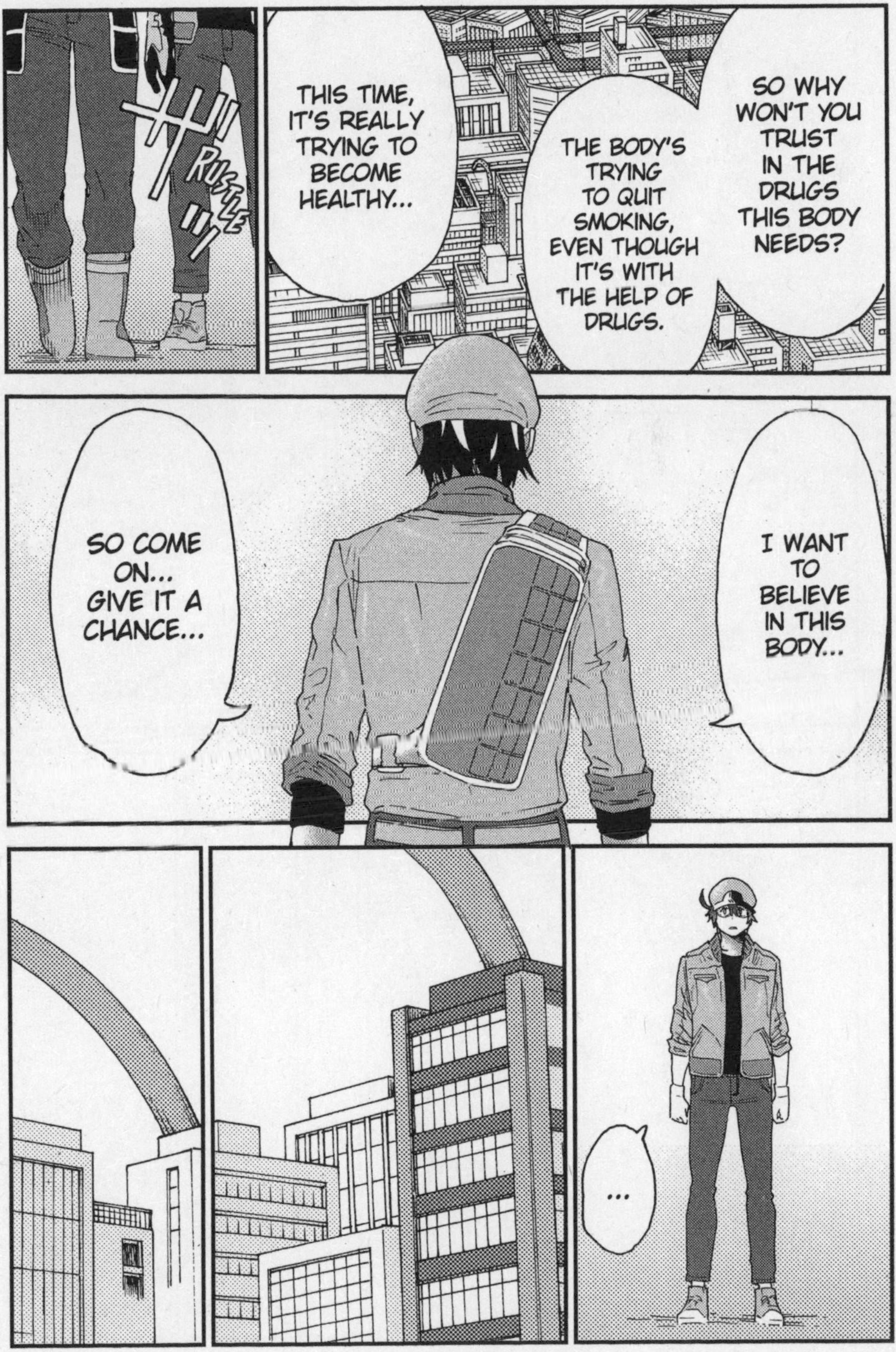
SO WHY WON'T YOU TRUST IN THE DRUGS THIS BODY NEEDS?
THE BODY'S TRYING TO QUIT SMOKING, EVEN THOUGH IT'S WITH THE HELP OF DRUGS.
THIS TIME, IT'S REALLY TRYING TO BECOME HEALTHY...
RUSTLE
I WANT TO BELIEVE IN THIS BODY...
SO COME ON... GIVE IT A CHANCE...
...

MS. WHITE BLOOD CELL... I DON'T KNOW WHAT'S RIGHT ANYMORE...

MS. WHITE BLOOD CELL HASN'T AWAKENED SINCE THE BATTLE WITH PERIODONTAL DISEASE...

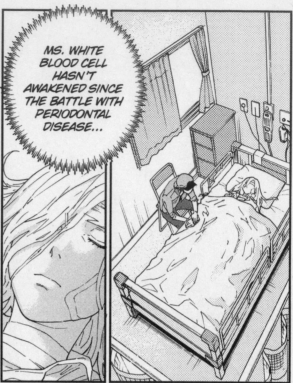

PLEASE...

COME BACK...!

HEY, CELLS! WE'RE BACK!

!

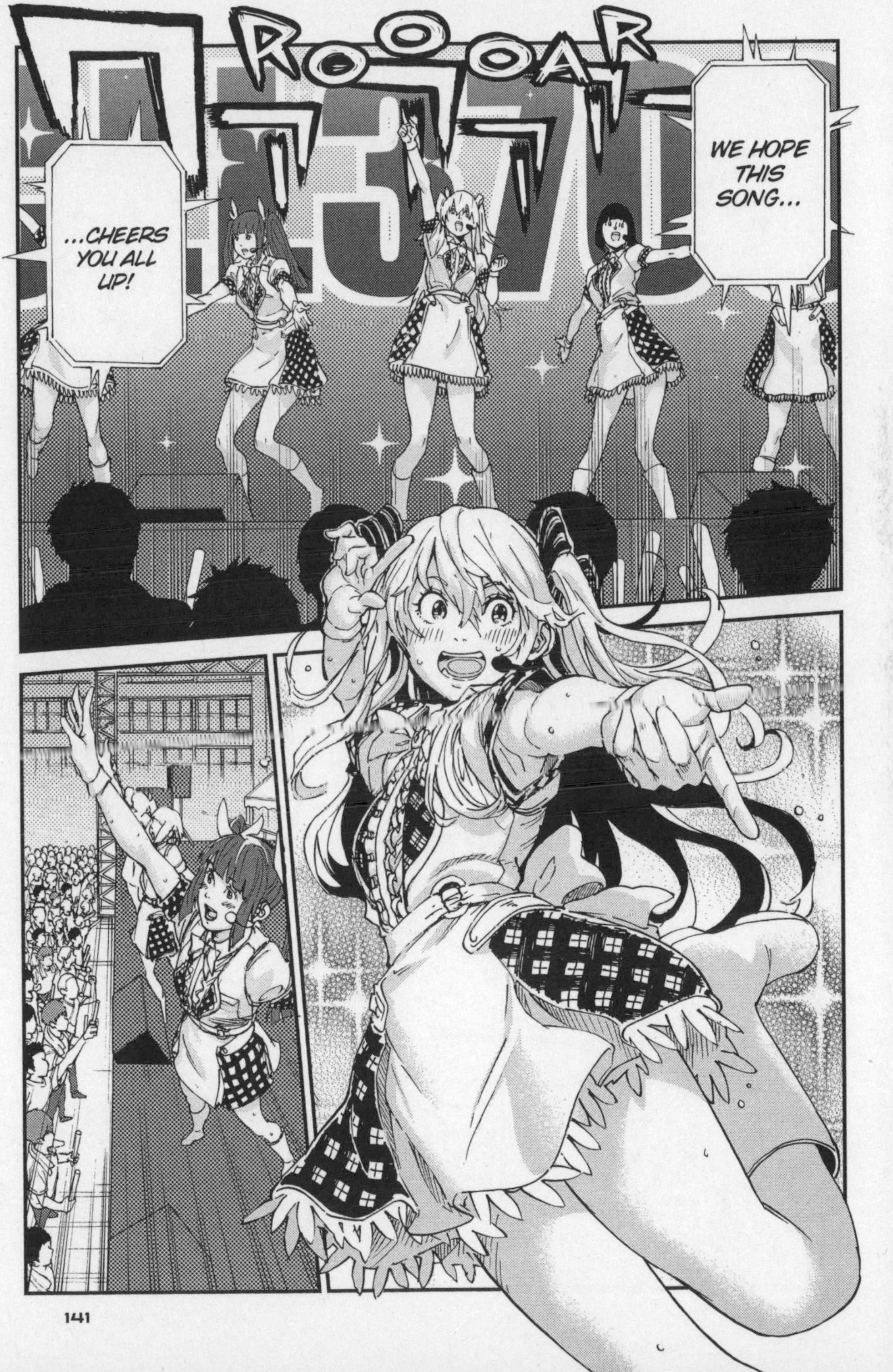
ROOOAR
WE HOPE THIS SONG...
...CHEERS YOU ALL UP!

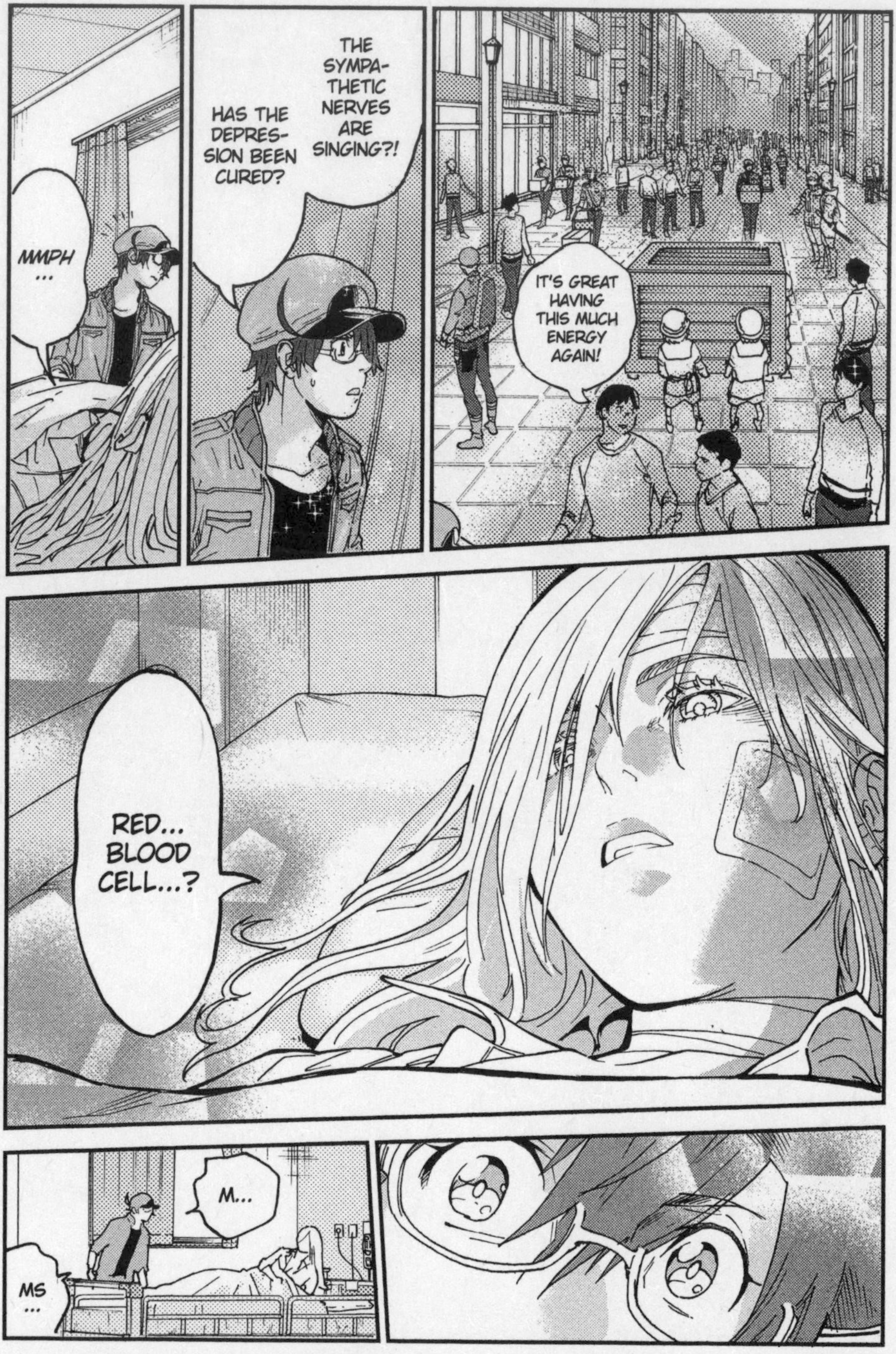
IT'S GREAT HAVING THIS MUCH ENERGY AGAIN!
THE SYMPA-THETIC NERVES ARE SINGING?!
HAS THE DEPRES-SION BEEN CURED?
MMPH ...
RED... BLOOD CELL...?
M...
MS ...

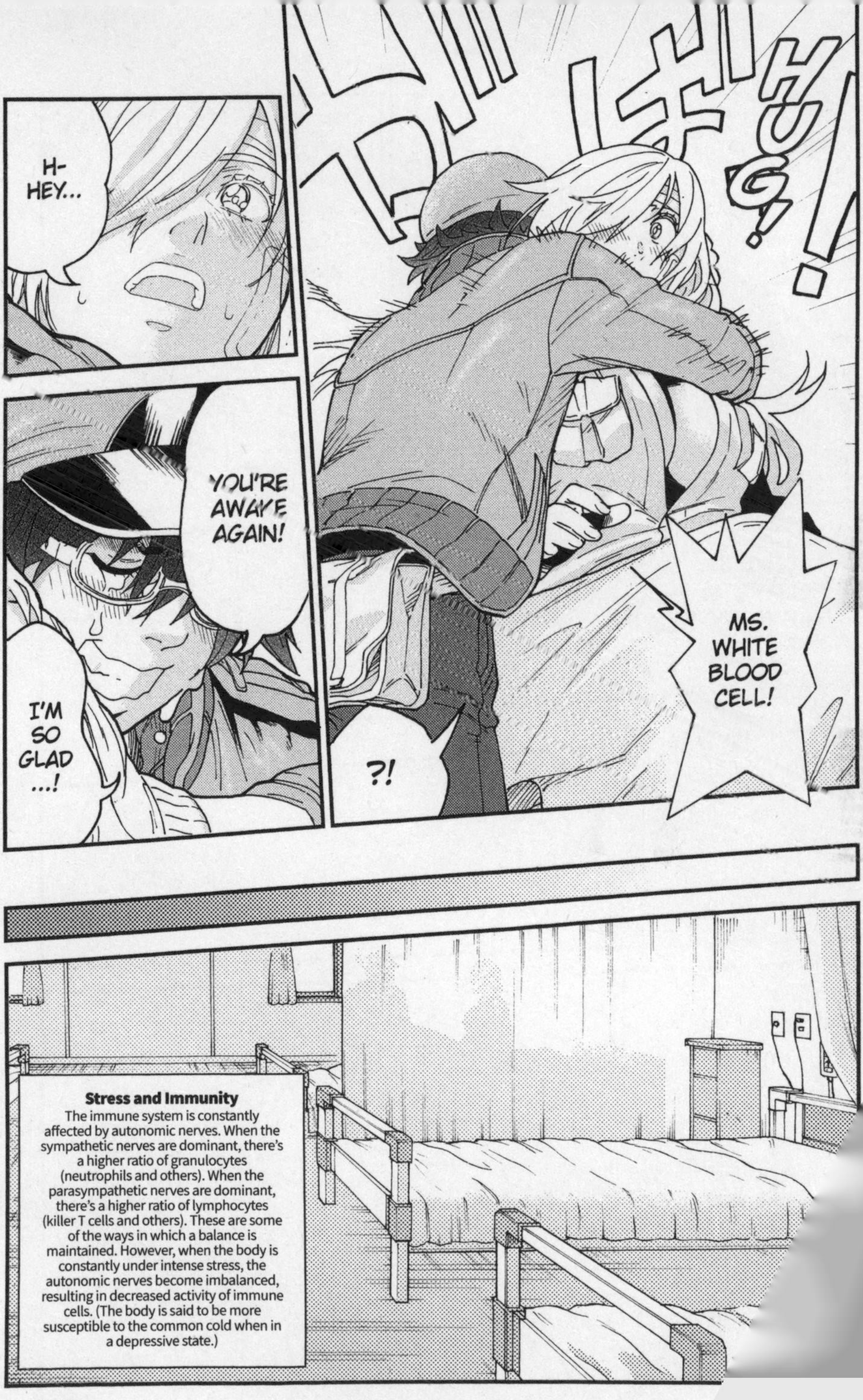
HUG!
MS. WHITE BLOOD CELL!
?!
H-HEY...
YOU'RE AWAKE AGAIN!
I'M SO GLAD ...!
Stress and Immunity
The immune system is constantly affected by autonomic nerves. When the sympathetic nerves are dominant, there's a higher ratio of granulocytes (neutrophils and others). When the parasympathetic nerves are dominant, there's a higher ratio of lymphocytes (killer T cells and others). These are some of the ways in which a balance is maintained. However, when the body is constantly under intense stress, the autonomic nerves become imbalanced, resulting in decreased activity of immune cells. (The body is said to be more susceptible to the common cold when in a depressive state.)

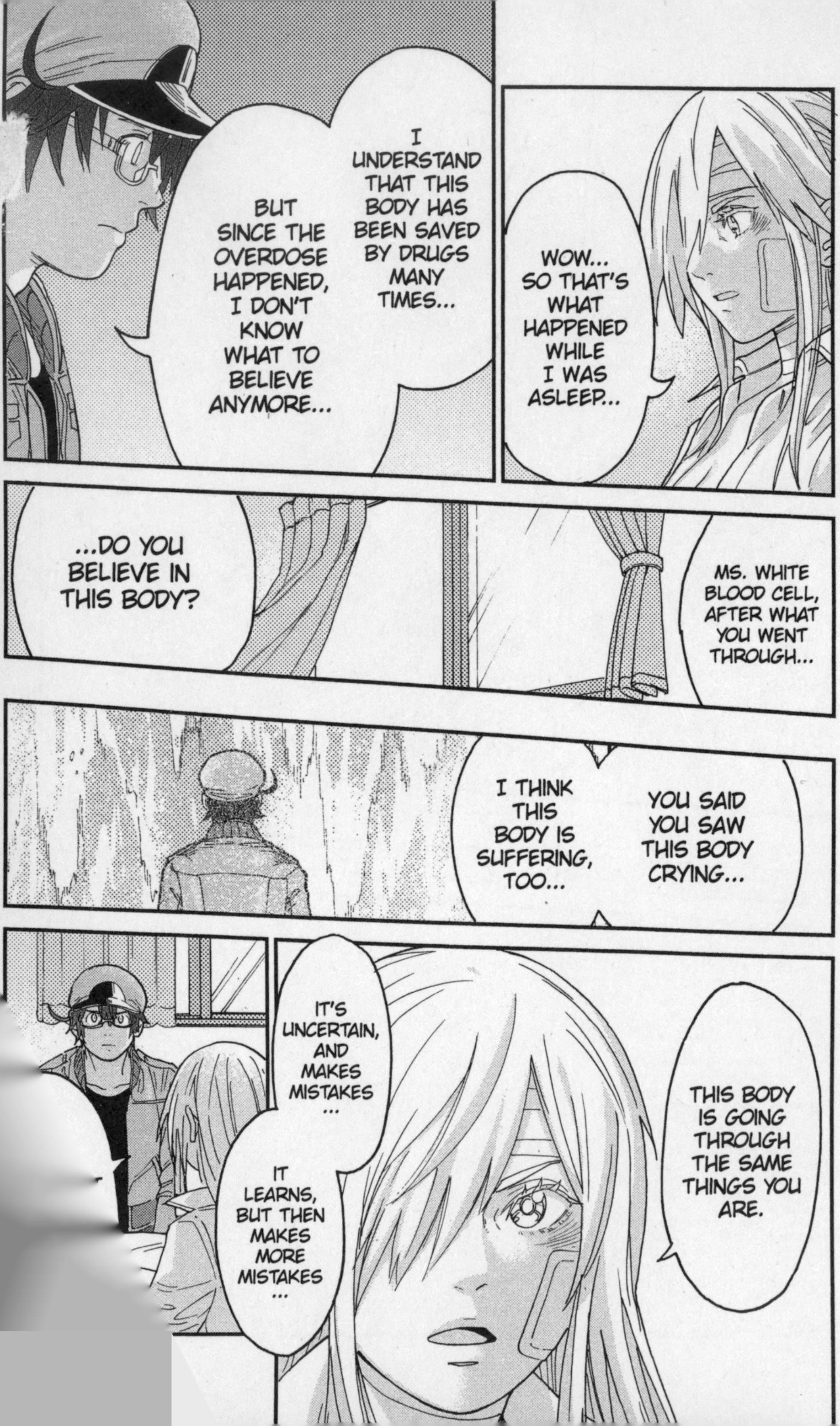
WOW... SO THAT'S WHAT HAPPENED WHILE I WAS ASLEEP...
I UNDERSTAND THAT THIS BODY HAS BEEN SAVED BY DRUGS MANY TIMES...
BUT SINCE THE OVERDOSE HAPPENED, I DON'T KNOW WHAT TO BELIEVE ANYMORE...
MS. WHITE BLOOD CELL, AFTER WHAT YOU WENT THROUGH...
...DO YOU BELIEVE IN THIS BODY?
YOU SAID YOU SAW THIS BODY CRYING...
I THINK THIS BODY IS SUFFERING, TOO...
THIS BODY IS GOING THROUGH THE SAME THINGS YOU ARE.
IT'S UNCERTAIN, AND MAKES MISTAKES ...
IT LEARNS, BUT THEN MAKES MORE MISTAKES ...

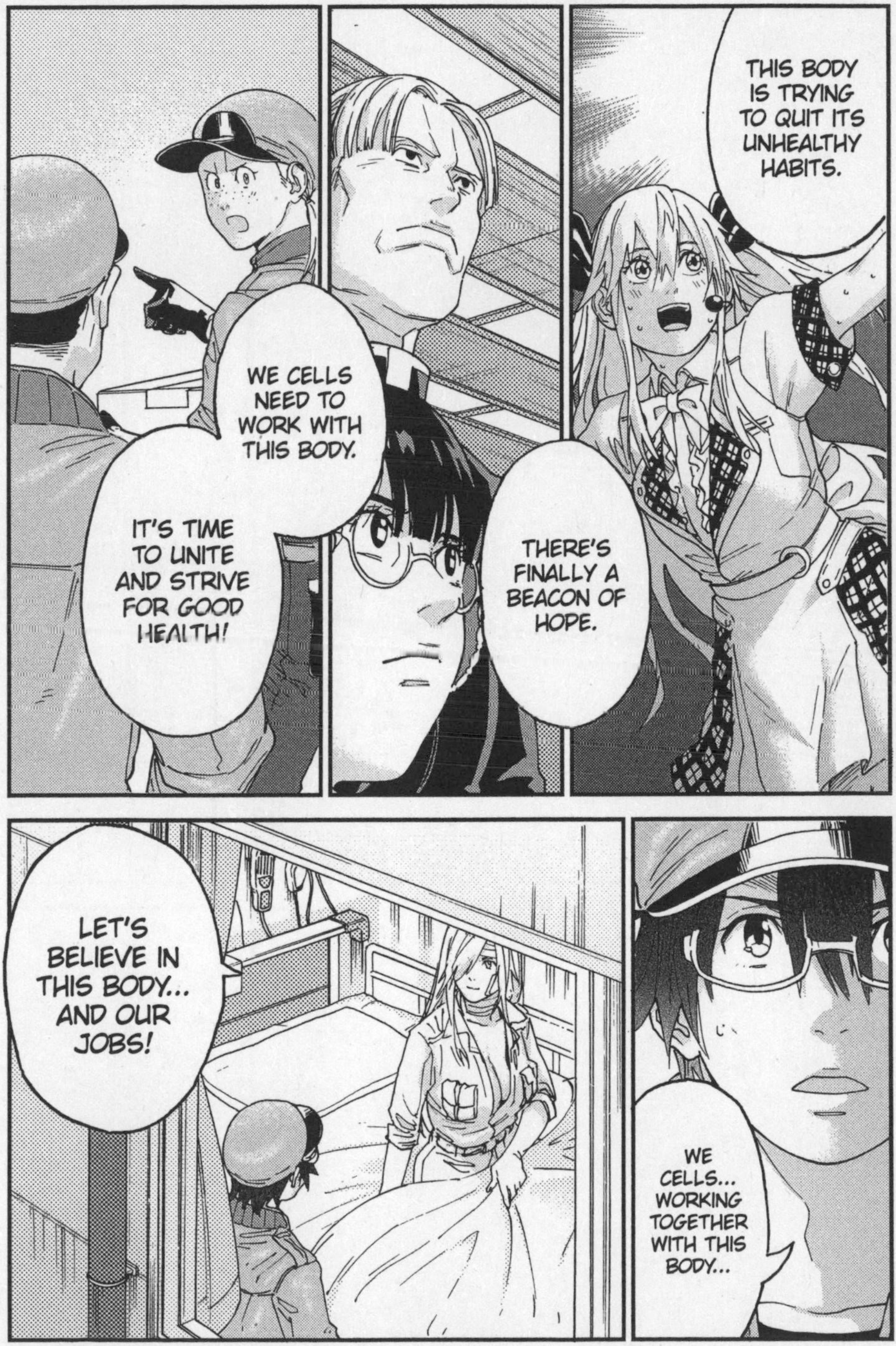
THIS BODY IS TRYING TO QUIT ITS UNHEALTHY HABITS.
THERE'S FINALLY A BEACON OF HOPE.
WE CELLS NEED TO WORK WITH THIS BODY.
IT'S TIME TO UNITE AND STRIVE FOR GOOD HEALTH!
WE CELLS... WORKING TOGETHER WITH THIS BODY...
LET'S BELIEVE IN THIS BODY... AND OUR JOBS!

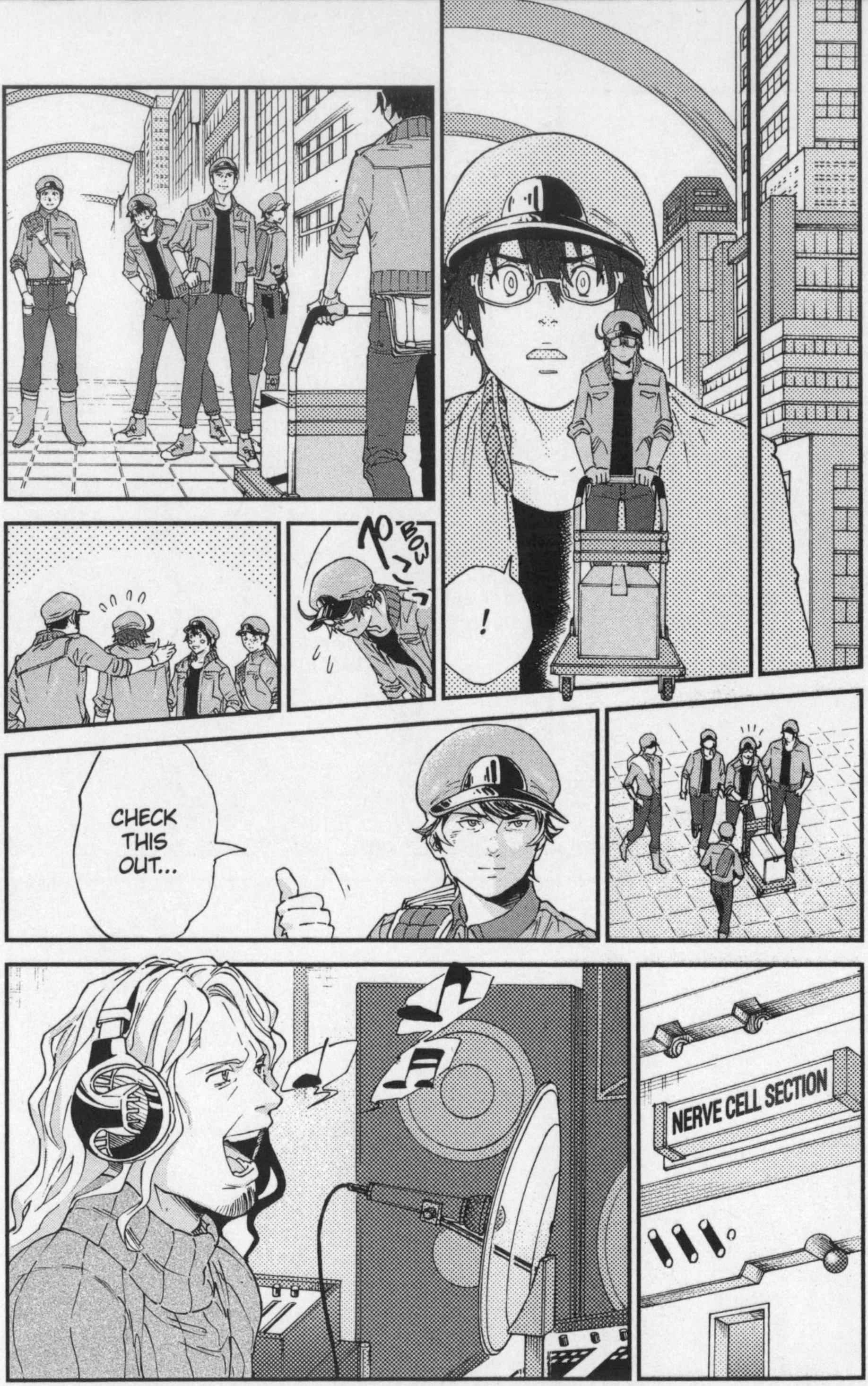
!
BOW
CHECK THIS OUT...
NERVE CELL SECTION

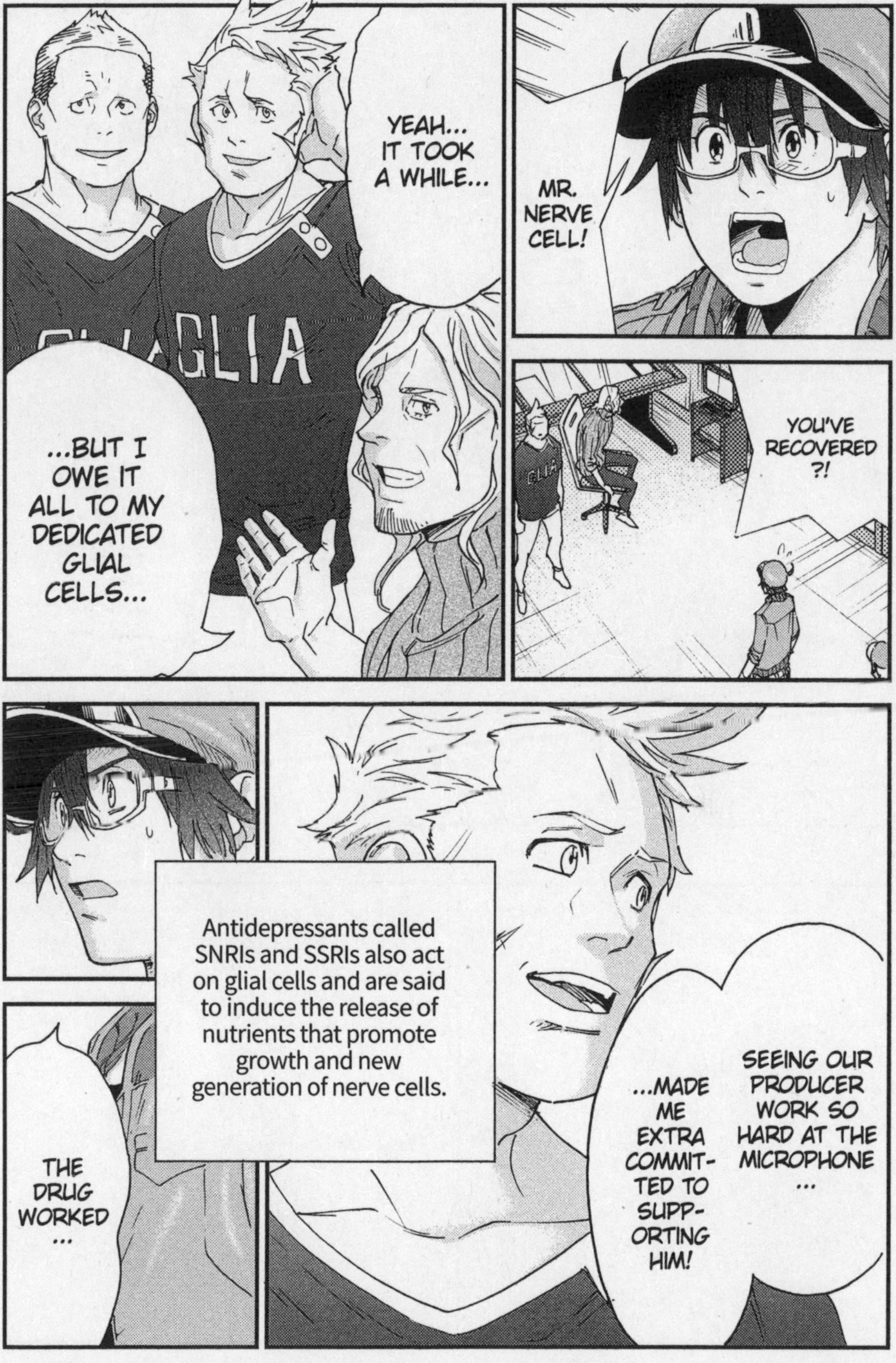
MR. NERVE CELL!
YOU'VE RECOVERED ?!
YEAH... IT TOOK A WHILE...
GLIA
...BUT I OWE IT ALL TO MY DEDICATED GLIAL CELLS...
SEEING OUR PRODUCER WORK SO HARD AT THE MICROPHONE ...
...MADE ME EXTRA COMMIT-TED TO SUPP-ORTING HIM!
Antidepressants called SNRIs and SSRIs also act on glial cells and are said to induce the release of nutrients that promote growth and new generation of nerve cells.
THE DRUG WORKED ...

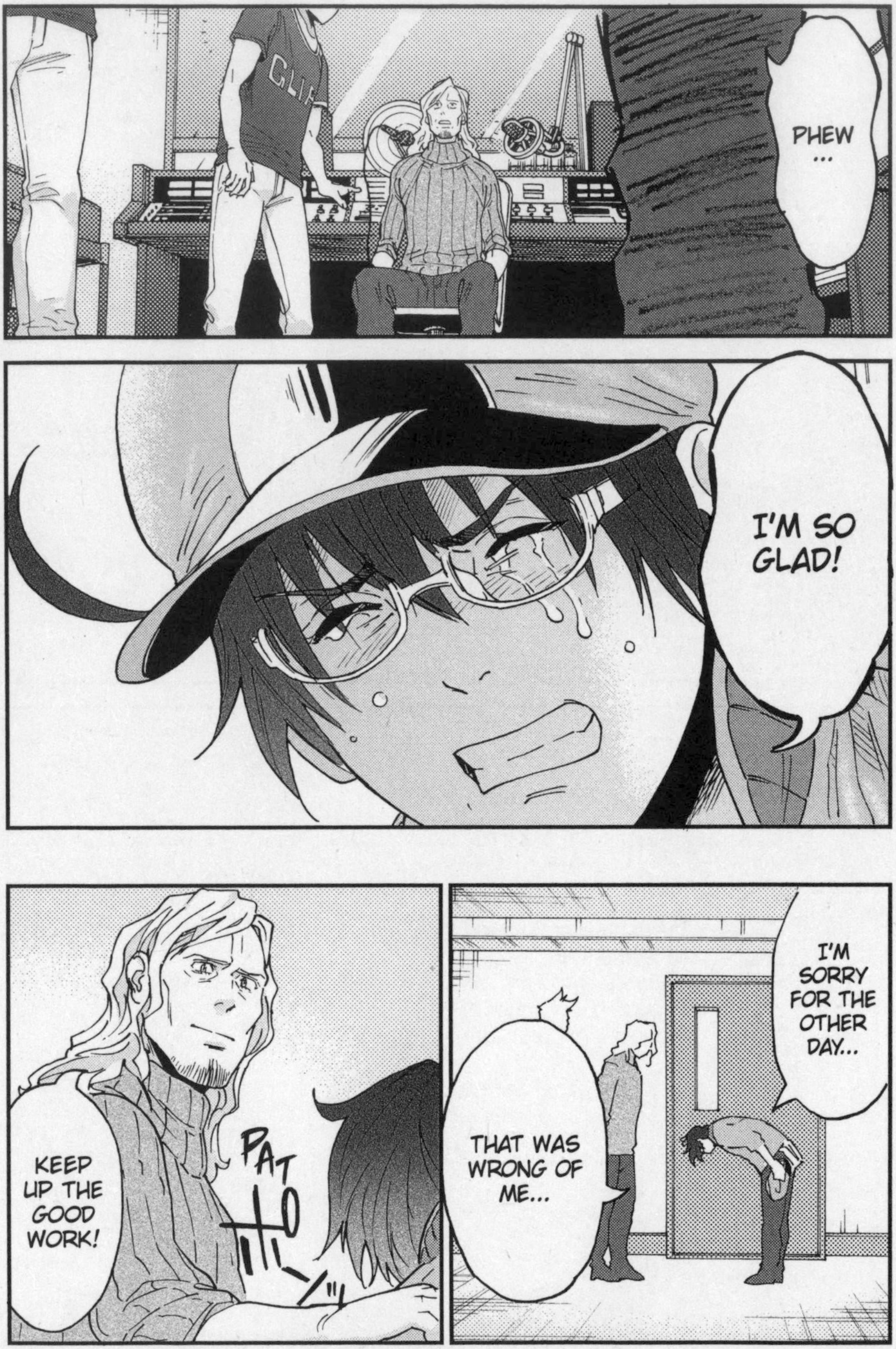
PHEW ...
I'M SO GLAD!
I'M SORRY FOR THE OTHER DAY...
THAT WAS WRONG OF ME...
PAT
KEEP UP THE GOOD WORK!

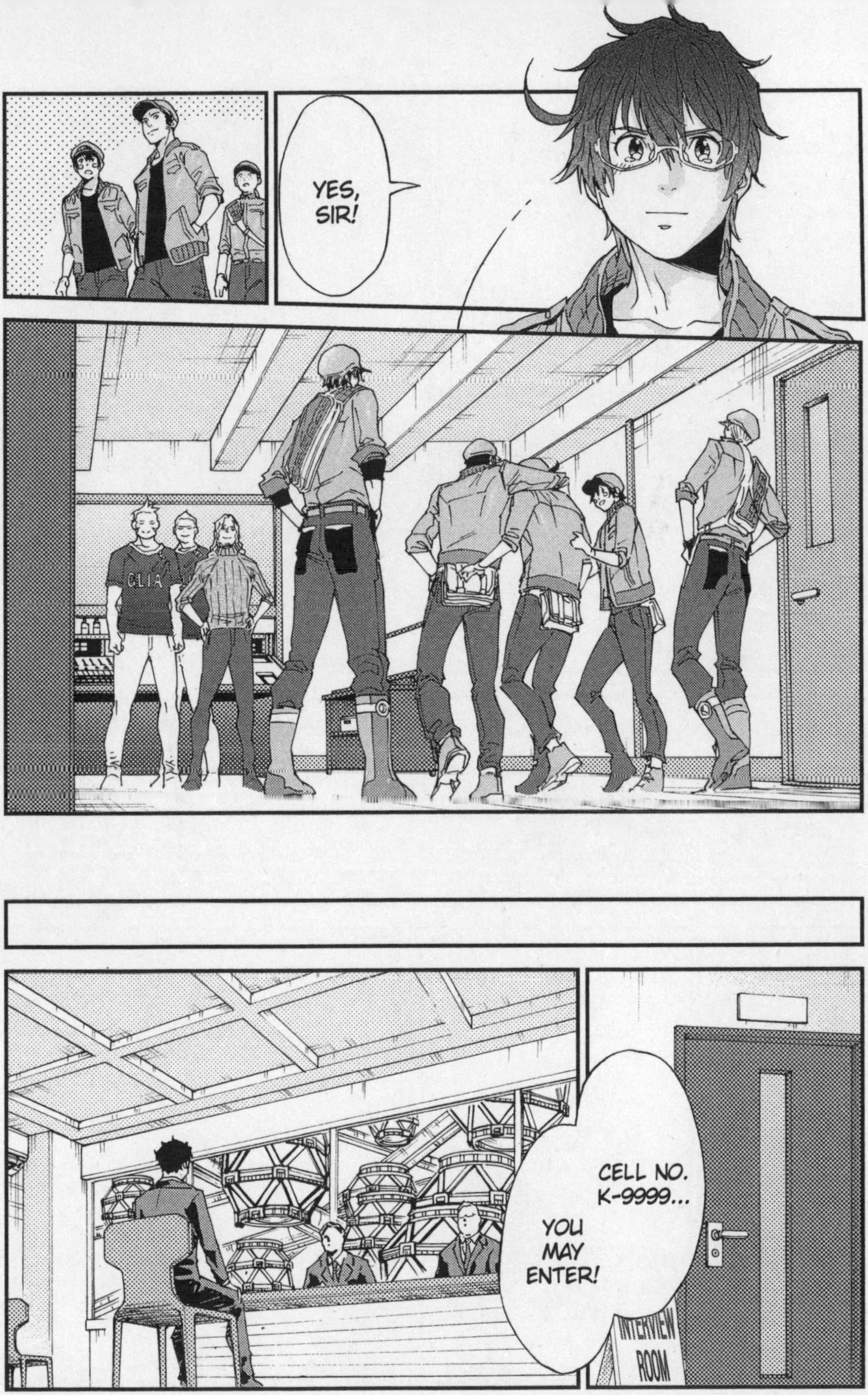
YES, SIR!
CELL NO. K-9999...
YOU MAY ENTER!
INTERVIEW ROOM

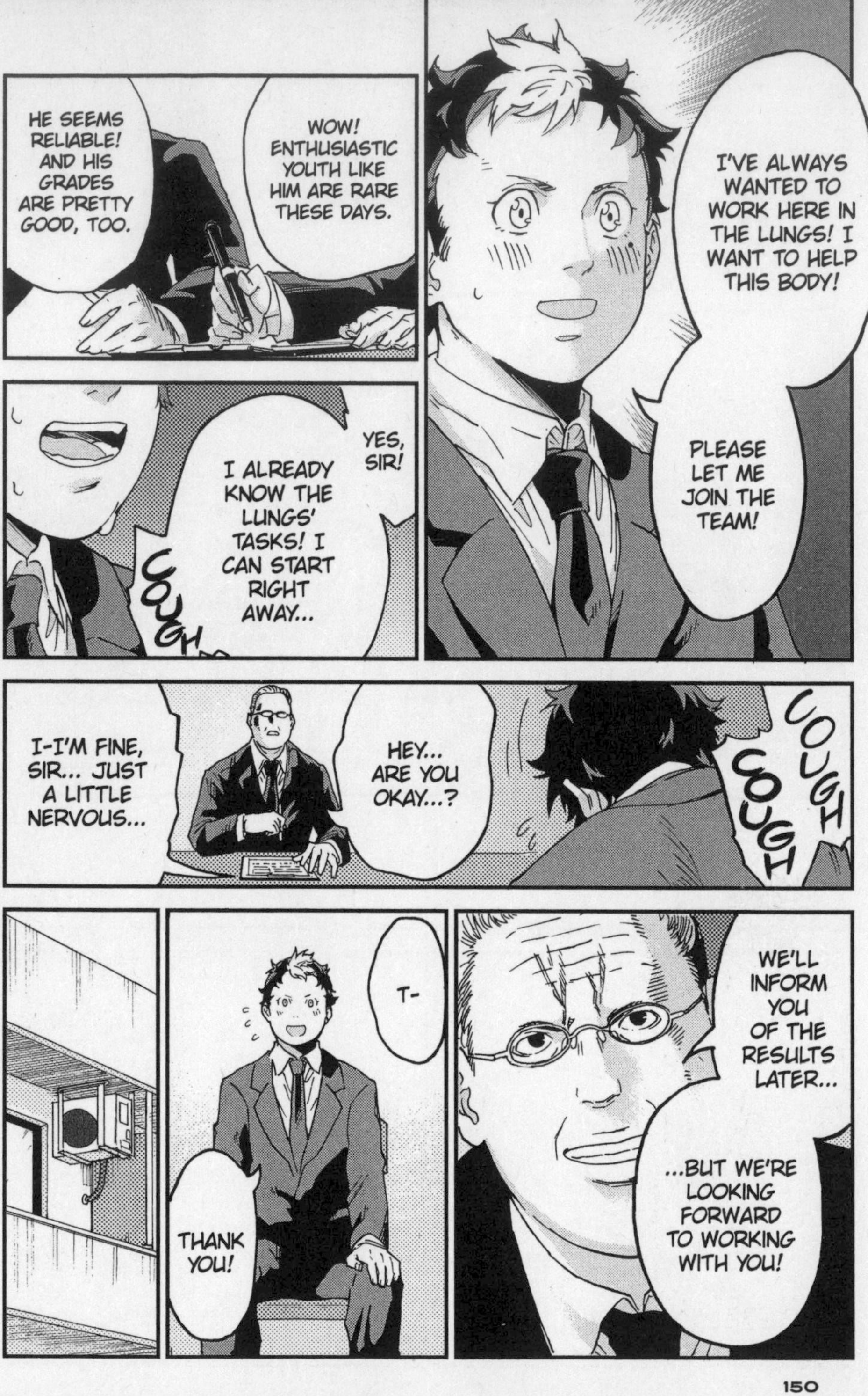
I'VE ALWAYS WANTED TO WORK HERE IN THE LUNGS! I WANT TO HELP THIS BODY!
PLEASE LET ME JOIN THE TEAM!
WOW! ENTHUSIASTIC YOUTH LIKE HIM ARE RARE THESE DAYS.
HE SEEMS RELIABLE! AND HIS GRADES ARE PRETTY GOOD, TOO.
YES, SIR!
I ALREADY KNOW THE LUNGS' TASKS! I CAN START RIGHT AWAY...
COUGH
COUGH
COUGH
HEY... ARE YOU OKAY...?
I-I'M FINE, SIR... JUST A LITTLE NERVOUS...
WE'LL INFORM YOU OF THE RESULTS LATER...
...BUT WE'RE LOOKING FORWARD TO WORKING WITH YOU!
T-
THANK YOU!

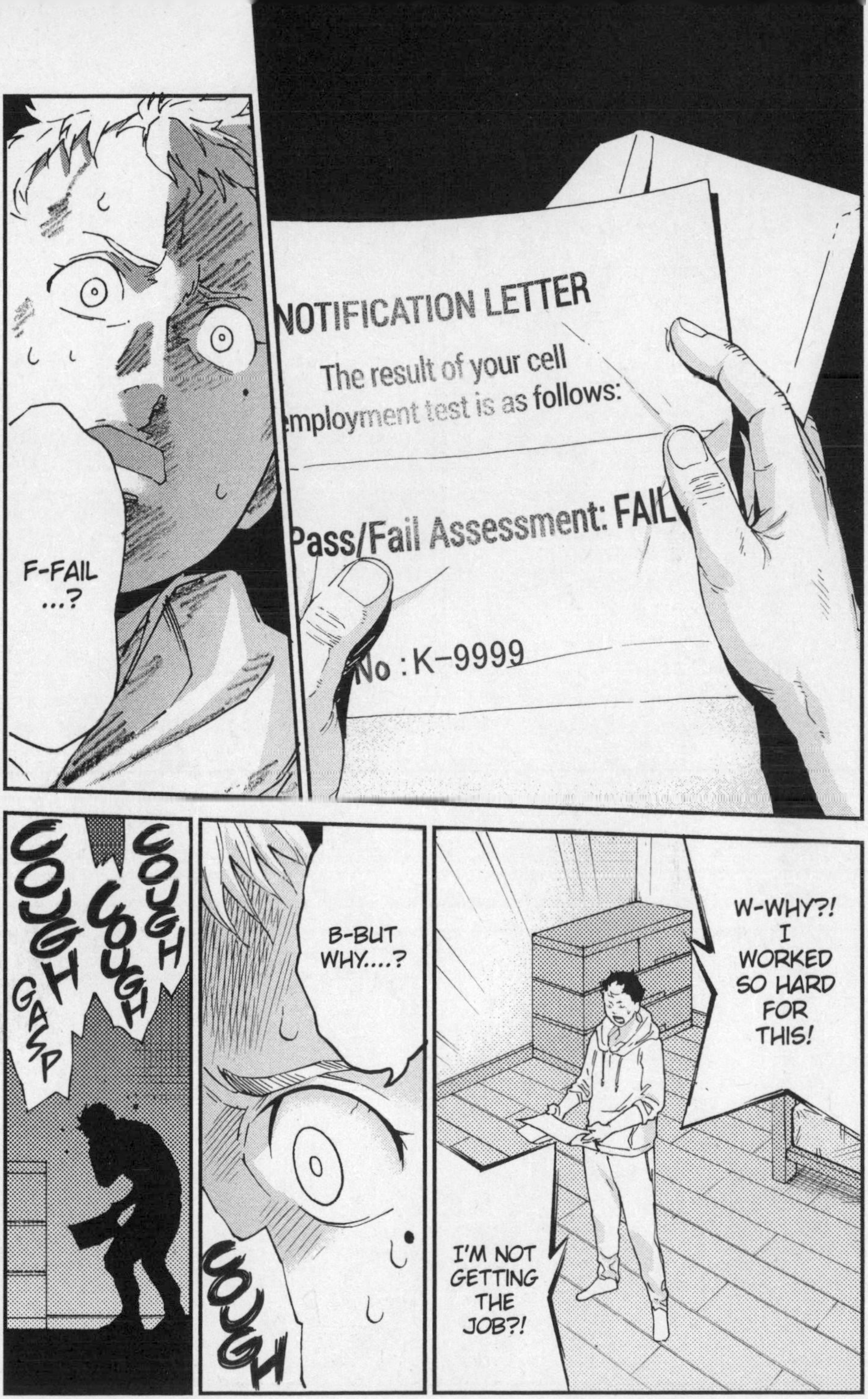
NOTIFICATION LETTER
The result of your cell employment test is as follows:
Pass/Fail Assessment: FAIL
No : K-9999
F-FAIL ...?
W-WHY?! I WORKED SO HARD FOR THIS!
I'M NOT GETTING THE JOB?!
B-BUT WHY....?
COUGH
COUGH
COUGH
COUGH
GASP

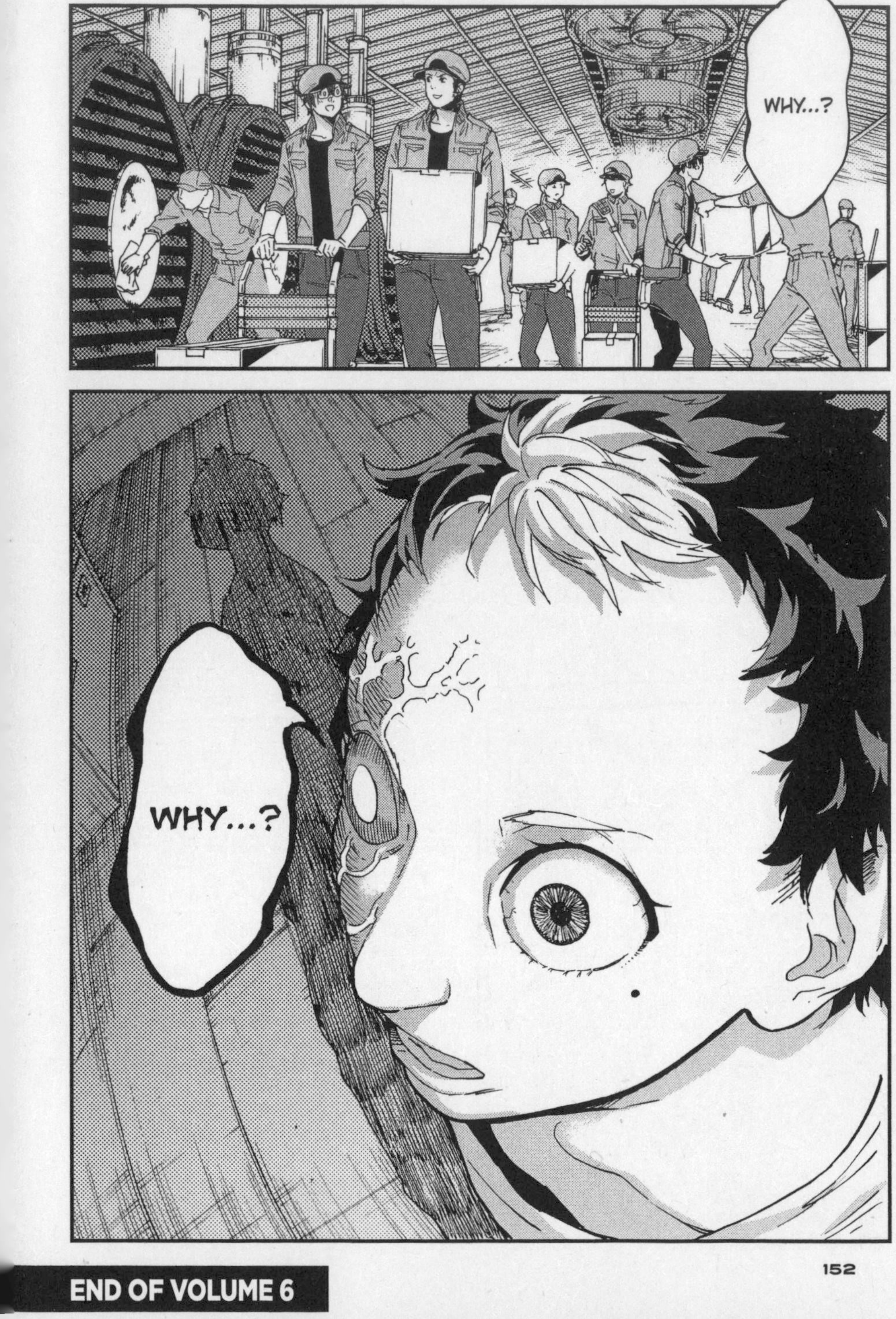
WHY...?
WHY...?

END OF VOLUME 6

Cells at Work!

はたらく細胞

CODE BLACK

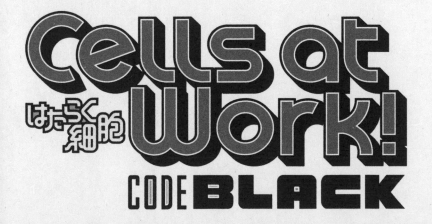

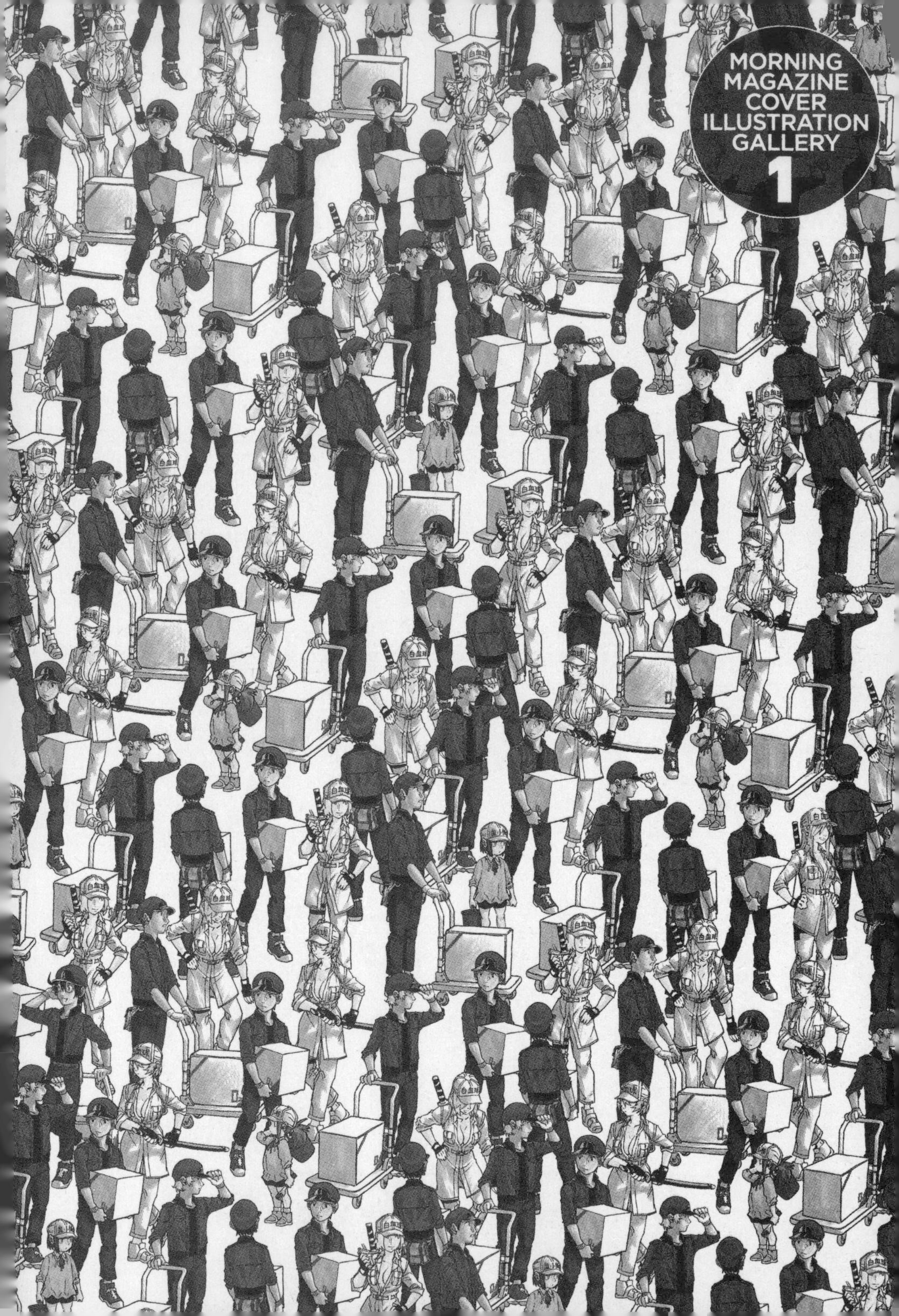
MORNING
MAGAZINE
COVER
ILLUSTRATION
GALLERY
1

MORNING MAGAZINE COVER ILLUSTRATION GALLERY 2

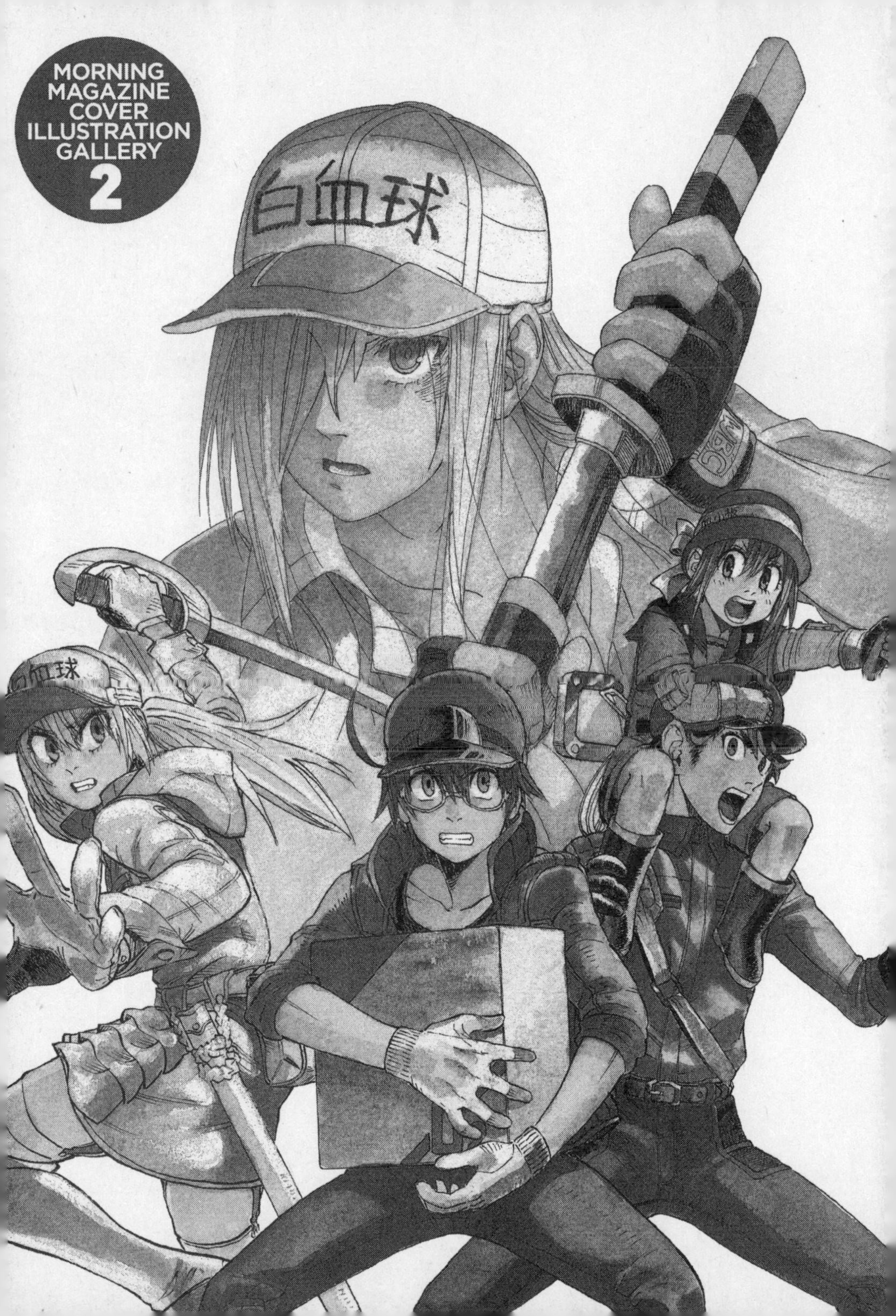

白血球
白血球

MORNING MAGAZINE COVER ILLUSTRATION GALLERY 3

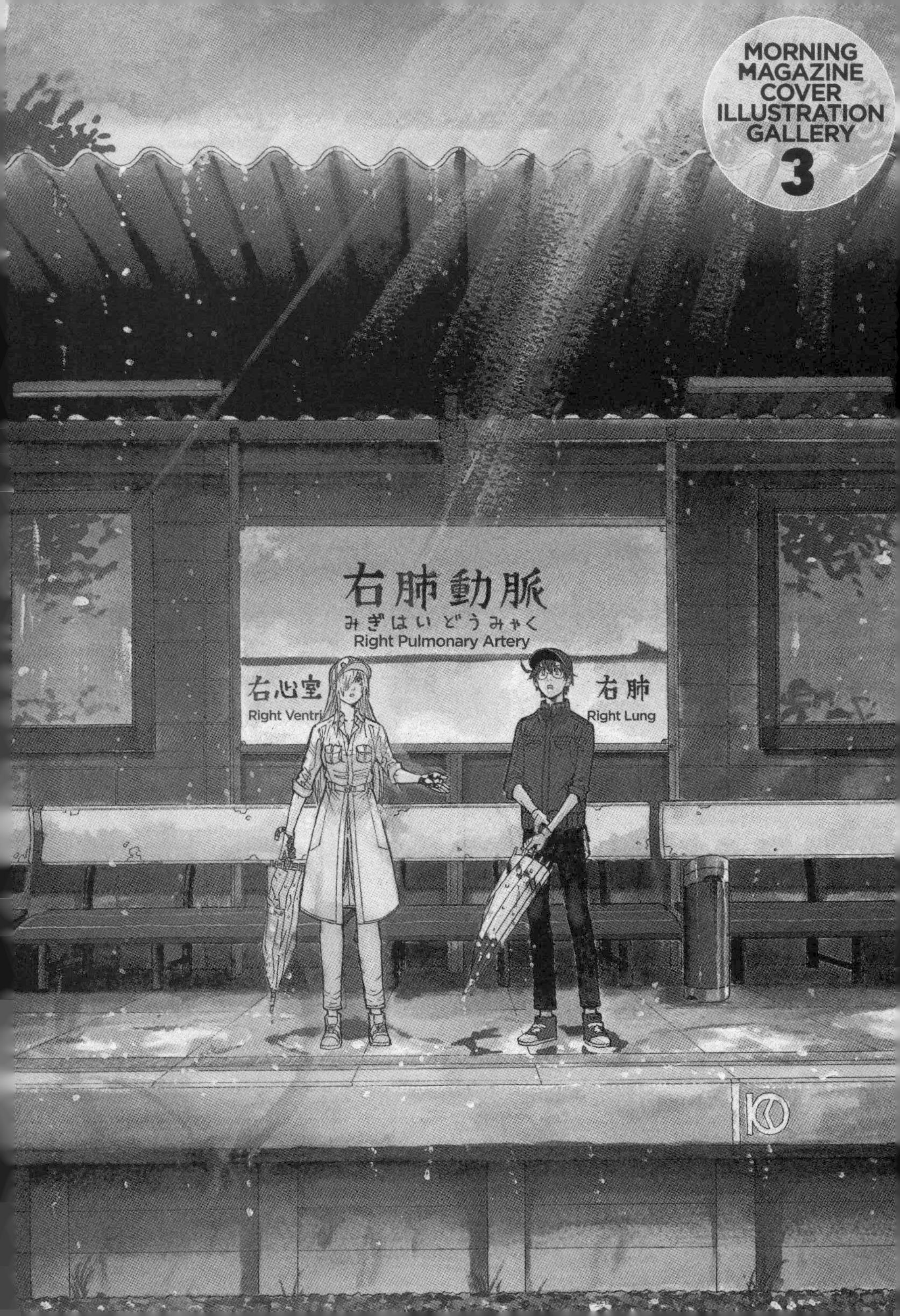

MORNING MAGAZINE COVER ILLUSTRATION GALLERY 4

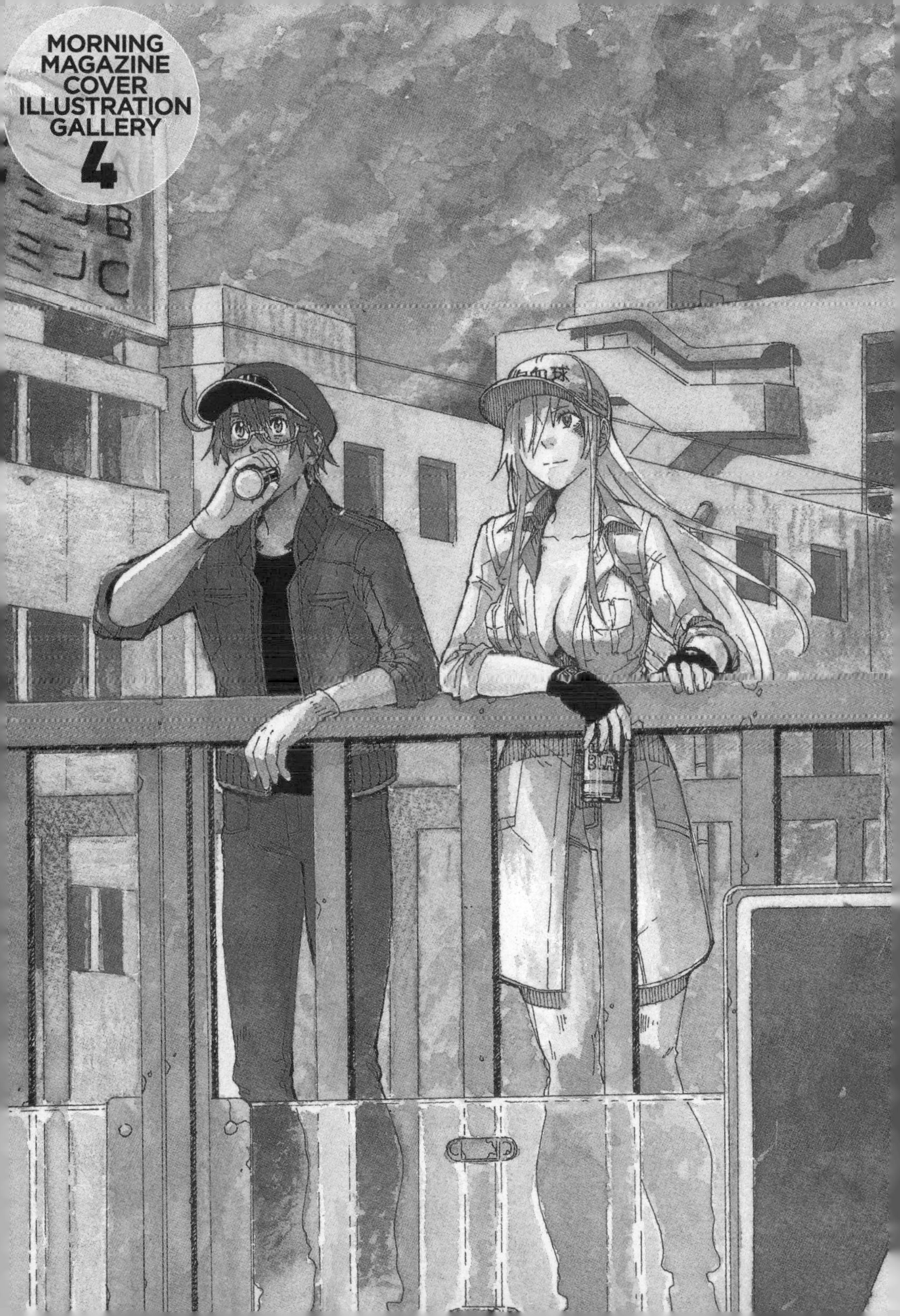

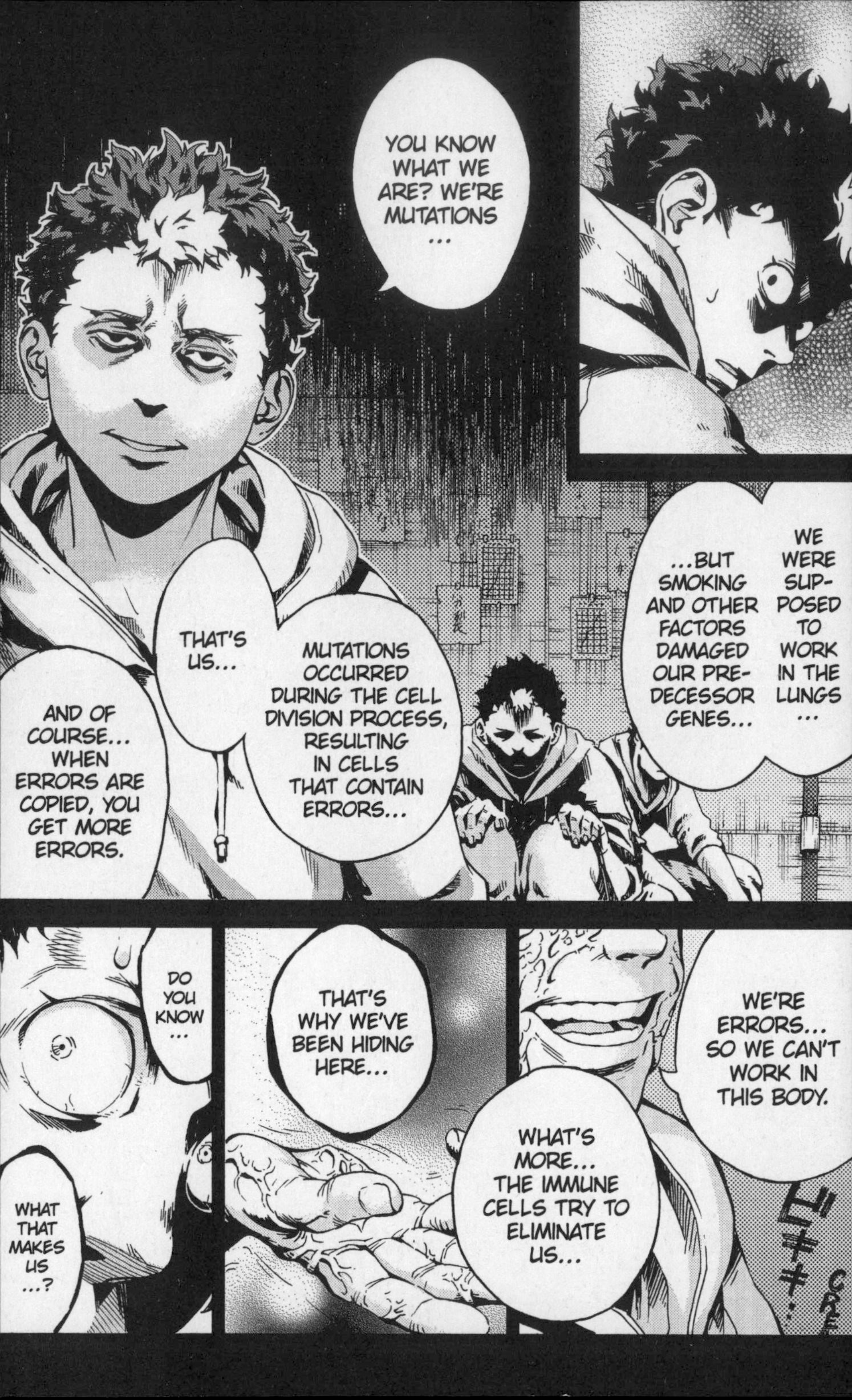

YOU KNOW WHAT WE ARE? WE'RE MUTATIONS ...
WE WERE SUP-POSED TO WORK IN THE LUNGS ...
...BUT SMOKING AND OTHER FACTORS DAMAGED OUR PRE-DECESSOR GENES...
MUTATIONS OCCURRED DURING THE CELL DIVISION PROCESS, RESULTING IN CELLS THAT CONTAIN ERRORS...
THAT'S US...
AND OF COURSE... WHEN ERRORS ARE COPIED, YOU GET MORE ERRORS.
WE'RE ERRORS... SO WE CAN'T WORK IN THIS BODY.
WHAT'S MORE... THE IMMUNE CELLS TRY TO ELIMINATE US...
CRE
THAT'S WHY WE'VE BEEN HIDING HERE...
DO YOU KNOW ...
WHAT THAT MAKES US ...?

WHO... ARE THESE GUYS?

WHO... AM I?

VOLUME 7 – COMING JANUARY 2021

Cells at Work! CODE BLACK 6 is a work of fiction. Names, characters, places, and incidents are the products of the author's imagination or are used fictitiously. Any resemblance to actual events, locales, or persons, living or dead, is entirely coincidental.

A Kodansha Comics Trade Paperback Original

Published in the United States by Kodansha Comics, an imprint of Kodansha USA Publishing, LLC, New York.

Publication rights for this English edition arranged through Kodansha Ltd., Tokyo.

First published in Japan in 2020 by Kodansha Ltd., Tokyo as *Hataraku Saibou BLACK*, volume 6.

ISBN 978-1-64651-149-5

Printed in the United States of America.

www.kodanshacomics.com

9 8 7 6 5 4 3 2 1
Translation: Iyasu Adair Nagata
Lettering: E. K. Weaver
Editing: Ben Applegate
Kodansha Comics edition cover design by Phil Balsman

KC
KODANSHA COMICS

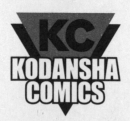

Publisher: Kiichiro Sugawara

Director of publishing services: Ben Applegate
Associate director of operations: Stephen Pakula
Publishing services managing editor: Noelle Webster
Assistant production manager: Emi Lotto, Angela Zurlo